The World's Leading Experts Reveal How They are Using the Classic Principles of Napoleon Hill to

THINK &GROW RICH TODAY!

Published by CelebrityPress®, Orlando, FL
A division of The Celebrity Branding Agency®

Celebrity Branding® is a registered trademark
Printed in the United States of America.

ISBN: 978-0-9886418-5-3
LCCN: 2013936369

This publication is designed to provide accurate and authoritative information with regard to the subject matter covered. It is sold with the understanding that the publisher is not engaged in rendering legal, accounting, or other professional advice. If legal advice or other expert assistance is required, the services of a competent professional should be sought. The opinions expressed by the authors in this book are not endorsed by CelebrityPress® and are the sole responsibility of the author rendering the opinion.

The title of this book is used pursuant to a license from The Napoleon Hill Foundation, however the content in this book is not endorsed, sponsored or approved by, or in any other way affiliated with The Napoleon Hill Foundation or Napoleon Hill.

Most CelebrityPress® titles are available at special quantity discounts for bulk purchases for sales promotions, premiums, fundraising, and educational use. Special versions or book excerpts can also be created to fit specific needs.

For more information, please write:
CelebrityPress®
520 N. Orlando Ave, #2
Winter Park, FL 32789
or call 1.877.261.4930

Visit us online at: www.CelebrityPressPublishing.com

The World's Leading Experts Reveal How They are Using the Classic Principles of Napoleon Hill to

THINK & GROW RICH TODAY!

FEATURING NAPOLEON HILL & LEADING EXPERTS FROM AROUND THE WORLD

CELEBRITY PRESS
Winter Park, Florida

CONTENTS

The classic Napoleon Hill book

Think and Grow Rich

is appended at the end. It follows the contemporary
authors compilation for reference, research or analysis
by the reader. Its Contents follow on the next page.

THINK AND GROW RICH

By Napoleon Hill

CHAPTER 1

PRINCIPLE 16: BUDGET YOUR TIME AND MONEY

BY INDIRA AMLADI CFA

Napoleon Hill's teachings on "Time and Money" have transformed my life. I now manage investments in excess of $1.5 Million. If I can do it, you can do it!

BACKGROUND

I came to the United States on a PhD graduate scholarship in 1988, with two suitcases and less than $100. As a full time student and graduate assistant to professors, I worked late nights. Managing scarce time with a meager budget left no room for error.

INITIAL FAILURE

While in the PhD program, being an "A" student in Biochemistry theory wasn't sufficient for laboratory research involving test tubes and mice. I quickly realized it was not my purpose and opted for a MS degree instead.

DEVELOPED A NEW PURPOSE

"To have a career at Procter and Gamble." I obtained a scholarship from Miami University (Oxford, Ohio) for an MBA. After graduating in 1992, Procter and Gamble, one of the world's best companies hired me and shaped my thinking, and for that I am forever grateful. I managed brand research and strategy for Jif Peanut Butter, Folgers, Old Spice, Sure and Secret deodorants, and volume forecast modeling, where I learned: (i) the importance of having a strong value system, (ii) commitment to customers, and (iii) commitment to shareholder wealth building. In 1998, I was hired by Kraft Foods Innovation, and in 2002 joined Johnson & Johnson as Associate Director, leading innovation and research for Oral Health brands such as J&J Floss and Reach.

SOUL SEARCHING: WHAT IS SUCCESS?

In spite of professional progress, I wasn't fulfilled in corporate life. I developed the purpose of "wanting to make money from investing full time" only in 2004, for which I resigned from J&J. I started rigorous formal investment training and testing that lasted 8 years, including: (i) Value Investing education from Columbia University; (ii) 3 years of certification exams to achieve the CFA charter; (iii) investing in US companies; and (iv) building a proprietary database of over 1,500 companies. Additionally, I did some consulting on the side to earn income.

USED CRITICAL HILL PRINCIPLES OF SUCCESS:

(a) **Mind Control**: Realizing daily that my mind must be steady and free of negative emotions, and waking up to my own purpose has been critical to my success.

(b) **Mastery:** Taking the best training to master the art of investing: Investing in the best companies at the right price has been critical to building wealth for my clients and my family.

(c) **Budgeting Your Money:** Time and money are precious resources that I always want more of. As a dual income couple, we saved at least 1 income every year and maxed out our 401K plans.

THE LIST BELOW ANSWERS HILL'S PERSONAL INVENTORY QUESTIONS, IN ORDER.

1. **Major definite purpose:**
   It was only in 2004 that it became a full-time purpose. The excitement and passion I felt was immeasurable. It was only after serious contemplation that I resigned from Johnson & Johnson.

2. **Burning Obsession:**
   Yes, the obsession "Investing to make money" grew each year. I fan its flames every day. I wake up each morning with a passion to fulfill my purpose!

3. **Giving in return for realizing your definite major purpose:**
   I took the required license (RIA) and registered my company in New York State. With an 18-year successful track record with 14.61% annualized return, I invest for others as a way of giving back to my community.

4. **Steps to build your mastermind alliance:**
   I read books about my success idol, Warren E. Buffett, and identified related experts in the investment field. Dr. Bruce Greenwald at Columbia University was an expert teaching the course taught by Benjamin Graham, (founding father of long term investing)—and Warren's teacher. After training with Dr. Greenwald in Value Investing, I asked him to be on the Advisory board of my company "Princeton Ivy Capital Advisors." I also attend conferences in my field to meet like-minded people.

5. **Have you made a habit of accepting temporary defeat as a challenge to greater effort?**
   My investment goal is to be right at least 95% of the time, willing to lose 5% of the time. With 18 years of trial-and-testing investing in the best companies the 14.61% annualized return (GIPS verified by 3rd party CPA firm) has beaten the S&P500 benchmark, which is at about 10.61%.

6. Time management = carrying out plans, not brooding over obstacles:
My ongoing aim is to focus on strategy/planning and execution, seek ideas and overcome obstacles, believing that our universe has more solutions than problems.

7. Sacrificing personal pleasure for the plan?
I work long hours in pure enjoyment of my purpose. I believe I'm a better wife and mom, as my purpose energizes and nourishes me.

8. Do you seize every moment of time as if it were the only one you were sure you had?
Definitely. Since my thoughts are time-consuming, I must create positive thoughts and solutions.

9. Have you looked at your life as the result of the way you spent time in the past? Are you happy? Do you wish you had spent it some other way?
My life is definitely the result of the way I spent time in the past. Overall happy, as there are less fortunate people in the world. However, I wish I could spend more time with all family members. I've also made some mistakes in family matters, and seek to make it right.

10. How positive is your mental attitude?
Humility and being positive are essential. Sometimes I have to "let go" of an upset, to refresh my mind in being creative and focus positively on my purpose. I have to hold myself to a higher standard in fulfilling my duties.

11. How often do you display personal initiative by backing your positive thoughts with action?
I add action steps to my calendar during meetings, and execute actions daily.

12. Do you believe that you will succeed by luck or a windfall?
I believe I am already succeeding, by effort + windfall. They are inseparable. As Thomas Jefferson said, "The harder I work, the luckier I get." I met excellent collabo-

rators at a recent conference and have already made investment alliances with them. Luck is being at the right place + right time.

13. Do you know anyone who inspires you with his or her personal initiative?

I have been inspired by Warren Buffett since the dotcom bust in the early 2000s, when I first read about him. Since then I took the same Value Investing training that he took at Columbia University, and researched his investments to understand his strategy. I read and model my behavior to reflect long term value investing made famous by him. Using this, I developed the proprietary investment return-drivers database.

14. When do you go the extra mile?

I go the extra mile in being helpful to people and investing with conviction. Good, honest character comes first, and is a requirement for survival in my line of business. It takes only one dishonest act to ruin an entire life. It does not matter whether someone is paying attention. I feel blessed in being able to find great investments.

15. How attractive is your personality?

I believe I am pleasant and humble, brown-skinned as I am, from India. I dress professionally and maintain professional speaking.

16. How are you applying your faith? Do you act on the inspiration from Infinite Intelligence?

Being humble is an infinite source of joy. I pray at least once a day. God is the source of Infinite Intelligence. If I sense obstacles, I tell myself that obstacles are also part of God's plan and I try to turn them into something good. I believe in Good Karma, and try to be good to all others regardless of their status.

17. Are you building your self-discipline? How often do uncontrolled emotions cause you to do something you quickly regret?
Self-discipline is tough, but has produced good results. I try "sleeping over" tough issues to clear my mind. Also try to speak slowly and with few words to clear my mind. Vipassana is a form of Buddhist Meditation with a focus on breathing, a calming force that has helped immensely!

18. Have you mastered your fears? How often do you display their symptoms?
I try to master my fears everyday. My biggest fear is for my mother's health, as she lives in India and I am in the US. I visit her at least once a year, and although she has other family members nearby, as a daughter, I cried with worry when she was undergoing surgery. The way I try to master my fear is by praying and telling myself that I have to work harder now, so I can be of use to her when she would need me.

19. How often do you accept other people's opinions as fact? How often do you call on accurate thinking as the solution to your problems?
I try to be rational and analyze the situation. I don't question openly, as I prefer to communicate solutions and options as a way to validate and help others. If an unimportant argument develops, I try to disengage with a quick solution. For important matters, such as investments or legal and regulatory requirements, I analyze the situation. If the situation is complex, I may take a swim to refresh my mind before analyzing.

20. How often do you inspire cooperation by giving it? Are you doing it ...at home? ...at the office? ...in your mastermind alliance?
Validating and helping others authentically has produced great results for my peace of mind, and also developed the mastermind alliance. My husband is the

original mastermind; he has been a blessing, a strong source of inspiration, and is also an expert in the field of finance and investing. We draw inspiration from each other and validate each other.

I have found that introducing smart honest people to each other and planning collaborative sessions to create opportunities is a great way to grow a mastermind alliance.

21. What opportunities do you allow your imagination? When do you apply yourself to problems with creative vision? What dilemmas do you have that need to be solved this way?

To encourage fresh thinking and to think "outside the box," I recently studied and started a new investment strategy envisioned by a successful entrepreneur. I am also inspired by reading *The Financial Times*, database analysis, and movies.

22. Are you relaxing, exercising, and paying attention to your health? Were you planning to start at the New Year? Why can't you start right now?

Yes, I feel relaxed daily with swimming and pelvic tilts that were recommended for strengthening my lower back.

MY DOER CHECKLIST

Mr. Hill's principles have taught me that *Doers have* a definite major purpose. Doers:

✓ Manage circumstances and resources

✓ Examine every idea they encounter before they adopt or discard it

✓ Take risks and assume responsibility

✓ Learn from their mistakes

✓ Go the extra mile

✓ Control their habits

✓ Have positive mental attitudes

✓ Apply their faith in their own success

✓ Create mastermind alliances to expand their knowledge and experience

✓ Recognize their weaknesses and take steps to correct them

THE DIVISION OF MY DAY: MY GOALS

8 hrs: Sleep.

8 hrs: Work

8 hrs: Weekdays: Spare time:

✓ Meditation (1 hr): To regain contact with God's Infinite Intelligence, affirming my gratitude for God's blessings. Self-analysis by identifying fears I must master, making plans to master. Ways to increase harmony in all my relationships. My needs vs. wants.

✓ MuHan foundation (1 hr)

✓ Read for self-improvement (1 hr)

✓ Spend time with family, friends, mastermind alliance (3 hr)

✓ Daily Chores (1 hr): Cooking + dishes, mail, organize.

✓ Swim (1 hr)

✓ Weekends – with family and friends, chores

TIME MANAGEMENT ON THE JOB

Prioritizing Your Tasks

Scheduling commitments on electronic-calendar, I mark each with an "IN" if it's Important and Not-Urgent, "IU" if Important and Urgent. I delegate or don't schedule if the task is "Not Important." All family matters are Important, doctor visits, birthday parties, and talking and being with Mom are Important.

Handling Paper
Felt like a chore, now I try to have fun with it.

I prefer clean rooms without clutter. Try to deal with mail daily, recycle all non-confidential mail, file important pages in folders, and shred the rest.

Budgeting Money
I love the sight of growing the investment accounts for my clients and always recommend, "Pay yourself first" by maximizing "Growing money." As a Registered Investment Adviser, I try to maximize money invested for long-term growth, and park short-term cash in a checking account for immediate needs. Inflation is dangerous long term, and longevity risk (the risk of outliving assets during old age) can be worse than death.

I strongly believe in Mr. Hill's quote – "Like time, money should be spent with a definite purpose in mind. You must create a budget for all your expenses, and you must use self-discipline in sticking to it… A strong and growing savings cushion is an important weapon in your fight against the fear of poverty."

Pay debt off. This is Mr. Hill's principle and what I learned growing up. The only debt I may accept is less than 20% of total assets and less than 2.5% in interest after taxes, provided it is used in growing assets at over 8% a year by investing carefully.

Emergency Fund Account: keep some cash for emergencies.

WEALTH ISN'T MONEY

I agree with Mr. Hill that – "Your greatest asset is who you are. Wealth isn't money, but people who are wealthy often have money. They have money because they believe in their capabilities and inspire others to believe in them, too!"

THE R2A2 PRINCIPLE: RECOGNIZE, RELATE, ASSIMILATE AND ACTION:

An example below:

Recognize: I recognized that great companies were available at cheap prices, and their value would grow over time. I researched to find the best metrics to select great companies / investments.

Relate: I realized from my experience at Procter and Gamble that high-repeat businesses are successful and tend to be low-risk for long term investing.

Assimilate: Investing in great low-risk companies at cheap prices could provide great investment returns over the long run, so I must be patient.

Action: I developed the proprietary screener to select investments with high certainty of outcome, and use it regularly to buy shares of strong businesses for the long term and monitor results. Also, hired a team to serve clients better.

THINK ... AND ACHIEVE YOUR GOALS

Thinking seriously, analyzing my life, and declaring my purpose, were critical steps in focusing my time, training and experience for success.

IS IT WORTH IT

Definitely, Yes! My life now has a jingle in every step! Happy that I can invest and make others wealthy as well. It helps that my husband also focused on his purpose! I try to spend time with my Mom in India. We are able to live comfortably, fund our daughter's college, and have a daughter who is also inspired to succeed!

About Indira

With an 18-year investment track record of 14.61% annualized return, and recently published in Forbes magazine for her forecast and strategy, Indira Amladi is the CEO and Investment Portfolio Manager for Princeton Ivy Capital Advisors. Ms. Amladi trained with Dr Bruce Greenwald in Value Investing Executive Training at Columbia Business School, and has 17 years of corporate experience at Fortune 100 companies such as Johnson & Johnson, Procter and Gamble and Kraft Foods.

Ms. Amladi analyzed and provided valuations for 10 Large Cap consumer companies as Consultant Sell-side Researcher for client Deutsche Bank at New York, NY (10/2009 to 4/2010). Prior to that, she has held several leadership positions such as Innovation and new product commercialization for Post Foods, Parsippany, NJ (1/2009 to 10/2009); Director of Marketing as a consultant for Value Investor Media, Vienna, VA (1/2008 to 1/2009); Consultant for Unilever at Trumbull, CT (7/04 to 1/2008); Associate Director Market Research/Oral Health Category, Johnson & Johnson PPC, Skillman, NJ (6/02 to 7/04); Market Research Manager for Kraft Foods, Glenview, IL (9/00 to 5/02); and Market Research Supervisor for The Procter & Gamble Co., Cincinnati, OH. (6/93-5/98).

As Associate Director at Johnson & Johnson 2002-2004, Ms. Amladi analyzed and recommended candidates for Mergers and Acquisitions, and led Best Practice Innovation Processes. In those roles, she provided consultation to the Personal Products Company's Board regarding consumer insights, volume forecasting and commercialization of new product launches.

As a consultant at Deutsche Bank, on Wall Street in 2009/2010, Ms. Amladi conducted Valuation Analyses for 10 consumer-goods sector companies.

Ms. Amladi accomplished her CFA charter in October 2010. She received her M.B.A. via graduate-scholarship, magna cum laude, from Miami University, Oxford, OH, in 1992, with a concentration in Marketing and Finance. In 1990, she received an M.S. degree (Biochemistry) via graduate-scholarship from the University of Cincinnati, Cincinnati, OH. She also holds a B.S. degree (Biochemistry and Microbiology), First Class with Distinction, from University of Bombay, India, 1987.

Ms. Amladi is engaged in foundation and charitable work, as the volunteer and co-founder of MuHan (means "The Great People" in India), the Foundation for the Multiple Handicapped. Additionally she envisioned and was responsible for initiating Reliance Capital's full sponsorship, hosting and organization of its conference for Columbia University's Investment delegation to India. Reliance Capital is one of the largest mutual funds in India.

CHAPTER 2

PERFORMANCE BASED HEALTH PLANS™:
A Business Strategy for Healthcare

BY CRAIG LACK

Napoleon Hill, in his renowned book, *Think and Grow Rich*, reinforced the message that people, and businesses, become trapped by their habits – either by lack of ambition, lack of specialized knowledge or lack of imagination. The proof of Napoleon Hill's message can be seen repeatedly in businesses everywhere today.

Take for example, the massive shift throughout the world from analog to digital solutions. There is hardly an industry or product that hasn't been transformed from analog to digital. Think of the music, movie, telephone or banking industries and see how everything has changed.

One of the most ironic examples of a business becoming trapped by its habits and success is the story of Eastman Kodak. Kodak was a very successful and profitable company for decades. They dominated the film industry and the portable camera market. Their financial success came from selling an inexpensive camera and then selling consumers all the film to use inside. Of course, they also processed the film to provide consumers the photographs that they would place in their albums. Every click of every camera meant money for Eastman Kodak.

The story becomes almost unbelievable, but in hindsight everything seems so obvious. Kodak invented digital photography. Unfortunately they were trapped by their past successes and were locked into their entrenched habits and lack of ambition. No one could overcome groupthink and the mantra of historical best practices. Internally, the dialog inside the company was that nearly all profits came from film, so why waste profits on developing digital. We all know how that story ended.

Despite today's tsunami of change to the digital world, there are still two remaining enormous industries in the United States that are resisting and fighting the inevitable: Our public education system and our healthcare system. The healthcare system in America is a $2.8 trillion industry and is inherently and systemically inflationary. Despite twenty-five years of Managed Care (Costs) we are no closer to controlling costs than before PPOs, HMOs and Rx cards were created.

We have now reached a point in time where government intervention has created laws making health insurance a regulated industry and a mandate for its citizens under the threat of taxation. Nowhere is the HealthCare Reform impact felt more than in the middle market companies throughout America.

Middle market companies are stuck with out-of-control trend increases in their healthcare spend (cost). At first you make your habits, and then your habits make you. A perfect example of this can be seen in how middle market companies purchase their healthcare. Think of it as the trap of experience. Lacking specialized knowledge, executives rely on their developed habits over years of repeating the same buying strategies and tactics.

There is a behavioral economic theory called the rule of first knowledge which states that most people have a difficult time unlearning the very first thing they learned about any particular subject, or process. More importantly, people find it very hard to change. This is evident in the repeated status-quo process of middle market companies purchasing and renewing their healthcare.

Napoleon Hill references habits and a lack of specialized knowledge as being two roadblocks to successfully making the change that you need in order to have success. Our experience with over 1,000 healthcare renewals leads us to the following conclusions. The vast majority of middle market companies look at their healthcare as a liability. Liability thinking is extremely limiting and diminishes the results and the outcomes that a company can expect to achieve. The majority of time is spent attempting to manage and control costs because, after all, healthcare is a liability.

Hill speaks about getting into a rut – which means that we accept our fate because we form the habits of daily routine. With respect to managing the healthcare spend, executives at middle market companies have become habituated and fear change, and typically prefer to hold onto the status quo liability thinking. Mistakenly, they rely on broker/consultants who mirror the same 'stuck' thinking. Excessive rate increases are costing middle market companies millions of dollars in lost profits. Employers are trapped using historical best practices that result in shifting costs to the employees, reducing benefits or limiting access to care.

Lack of ambition is described in *Think And Grow Rich* as a universal weakness. It's noted that lack of ambition was especially prevalent with salaried employees, and in our experience there are common parallels with many of the executives in charge of the healthcare budget at middle market companies today. The executives tend to manage healthcare as a liability and therefore focus their buying criteria on the price of insurance, much like a purchasing manager. The purchasing manager mentality is exhibited throughout the middle market, which results in companies being forced to react to their renewals each year. If managed correctly, EBITDA can be created from the current healthcare spend by reducing trend!

Because the insurance carriers and HMOs play hide and seek with the key utilization data, companies rely on their broker/consultants to go shopping for sales on insurance every twelve months. We fondly refer to the process as the Ground Hog Day renewal process. As Peter Drucker once said, "If you can't measure it, you can't manage it." Therein lies the biggest problems for the middle market who are fully insured. The annual benefits renewal meeting looks and feels an awful lot like this cartoon.

For those middle market companies who are self-funded, most are operating on old maps that don't provide the directions they need moving forward. Quite simply, your outcomes are a function of your design. And, your design is representative of the knowledge and understanding of your internal staff and your outside broker/consultant. Since 99% of those professionals manage healthcare as a liability then you can be assured of continued unmanaged excessive trend increases. When you are lost in the woods, you have to stop looking for signs that confirm you know where you are – just admit that you are lost.

Here's a story about being open to learning and changing your perspective, despite your illusions of expertise, which evolved over time, primarily because you have been involved with a health care purchasing process for your company twenty times over twenty years.

A karate master came to Bruce Lee and asked Bruce if he would teach him everything he knew about karate. Bruce Lee filled two cups of water and handed one to the karate master.

Bruce Lee said, pointing to his cup, "This represents everything I know about karate." And then he pointed to the eager master's cup, and said, "This represents everything you know about karate. If you are to learn anything from me, you must first empty your cup to make space for what comes from mine."

One thing that we've learned after 25 years of managed care is that we can't control the supply-chain side of the healthcare equation. Lack of ambition is particularly common in the healthcare renewal scenario because of the competing demands that often face executives who are charged with the management of the healthcare spend. For example, competing demands include making the boss happy, other job responsibilities that have to be borne by limited staff, keeping a lid on costs or just trying to keep everything as close to the *status quo* as possible!

Since nearly everyone involved in managing the healthcare spend believes it is a liability, there are also common errors made. Too often there is a reliance on the mythology of national brands and the perpetual launch of another outdated best practices initiative from other liability thinkers, who are often the consultants that are being paid to provide tactics on controlling costs.

LAUNCH THE NEW INITIATIVE

The primary expectations of the middle market are just to have their broker/consultant at least negotiate a renewal that's below national published trend and below the first carrier/HMO renewal offer. The whole process has lead to the normalization of pain for middle market companies. In today's world, healthcare rate increases are a foregone conclusion and a "less bad" renewal is the new good renewal.

All the while for the last decade, the premium increases and cost shifting to the employees in most middle market companies has exceeded the rate of pay increases, so that the net result, is employees are working for less money than they did five years ago. The renewal experience usually results in cost shifting to employees' paychecks like the cartoon on the next page.

The problem to solve is not on the supply side, but in fact, the demand side. If we reduce the demand for services we will incur

lower claims. If we incur lower claims we will have lower rates. It doesn't matter whether we're fully insured or self-funded or partially self-funded - the formula works.

One of the biggest problems we have today is the American idle. Nearly 69 percent of adults in the U.S. are overweight with nearly 40 percent considered obese. The question the middle market companies have to ask themselves is - do you want to eliminate disease, or do you want to promote health? Think of it the same way as in the financial world - do you want to eliminate poverty, or do want to promote wealth?

The future is going to be about the redistribution of health, not wealth. It's not about controlling the health premiums! Success in the future is about maintaining the health of the employee!

Creating measurable data points around the health status of the employee population will have the largest impact on future rates.

Middle market companies who can create Performance Based Health Plans™ based upon data, employee participation and engagement in health promotion will be the winners – whether fully insured or self-funded.

When the Centers for Disease Control says that 50% to 70% of all claims are preventable and modifiable, because they're based on lifestyle and behavior choices, then we can see that there are big changes afoot. Additionally, the Institute of Medicine recently released a report that said 30% of the money spent in the US healthcare system is fraud, waste, bureaucracy and unnecessary care.

One can see the coming attractions in healthcare by studying the Affordable Care Act. Starting in 2014, employers are allowed to charge a 30% healthcare premium differential to employees based on participation or performance in health promotion, and smokers can be charged up to a 50% difference. Currently HIPAA allows for a 20% healthcare premium differential based on participation or performance in health promotion.

The majority of middle market companies have yet to build a healthcare business strategy around the future direction of healthcare, and that is a costly mistake. Whereas, most of the largest and smartest companies in America have been implementing health promotion for many years, and in some cases for decades. The proven results have been published extensively in academic, medical and business journals.

The obvious parallels can be seen in all other insurances. Non-smokers pay less for life insurance and good drivers pay less for auto insurance. As a matter of fact, the newest innovation in auto insurance is the offer to attach a computer-monitoring device that records your driving habits and performance in exchange for the lowest possible rates.

Middle market companies have been practicing for years many of the same health care culture changes that we are espousing, but they have instituted these changes in the management of their workers' compensation program. Think of your workplace safety program and the reasons you created a focus on preventing workplace injuries. What about your IT, Capital Asset, Auto or Fleet maintenance programs?

Are you starting to see the enormous blind spot in seeing healthcare as a liability? Now ask yourself why you don't have a similar prevention program for your employees. The time is now for middle market companies to align incentives, engagement and responsibility in their health care program! The solution is called Performance Based Health Plans™.

More data equals greater transparency and greater correlation to measuring future risk. The same equation holds true for healthcare claims. With more data points measured over time and supported by a health promotion program, insurance carriers can deliver better rates and for longer than twelve months.

Conventional wisdom surrounding the healthcare spend at middle market companies is outdated. It's a classic analog solution in a modern digital world. We operate a 19th century medical system with 20th century physicians and 21st century employees.

The future of healthcare in America is undergoing a major transformation from B2B to B2C. The primary focus is no longer about the providers of medicine. Instead, the future of medicine is about the patients, their health and their outcomes.

When insurance carriers/HMOs are receiving over one thousand RFPs per month, why exactly will they view your company as a preferred risk? Successful middle market companies have to partner with professionals who can position their risk profile to a prospective insurance carrier/HMO in a way that reduces the perceived risk. The carriers/HMOs are mostly for-profit and their primary objective is to earn an underwriting profit off of your premiums.

If companies continue with their current design and current tactics, they will continue to receive excessive trend renewals. Risk management, or lack thereof, makes most employers look like every other employer. If you are fully insured then you're not doing anything except transferring the risk to the insurance company/HMO. They control all the data and they set the pricing. Is it any wonder that employers feel trapped by the uncertainty and total lack of predictability?

Remember, the insurance companies/HMOs have some data based on a clinical intervention or ongoing prescriptions for your employees that have been diagnosed with a mild, chronic, critical or degenerative disease. For an average group that means around 25%-40% of the employees. Here's a little news, most health plans ignore the 60%-75% of the employee population because they are not symptomatic and they get paid to treat sickness.

So when your broker/consultant tells you in your quarterly claims review meeting that their predictive analytics software has correlated what happened last year to 25%-40% of your population, into a forecast of next year's estimated utilization, don't be surprised later. Take a look at your 401(k) disclosures from the mutual funds – past performance is no guarantee of future performance. Those claims reviews tell you what already happened but provide little actionable intelligence for management to use. Even though the analytics reports are three inches thick that doesn't make them useful.

The digital solution is to measure your emerging risk to see what's coming around the corner, or over the horizon. By focusing on the ignored 60%-75% of the employees we can impact future claims dramatically. For example, the CDC states that 59% of next year's high claims will come from this year's low claims. That means you never see it coming and the carrier never sees it coming, because you're not measuring the emerging risks. Proper design can stratify future risks up to three years in advance.

By identifying risk factors before employees become symptomatic and creating engaging incentives, employers can dramatically influence currently unmanaged future claims. Health status is a continuum. Just like we get another year older each year, our health changes as well. If left unmanaged we slide along the natural continuum from asymptomatic to symptomatic to chronic to critical to expiration. Of course, there are varying degrees to all stages. …Who wouldn't want information on how their lifestyle and behavior choices were contributing to their own premature expiration date?

With more useful data that the employer can control it is possible to influence the reduction in the demand for services through a reduction in the number, size and frequency of claims. So, the natural conclusion is that we promote health not eliminate disease, and, therefore, over the long run, we prevent the preventable.

By reverse engineering the outcome that you want, one can design small incremental, repeatable, sustainable improvements to a multitude of areas and components in your healthcare program –whether it is fully insured or self-funded. The impact of those improvements will ultimately lead to lower utilization, lower healthcare rates, lower healthcare renewals and lower trend.

The natural consequences of a lower trend results in higher profits, lower workers' comp costs, lower absenteeism, greater employee productivity, less 401(k) hardship loans, less turnover and happier and healthier employees. By focusing on promoting health as an outcome and preventing the preventable, we end up with the outcome that we're looking for, because we've changed the perspective to investing in healthcare asset management versus attempting to manage by controlling the spend.

Performance Based Health Plans ™ identifies and measures the emerging healthcare risks of middle market companies – which improves the predictability and control over costs. The needs of the Company, employees and insurance carrier are aligned by promoting and incentivizing employee health responsibility. The results are higher earnings (EBITDA) by lowering the health care trend.

TOP 10 Questions To Assess Your Healthcare Management

1. Do you have a three-year healthcare business strategy in a blueprint to guide you in converting healthcare from a liability to an asset?

2. Explain how you currently identify your population's emerging health risks up to three years in advance?

3. Other than paid claims analysis, what else do you use to predict next year's healthcare spend?

4. Exactly what data does your insurance carrier really have, and is it the best data to determine your future risk?

5. Exactly what metrics do you use to manage your healthcare spend?

6. How much is adverse selection costing the company in unnecessary claims?

7. How much does your carrier provide you in financial incentives for your health promotion?

8. If you are a preferred risk company, what strategies are you currently using to design 5% to 20% fully insured premium reductions, or similar savings to the fixed and variable cost on your self funded plan?

9. Exactly what are you using to reduce the number, size and frequency of medical claims?

10. How would engaging 75% to 95% of your employee population improve your health care business strategy?

BONUS: How to calculate the new sales revenue necessary to replace lost profits from excessive trend increases:

$ Amount of Increase

Example:

$500,000 = $5M New Sales

Net Profit Margin (%) .10

About Craig

Craig Lack, the creator of Performance Based Health Plans™, will be featured in an *Inc. Magazine* spread entitled "The Next Big Thing" speaking about how Craig's exclusive program, Performance Based Health Plans™, is designing a business strategy around managing health care and building three year benefit strategies that reduce healthcare trend. Middle market companies around the country are looking for certainty and predictability to deal with the excessive trend increases they have suffered for nearly a decade.

Craig Lack is the Founder and President of Employer's National Expert Resource Group Inc., doing business as ENERGI and brings over 20 years of employee benefits insurance experience working with middle market companies nationwide. His experience includes well over a 1,000 group medical renewals that have generated millions of dollars in additional profits for clients.

The purpose of ENERGI is to fundamentally change the perspective of the middle market on Health Care. Instead of viewing healthcare as a liability, where treatment costs have to be controlled, healthcare is redesigned and reframed as an asset where investment in employee health promotion is measured and managed. ENERGI has named its strategy Performance Based Health Plans™. We are changing the narrative on how to manage healthcare.

ENERGI creates EBITDA from health care by converting unmanaged liabilities into performing assets. The company's focus is on providing companies a step-by-step road map on how to manage health care as an asset and deliver a lower trend. The exclusive program guarantees savings in advance for qualifying fully insured and self-funded middle market companies.

Craig Lack earned his MBA and Bachelor's degrees in Finance from Long Beach State University while playing basketball for Tex Winter. Married for over 27 years to his college sweetheart, Sandy, they have two sons, Ryan and Mark. He has served on the Board of the Boys and Girls Club and financially supports the Bike Foundation, the Eric Trump Foundation, Boy Scouts of America and the American Red Cross. He is currently sharing company profits in support of the Second Harvest Food Bank by feeding 10,000 meals to neighbors in Orange County, CA.

ENERGI
33302 Valle Road, Suite 250
San Juan Capistrano, CA 92675
888-636-3744
www.performancebasedhealthplans.com

CHAPTER 3

SPECIALIZED KNOWLEDGE:
The CELEBRITY BRANDING®
Secret of Success

BY NICK NANTON & JW DICKS

Napoleon Hill calls "specialized knowledge" the fourth step to riches in his pioneering self-help book, *Think and Grow Rich.*

For anyone who wants to establish their own Celebrity Brand, however, specialized knowledge is actually THE key to success.

At our Agency, we know what makes our clients special and stand out from the rest *is* their specialized knowledge. The trick is to make their potential leads (and the general public) aware of what they have to offer – and how it can improve the lives of those who hire them.

In this chapter, we're going to pull back the curtain and let you in on some of the "magic" behind our biggest Celebrity Branding® secrets. We'll discuss the power of specialized knowledge, why it's important and how to promote it in credible and impactful ways that lead to a new level of success.

41

In the words of Napoleon Hill himself, *"There are two kinds of knowledge. One is general, the other is specialized. General knowledge...is of but little use in the accumulation of money.... the accumulation of great fortunes calls for POWER, and power is acquired through highly organized and intelligently-directed specialized knowledge."*

Sounds good to us!

THE LASTING VALUE OF SPECIALIZED KNOWLEDGE

None of us can be experts on everything. Now, we've certainly met people who actually *did* know a little bit about everything. They can be very interesting to talk to. But, when you actually need some *real* in-depth advice for a specific concern, you need more than a stimulating conversation. You need expertise – the expertise that comes from *specialized knowledge.*

Think about it. When you have a tax problem, are you just going to listen to your cousin who got audited six years ago and thinks he knows everything about the IRS? Or are you going to listen to a tax attorney who keeps current with all the latest legislation?

When you have a specific pain, are you going to listen to your friend who played college basketball about what he learned when he pulled a hamstring – or are you going to go to a specialist whose practice involves the area of your body that's currently plaguing you?

When there's something important going on in your life that affects your business, your finances, your health or even your relationship, you want to go beyond casual talk with people who have had limited experience in your "area of pain." You want to talk to someone who knows everything there is to know about the specific concern you need addressed. You want to see THE expert in solving the problem you have.

That's why specialized knowledge is so valuable. As Napoleon Hill makes clear in his chapter about specialized knowledge, it *always* has a value to those who, at the time, desperately need it. Even when it comes to the act of making money, Hill writes, "Before you can be sure of your ability to transmute DESIRE into its monetary equivalent, you will require SPECIALIZED KNOWLEDGE of the service, merchandise or profession which you intend to offer in return for fortune."

But, as Hill also makes clear, many do, in fact, have vast amounts of specialized knowledge – and yet they still don't profit greatly from it. In his words, "The faculties of the great universities possess, in the aggregate, practically every form of general knowledge known to civilization. *Most of the professors have but little or no money.*"

Those italics are courtesy of Hill, not us! While we respect men of learning, we also believe they should be able to profit from that learning. Specialized knowledge can be, to use Hill's word, "transmuted" into healthy profit.

Let's talk about how you can make that happen.

MARKETING SPECIALIZED KNOWLEDGE

So what's the difference between a successful businessperson and a doctor, attorney or other professional who has the kind of specialized knowledge people need on a regular basis?

Simple. The businessperson's specialized knowledge usually has to do with *how to make money.* The focus is completely on the bottom line – whereas the professional is usually focused on whatever his or her area of expertise is all about. The doctor or lawyer, for example, spends many extra years beyond the standard four years of college learning his or her profession; the typical entrepreneur, by contrast, could easily be a high school drop-out (and, as a matter of fact, many of our biggest titans of industry over the years never got their high school diploma).

Hill addresses this point by recounting the story of Ford Motors founder Henry Ford, who was one of those super-successful men who had little formal education. Ford was embroiled in a lawsuit and was being challenged by a group of lawyers who were out to prove that he was not too smart. They began peppering him with simple history questions that any schoolboy might know – the problem was, Ford didn't spend a whole lot of time being a schoolboy.

Fed up with the taunting, Ford finally replied, "If I should really WANT to answer the foolish question you have just asked, let me remind you that I have a row of electric push-buttons on my desk, and, by pushing the right button, I can summon to my aid men who can answer ANY question I desire to ask…WHY should I clutter my mind…when I have men around me who can supply any knowledge I require?"

This reflects a very traditional view of specialized knowledge - the "big fish" like Ford made all the money and simply paid for that kind of expertise when they needed it.

But why shouldn't those with specialized knowledge be big fish too? They worked hard to obtain their knowledge and experience – shouldn't that entitle them to more?

ENTER THE CELEBRITY EXPERT®

That's why we enjoy elevating those with their own unique specialized knowledge to a new position in their industry – and in the public's eyes. The Celebrity Expert® is famous and successful precisely because he or she has a certain kind of specialized knowledge that's in demand. People seek out Celebrity Experts®, instead of vice-versa, simply because their reputations precede them.

Think of people like Dr. Oz and Dr. Phil – they're the ultimate in Celebrity Experts®, and, of course, they really don't have to go knocking on anyone's doors – the public comes knocking on theirs. With all due respect to those two gentlemen, though, we have to say we're sure there are thousands of doctors out there that are just as qualified as them – just not as rich and famous.

Why? Because *millions* know who Dr. Oz and Dr. Phil are – while, in comparison, very few people know those other doctors. The fact of the matter is that the difference between Celebrity Experts® and their peers doesn't necessarily have anything to do with them being *better* at what they do – no, it's often just a question of *effective marketing of their positioning.*

This is the point where many professionals sigh and say they don't want to market themselves. They feel it somehow demeans them. They feel it should be enough to be able to excel at what they do – that alone should bring people in through their doors. Our experience is that's a very risky way to think. At best, unaided word of mouth takes years and years to build – and, at worst, someone who doesn't effectively market themselves never gets new clients to replace the old ones who either move on or pass away.

Frankly, with all the economic upheavals of recent years, everyone is looking for every possible advantage in the marketplace. That means if you're *not* marketing yourself, odds are your competitors *are* – and your potential clients or customers, not knowing any better, are going to end up going with the ones making the best case for themselves, i.e., the ones that are doing the best marketing, as opposed to you.

Imagine a lawyer finishing a difficult case – and choosing not to make a closing argument. What's the jury supposed to think? Well, that's kind of the point of a closing argument, isn't it? – to frame the case so the jury looks at it from your point of view. Without that kind of guidance, those twelve men and women are probably just going to latch on to what the opposing lawyer is saying.

Well, that's basically the situation in which professionals and entrepreneurs who refuse to market properly are putting themselves; they're not making a case for their specialized knowledge and those that might have hired them *never find out that they should.*

CELEBRITY EXPERTS® REQUIRE EXPERT MARKETING

Part of the reason professionals don't feel comfortable with marketing is that the word "marketing" immediately makes them think of the worst TV commercial they recently saw. Maybe it was a cheesy infomercial for the latest glued-together combination of metal and springs that's supposed to give you super-abs – or maybe it's some famous football player yelling at you from the TV about how to get your prostate in shape with his brand of vitamins.

We're the first to agree that this is not the way to market a Celebrity Expert®. No, the way to market a Celebrity Expert® is to take advantage of the most important thing he or she has to offer – which takes us right back to the subject of this chapter, *specialized knowledge.*

In other words, we're not suggestion they should be out there doing TV commercials where they wear cowboy hats and ride on elephants (don't laugh, a car dealer in California used to do that!)—and we're not discouraging it either....if it aligns with your brand. Instead, they should appear in *venues and in situations that fit their brand, offering their expertise.*

We do this through several media channels for our Celebrity Expert® clients. In this next section of the chapter, we're going to share some of the main ways we market them in a way that doesn't embarrass them (or us!) – and how you can easily take advantage of them yourself:

- **Newspapers and Magazines**
  It would be awesome to find yourself profiled in an article in a major periodical like *The Wall Street Journal, USA Today* and *Forbes*, right? Especially if that article focused on all the good stuff about you and featured quotes from you that demonstrated your specialized knowledge. Well, that's just what we do for our clients

– and it's easy enough to do on your own in your community. There are always local newspapers and magazines that are hunting for good content; just provide it to them in the form of an interview or by writing an article on a subject that you're an expert on and that their readers will want to read about.

- **TV and Radio Shows**
  We produce many television and radio shows, such as our *America's PremierExperts® programs*, in which we feature our clients being interviewed about their work by media professionals. These shows air on ABC, NBC, CBS and FOX affiliates across the nation. For your part, there are always local "talking head" radio and TV talk shows that are anxious for guests that are interesting and have informative content to share. Look for topics that will work for them and you and contact them about a possible interview.

  And don't forget – you can even do your own podcast and put it up on iTunes!

- **Blogs and Articles**
  Online blogging (and article posting) still definitely makes an impact; we help our clients place their content on such popular sites as *The Huffington Post* and *Fast Company*. You should consider blogging on your own site and also posting articles on other sites that accept your kind of content (always make sure you include a link back to your site when you do that).

- **Books**
  Nothing says "expert" more than showing a potential client a book authored by you. And it's not all that hard to pull off, even if time is at a premium in your schedule. There are a myriad of publishing options out there, as well as affordable ghostwriters who will actually help you complete the work. We're proud to say we've

helped over 1000 professionals become Best-Selling authors – and most of them are ecstatic that they're able to use that fact in their marketing to help boost their profile and their prestige with their clientele. Think about it, who would you rather hire, the Best-Selling author….or the other guy? Easy choice right!

- **Videos and Branded Films**
  Using online video is a giant industry that's getting even bigger with each passing year. Here are two important stats that prove it, according to a recent Content Marketing Institute (CMI) survey:

  - Over 85% of online users viewed video content in September 2012 alone.

  - About 46% of people are more apt to research a product or service after watching an online video about it.

Video and film are also great for showcasing your personality and establishing a personal connection to potential clients and customers: They bring an extra dimension to marketing that can be invaluable.

This kind of content can be as simple as "How-To" videos on YouTube, featuring you talking directly to the camera about a subject in your area of expertise, or they can be fully-produced branded films that tell your story, as well as the story of your business or practice, so viewers understand what you're all about. We've produced many of these for clients, who have seen outstanding results from them.

In all of the above marketing examples, you may notice there's not a lot of hard sell. We don't believe that's effective for most professionals and entrepreneurs. What we do believe is most effective, in terms of marketing, is for a Celebrity Expert® to: (a) demonstrate they have a high level of specialized knowledge, and (b) provide a taste of that knowledge (with some personality infused) to give those exposed to the marketing some *value* from having seen it, making it a win-win.

Whether you're an entrepreneur who's achieved a high degree of success or a professional who has worked hard to build your expertise to an outstanding level, you have specialized knowledge that will benefit others. When you use high-level marketing to successfully *convey* that specialized knowledge through your own words, you not only boost your recognition factor, but you also create *credibility* and the beginnings of a personal bond.

A Celebrity Expert® is someone who knows the value of their specialized knowledge and has successfully communicated it to the world. And there's no reason you can't join their ranks.

In other words, you can not only *Think and Grow Rich* – but you can also *Know* and Grow Rich!

About Nick

An Emmy-winning director and producer, Nick Nanton, Esq., is known as the top agent to celebrity experts around the world for his role in developing and marketing business and professional experts through personal branding, media, marketing and PR to help them gain credibility and recognition for their accomplishments. Nick is recognized as the nation's leading expert on personal branding as *Fast Company* magazine's expert blogger on the subject and lectures regularly on the topic at major universities around the world. His book *Celebrity Branding You®* has also been used as the textbook on personal branding for university students.

The CEO of The Dicks + Nanton Celebrity Branding Agency, an international agency with more than 1000 clients in 26 countries, Nick is an award-winning director, producer and songwriter who has worked on everything from large-scale events to television shows with Bill Cosby, President George H.W. Bush, Brian Tracy, Michael Gerber and many more.

Nick is recognized as one of the top thought leaders in the business world and has co-authored 16 best-selling books alongside Brian Tracy, Jack Canfield (creator of the "Chicken Soup for the Soul" series), Dan Kennedy, Robert Allen, Dr. Ivan Misner (founder of BNI), Jay Conrad Levinson (author of the "Guerilla Marketing" series), Leigh Steinberg and many others, including the breakthrough hit *Celebrity Branding You!*

Nick has led the marketing and PR campaigns that have driven more than 600 authors to best-seller status. Nick has been seen in *USA Today, The Wall Street Journal, Newsweek, Inc., The New York Times, Entrepreneur Magazine* and FastCompany.com and has appeared on ABC, NBC, CBS, and FOX television affiliates around the country, as well as on FOX News, CNN, CNBC and MSNBC, speaking on subjects ranging from branding, marketing and law to "American Idol."

Nick is a member of the Florida Bar and holds a J.D. from the University of Florida Levin College of Law, as well as a B.S./B.A. in Finance from the University of Florida's Warrington College of Business Administration. Nick is a voting member of The National Academy of Recording Arts & Sciences

(NARAS, home to the Grammys), a member of The National Academy of Television Arts & Sciences (home to the Emmy Awards), co-founder of the National Academy of Best-Selling Authors®, and an 11-time Telly Award winner. He spends his spare time working with Young Life and Downtown Credo Orlando and rooting for the Florida Gators with his wife Kristina and their three children, Brock, Bowen and Addison.

About JW

JW Dicks, Esq. is America's foremost authority on using personal branding for business development. He has created some of the most successful brand and marketing campaigns for business and professional clients to make them the credible celebrity experts in their field and build multi-million dollar businesses using their recognized status.

JW Dicks has started, bought, built, and sold a large number of businesses over his 39-year career and developed a loyal international following as a business attorney, author, speaker, consultant, and business experts' coach. He not only practices what he preaches by using his strategies to build his own businesses, he also applies those same concepts to help clients grow their business or professional practice the ways he does.

JW has been extensively quoted in such national media as *USA Today, The Wall Street Journal, Newsweek, Inc.*, Forbes.com, CNBC.com, and *Fortune Small Business*. His television appearances include ABC, NBC, CBS and FOX affiliate stations around the country. He is the resident branding expert for *Fast Company*'s internationally syndicated blog and is the publisher of *Celebrity Expert Insider*, a monthly newsletter targeting business and brand building strategies.

JW has written over 22 books, including numerous best-sellers, and has been inducted into the National Academy of Best-Selling Authors. JW is married to Linda, his wife of 39 years, and they have two daughters, two granddaughters and two Yorkies. JW is a 6th generation Floridian and splits his time between his home in Orlando and beach house on the Florida west coast.

CHAPTER 4

13 STEPS TO ENRICHING YOUR LIFE

BY FOREST HAMILTON

> *"Whatever your mind can conceive*
> *and believe, you can achieve."*
> ~ Napoleon Hill

That's it.

Right there.

You just received *THE SECRET* to mind-blowing, world-chang-ing, *nearly*-incomprehensible successes...in a little bitty nutshell.

These ten words have been the catalyst of every great invention, business, and personal success story for all of history.

Whatever your mind can conceive and believe, you can achieve? Surely, it can't be that simple? Can it? The answer is yes. It IS that simple, and it IS true.

Here is another truth:

If you are mentally, emotionally, and spiritually ready for what you are going to read in this book, you and your life will change drastically, never to be the same. If you are not ready, the lack of massive, positive change that you will experience will be all the evidence that you will need. Unfortunately, you are probably not ready, so this evidence will probably cement in your mind long-standing societal beliefs that you are not in control of your life, nor are you in control of the successes and failures that you are "destined" to experience. Many will read this book and "succeed" in proving its principles wrong, for this is the Law of Reversed Effect. The Law of Reversed Effect states that when you attempt to plant a positive idea in your mind, if the subconscious already harbors a negative towards that idea, it will dig in its heels and become obsessed with defending its already established idea.

Ok, now go back to the beginning of this chapter and read it again, savoring each word and paying attention to your thoughts and feelings. Think about how it made you *feel*. When you were reading about how simple the secret was, did you roll your eyes and think something like, "Oh yeah? Well, I'm conceiving and believing a million dollars right now and I don't see it!" or when you read about not being ready, did you nod your head and think, "Yeah, it probably won't work for me either." If so, you are not ready and you can stop reading now. Come back when you are genuinely seeking solutions to your problems and only then will you find them in these pages.

If, on the other hand, you came here because you ARE ready to fully immerse yourself in the system of Thinking and Growing Rich, you may continue. If you nodded your head as you read and thought, "I never thought of it that way!" or felt yourself getting excited thinking that maybe your dreams and goals were closer than you thought, keep reading. If you felt a twinge of competitiveness when I challenged you by saying you were probably not ready, please, prove me wrong. Go ahead and show me, show you, and show the world that you ARE ready to set down your preconceived notions and pick up the proven system used by all of the great men and women in history.

My *hope* is that I got your attention. My *wish* is that you will study and apply these Success Principles for the rest of your life. My *prayer* is that you will pass them on as I am doing so that others may benefit from the power of the truths that they hold.

That being said, it will take more than a Hope, a Wish, and a Prayer to make your dreams come true, so let's get started!

In the following pages I will break down the 13 Steps to Riches that Napoleon Hill spent his life studying, learning, and teaching. By following these same 13 steps, my life was transformed from literal rags to enlightened riches.

THE 13 STEPS TO RICHES

1. Desire

2. Faith

3. Auto-Suggestion

4. Specialized Knowledge

5. Imagination

6. Organized Planning

7. Decision

8. Persistence

9. Power of the Master Mind

10. The Mystery of Sex Transmutation

11. The Sub-Conscious Mind

12. The Brain

13. The Sixth Sense

A BURNING DESIRE
The Starting Point of All Achievement

At this juncture I feel that it is important to define "riches." *Think and Grow Rich* is primarily focused on the attainment of money, but do not be turned off by this. Every concept that Dr. Hill describes is applicable to any desire that you may have. Financial, philosophical, and physical dreams all are achieved using this same 13-step recipe. Many of the world's greatest culinary dishes require that you follow a recipe within a recipe. In other words, there are often steps that you must take and certain ingredients that you must mix together at specific times in order to get the desired result in the end.

Hill's 13 Steps to Riches are designed to be followed in order. In many cases it is difficult or even impossible to understand a step until you grasp the one before it. It is a progressive unfolding of the truth. He states clearly in his teachings that you must follow all of the steps or you will not succeed in truly fulfilling your potential. That being said, it is unfortunate how many people become wealthy by simply learning and practicing the chapter on desire. This is possible because it contains six definite, practical steps by which a desire for riches can be transmuted into its financial equivalent. Sit down in a quiet place with a pen and paper and fully engage in this process:

1. Fix in your mind the exact amount of money (or the specific thing) that you desire. It is not sufficient to say "I want lots of money!" or "I want a promotion." Be definite as to the amount or the specific thing that you desire.

2. Determine exactly what you intend to give in return for the money (or the thing) that you desire. (There is no such thing as something for nothing.)

3. Establish a definite date when you intend to possess the money (or the thing) that you desire. Set a deadline!

4. Create a definite plan for carrying out your desire, and begin at once, whether you are ready or not, to put this plan into action.

5. Write out a clear, concise statement of the amount of money (or the thing) that you intend to acquire, name the time limit for its acquisition, state what you intend to give in return for it, and describe clearly the plan through which you intend to acquire it.

6. Read your written statement aloud, **twice daily**, once just before retiring at night, and once after arising in the

morning. AS YOU READ - SEE AND FEEL AND BE-LIEVE YOURSELF ALREADY IN POSSESSION OF THE MONEY (OR THE THING).

You are probably asking yourself how you can see and feel and believe yourself in possession of the money or the object of your desire before you actually have it. Your desire for this achievement cannot be a passing whim, it must be a *burning* desire that allows you to overcome the doubt that has kept you from it up until now. This idea will quickly grow from *wanting,* to *believing,* to *having* faith that moves mountains if you are disciplined enough to follow these steps.

DEVELOPING FAITH THROUGH AUTO-SUGGESTION
How to Visualize and Attain Your Burning Desire

Faith is the "eternal elixir" which gives life, power, and action to the impulse of thought. I love how Dr. Hill describes the method by which one develops faith where it does not already exist. He states that it is almost as difficult as it would be to describe the color of red to a blind man that has never seen color, and has nothing to compare what you describe to him. He goes on to say that faith is a state of mind which you may develop at will, after you have mastered the 13 principles. Faith may be induced, or created, by affirmation (repeated instructions) to the subconscious mind, through the principle of auto-suggestion.

Man is the master of his own destiny because he has the power to influence his own subconscious mind. Our greatest weakness is often a lack of self-confidence. By using a simple, five-step process of auto-suggestion, you will be able to rewrite your negative script with a more functional and positive script. You will accomplish this by arranging thought impulses stated in writing, memorized, and repeated, until they become a part of the subconscious faculty of your mind. Dr. Hill calls this the Self-Confidence Formula.

SPECIALIZED KNOWLEDGE
Knowledge is NOT Power!

If knowledge alone was the secret to success, then college professors would be the most powerful, wealthy, influential people on earth. Knowledge is simply potential power. The true power lies in the organization and intelligent use of *specialized* knowledge. Henry Ford had less than a sixth grade education, but because he had specialized knowledge in his field and the awareness to hire others with specialized knowledge in areas that he did not excel in, he became one of the wealthiest men in America. Find and fortify the specialized knowledge that can best help you to carve out a niche in *your* market!

IMAGINATION AND THE BRAIN
The Workshop of the Mind

All ideas take form in the imagination. You can create anything that you can imagine. There are two forms of imagination, synthetic imagination (arranges old concepts, ideas, or plans into new combinations) and creative imagination (all the new ideas that come from being connected to our purpose, i.e.. hunches and inspiration.) You must learn to use the two in harmony in order to achieve your imagined vision.

ORGANIZED PLANNING AND THE POWER OF THE MASTERMIND
The Crystallization of Desire Into Action

One of the steps from the chapter on desire was to form a definite, practical plan, through which your transformation would occur. In order to create and implement the best possible plan, Dr. Hill suggests you ally yourself with a group of like-minded individuals. The Mastermind group blends all of the strengths of each member into a powerful, connected, synergistic force that is able to plow through obstacles that none of the individuals could defeat alone. The combined passion and multi-faceted perspective of the Mastermind group helps in the organization, planning, and implementation of the plan. You automatically take on the habits and power of the people that you associate with, so be careful in the choosing of your Mastermind group. Be sure that all members add value and strength to the group.

DECISION AND PERSISTENCE
The Mastery of Procrastination and The Sustained Effort Necessary to Induce Faith

Successful people have the habit of reaching decisions very quickly and changing them slowly, if ever. This does not mean that the plans don't change in the face of temporary failure, it simply means that the commitment to succeed in the agreed-upon mission does not waver. In fact, temporary failure is a signal that something must be changed, not a time for head-hanging or tail-tucking. One of my favorite stories is from one of Napoleon Hill's conversations with Thomas Edison. When asked how he was able to push through the 10,000+ documented laboratory failures in order to finally perfect the incandescent electric light bulb, Edison simply replied, "That's easy, I ran out of things that wouldn't work!" He was so convinced that he was going to figure it out that he genuinely believed every failure got him one step closer to the answer he was looking for. A quitter never wins and a winner never quits. Will-power, desire, and persistence are essential for the transmuting of desires into their monetary equivalents.

THE MYSTERY OF SEX TRANSMUTATION

Sex transmutation involves the transfer of sexual desire into a motivating force for financial achievement. Many people still have such insecure emotions about Sex that they never are able to utilize one of the most powerful forces in nature to their advantage. Behind the emotion of sex lie three constructive potentialities:

1. The perpetuation of mankind.

2. The maintenance of health as a therapeutic agency.

3. The transformation of mediocrity into genius through transmutation.

Sex Transmutation is the act of using your mind to channel the natural physical desires at your core into creative action. Through the use of will-power, you choose to focus your mind on that which is truly important to you, allowing you to tap into levels of passion and desire that are unattainable by those that submerge, eliminate, or use only physical outlets for the expression of this emotion.

THE BRAIN AND THE SUB-CONSCIOUS MIND

The brain is merely a broadcasting station that sends and receives thought. The Sub-Conscious Mind is the key to all consistent joy, success, love, and riches. It is working 24 hours a day, 365 days a year. It functions voluntarily, whether you make any effort to influence it or not. If you fail to feed your subconscious mind the desires of your choosing, it will instead feed upon the negative thoughts which reach it as the result of neglect. The subconscious mind can be directed only through habit, under the persistent planting of specific plans, desires, and purposes which you wish to be transformed into their physical counterparts. Positive and negative emotions cannot occupy the mind simultaneously. If you habitually choose the positive, there will be no room for the negative.

THE 7 MAJOR POSITIVE EMOTIONS

1. Desire
2. Faith
3. Love
4. Sex
5. Enthusiasm
6. Romance
7. Hope

THE 7 MAJOR NEGATIVE EMOTIONS

1. Fear

2. Jealousy

3. Hatred

4. Revenge

5. Greed

6. Superstition

7. Anger

THE SIXTH SENSE
The Door to the Temple of Wisdom

The Sixth Sense is "the apex of the philosophy. It can only be assimilated, understood, and applied by first mastering the other 12 principles." It is a mixture of both the mental and the spiritual and the place where you get inspirations, hunches, and epiphanies. It is nearly impossible to fathom until you fully immerse yourself in the entire process, but becomes a natural and effortless addition to your mind and heart through the application of the first 12 principles.

OUTWITTING THE SIX GHOSTS OF FEAR

I started this body of work by attempting to get your attention. By making you aware and increasing the vibration of your thoughts, I was attempting to prepare your mind to receive the philosophy that I have laid at your feet. You will not be able to use any portion of this until you remove indecision, doubt, and fear. Study your fears in order to know them. Once you know them, you will see that they are not real, they are simply states of mind. Since we have the power to change our state of mind, we have ultimate power over our fears. This is a simple secret that once practiced, removes all clutter, leaving only clarity. That is when you will no longer have to fight to follow the 13 steps, you will float along in the current as your freed subconscious sings your favorite tune.

FROM MESS TO SUCCESS

Always remember, it doesn't matter where you currently are in your life! The only thing that matters is what you do from this point forward. You become and achieve what you think about all day long. Both poverty and riches are the direct results of your dominant thoughts. The way you have been thinking has gotten you to this exact place in your life, good or bad. One of my favorite quotes about change is, "If you always do what you've always done, you will always get what you've always got." Every great success story tells of how things went from a Mess to a Success. If you are currently struggling, simply realize that this is the Mess part of your story that must exist before the Success part can become possible.

I chose not to spend a lot of time in this chapter telling you my Mess to Success story in order to fill this precious space with life changing principles uncovered by Napoleon Hill. Take a few minutes and read my bio or send me an email if you would like to hear about how drastically my life has changed since I applied his 13 Steps. I am happy, healthy, wealthy, and living a life far beyond my wildest dreams. I read "Think and Grow Rich" at least once a year and get something amazing from it each time. Buy it, read it, apply it, and you too will think, and grow rich.

About Forest

Forest Hamilton was literally delivered into his father's hands. When the midwife was late in arriving, David Hamilton had to find a way to bring his boy into this world. Through fear, uncertainty, and an umbilical cord wrapped around his son's neck, he found a way. Raised without running water or electricity into his teens, Forest followed his father's example and continued to persevere. His father taught him to be the hardest worker on the farm, the most competitive athlete on the field, and the most dedicated student in the classroom. This work ethic, coupled with his mother's consistently encouraging ways, helped him find his way to Texas to pursue his dreams at an early age.

Forest Hamilton is a two-time Best-Selling author, award winning speaker, and a serial entrepreneur. He recently received the Thought Leader of the Year Award from the National Academy of Best-Selling Authors. He is one of America's PremierExperts™ and has been featured in USA Today, CNBC, Yahoo! Finance, and MarketWatch online, among others.

Forest now resides in Beaumont, Texas and is the Assistant Director of Universal Coin and Bullion, Ltd. He has held many positions in his nearly 20-year career with UCB, one of the world's largest gold, silver, and rare coin investment firms. Beginning his career at UCB as a teenager, Forest has been awarded numerous honors for sales, teamwork, and customer service on his way to becoming an invaluable resource in every department. He has helped propel his company from a five million dollar a year business into a multi-national, award winning, sixty million dollar a year industry leader.

Forest is the Founder of Poor Kid Enterprises, LLC, Poor Kid Films, LLC, and Poor Kid Real Estate, LLC. He is an Executive Producer of the Hollywood film, SNAP and is also a partner and co-founder of David Hamilton Winery, LLC in Mt. Vernon, Oregon. This family-run winery specializes in organic fruit wines of the Northwest. He truly enjoys helping his family find ways to acquire, produce, distribute, and drink their unique wines.

Forest and the love of his life, Stormy, have three beautiful daughters, Taylin, Tinsley, and Trinity. He is a dedicated husband and father and applies the same passion to his personal life that he does to his business life. His true purpose is to help others realize that happiness and success are the results of choices, not chances. He is constantly studying, living, and teaching a simple, proven system that can take anyone from wherever they are to exactly where they want to be.

If you are interested in having Forest Hamilton help YOU find a better way in life or business, he is available for speaking engagements, gold and silver portfolio planning, and personal/business coaching. Please visit: foresthamilton.com or universalcoin.com to set up your free consultation and determine what he can do for you and your business. You can also call 800-248-2223 or email Forest directly at: foresthamilton@universalcoin.com

If you are interested in learning more about organically grown fruit wines with no added sulfites, visit: davidhamiltonwinery.com or call 541-932-4567.

CHAPTER 5

FOR ADULTS ONLY:
Transmutation and the Mastermind Marriage

BY RICHARD SEPPALA

There is one chapter in the original *Think and Grow Rich* book that not a lot of people reference. And I can see why.

Let's face it – it's easy to apply such principles as "Organized Planning," "Imagination" and "Persistence" to wealth-building. But the subject of Chapter 11 of Napoleon Hill's groundbreaking volume isn't maybe quite as easy to connect. Its title is "The Mystery of Sex Transmutation" – and that's a topic that doesn't come up very often in learning how to become successful.

Of course, I could be going to the wrong seminars…

Anyway, don't worry, I'm not here to give a sex talk – and this chapter is not going to venture beyond a solid PG. Napoleon Hill's point wasn't that you should watch porno to improve your negotiating skills – no, I believe he was actually talking about how your true love can inspire you to heights you wouldn't otherwise achieve.

To make this understandable in terms of my role as "The ROI

Guy," I believe when you partner up with the right significant other, not only does your personal Return on Investment goes through the roof – your professional one does as well.

TRANSMUTATION AND YOU

As Hill wrote, "Transmute is, in simple language, the changing, or transferring of one element or form of energy, into another." His further point is that sex is the most powerful of human desires – and that, "when driven by this desire, men develop keenness of imagination, courage, willpower, persistence, and creative ability unknown to them at other times."

You'd think I would've gotten a lot more from watching *Baywatch* when it was on, right?

I frankly believe that it isn't just the physical act of love alone that creates this kind of productive "transmutation" – I think the emotion of love has a whole lot to do with it too. And, if you read Napoleon Hill's original chapter, you'll see that he more than agrees.

In it, Napoleon talks of the other Napoleon – remember that short guy from France that almost conquered the world? Well, according to Hill, during the period when that earlier Napoleon was inspired by his first wife Josephine, he was "irresistible and invincible." When he divorced her, however, that's when his fortunes took a decisive turn for the worse.

That's because Hill believes that the kind of energy that is created by the right couple is the most powerful: "When the emotion of love begins to mix itself with the emotion of sex, the result is calmness of purpose, poise, accuracy of judgment and balance…. Love is the emotion which serves as a safety valve and insures balance, poise and constructive effort."

I have to say I totally agree with Mr. Hill – because I've experienced this miracle in my own life.

BRIDE OF THE ROI GUY

I was alone with my oldest son Cole when my wife Lisa came into my life. It was a time of great change for me; because of my personal situation, I had made a big shift from a prominent role in corporate marketing (which required a great deal of travel) to becoming a sole entrepreneur. As almost everyone reading this book knows, that takes a massive change of mindset in order for you to succeed. Generating your own business success, as opposed to following the *dictums* of a company, requires approaching everything from a very different angle.

When I was in the midst of making that particular turn in my road, I met Dr. Lisa Peters – she was a dentist with a son of her own. We had a lot in common and a lot to offer each other. The "transmutation" (I'll spare you the details!) quickly kicked into gear and soon, I was applying my marketing smarts to helping her grow her dental practice – while she helped advise me on my new business.

Just in the past few months, our brainstorming (not to mention our four kids) has resulted in the birth of the "ROI Kids Club" – an organization that we created to help children at an early age learn the value of becoming an entrepreneur as well as giving back to the community (you can find out more about it at ROIKids.com – where you can also see all of our smiling faces). We combined forces to throw an awesome charity ball to benefit clean water for impoverished communities around the globe - and we're planning more special events for the ROI Kids Club in the future to both attract new members and to make the world a better place.

The ROI Kids Club is just another benefit I've found in my relationship with Lisa. What I've discovered over the six years we've been married is that when you finally hook up with the person you're supposed to be with, it takes your thinking – and your living – up to the higher level that Napoleon Hill wrote about in that "notorious" Chapter 11 of his. According to him, "The men who have accumulated great fortunes and achieved outstanding recognition in literature, art, industry and the professions were motivated by the influence of a woman."

Of course, back in 1937 when *Think and Grow Rich* was written, conventional thought had it that only men achieved great things. I'm proud to say things have changed major league since then, and that both of us want to land in the winner's circle together.

The intimacy provided by a rich and real relationship, such as the one Lisa and I enjoy, enables both of you to 'fire on all cylinders.' You create the vital and supportive team that frees you to come up with all kinds of ideas (and makes you unafraid to share those ideas, even though some of them might be dopey!). Our combined creativity, experience and expertise makes us much more than we would be on our own – and I honestly feel that in our case, one plus one equals…well, about a million.

That formula might not add up in math class, but that's how the numbers work in our home!

THE MASTERMIND MARRIAGE

One of the other famous concepts that Napoleon Hill put forth was that of the Mastermind group – in which people at advanced levels in an industry would form an informal roundtable of sorts in order to help each other find new levels of success. The theory is that each person in the Mastermind Group would have different skills and specialties that the others might lack – so everyone finds a real, lasting value in the group interactions.

Well, I've never heard a better description of a great relationship. The fact is, the right couple can put together their brains and talent to create the "Ultimate" Mastermind Group – what I call a Mastermind Marriage.

Why do I call a Mastermind Marriage the Ultimate Mastermind Group?

There are a few reasons – and number one is *time.* Think about it:

With a traditional Mastermind group, you're limited to an hour or two for a meeting once a week or month (or even just once a year, in some instances). At best, you might have an entire Mastermind weekend at some resort. While I'm certainly not discounting the value of that time (I participate in these groups myself), it can be a little frustrating not to have enough time to fully work through an idea or problem with the group.

That's not a problem with a Mastermind Marriage. When you're married to your Mastermind partner, you have the ability to share ideas and thoughts pretty much 24/7. And, if you are on the verge of an awesome breakthrough, you don't have to worry about the clock running out – you can easily pick up where you left off when you see each other next during the day.

Another reason you can't beat a Mastermind Marriage? *Security.* As I noted, you can feel safe saying out loud the stupidest idea in the world with someone you have a great relationship with. Of course, you might be thinking, "Why should you want to be able to do that?" Simple. Sometimes the dumbest things spur some thinking in the right direction, enabling you to come up with some incredibly *smart* ideas and new ways of looking at problems. I've seen it firsthand. You never know where an idea will take you – that's why it's great to feel okay about saying *anything* to your significant other. Whereas, if you're with a traditional Mastermind group, you're going to think twice about what you say – you don't want to appear dumb in front of other heavy hitters, so your ego starts to get in the way because you want to impress them. That automatically means you're going to be extra-careful about what you say and how you say it.

Here's another big reason the Mastermind Marriage makes you into a real power couple – *intimacy,* which I touched on earlier. We may be back into Napoleon Hill's transmutation theory here again, but the love and commitment a real Mastermind Marriage should have as its foundation gives every interaction its own unique power and intensity. Of course, when you have a fight, that power and intensity might get a little scary – but, most of the time, it instead spurs you both on to achieve.

As Hill wrote, "...it has the effect of lifting the individual far above the horizon of ordinary thought, and permits him to envision distance, scope and quality of THOUGHTS not available on the lower plane, such as that occupied while one is engaged in the solution of the problems of business and professional routine."

I would have said the same thing, but he said it first.

The final reason a Mastermind Marriage excels? Well, there's the little matter of *accountability* – which isn't a little matter at all. When people are held accountable, when they know someone is going to be around to see if they do what they say they're going to do, there's a much greater chance of that follow-through actually occurring.

If action is the key to success (as I believe it is), a Mastermind Marriage is definitely the best way to make things happen. A Mastermind Marriage means that if you tell your partner you're going to do something, whether it's picking up a gallon of milk from the store on your way home, starting a diet to lose ten pounds or putting an exciting new business idea into action, you know you'd better do it – or your partner is going to be eyeing you and wondering why you didn't.

This isn't meant to imply that, in a Mastermind Marriage, you should always be watching each other like a hawk – and more than ready to pounce on your partner's failures. It's more about the fact that, if you truly love and respect each other, you'll *want* to follow through on your promises simply to keep that love and respect alive. But, of course, you always have to be ready to forgive when the other party, for whatever reason, doesn't make something happen as expected.

CRAZY LITTLE THING CALLED LOVE

Not many people ever read *Think and Grow Rich* for romantic advice. But maybe they should – because Hill is clearly a believer in the power of love.

"When the emotion of romance is added to those of love and sex," he writes, "the obstructions between the finite mind of man and Infinite Intelligence are removed. Then a genius is born!"

Now, I'm not claiming to be a genius by any means, but I know what he means. I've been lucky enough to see for myself how a Mastermind Marriage contains the best of all possible worlds. It is possible to combine work with pleasure – in fact, with a Mastermind Marriage, it's the ideal – and when you do, that's when the real "transmutation" gets kicked into high gear.

One final note from Mr. Hill: "NO MAN IS HAPPY OR COMPLETE WITHOUT THE MODIFYING INFLUENCE OF A WOMAN." Wow, Napoleon, you don't have to shout – we get it. At least I do. But, to be more politically correct, we probably need to amend that statement to "No *person* is happy or complete without being in a Mastermind Marriage of their own."

The right relationship inspires us, motivates us, and lifts us up to the heights we want to reach. The right relationship does indeed complete us. Here's hoping you are in – or are able to find – the Mastermind Marriage you were destined to be in.

And here's hoping the S-E-X is pretty good too!

About Richard

Richard Seppala, also known as "The ROI Guy™," is a marketing expert, business consultant and Best-Selling author who helps companies maximize their profits by accurately measuring the ROI (Return on Investment) of their marketing efforts. His latest revolutionary tracking system, "The ROI Matrix," measures to the penny just how much revenue each specific marketing placement generates for a client.

Richard founded his "ROI Guy" company in 2005. In addition to his acclaimed marketing tracking systems, called "The Holy Grail of Marketing," he also supplies businesses and medical practices with cutting-edge sales solutions designed to facilitate the conversion of generated leads to cash-paying customers.

By identifying marketing strengths and weaknesses, The ROI Guy™ is able to substantially boost his clients' bottom lines by eliminating wasteful spending on ineffective marketing, as well as leveraging advertising campaigns that prove the most profitable. By providing "all-in-one" automated systems that allow for the real-time tracking of each generated lead, a business can easily access valuable marketing data with just a few keystrokes.

Richard's marketing expertise is regularly sought out by the media, which he's shared on NBC, CBS, ABC and FOX affiliates, as well as in The Wall Street Journal, USA Today and Newsweek. He's also launched his own television show, "ROI TV," which features interviews with other top marketing specialists.

To learn more about Richard Seppala, The ROI Guy™, and how you can receive free special reports and other invaluable marketing information from one of the country's leading experts, visit: www.YourROIGuy.com
Or call Toll-Free 1-800-647-1909.

CHAPTER 6

THE MASTERMIND...

BY RICHARD McFARLAND

It was a cold, dark and stormy night and the wind and rain were beating against my body with no end in site. I struggled to keep walking forward towards the lighted city in the distance. I knew that if I could just reach the city limits I would survive and make it through the night.

Each step I took I knew in my mind would bring me closer to safety and security. However, the howling wind and beating rain seemed to make my progress seem backwards and the city lights just would not get closer. Every hour that passed was perceived as years to my body and my weary mind as I strived to follow the path given to me. After what seemed an endless trek towards and many stumbles of failure, I managed to reach a small hut upon the path and a very small light in the window. This meant someone had to be home and I longed for a warm drink and to get out of the storm.

As I reached the porch and lightly rapped on the door, I could hear footsteps coming towards the door. Slowly the door opened and a small but muscular, white-haired man smiled and welcomed me in. I gratefully accepted and as we stepped towards the back of the cabin, it opened up into a great room with a welcoming fireplace and table with food, drink and several beings which appeared to be human – yet had something greater and lighter shining around them. There was almost a green aura that glowed in the night and it seemed to be even warmer than the fire, yet it did not burn as brightly.

As I sat down at the table I was offered warm drink and bread and dry towels to comfort my aching body and sooth my weary mind. No words were spoken and I felt as if nothing was expected of me until I was ready. As I began to warm up and get comfortable in my chair, one of the beings spoke to me and asked me about my journey. As I explained to him my goals and aspirations once I reached the city, he just smiled warmly and seemed to understand and already know what I was about to say with each word.

After I completed my story and life plan and how I wanted to change the world, all of the beings surrounding the table smiled, applauded and somehow assured me without even speaking that it would all be well and that my journey was not in vain. Then, one by one, they went around the table sharing their story with me about how they had struggled through great storms and had reached their destinations, and the great victories and failures that ensued during the trip.

As I listened carefully and soaked in the great stories from each one, I seemed to become part of the group and I could feel my spirit literally merging with each one as if we had known each other for ages, and each of us had a similar experience to share. After all had spoken, I had a comforting feeling rush over me as if a large warm blanket had been given to me for protection. I felt as if I could easily share my most difficult challenges and darkest secrets to this group of experienced beings that I had never met in this world, but seemed as if I had known them for all time.

The conversation turned to laughter and then a bit of dancing to great music from the small music box in the corner of the room by the fireplace. And at nights end, the camaraderie seemed inseparable. I was so very grateful that I had found this place along the path that at first seemed so dreary and impassable. I knew in my heart I had found a place where I belonged, and that I could obtain great experience just by being there.

The next morning the storm had seemed to subside, or maybe it was the same, but my perception of the storm was that it was much smaller and appeared more of a light rain with sunshine in the near distance. I knew it was time for me to go. The group I had grown so close to the evening before all made it clear it was time for me to venture out on my own, but this time not alone.

I thanked them for their kind hospitality and great stories of things that would certainly be useful to me on my trek (and some life saving). As I stepped out into the windy path I experienced a feeling of great calm and gratefulness. I knew that I was now prepared mentally and spiritually to take on a new strength as I headed towards the city and all of its offerings and challenges. As I reached the city gates, I was welcomed and smiled upon, and it appeared that each person I met noticed my genuine caring about them and my newly-learned language that allowed me to speak to them about things they were already thinking – creating instant agreement and trade between us.

As I began to realize my goals and dreams over the coming months and years, I realized that without that chance meeting in the night during the worst part of the storm, I might have never made it to the city at all. Or when I did I would have a very dark experience due to my hate and spite of the storm, and my weary soul from the brutal travel. Instead I felt a strength that is difficult to describe in words, and certainly more complex to apply monetary value to. Nonetheless, I knew in my own heart that the valuable lessons and stories shared with me that night were priceless and have stayed with me ever since.

Okay so this might sound to you like some romantic novel or some mysterious dark saga of some lost soul. And in fact, that is how I view our lives. Each of us is our own author of our life story and we can write it any way we see fit.

Most of us will be non-fiction documentaries following a pre-dictable path already told my millions. It is not evil or wrong, just predictable. Fewer will write their own fiction about a life well-lived and full of adventure. Good vs. evil, long treks to far away places, lost treasures found in exotic lands, and new inventions never before experienced by mankind. The latter is the one who can read this book, this chapter, and these words and know exactly what I am saying. You see I am that lost soul trying to find his way. I have travelled the past 30 years through darkness, thick forests, dry deserts and heavy storms. Along the way I have enjoyed great times and some very dark times when I thought the city lights would never be attainable.

The story I share above is one of the masters. The beings I speak of are what is best known as the mastermind. If you read, com-prehend and believe in what Napoleon Hill found during his great adventure studying some of the most successful people in our civilization's history, then you know that none of them did it alone. It was quite clear in fact to Mr. Hill and to those who have found success that having a mastermind to learn from, share with and be of service – to be literally one of the fastest ways to the successful destination.

The mastermind does not have to be people that you see and interact with everyday or now and then. Although that is a re-quirement to reset your own internal issues and downplay the perceived demons within us. Even long passed masters who have left behind their expertise in the form of written word or recorded voice can become integrated into our lives, our being, and our beliefs.

It is that combination of the mastermind that generates new ideas, new opportunities as well as providing safe harbor for the concepts, and feelings that we nurture inside not knowing if the world will accept our philosophies or us.

Each of us who long for success regardless of that definition, must reach out and find that group of like-minded beings that will not scoff at us for our wishes or desires. But who will welcome us with open arms and valuable lessons to help us shorten and ease the journey ahead of us.

I am tremendously grateful for the masters that welcomed me and taught me so many valuable lessons and shortcuts in my professional career and personal life. From the greats who have passed such as Earl Nightingale, Jim Rohn and Zig Ziglar to the recorded greats of current times such as Tony Robbins, Dan Kennedy, Brian Tracy, Bob Proctor and Harvey Mackay. Some of these people I have had the pleasure to meet in person and even work with or for. Others I feel as if I have known forever. These beings mean so much to my life and my success. I owe them a great debt of gratitude as they have shaped my entrepreneurial successes and have saved me from great mental failure and breakdown during my toughest of times in business and in personal life.

Today I enjoy the company of some really great mastermind beings – such as Jeff Walker who has managed to put together a very tight knit and uber-successful group of people in our mastermind. Joe Polish, the great carpet man turned marketing guru who also learned from the great masters. Brendon Burchard who wrote the best selling book *Millionaire Messenger*. And Dan Kennedy who is one of the most prolific millionaire makers on the planet who offers a "scared straight" delivery that leaves us all in awe, yet ready to conquer.

These are people who have impacted my own personal success just by being in the same room with them, learning of their journey and sharing their story of adventure and success. They pave the way for us who strive to stay fresh and young about the latest in business, marketing and personal life success while keeping us on track on tried and true lessons that are timeless, and always work regardless of the generation or market we live in.

Having this mastermind available to me in my most critical time of need has not only saved me from certain failure, it has allowed me to trek forward and succeed in manners that I would not have even dreamed of before meeting them or hearing them. I can easily attribute many direct lessons of professional and personal achievements to the people who have passed before me and who share their life experience with me today. I am grateful to all of them, named and unnamed, for my great life.

So, for those of you reading this passage that have yet to attain your dreams or those of you who have tried and feel as if the dark is taking over the light. Reach out to your mastermind and get involved. Be of service to them. Listen to them. Do not try to learn with any specific expectations. Let go of the outcome and become part of that group of beings that together creates an unbreakable bond of triumph and strength that cannot be matched going it alone.

If you do not have a mastermind, then start with the masters who have passed before us. The best place to start is at Nightingale Conant (www.nightingaleconant.com). There you will find a myriad of resources available to you from business to personal to spiritual teachings. This is where I purchased my very first Earl Nightingale tapes (remember tapes?) and that program was the launching point for my first multi-million dollar business. I even found the name for my company in that program. Every single one of Earl's programs are priceless additions to any entrepreneur's library. From *Acres of Diamonds* to *The Strangest Secret* and *Leader of the Field*. You come away with timeless philosophies and guidance to the life of your dreams.

Then, if you are trying to build or run a successful business today you must get to the millionaire-maker himself, Dan Kennedy (www.dankennedy.com). Here you will find a group of welcoming resources that will grant you access to untold wealth and treasure for marketing and building any business in any industry or trade. Start with his *World's Greatest Free Gift* and they will take it from there. Read every single *No BS* book he has written, because you will get an instant MBA and begin to run circles around your competition.

Do not be afraid or apprehensive about spending money on this training and interaction. Each dollar invested will return a million-fold as you entrench yourself into the "belief" of success and wealth. Choose your live masterminds wisely. Make sure you pick a group that is farther along that you in some respects, but also one that you have something to offer as well to ensure that you are truly a contributing part of the mastermind and not just a parasite of information.

And this is an important point. The best mastermind groups are those where each person has something to offer and is openly willing to share their experiences, good and bad. It is a safe harbor for like-minded entrepreneurs to unload their true feelings and desires while applauding each other's achievements and triumphs. It is meant to be an unselfish place of warmth where advanced beings come together to generate success and create wealth in order to realize their hopes and dreams.

Napoleon Hill wrote about the mastermind group principle as *"The coordination of knowledge and effort of two or more people, who work toward a definite purpose, in the spirit of harmony."*

Just as Mr. Hill found through countless hours of study and years of effort, the greatest and most successful business icons of the last two centuries have used many ways to get to their place of success in the world. And the most common (and fastest) way to that success was through the participation of a mastermind group. Once you find the right group and become an integral part of that group you will see your business, and your life, grow beyond the darkness and into the light of success and wealth.

About Richard

Richard McFarland is a 30-year veteran of building software systems that help companies better serve their customers. As a seasoned systems designer, Best Selling author and leading authority on contact centers in many different industries, he brings a wide range of expertise to each client. Rich is a sought-after resource for bringing multi-media communications and business process automation to the enterprise. His experience, combined with the latest technologies provided by his company, Voice4net, allows organizations to realize a major return on assets used in the contact center.

His primary mission is to eradicate bad customer service worldwide and create a "pleasant" experience for both customer service staff and customers alike – thus creating an instant bridge of communications that empowers the end user with easy-to-use tools and toys that make doing business more fun.

To learn more about Richard McFarland and creating the best possible service experience for your customers, visit: www.voice4net.com/bioreport to get your free report on how to create a "pleasant" customer experience with your clients regardless of the industry you are in.

CHAPTER 7

TAP INTO YOUR SIXTH SENSE - PROPEL YOUR LIFE TO THE NEXT LEVEL

BY GAYLE E. ABBOTT

Have you ever sensed something about a situation and failed to follow through only to find later that your sensing had been right on target? Have you ever had an idea for a product or service and dismissed your thought only to find someone else did something just like it and became successful? Have you ever had a thought pop into your head on how to solve a problem, handle a difficult situation or overcome an obstacle when you were sleeping or walking or in the shower? If so, you have experienced the power of the sixth sense...or intuition if you will.

Acknowledging and using that sixth sense can be one of the most powerful forces and tools in our life – if we are willing to open up and leverage the possibilities and options it provides us. It has made all the difference in my personal and business life.

Awareness of my sixth sense has truly been a journey – it came slowly and I battled and doubted it along the way. Initially, I dismissed anything that wasn't totally logical, rational and practical. I wanted to see and hear the facts because that was what I was taught I was supposed to do and besides anyone who didn't was flaky, woowoo or weird. While I was not naturally drawn to or maybe even gifted with the truly theoretical, I valued learning and was very tied to the down and dirty practical and common sense.

But over time I began to realize how my sixth sense had been there and guiding me even though I hadn't acknowledged it and didn't always listen. I'd have a flash of insight but I'd go ahead and do something anyway only to find myself, loosely speaking, "in trouble." Then, even as I became cognizant of what it was and that it was part of me, I fought it and questioned it. I remember a job interview – I walked into the offices and just sensed it wasn't right for me but every fact and piece of information I had said: "to 'succeed' I need to take this job," so I dismissed my sensing. As it turned out I didn't stay long because despite all the logic and facts, I was miserable and the job really wasn't right for me.

Over time, due to a series of truly challenging incidents in my life, I slowly came to listen and appreciate the power and value of my sixth sense. One of my early "wake up" calls to pay attention to my sixth sense occurred in a strictly personal situation. My husband, daughter and I had made a practice of going to our beach condo every New Year's weekend beginning in the late 90's. We really enjoyed getting away, hearing the sound of the surf, feeling the brisk ocean wind and smelling the fresh ocean air. We'd walk, read and just plain relax. One year we decided not to go – it was just going to be too cold. We decided to stay home and sit by our fireplace. On New Years day we decided to walk our Siberian Husky, who loved the cold, through the park in our neighborhood.

We had no sooner entered the park when I turned to my husband and said we have to go to the condo. Needless to say he just looked at me. I said, "No really. I don't know why, but we have to go back to the house, throw a few things in an overnight bag and drive over there now." My husband, being the incredible person he was, went along with my sense and three hours later we were there. Upon arrival we discovered the heating system had totally stopped working. If we hadn't been there we would have had frozen pipes that burst! It would have flooded our unit and others! It was the first time I simply listened to my guiding sense and it saved us from a huge crisis.

Another hint of the power of the sixth sense came when dealing with a situation with my daughters' father from whom I'd been divorced since she was small. A "major" problem arose that threw me for a loop and after weeks of losing sleep, feeling angry, frustrated and fighting to resolve the situation logically, I was walking through the park alone in the middle of the day to try and clear my mind. Here I was amidst the beauty of nature with absolutely no one and nothing around but the sound of birds in the background, trees and a beautiful blue sky with a few clouds when all of a sudden I heard… "I don't know why you're worrying, I've always been with you, all you need to do is to let go and everything will be O.K." I looked around; there was no one around! I had no idea where the words had come from.

After gathering myself together, I thought well, why not give letting go a try, nothing else I've been doing has worked for me or given me any relief. As the process unfolded I was "tested" several times and had to persevere to remember what I'd heard. I had to walk in faith and listen. While the situation went to the 12th hour, everything worked out positively. It took me years to share this with anyone except my husband. What finally gave me the courage to share – and until now I still haven't shared it with many – was when I told my very left brained logical, rational, technically-oriented brother and he didn't question or ridicule or give me his usual "20" reasons it couldn't have happened.

Another big incident came professionally when I was giving a speech called "Achieve Your Summit" at a conference. I'm giving this speech and following the outline I'd prepared and adding stories along the way. Somehow, and I wasn't sure at the time, I was "in the flow" and just talking. All of a sudden, an attendee raised their hand and said, "Can you repeat what you just said? That was so powerful." I couldn't, because I had no idea what it was or where it had come from. Another participant shared what they'd written down and it hadn't been in my "speech" but it had flowed through me from my sixth sense as something I was meant to say.

Over time I started having and recognizing more experiences of my sixth sense coming into play.

I've worked with numerous organizations, leaders, teams and individuals through my consulting business. I've found that I have greater success when I pay attention to my sixth sense and pair it with other facts and data. I've also seen the gamut of individuals from those who I "know" have the capacity, but have not yet been ready to acknowledge or leverage it, to others who are aware but are afraid of it, and finally to those who recognize its value and power in their life and in fulfilling their potential.

I've spoken with several clients. One CEO I work with, someone I know has a strong intuitive capacity through a variety of things I've done with him including assessments, and he shared that he sensed it might be there but he wasn't sure he'd had the confidence to use it. He was just more comfortable relying on the facts, data and logical business processes. Yet, interestingly enough, the more we talked and I asked questions the more I found that his sixth sense did come into play regularly. That there were situations where he "just knew" or had a flash of insight while working out or sleeping or such, which he then logically thought about and found the facts, data, and logical approach to support the insight and move forward.

Another colleague and friend described her realizing how her sixth sense came into play when she came up against a problem or barrier or something that wasn't working, and where she was working through and forcing a very logical, rational analysis in her head. Only at that point, where she reached overwhelm, was mentally exhausted and forced to "walk away" from the issue, just let it go and try to allow that quiet space, did the solution or answer come to her from some unknown insight or source – her sixth sense.

While there are increasing numbers of individuals who are willing to publicly acknowledge their sixth sense and the role that intuition plays in what they do on a regular basis, there are still so many who, due to "programming" which has occurred in their life and naysayers in their environment, block it out and resist it. All of this makes the concept challenging to embrace, especially given natural human tendencies around fears of failure, not fitting in, not being liked or accepted, seeming strange.

However, as we look at really successful people, we find that they arrived at that point (even though they may not all admit it to the world at large), by using and integrating their sixth sense with their conscious intellectual brainpower. They have done so while staying persistently focused on achieving concrete practical results that are theirs to achieve. And they've found that once they give themselves permission, and allow their mind to float, that their subconscious or unconscious mind works on identifying opportunities where the universal power can flow through them in order to achieve practical outcomes and make a greater positive impact on society.

In fact, often our sixth sense can provide the insight into our purpose and where we can make the greatest contribution and have the greatest success. It's about listening, being open, moving out of our comfort zone and away from fear, and then just taking the action steps as they fall in front of us. As you look at your life, consider the following as just a few of the actions you can take to go to the next level.

1. Listen to your Intuition. Give yourself permission to do so. It usually has really important information that can advance you to new levels and save you grief. When you

get that insight at least test it. If you're not confident enough yet to act on your intuition, then at least start writing down what comes to you and see what happens. Part of working effectively with your sixth sense is to gain the confidence to do so – to understand that everything in this world isn't cold, hard facts and data and that sometimes you end up behind the curve when you wait until you have all the information that you want to be comfortable.

2. You never know when your sixth sense will kick in or how it will help you. My experience at the conference surprised me but moved me to a new level. And even then it took years for me to fully trust it and learn how to use it. In fact, it probably wasn't until a series of experiences around the totally unexpected death of my husband that I started consciously allowing myself to use intuition even more. So the first time your sixth sense kicks in, at the very least acknowledge it and see what happens next.

3. Your sixth sense plays a key role, but backing it up when it makes sense with facts and data can make your success even greater. As part of one of our businesses, we work with companies looking to increase the effectiveness of their selection processes. We were working with one firm benchmarking an investment analyst position and found, much to our surprise at the time, that a differentiator for really successful analysts was that their intuition pointed them in the right direction and then they used extensive research on the facts and data to support their decisions. This caused us to ask more questions of CEO's and others and found that the most successful ones got messages from their sixth sense and then many times, but not always, found the facts and data to support their "instincts."

4. Far more people have the capacity to use and tap into their sixth sense than consciously know it. We use tools such as TriMetrix® HD and the esoteric sciences to give individuals greater insight to their innate talents, most powerful direction and opportunities. We are finding higher percentages of people already have or are here to develop and better leverage their sixth sense. Become more self-aware and see what potential lies within you to tap into the power of your sixth sense.

5. Leaders who innately have and tap into their intuition can take their organizations and their careers to whole new heights. We have a number of leaders who have proven that the sixth sense is a powerful tool for them not only in running their business, but also in how they work with people. In fact, those that use their sixth sense when combined with rational thought in dealing with employees and other people, in addition to strategy, tend to be far more effective and respected. How can you develop your sixth sense in relation to reading, relating to and understanding other people?

6. Your sixth sense can be a thought that just comes out of your mouth. This often occurs to me when I'm facilitating a group or coaching someone. It's not planned but I'm listening and all of a sudden I just "know" what to say. Now that I've given myself permission to just say it, I frequently find that it totally resonates and grabs the attention of the group or person, and heads the discussion in the direction it needs to go in order to achieve the ultimate objective.

7. You can open your subconscious or unconscious mind to the concept of your sixth sense by making time to just let your mind "float". How can you make time for "the quiet" so your mind can "float"? Allow for the possibility of moments of inspiration by taking a walk outdoors, or sitting quietly in a room with no distractions, or walk-

ing through a museum, or any other number of situations where you can detach from constant activity and doing and hard thinking.

I went through a period when I was logically and rationally pursuing success and riches, following other people's models without listening to, or perhaps even ignoring, my sixth sense. Interestingly enough, those paths didn't work for me. I "knew" where I was meant to go and when I finally started "listening" to my sixth sense and got over my fear and self-doubt amazing things began to happen. Significant people came into my life who became part of my informal mastermind. I became more focused, persistent and decisive. Not only did I know I had a guide in my sixth sense and a brain with more capacity than I'd ever known, but I had the insights of others who were smart and successful – all contributing to my capacity to achieve more of my potential. I realized that persevering through things that are challenging and uncomfortable build the neural connections and pathways in our brains to use more and more of our potential, and move to greater levels of contribution and impact. Tapping into our sixth sense and then combining it with the capacity available in our brain, allows us to tap into our creativity in new ways – allowing us to step into more of our full potential.

About Gayle

Gayle Abbott, President and CEO, Strategic Alignment Partners, Inc. and Mind Soul Academy works with boards of directors, executives, leaders, high potentials and teams to fulfill more of their potential and facilitate their achieving their strategic initiatives and practical performance results. She is passionate about helping people and organizations move to new levels on their journey. In doing this, she uses her sixth sense, practical business techniques and tools, the esoteric sciences and her expertise in people, communication, critical thinking, practical results and business strategy and execution to help move individuals and organizations to the next level of performance.

Gayle is an entrepreneur and leader who has run a successful company for over 20 years. She has recently been quoted in several articles in CBS MoneyWatch, Business newsdaily.com and CEO Update. She has also been published in the magazine, *Dollars & Sense.* Ms. Abbott has delivered speeches on such topics as "Achieving Your Summit: Strategies for Personal and Career Success," "Strategic Alignment for Increased Productivity and ROI," "Selecting and Retaining Top Performing Talent in a Competitive Market," "Using Competencies to Develop and Get Better Results through People," "It's Not What You Know but What You Do," and "Increasing Your Leadership Effectiveness."

Ms. Abbott has served as an adjunct faculty member at Marymount University and American University. She has won several awards for outstanding leadership over the years and has been listed in Who's Who in America, Who's Who in the South and Southwest, Who's Who in Finance and Industry and Who's Who in American Women. She is certified as a Growth Curve Strategist and is TriMetrix® HD and Emotional Quotient™ certified. On her journey she has experienced extensive personal growth and achieved her successes to this point by seeing the opportunities in, and overcoming a variety of life challenges such as the bad manager, divorce, being widowed unexpectedly, and financial challenges to name a few. She has learned that while we are continually learning and growing, that if we leverage our gifts and get on the right path for ourselves, there's no end to the possibilities of what we can do and contribute.

A few of her other passions include spending time with her daughter and their two Huskies, travel, reading, visiting museums, and being in the outdoors – whether by water, in the woods or by mountains.

For more information, please visit:
www.strategicalignmentpartners.com and
www.mindsouljourney.com.

CHAPTER 8

PERSISTENCE

BY CATHERINE NEWTON

*Patience, persistence and perspiration make
an unbeatable combination for success.*

~ Napoleon Hill

Anyone who said doing business is easy, is obviously bluffing!
In all seriousness, there were times in the early days of building
my business where it seemed like one big uphill slog that was
going to take forever to climb.

Can you relate?

As I was getting started, people promised to call back and didn't.
Messages got left and not returned. Contracts got cancelled or
people just changed their minds. Banks reneged on loan promises. For certain obstacles no amount of intention setting and
meditating seemed to work.

So why did I push on? I did it for the same reason I'd hedge
my bets that you do. I'm passionate about helping people, about
making a difference and having an impact in the world.

Along the way there has been much to learn to grow, sustain,
and build a thriving business. The marketing skills to learn, my
mindset to constantly uplevel (we all do), and the way I learnt to
manage money was hugely important. Sometimes the learning

curve alone seemed like it was out of control!

But all of the knowledge I acquired, all the time and money I have invested into growing my business and growing myself wouldn't matter a bean – if I didn't have *commitment, enthusiasm* – and most of all, *persistence.* These three traits have been my driving force so that even when it felt hard, when things weren't going my way, or it was taking too long, I never gave up.

Ever.

People often ask what the turning point was when everything changed as I grew my now thriving business. And the truth is…

There was a period of time where I was going through money like it was going out of fashion, and worried that I would never 'make it' as I watched my nest egg dwindle. So I took a risk – I sold my home and poured it in to my business. There were times when it would have been easier to close up shop and get a J.O.B.

But I held my faith in what I was here to do. You see, I believe that each of us has a life purpose that has been pre-programmed in us. By listening to it and allowing our burning desire for it to manifest, to shine through, we get to be abundant and wealthy when we live into that purpose. Just as an acorn is pre-programmed to become an oak tree, so too have you been pre-programmed to act on your soul's mission once you make the decision AND act on it.

I remember sitting in the audience at a Think and Grow Rich conference in Sydney in 2009 and making a pledge to myself. They were looking to make 100 millionaires. I was going to be one of them…and then some! If the signs around me were anything to go by, I knew it was possible …you see, on my trip to Sydney I was invited to stay at a luxury mansion worth $65 million that my Aunt happened to be 'house-sitting.' So here I was, at a Think and Grow Rich conference, staying at one of Sydney's most stunning homes.

Call it synchronicity. Call it fate. Call it law of attraction. But it had called to me and shown me that ANYTHING is possible. And I was ready to act on it.

From that point on, I held my belief in myself that I could inspire and change people's lives the way mine had been changed, from single Mother to woman on a mission! I held onto the commitment I had made to myself and I never gave up. I stood my ground on what I was worth. I said yes to events, speaking engagements, leading workshops, trainings, writing – everything that was within my genius. I persisted with phone calls, meetings, events and networking – even when chaos, naysayers and discouragers came into my life.

Even then I didn't stop. Because I had found my BURNING DESIRE. And the 'magical' results showed-up in unexpected places as I learned to take my message to the 'masses,' and then monetize it.

In 2011, I spoke on stage to over 750 people at Mega Partnering, a US business conference, organised by the equally persistent JT Foxx. Before going on stage I spoke with one of my mentors, a highly successful entrepreneur, Dr. Nido Qubein. He said to me, "Catherine, you are in the right place, at the right time, with the right Mindset, and the right people – but you've earned that right because you have consistently shown up and said yes to opportunities."

My persistence had suddenly been noticed by others, and by the Universe. Doors were being opened for me that I could only have dreamed of, and I was NOW being richly rewarded. Make no mistake - there is a direct connection between the level of effort you put into it and the results you get out of it…You have to DO something about it. We are each given the tools to fulfill our mission and purpose in service to the greater good. So, when we align our business with our calling, and persistently take productive steps towards our goal, we can absolutely fulfill our mission.

The difference between being financially successful or not is the number of people whose lives we change along the way and the lessons we learn. THE secret to doing that is to figure out exactly how to monetize that calling within you, and then, not let setbacks get in the way of you accumulating your riches.

George Ross, Donald Trump's right hand man, broke success down to a simple equation as I lunched with him at the Trump Tower in New York in 2010. He said "success is simple if you remember this formula," and with that he said to me a statement that has been etched on my mind ever since. He said, "Failure plus persistence equals success. Not failure plus hand-outs, or setbacks plus giving up."

Failure, he went on to say, is that sick feeling you get when it's all gone wrong. He went on to say that your first loss is the best loss. Because it hurts so much – it hurts your pride, your ego, your reputation, your confidence. But it is in that moment the very thing you need to ask yourself is, 'What went wrong? What can I do differently?' To not learn from this would be unwise! Our success comes as a result of failures.

As Mary Kay has said:

> *"One of the secrets of success is to refuse to let temporary setbacks defeat us."*

It is the failings that help us learn, it is the false starts and the setbacks that grow you as you climb your ladder of accumulating riches and reaching goals that inspire you. But it is persistence that keeps you pushing through, …that keeps the faith against all odds, …that drives you to do whatever it takes.

Napoleon Hill spent 20 years studying many of the world's most successful people in his path to researching *Think and Grow Rich*. He noted that the only quality he could find in the most successful, in Henry Ford, in Thomas Edison, and in Andrew Carnegie that he could not find in others, was persistence. Hill suggested, "There may be no heroic connotation to the word persistence but the quality is to your character what carbon is to steel."

He is talking here about the habit of following through in your plans with persistence, letting no idea go until it comes to fruition. It is a common theme that difficulties, challenges and setbacks appear on a regular basis but because of persistence, we can achieve victory...

Sir Edmund Hillary, who in 1953 was the first person to climb Mt. Everest and return safely, didn't get to the top of Mt. Everest until his third attempt. He was fuelled by a burning desire to follow his passion and achieve his goal. Many asked "What kept him going year after year?" He believed it was possible; his burning desire to prove it so, coupled with his fierce persistence, meant that he would do whatever it took to succeed. He credited his success to the lessons he learned on the first two attempts. That's the kind of persistence that Napoleon Hill had in mind.

Jack Canfield, author of the *Chicken Soup for the Soul* series, speaks of being rejected by publishers not just once. He was rejected by more than 130 publishers before he got a yes. Here is a man who stands by the importance of persistence – without it, he would never have become the worldwide sensation that he is.

Canfield believes that persistence is probably the single most common quality of high achievers. "The longer you hang in there, the greater the chance that something will happen in your favour. No matter how hard it seems, the longer you persist the more likely the success," he writes in The Success Principles. Now the publisher who said yes has helped him sell over 100 million books.

Phillip Mills, former international track athlete and CEO of Les Mills, a New Zealand based international Fitness Company, explained his story of persistence to me recently as we talked about how he took the New Zealand business global.

Phillip's father, Les Mills, launched the company in 1968. Starting locally, it quickly became New Zealand's largest gym chain. Phillip followed his father into the gym business but by 1987 the company had hit rock bottom.

A year after Phillip took the helm, consumed by the stock market crash, the company took a massive hit and Phillip was faced with his darkest hour. "At the low point, in 1987, we had pretty much hit a wall," Mills says. "We had the banks expecting us to declare bankruptcy but there was no way I was going to let that happen." So Mills was faced with a decision – "I could either close the doors and let go of something that had been built over 20 years or borrow and pay back the debts that surmounted to over $5million." Mills chose the latter and fortunately the banks and the receivers were willing to loan him the money.

Phillip realised he had to really focus on the things that had to be done immediately to keep the business afloat. "It was a slow moving train-wreck over the next year" he remembers. "The last thing I wanted to do was to see people lose their money and staff lose their jobs. I felt that we could lose everything, but when you're on the verge of going out of business, you work hard to ensure you'll NEVER be in that position again, and it makes it tough. My wife was a full-time Doctor and we had 2 young babies who barely saw me. I was working 16 hour days, 6 days a week."

But Mills had a fierce love for the business; he had a vision, a determination and a drive that turned into a way out. After a 5 year recovery between 1987-1993, the privately held Les Mills is a global New Zealand success story ….It expanded from running clubs to licensing its fitness classes to 15,000 clubs around the world. Les Mills now provides inspiring, motivating and totally addictive group fitness workouts to millions of people around the world every year.

"People would fall in love with our products – our music, exercise, dance, fitness education… and we realised we had something more to sell than just memberships to clubs in New Zealand. The trick was how to get out there and sell it. After a few false starts we created an independent distributor model. WE found the best distributors for our products in each country and persuaded them to represent us. In most cases we were just a small product line for them, but we were fun to do business with, their staff fell in love with us and before long we became their biggest business - we were like a viral infection inside their companies."

A banner on my Auckland Les Mills gym wall says: *"It won't get easier, you'll just get better."*

"Any successful business has it's challenges," Phillip remarked as he explained, "Get a better business model than your competition, get great people on your side, learn everything there is to know about your industry, and with a little hard work it just might take you to the moon."

Mills persisted against so many odds, looked adversity in the eye and faced it head on.

Another inspiring individual was Steven Bradbury, 2002 Gold medallist. Bradbury went to his 4th Winter Olympics in Salt Lake City as a speed skate competitor. Fortunately, the man who had given the last 12 years of his life to Olympic training wasn't satisfied with leaving the sport without a medal. He HAD to give it one more go. He was hungry and he had a vision he was not letting go of.

On meeting Bradbury I could see he was a fighter – and fight he did. 18 months before his final Winter Olympics he broke his neck at training by crashing into a barrier. For most that would have been enough to give up. But not Bradbury – for he had well formed the habit of persistence. This is the man who in 1994 had his leg impaled by another skater and had almost lost his life as 4 litres of his blood flooded onto the ice.

But in 2002 at the Salt Lake City Winter Olympics, Bradbury had a strategy. He knew his best chance was to get on the ice, and stay out of the way. This tactic proved to be Bradbury's finest decision.

The world watched in disbelief as, one by one, the skaters ahead of him in the 90 second race fell, like dominoes. As Bradbury glided over the finish line he was the last man standing. He had won Gold. Was he the fastest man on the ice that day? No. But he took that Gold medal – not for the 90 seconds of the race, but for the 12 years that led up to that 90 seconds. Through a great deal of hard work, practice and persistence, he took the Gold.

Many people who consider themselves to be 'not as good as the others' would have given up before they even got started. These people aren't prepared for the battle. They get caught up in fear and can't cross the 'terror barrier.' Their desire is weak and so they stick to mediocre performances and justify to themselves that it wouldn't be worth the effort. They don't see that with persistence, you can succeed against all odds.

Many of life's failures are people who did not realize how close they were to success when they gave up. ~ Thomas Edison

The desire to achieve is the most necessary pre-condition to becoming a winner, to persist with your goal no matter what. This is the starting point of all success. And what of Thomas Edison's approach to success? He said that he never failed, he just discovered what didn't work. If we treated every outcome as a step closer to our success, we might find it easier to be grateful for it.

My mentor, Bob Proctor, the Master of Law of Attraction, and the star of the hit movie 'The Secret,' believes that ultimately persistence must become a way of life, but in order to develop the mental strength – persistence – you must first want something bad enough. It was during an event I attended with him in Los Angeles that he lent across, touched my arm and stated, "You have to WANT something so much that it becomes a heated desire... a passion in your belly. You must fall in love with that idea and magnetize yourself to every part of the idea." At that point, Proctor reminded me, persistence is virtually automatic.

Bob Proctor knows the impact persistence can have. In 1961,

he was first introduced to Napoleon Hill's *Think and Grow Rich* book and proceeded to read it day in and day out. At first he was sceptical. But in just one years' time, he soon witnessed miraculous changes in his life, and credits much of it to a BURNING DESIRE to wanting to understand and execute Hill's principles of success.

He started on his journey with little formal education and a job that barely paid the bills, and when Bob Proctor needed a $1,000 loan to start his first business, 21 straight banks turned him down. In his words "I discovered 21 banks that weren't right for me." The 22nd bank gave him the money, and the rest is history. He soon found himself making over a million dollars.

He went from being a high school dropout to now being known as the Grandfather of Personal Development, with over 50 years in the industry, turning over multi-millions every year. He is testament to the fact that behind extraordinary achievement you will always discover extraordinary effort, with or without a college degree!

In December 2012, Bob personally gifted me with my own copy of the Persistence chapter and inspired me to read the chapter every day for 30 days. It was while I was undertaking my 30 day challenge that I was invited to co-author for this book. When asked which chapter I would like to write on, I naturally chose the one on Persistence.

I had learned that lack of persistence was the reason 97% of people do not succeed the way they want to. If you give up too soon you'll never know the miracles that were waiting for you. Successful people DO what the average person isn't willing to.

They go deeper, farther and longer – EVERY time... When you are persistent you WILL become an expert in your field, a leader in your industry.

"Persistence," Napoleon Hill reminds us, "is a state of mind, therefore it can be cultivated."

FOLLOW THIS FORMULA TO ACCELERATE YOUR SUCCESS, AND INCREASE YOUR INCOME, SO YOU TOO CAN MAKE A POSITIVE IMPACT ON THE WORLD:

Your Purpose

(Your life purpose that is your calling – it's the most perfect fit for you that makes you feel in your genius.)

+

Your Burning Desire

(The passion in your belly that has you fall in love with the idea and allows you to turn it into reality.)

+

Your Vision

(Being clear and definite about your mission, your goal, your plan – so you can create a compelling vision of your future.)

+

Your Drive

(Self-motivation, steady persistence and a deep belief that you CAN do it, will help you realize your goals, despite obstacles.)

+

Your Personal Responsibility

(Have faith, and let go of non-productive actions, past patterns, fears and doubts – then be fully responsible for creating massive action.)

+

Your Gratitude

(Practice gratitude – even for the dead ends, false starts, and setbacks. It's a lot more productive to be grateful for the learning's than to whine about what went wrong.)

+

Your Decision

(Make a conscious decision to reject any and all negative suggestions that come from friends, relatives, or acquaintances who indicate the goal cannot be accomplished.)

+

Your Acceptance of Support

(Realize the possibilities and benefits of not doing it alone, of having a group of one or more people who will encourage, support, and assist you wherever possible.)

+

Your Continuing Journey

(Constant repetition of up-levelling yourself, growing and shifting who you are, and trusting in the process accelerates your success.)

=

Success

There is an interesting phenomenon that occurs when you get persistently serious about reaching your goals in a focused, consistent way and you follow this formula. There's a reason why successful people operate this way... It's the only way to become successful!

What I LOVE about being in business and surrounding myself with high-level mentors and successful people like I do, is that I have seen the power of the persistence in action.

What I have noticed is that it's the constant repetition that fuels it. It all started for me when I undertook these 10 Steps...

1. Review Your Goals and Affirmations Daily

2. Meditate Daily

3. Read Daily

4. Listen to Inspiring Audio Daily

5. Affirm Daily Your BURNING DESIRE and Your Belief IN Yourself

6. Keep a Gratitude Journal Daily

7. Surround Yourself With Successful People Daily

8. Mastermind Weekly

9. Plan Daily

10. Get Support

The magic happens when consistent DAILY actions occur. In the words of Yoda, "There is no try, only do."

When you take consistent daily actions that support your goals, it immediately graduates you from the slow road to the FAST TRACK! So what do you dream of doing with your life? You weren't meant to be average. Make the decision to be bold! Be willing to try new things even if it seems risky, and even if you're not sure it will work – Do it. Begin right now and never quit.

As Marianne Williamson says, "Who am I to be brilliant, gorgeous, talented, fabulous? Actually, who are you not to be?"

There is greatness in you. Spread your wings, and as you do, you in turn give other people permission to do the same.

Persist.

About Catherine

Catherine Newton is an International Award-Winning Coach, Teacher, Entrepreneurial Business Expert, Law Of Attraction Practitioner, and Master Educator And Trainer.

The Speaker

Since 2007, Catherine has spoken to over 5,000 people on various subjects including mindset, marketing, business and personal growth, and how using the Universal principles that Napoleon Hill and Bob Proctor talk about, can help you to create lasting success. She is passionate about passing on her successes to others and teaching 'helping entrepreneurs,' leaders and sales professionals how to increase their income and achieve their potential. She has recently been invited to speak on American television as a Premier Expert in the area of Success Mindset.

The Educator

Catherine is the founder and CEO of the mentoring, training and coaching firm, *Catherine Newton International* with more than 1,000 students worldwide. In the last six years, she has gone from strength to strength by first changing her thoughts and then doing exactly what she now does for others; finding a mentor and following their steps to success and happiness. She is currently being mentored by *George Ross* (Donald Trump's right hand man), *Bob Proctor* (considered one of the Masters of Law of Attraction) and serial entrepreneur *Dr. Nido Qubein,* as well as Big Idea Catalyst, *Melanie Benson-Strick.*

The Mentor

Catherine was named International Mentor of the Year at 2011's Top One Awards in Los Angeles, USA. As a world-class speaker, sales trainer, and success-mindset mentor, Catherine also privately mentors CEO's in their pursuit of quantum leaps. If you're ready to significantly add increase to your business and life, you'll love Catherine's mentoring style and her mastermind programs where step-by-step guidance meets expert spirit-rich coaching – leading to your abundant business and lifestyle.

The Workshop Leader

Catherine's genius shines when she leads workshops, trainings, presentations and online-classes. At any of Catherine's live events, be prepared to be inspired as she encourages, supports and challenges you to dare to dream bigger, increase your income and achieve greater success.

The Author

She is the co-author of Best Seller *Over-comers Inc.* and the author of the training systems *Your Life Enriched* and *Gain Clarity, Clients and Cash-flow* and *Your Money Blueprint. 'Think and Grow Rich Today'* is her latest co-authored book. Catherine is also featured in Inc magazine in April 2013 as a charismatic, transformational leader to watch.

The Heart-Centred Entrepreneur

Known as "The Entrepreneurial Success Coach," Catherine combines Universal principles with practical applications to get a results-focused, "how to" approach in implementing simple strategies to bring about expanded awareness and wealth and abundance consciousness to 'helping entrepreneurs' and sales professionals.

Catherine's mission is to teach them effective ways to increase their income more rapidly so they can lead their greatest possible lives and serve the greatest number of people while making a greater impact in the world.

If you're struggling to grow your business, Catherine can help! Get your FREE
resources and strategy session at: www.catherinenewton.com
Or email us at: support@catherinenewton.com
Or phone +64 21 360 891

CHAPTER 9

PASSION IN ACTION CAN CHANGE THE WORLD

BY BONNIE KANNER

People often ask how I came to this amazing place in life—a place that many yearn to be and many only dream of. Someone once said, "Bonnie, there are good days and there are bad days, but you never know which is which until sometime down the road." I came to fully understand the wisdom of that statement during a point in my life when I had been lying in bed feeling sorry for myself. Like many single parents, I was financially strapped, surrounded by stacks of bills, with no help in sight. This was devastating place to find myself in because I wanted to take care of my children and provide for them without worry.

As destiny would have it, my children were the ones that set me on the road to success. One day, which seemed like every other, turned out to be quite an extraordinary day that changed my life forever. A couple that my daughter had recently introduced me to invited me to attend a meeting of their private group called "The Secret Knock." The gathering was filled with amazing people from around the world. One gentleman in particular captured my attention when he spoke about **"vision boards"** and how to map out our wishes, hopes and dreams. I created a vision board with my daughter that night and like a bolt of lightning from the heavens, everything started to fall into place. A vision board was the roadmap that I needed.

I realized I had been driving on dreary roads that continually led me to an existence of living paycheck to paycheck, which certainly did not bring out the best in me. To see the changes I wanted for my life, I couldn't go out and find another job. A job is merely an exchange of energy on a material level and puts someone else in charge of my life as they can fire me whenever they want. At this point in my life, I was ready for more. I was ready for the super highway, a high road to a destination that would bring out the deepest aspects of who I am, and reward me financially. I was ready to find my calling; my divine purpose for being.

My son and I went to a casting session at a friend's house. When we were getting ready to leave, my friend yelled out, "Wait, I have something for you!" and handed me a book called "The Vision Board" because she had seen the one I created. That night, I started reading a chapter on how to activate a vision board and I learned it would require a group of people. I immediately thought of my friend, Tony Jabbour, host to a wonderful meditation group at "The Body Sanctuary" in Westlake, CA. I called to see if he was familiar with activating a vision board. Tony said he was, so I scheduled an appointment. At this special meeting, he asked me to pose a question to the group. My question was, "Why do so many people keep coming to me to help them with funding their company's projects? These are amazing life-changing opportunities that the world needs to see, and I want so badly to help them. Please tell me what I can do to help them." Tony gave a crystal to the woman to my left and asked the group to meditate on my question. He said whoever holds the crystal holds the floor and is not to be interrupted. Each person sequentially spoke the words that came to mind: "**Illuminate, Illumination, Global, Universal, Trust, Pied Piper, Children's Education, Equali, introduce the people you meet to each other, it is your purpose. Introduce people that are coming back**

from the past, they are to be included. Fun and travel." I was in shock. Those words may not have meant anything to someone else, but to me, they meant everything. I knew they were the street signs and mile markers on the road to my destiny!

At a time of severe economic challenges, when people everywhere were losing their jobs, I was determined to stay on course with the hopes and dreams mapped out on my vision board. A job that was safe and comfortable would have been easier, but I chose to believe that we are all destined for greatness and I was determined to find mine.

Most of my previous "jobs" were in the entertainment industry, where I've received over **80 major on-screen credits** in various levels of production. Even though my years in the business may sound quite glamorous and were financially rewarding by most standards, I didn't feel that I was living my life on purpose. It was only when I launched my own company, "**Shooting Star Entertainment**" and decided to produce projects that I would select, not someone else's, that I began to feel I was doing what I was called to do. (http://ShootingStar-ent.com)

It's interesting when one decides to be in the divine flow that the people and the opportunities to make things happen just seem to show up. I received a message from a very persistent gentleman named Donald Delaney. "I know you are very busy, Bonnie, but please read this script I have. I know you will love it. The story is about Angels saving Humanity and reminds me of you and your mission to transform the world!" His passion and persistence paid off. I read the script and fell in love with the story. Within a week, Gina E. Jones (the writer) and I met and agreed to work together. What happened to Donald? Well, he is now my Co-Executive Producer for "Flying Between Heaven and Earth" which is also going to be a television series.

Flying Between Heaven and Earth, an adaptation of the award-winning novel by Gina E. Jones, is about the trials and tribulations of an innocent angel when she volunteers to help Archangel Michael and his airline of angels save humanity from the evil Lord of Darkness. Infinity Airways seat assignment system specifically provides passengers the opportunity to balance their heavy karmic and emotional baggage with their assigned seat-mate—not only from this lifetime, but from past and future lives as well. With the right person sitting on the right flight in the right seat, the traveling public is unaware that they are being served by angels and are being given the opportunity to learn their soul's most important lessons before they reach their destination. (http://FlyingBetweenHeavenandEarth.com)

Now there is more to this than just optioning another movie. One day when I was on a conference call, Donald called and I clicked over. All he said was, "When is your birthday? Gina wants to know." As fate would have it, Gina is also Certified Magi Counselor of the Cards of Life. In this system, my card is the Queen of Hearts and hers is the Queen of Diamonds. Looking into our relationship connections, Gina said we are destined for great success. The information she gave me about who I am and why I am here confirmed my inner knowing and now fuels my burning passion to help people and help improve our world. (http://TheCardsofLife.com)

The story doesn't end there because Gina asked me to be the Executive Producer for another project of hers called *The Great Secret*. It is a transformative documentary that pulls back the curtain to reveal who we REALLY are and what is REALLY playing out on the world's stage. After digging through the mysteries of life and death, searching through ancient glyphs and numerous codes, and delving into fractals and the Fibonacci spiral, the hidden secret about humanity and how the world operates is ready to be seen by all. Our lives, calendars, DNA, pyramids, seasons of the year, and even time itself are all encoded and all connected. *The Great Secret* reveals that our lives—past, present and future—are written in a simple code. And it is not what you think! (http://TheGreatSecretofLife.com)

When I attended *The Enlightened Entrepreneur,* Steven Sadleir was on stage and he felt so familiar to me. I pulled out my cell phone and pulled up my vision board picture. Lo and behold Steven looks just like the man I put on my vision board with a caption that reads, "A divine relationship inspires others" and another that says "Let's grow together." It was unbelievable. There was Steven speaking about the power of meditation, The Self Awareness Institute, which he founded, and some of his books including *Money and Power* and *Christ Enlightened.* Once Steven was off stage, I showed him the picture and told him about Unified Field Corporation, the new model of banking that I am involved with. Steven said, "My dream has always been to have a Unified Field Bank." Several months later we met to discuss business opportunities and he said "I don't want to scare you, but I knew when I met you that we are supposed produce this movie." Right then I knew with all my heart that I was, in fact, the one to bring *The Lost Teachings of Jesus Christ* to the world. *The Lost Teachings of Jesus Christ* is a screenplay written by Steven Sadleir based on his book *Christ Enlightened* that tells the story about Christ's missing years, who he was and why people followed him, his teachings, the son, friend, and the healer. It's the greatest story never told about the greatest story ever told.
(http://TheLostTeachingsofJesus.com)

Another exciting Shooting Star project is *System-Upgrade* [Action Thriller Film Project]. As Executive Producer/Producer, I am working with writer/producer Chris Rossen to launch this high power action/thriller that really challenges the way we think about technology. *Logline*: An undercover CIA agent discovers that the company he is investigating produces a product that manipulates the behavior of the general public and he must prove it to the media before he is killed by a powerful political conspiracy. This movie draws an analogy to our existing relationship to mass media manipulation. It has multiple revenue streams, including an interactive game, product placement and an online community. For more info see:
http://System-Upgrade.com/welcome/

Remember the Pied Piper? I wondered what that meant when it came up in my vision board activation. Well, here it is. *The Pied Piper Meets The Bone Man* (performed by Grammy-nominated trombonist Jim Moseley) is a happy ending to the original story. It is to the original Pied Piper story what "Wicked" is to *The Wizard of Oz*. It is a fun, energetic family musical that does more than just entertain. It creates smiles and that's exactly what I, as the Executive Producer to the new Jim Moseley musical, want to do. By incorporating Operation Smile kids who have found "their voice" through the miracle of a simple 45-minute operation and only $240 becomes quite powerful. The storyline has the potential to be far more than an evening of great entertainment. Nightly performances will translate into significant funding and awareness that could transform many lives offering another benefit to the viewing audience. (www.BoneManMusic. com/ShootingStar/)

I love to see people happy and fulfilled. Throughout my life I have always been very social, often referred to as a "social butterfly," and even called a "matchmaker" – since I love introducing people to each other on both a personal level and a professional level. Staying on course to my calling, I want to learn as much as I can, so I started to attend numerous conferences and meetings. Almost everyone in attendance was either a Venture Capitalist, Angel Investor, SEC expert, Grant Writer or EB5 Attorney. At the first conference, I was introduced by a friend to David Sinclair, President of Axiom Capital. At the third conference, David offered me a position as VP of New Business Development for **Axiom Capital USA** (www.AxiomCap.co.uk) to bring in new business opportunities that would have global appeal. Since finding great companies to present to Axiom came naturally to me, I decided to present David with an opportunity which enabled us as partners to acquire an 18.5 million person database. Thus was born http://ChosenForChange.com. The focus of our new joint venture is to market products, services, and life-changing inventions that will have a positive impact on the world. Isn't it ironic that what had seemed like small and insignificant parts of my personality are actually my strong suits and part of my true calling in this lifetime? I've discovered that my gifts include building international strategic alliances for corporations.

As everything at **Shooting Star** was taking off, my **Axiom Capital USA** business networks were simultaneously expanding and I was promoted to **President of New Business Development**. When I first started this road to success, I often felt I was going around in circles, but now I'm driving a bullet train moving at the speed of light and stopping along the way to pick up lots of brilliant and innovative people and their amazing projects.

I am now sought out by many companies seeking assistance with joint ventures and marketing of their projects and inventions. Most of these companies have amazing, life-changing products and services that the world needs to see! I am dedicated to helping them take their projects and services to the next level. Just like my film projects, the following are like my babies and I'm very passionate about them.

Distribution is a key component to the success of any media project. Therefore, movie producers are always looking for alliance partners for new forms of distribution. Once **Kiosk Co.** and **WhiteHatt** are funded, I will use my extensive entertainment industry relationships and databases to develop the necessary alliances.

Kiosk Co. – Owns and operates automated retail kiosks that dispense DVD rentals and DVDs for sale. Our plan is to acquire content and strategically choose locations to deploy 30,000 units over the next 5 years. (http://Kiosksol.com/ShootingStar/)

WhiteHatt Internet Television – VP of Marketing and New Business Development. WhiteHatt is a return to television before Cable TV, when television was free and commercials were limited. WhiteHatt combines the comfort and convenience of the "Cable Experience" with all that current technology has to offer. WhiteHatt Internet Television is an all-in-one, portable, home entertainment component that integrates live television with built-in DVR, Internet Television, social networking and Blu-ray/DVD w/ 3-D, combined into one high-quality consumer electronic. (www.Whitehatt.com/ShootingStar/)

Unified Field Corporation (UFC) – As Business Development and Marketing Advisor, I market the company's Regenerative Community Initiative (RCI). RCI partners with community stakeholders to develop sustainable local infrastructure projects, create green jobs and local resiliency in food, energy, housing, water, waste recovery, transportation, communication, education, the arts and wellness. RCI project funding is completely independent of other aspects of UFC's work that include eventually submitting applications for permission to organize sustainable banks. UFC's systems will support healthy local economies, rebuilding a sustainable infrastructure to provide for our community's needs. (http://UnifiedFieldCorporation.com)

Life Cube – I am the VP of New Business Development/Strategic Alliances and International Sales. Life Cube has many uses from emergency shelter to "green" location production offices. These rapidly deploying shelters transform from a 5 foot cube to a 144 square foot shelter complete with food, water, communications, first-aid, electricity, lighting, heating and cooking within 5 minutes. With the multiple doors, units can be clustered together to create multiple room live/work space making the Life Cube the ultimate shelter for instant response. (www.LifeCubeinc.com/ShootingStar/)

4EVERPWR SYSTEMS LTD 24/7/365 Power & Lighting - As Director of Business Development and Strategic Relations, I help promote their lamps with no cords to plug in, lighting fixtures that work without wires, and battery power generation and backup that can work anywhere, anytime and with any type of system, portable or fixed use. This is a true game-changing technology that will impact our lives, from small applications to large uses of energy and lighting. (http://4everpwr.com/ShootingStar/)

SunSeeker Fire Blanket Technology – Since my own home was destroyed in a Malibu fire, saving lives and homes is extremely important to me. After watching a Fire Blanket draped over the arm of a friend with a 3,000°F blowtorch directly on it, I decided to join SunSeeker as Director of Business Development. I am involved in creating new and innovative ways to market a patented fire protection technology for individuals, businesses and government organizations. (http://SunSeekerFireBlanket.com/ShootingStar/)

ClickN KIDS Children's Online Educational Company - Advisory Board Member and Executive Producer for Creative Content and Distribution. ClickN KIDS goal is to become a premier online educational resource for parents, teachers and kids. The company seeks to use its research-based tutoring tools to stop illiteracy. A unique partnership with Warner Bros. also allows for the world famous Looney Tunes characters to make learning engaging and fun.
(http://ClicknKids.com /ShootingStar/) and
(http://OneWorldLiteracyFoundation.org)

Slimmer Silhouette® Body Wrap - Recommended by Dr. Mc-Coy specializing in less-invasive cosmetic treatments, weight-loss, and natural bio-identical hormone therapy since 2003. Advisory Board VP of New Business Development - the world needs to know these products exist! With over a decade of development, spa testing, and over 50,000 treatments, Slimmer Silhouette® is proven to help lose inches, detoxify, look and feel better. After only being available as in-spa treatments for years, founder Meggie Hale has now made these wraps available for in-home purchase at a fraction of the cost.
(www.SlimmerSilhouette.com)

Enter this PE number for a special bonus **99481153.**

The IDENT-EYE-FIER - As a Partner and Business Development Consultant, I help forge relationships to license the technology and build prototypes. Inventor Ron Klein, creator of the credit card magnetic strip, created a patent-pending product that enables the visually impaired to identify a person wearing a badge with a QR code or item with a QR code when in physical range. The glasses have a small camera and a retractable ear piece that interfaces with a Smart Phone to read the QR codes. More than 21.5 million Americans experience vision loss that renders them unable to read prescription drug labels and face a greater danger of taking the wrong medication, consuming an incorrect dosage or overlooking potentially serious drug interactions. (http://4ronklein.com/ShootingStar/)

EqualiTV - Canadian Cable TV channel licensed to broadcast content that is by, for, or about people with disabilities to encourage their full inclusiveness in the media industry worldwide. The channel features international co-productions with more than 53 countries. As Special Advisor and Executive Producer, my mission is to develop strategic alliances to further the EqualiTV cause and help them become known internationally. (http://Equali.tv/ShootingStar/)

My days are full and I feel fulfilled, I am so grateful to finally know what I am here to do. I am passionate about making the world a better place and dedicated to transforming communities into collaborative, problem-solving environments.

As an established Hollywood movie producer, entrepreneur and strategic alliance expert, my mission is to transform lives by developing awareness of innovative inventions, products and services. I create various forms of media and strategic alliances, and market unique opportunities to my extensive relationships and databases. I'm dedicated to producing thought-provoking entertainment focused on inspiring positive change that makes the world a better place. Nothing feels better than earning a living doing something that truly makes a difference and creates positive change in the lives of others.

Today I continue on the high road, driving through a world full of magic and surprises at every corner. Sure, I still have an occasional bad day, but I stay focused on my destination and enjoy the scenery and the company of others journeying on the same road to success. Opportunities are everywhere if you open your heart, give back, and open your mind to receive. If you don't have the life you want, there are usually two things standing in the way:

1. **Not knowing what you want....** It's like getting in your car to drive somewhere and having no idea where you are going.

2. **Self-limiting beliefs....** How can you have what you want when your focus is on what you don't want or don't have?

Here are some tips for the road that may help you find your true destination in life. First, imagine what you do want, see it as if you already have it. Next, take action and the road map will appear. Pay attention to the signs along the way and avoid unnecessary detours and roadblocks. Whatever you do, stay away from the naysayers and other people's dramas. Remember, you don't have to be the lone ranger; collaboration can be the key to your success. Believe me, like-minded people coming together are very powerful!

Opt-in at http://ChosenForChange.com to learn more about these and other exciting products and services.

About Bonnie

Bonnie Kanner grew up in California as the oldest of six children (five full brothers and one half-sister) and was considered the "responsible" one. She had her first job at age 12 and by 17 had moved into her own apartment.

At 24, she married her best friend and they were together for 11 years. When Bonnie's father passed away from cancer, something inside drastically changed and she decided to have a more fulfilling life—one that would make a difference in people's lives and leave a mark on the world. In 1997 she divorced, leaving her with a 4 and 8-year old. As a single mother, Bonnie yearned for a job that paid well and had flexible hours so she could be with her children and provide for their needs.

Bonnie produced four charity golf tournaments called "Shoot for the Stars" for Jewish Big Brothers and Camp Max Straus and the Hollywood Post Production Community. Bonnie filled the tournaments with players from Sony and Disney and was a big success. Doors began to open, leading to several job offers including a position in the Visual Effects industry. Bonnie worked for over 8 years with a company and received over 80 major screen credits for theatrically released films, serving as the Executive Producer. Bonnie is an active member of the Producers Guild of America, Visual Effects Society, Women in Film and the Screen Actors Guild and listed on IMDB: http://www.imdb.com/name/nm0437801/

In March, April and May 2012, Bonnie attended 'Crowd-Funding' conferences. At the first conference, she was introduced by a friend to David Sinclair, President of Axiom Capital USA. By the third conference, David offered Bonnie a position as VP of New Business Development, with the flexibility to maintain her production company, Shooting Star Entertainment.

Bonnie Kanner, now a world-renowned Hollywood Producer and Entrepreneur, is focused on producing films and advancing companies whose goal is to make the world a better place. She strives to produce thought-provoking films that spread a positive message like her upcoming films: "The Lost Teachings of Jesus Christ," "The Great Secret," "System Upgrade," and "Flying Between Heaven and Earth" based on the award-winning novel by Gina E. Jones.

Bonnie's unique life experience allows her to create a very influential network of companies and individuals who rely on her as a Strategic Alliance Expert; bringing them together to fulfill their mission to solve a problem in the world. These "Projects for Good" are Bonnie's passion and she is the go-to person for filling any gap the companies needs to make their vision a reality. She works with innovative companies like: Life Cube, ClickN KIDS Online Educational Community, and IDENT-EYE-FIER...Glasses that will read QR codes and translates them to audio for the visually impaired.

Monika Wiela, Founder of the "Give Back Box" asked Bonnie to join the board as a founding member of "Give Back Box." This concept substantially changes how people make charitable donations. If you received a box from an online order, you will have the opportunity to refill the box with other items that you would like to donate to charity and your Give Back Box™ will then be sent free of charge with your items to be donated. The Give Back Box™ allows you to give back to the people in need from the comfort of their own home. www.givebackbox.com/bonniekanner

Bonnie Kanner's impact has not gone unnoticed. She will be featured in the forthcoming Inc. Magazine entitled "The Next Big Thing" as a leading expert in Strategic Alliances and will be seen on ABC, NBC, CBS, and FOX affiliates around the country later this year on "America's Premier Experts."

CHAPTER 10

VISUALIZATION

BY CHARLIE BAKER

It's funny how we all start out in life as the young dreamer, dreaming of what we want to be, do and create when we get older. Before we know it, we are older and only a few of us achieve, do and create what we set out to do or become. That shouldn't be so. All, not just a few, should achieve their personal accomplishments, as large or small as they decide. In his original book, Napoleon Hill grouped this second step towards riches into a chapter titled *Faith Visualization Of, And Belief In Attainment Of Desire*. The focus here is on the visualization, a current version of a required step to prosperity that all should practice, achieve and master.

I was in real estate selling commercial property to investors on Long Island and Manhattan at the time, when I came across a business owner who I thought had money and needed to expand his business by buying a building. Well, even though I was a successful agent and closed a good amount of deals in 2008, what I didn't know was that I had been sold. ...Instead of selling a building, I was sold a business opportunity. My now ex-partner, had found a new product for a client that had to be imported in from Europe. This product was not being produced in the United States, and after some extensive research on my part, I realized we could reverse engineer the product and build it here in New

York. So I accepted the opportunity. The opportunity for me was to grow a business from a single product. I knew the minute I saw it, that it was more than a product, it solved a problem. The problem was keeping a visual display board clean, new looking and fresh before each use. The product was the "Glass White-board." The business is Krystal Writing Boards, Inc.

I knew from the minute I saw the product – which came to us in a crate from Sweden. The glass was clear, the surface was smooth and when we hung it on the wall to test, I saw the vision. A glass writing board that was so _needed_ in America's boardrooms.

I started out as a college graduate with a Bachelor's in Accounting and a Master's in Information Technology. Both degrees have served me well during my first 15 years in business. I contributed to the companies I had worked for and helped them grow and earn money. All the time, I knew in my heart of hearts I wanted to own my own business, and when the last company I worked for was bought out, I had the opportunity I needed to seize the moment. Unfortunately, that moment only included a severance not a business. I still maintained my dream. I worked hard during the exploration and business modeling period. After two months, I settled on the business of commercial real estate but after three years of working hard, I didn't feel that I had found my calling. I realized I didn't own or control the buyer, I didn't own or control the seller and I certainly didn't own or control the financing. As my dad often said to me, "always keep your doors open and don't burn bridges. Who you meet on the way up, you meet again on the way down. The keys to success are: follow your dream, listen to your heart, and do what you like to do."

Well, I liked to build value, build businesses, and build relationships. I visualized owning a company and speaking to my clients, going to conventions and working with my employees creating an environment that was fun and productive. All I needed was a product or service. That product came to me in a way I did not expect, in a way I did not plan. Each day I had visualized my company, the employees, the clients and the office setting.

I believe on that special day my subconscious mind alerted my conscious self that the glass writing board was that product that would fulfill my calling.

At the time we started the business venture, it was the beginning of the recession, ...companies were pulling back from spending, ...not many small companies were hiring, ...lending was tightening. With my faith, vision and belief intact, I acted. My dream was to own a company, not to work in one. I began to implement the business models that I had observed and studied. The small accounting firms where I had worked provided the starting point and base to build upon. Then I looked at Microsoft's support team, UPS's distribution structure, Home Depot's product identification and organization, Zappos's customer service, GKIC's information marketing and Marriott's model of building success one hotel at a time. I watched how they interacted with prospects, turned them into clients, and grew their businesses through joint ventures and long-term relationships. I watched how they communicated, invoiced, followed up, closed transactions, performed customer service and built their infrastructure through their employees and work environments. There were many other firms I examined, many smaller and more local. It was the visualized planning that paid the dividends of today.

By taking the time each day to visualize what I wanted to accomplish, plan the next step, write it out, cross examine it and utilize my peer group. I was able to determined whether it was a good fit within the overall plan. Even though each step had many more obstacles and partial road blocks, I knew if I kept my faith in myself, saw myself achieving success and believing I could do it, that it would happen. This three-step process was vital – (1) have faith, (2) visualize and (3) believe it will happen. There is a reason why so many people have written books about this topic. It is why Napoleon Hill is still read today and why the book *The Secret* was such a success, because it works. Your subconscious mind will achieve what you tell it you want to achieve. Whether it is a negative thought or a positive thought.

You dictate that part and need to stay positive. The subconscious mind cannot tell the difference, it just wants to do, achieve and fulfill the thoughts you feed it. Mine told me "here is your product, here is your company." Had I not been practicing visualization on a daily basis I would have missed that opportunity and then only wished I had been lucky enough to have something like that happen to me. Instead I was aware, alert and ready. I made it happen.

Now my tool today for visualization is the glass white board. A tempered, polished, innovative, elegant, branded, frameless writing board. It's mounted to the wall with standoff anchors that allow the board to float. The truly innovative aspect of the glass writing board is that it doesn't stain. With a little glass cleaner it will stay new, brand new, for a long time. It's a touch of class with a touch of glass. No more need to constantly replace the old stained whiteboard. No need to buy an expensive cabinet to hide the stained whiteboard. Many boardrooms were furnished with the dark wood cabinet that housed the whiteboard. It was sold to them with the value of prestige. Having this piece of furniture was a necessity. Well not any more. The glass writing board can be personalized, offering a branding aspect to the boardroom. Visiting prospects, clients, vendors, students, patients all see the image, the brand , the elegance, and the innovation. They visually feel the effectiveness of what is written and the accuracy of the information. What they don't see is the remnant of what was written yesterday, last week or last month. The stunning beauty of the glass writing board has purpose. All it took was for the vision to see the adaption of a product put into business.

Napoleon Hill was instrumental in the creation of the Krystal Writing Board, Inc. company. The book *Think and Grow Rich* was part of my required reading as I modeled successful people. There is one poem from the original book that needs to be brought forward into this writing.

"The law of auto-suggestion, through which any person may rise to altitudes of achievement which stagger the imagination, is well described in the following verse:

> If you think you are beaten, you are,
> If you think you dare not, you don't
> If you like to win, but you think you can't,
> It is almost certain you won't.
>
> If you think you'll lose, you're lost
> For out of the world we find,
> Success begins with a fellow's will-
> It's all in the state of mind.
>
> If you think you are outclassed, you are,
> You've got to think high to rise,
> You've got to be sure of yourself before
> You can ever win a prize.
>
> Life's battles don't always go
> To the stronger or faster man,
> But soon or late the man who wins
> Is the man WHO THINKS HE CAN!

Observe the words which have been emphasized, and you will catch the deep meaning which the poet had in mind."

To be successful today using visualization, you need to understand and utilize the following five points:

1. It all begins with a desire. Ask yourself this important question, "What do you want to do, be, achieve in this lifetime?"
Whether you are five or ninety-five years old your desire is what motivates and inspires you as a being. Today we live longer and a good part of that longevity is the simple desire to live longer. We are driven in science to cure disease, we are driven in education to learn from generations past and we are driven today to be responsible and live healthy, active lives. We are driven by our companions, friends and co-workers. As a society we want to provide more for our children than was provided

to us. We want our companies to provide more than they did the year before. That desire should be nourished, encouraged and strengthened every day. The desire can change from day to day. One day your desire can be health related, one day it can be relationship growth and another day it can be about a certain goal. The key is to have the want and desire to do something positive. Don't take any given day for granted, but rather look at each day as a new beginning and the opportunity to make a difference.

2. You must believe in yourself - have faith.
Faith too needs to be fed daily. The belief that one can succeed at one's desires is the building block to success. Take the time to practice a daily routine of asserting the notion that you believe in yourself – that you are a good person. You're in the right place in your life. That you are looking to do good things and create good outcomes. If you need to acquire skills or assets you have the faith that you will obtain those skills or assets. If you need to find that right path, keep your faith set on obtaining that path and one day you will achieve what it is you seek. This daily reinforcement of having the courage and belief that you can accomplish anything you set out to do has been proven time after time. It is as applicable today as it ever was before. The skills you possess will guide you down the correct path and help you choose the course that fills your heart. Faith will greatly expand your skills. One enhances the other.

3. You must see yourself in the present as owning what you are after. You must visualize this thought.
Visualization is the art of making "It" happen before it happens. By seeing in ones mind's eye the reality of having what it is you seek, you instruct the subconscious mind to seek out what it is you are after. The more you touch your subconscious mind with the right thoughts,

the more adept the subconscious mind will be at obtaining that thought. As I mentioned before your subconscious mind will achieve what you tell it you want to achieve. Whether it is a negative thought or a positive thought. You dictate that part and need to stay positive. The subconscious mind cannot tell the difference, it just wants to do, achieve, and fulfill the thoughts you feed it.

Whether that vision is written down on paper, a glass whiteboard, in your tablet or within your mind, you must see it, …visualize it every day.

4. You must Act. Without action there is only the thought.

Some of the most successful students of visualization use it more than twice a day. Any professional, whether they are an Olympic athlete, successful salesperson, business owner, teacher, pilot, doctor, policeman, fireman or professional athlete, they must visualize their performance. They must see it happen before it happens. Then when it does happen they can measure the success and make any adjustments. The performance review of the action helps to judge the success. This allows you to create a more detailed visualization – which in turn will become more realistic and heighten the senses. In order to perform with high success, they must work at taking that desire, believe they can do it, see it in their mind's eye and then act. They must work at developing the skill of seeing what they desire as already having it, and then going out and doing it. This action will create a positive experience and provide lasting fulfillment to life, their life and anyone they touch.

5. You must never stop visualizing. You can change your vision but you cannot stop. For if you are not growing, you are dying.

This is the foundation of improvement. Where practice makes perfect and where perfect practice makes perfection. The people at the top of their professions, the ones with the highest self-esteem, the most sound relationship, the 1% income producers, and the tops in their field all obtain this level through constant practice. The behind-the-scene planning, preparing and practicing after each failure or success is what truly drives the best to be the best.

I encourage you to re-read the original book by Napoleon Hill and re-read this version. Take the pointed lessons and put them into your skill set. Don't wait for tomorrow, visualize having it today. Make the necessary preparations and act. I promise you that you won't regret the effort and you certainly won't regret the reward. It has been my privilege to impart my experience and my interpretation in hopes that others can achieve their goals. Mastering these key concepts of visualization will greatly increase the chances of your success. Wishing you all the best!!

About Charlie

Charlie Baker, President of Krystal™ Writing Boards, Inc., is a lifelong New Yorker. After visualizing the tremendous use for glass writing boards, he built Krystal from the ground up. Throughout his career he spent many meetings in both boardrooms and classrooms, he succinctly realized the great benefits of using a tool such as a glass writing board. The innovative change in the functional use for glass created an industry that wasn't there before. Charlie states: "My ability to communicate is greatly improved when my audience can see the subject matter clearly. Our boards do not stain or ghost, and they are elegant, yet functional. I love building a superior product for a marketplace that appreciates quality."

Prior to starting Krystal Writing Boards, Inc., Charlie started his own Commercial Real Estate Brokerage Company and worked with business owners to secure the appropriate commercial property for their current and future needs. Additionally, he has 15 years of financial and accounting experience, working in mid-to-large size Long Island corporations including two Fortune 500 Companies, building financial and accounting systems, and was a public accountant.

Charlie is the acting President for Patchogue Lion's Club and a past President of the Patchogue Chamber of Commerce. He has a Masters Degree in Information Systems Management from Dowling College and a Bachelor of Science Degree in Accounting from Marist College. He has a passion for helping other local companies grow nationally and devotes time to building two other businesses: A local accounting software service business and Freshana Organic Solutions, LLC. Freshana is a revolutionary, 100% organic compound cleaner that microencapsulates and removes carbon waste 1000 times faster than nature. This too will change an industry, so stay tuned.

Charlie is married to his high school sweetheart Cheryl, and they have two children Nicholas and Rylee. They love to go camping in their RV with their three dogs Skippy, Oreo and Bella.

To learn more about Charlie Baker, Krystal Writing Boards, Inc. and how you can receive his free Special Report *The Five Silent Threats Damaging the Image and Efficiency in Organizations Today,* go to www.krystalgwb. com, select Contact Us and enter "Send the 5 Silent Threat Report" or call 1-877-FOR-KRYS (1-877-367-5795).

CHAPTER 11

SUCCESS:
How Bad Do
You Really Want It?

BY GARY MARTIN HAYS

Fight like you are the third monkey trying to get on the ark.
~ Some Clever, Unknown Person

Visualize this scenario for a moment: some man named Noah is predicting a major flood. He tells everyone the floodwaters will cover the face of the earth. But he has a plan. He is building an enormous boat that will weather the storm. He puts an ad in the newspaper that he needs a male and female of each kind of animal "to keep the species alive on the face of all the earth."[1]

You are a monkey. You see the ad. It is your desire to be "THE" male monkey to board that boat and help procreate the monkey race. You get out a map and you plot your course to Noah's shipyard. For days, you swing from branch to branch to get to the ark. Thoughts about the future "Mrs. Monkey" and that 3 bedroom, 2½ bath tree house occupy your mind during the trip. You are focused on getting to the ark, boarding it, and romancing Miss Monkey.

---

1 Genesis 7:2-3.

After days and nights of travel, you finally arrive at the loading dock of the shipyards. The magnificent ark is before you. It is huge - several stories high. You sit down on a crate full of bananas on the loading dock to rest - and you wait...

Then it happens. The gangplank lowers. Noah and several of his family members begin loading the animals. He takes the giraffes in, and then the elephants and the zebras. You hear Noah shout "Time for the monkeys to board." You get up and start walking towards the ark. But much to your surprise, you see two monkeys being introduced at the base of the gangplank. You watch them exchange greetings and then see them turn and start to head up the ramp towards the ark. They are holding hands...

What do you do, Mr. Monkey?

Just ask yourself: how bad do you want it? Do you just "want" it, or has this become " the one CONSUMING OBSESSION" of your life", a "keen, pulsating DESIRE, which transcends everything?"

How will you answer this important question?

Do you fight like you are the third monkey trying to get on the ark, or do you sit on the dock and let your ship sail?

If you are like most people, you stay on that dock only to drown in your sorrow of "what could have been." It is always someone else's fault they did not succeed, or they simply blame it on bad luck.

So how do you change the course of your fate? What do you need to do to turn yourself into the successful, winning, "Ark Monkey" that waves goodbye to all the other monkeys while sipping champagne on the Lido Deck of the Ark at the Bon Voyage Party?

You need to have a **DESIRE** for something. Napoleon Hill's classic work, *Think and Grow Rich*, gives us a great road map that we can follow to find that desire, as well as practical steps we can take to see that your desire becomes a reality. Hill felt that "desire" is the starting point of all achievement.

So what is "desire" and how does one use it to achieve goals?

Merriam-Webster defines "desire" as "to long or hope for; to express a wish for."[2] But if success were simply about "longing" or "hoping" or "wishing" for something, there would be a lot of successful people in this world. Napoleon Hill tells us that, "Wishing will not bring riches. But desiring riches with a state of mind that becomes an obsession, then planning definite ways and means to acquire riches, and backing those plans with persistence which does not recognize failure, will bring riches."[3]

There are a lot of great inspirational quotes about "desire":

- "It's not the size of the dog in the fight, but the size of the fight in the dog."- Mark Twain

- "Desire is half of life; indifference is half of death." - Khalil Gibran

- "Burning desire to be or do something gives us staying power - a reason to get up every morning or to pick ourselves up and start in again after a disappointment." - Marsha Sinetar

- "A creative man is motivated by the desire to achieve, not by the desire to beat others." - Ayn Rand

- "The will to win, the desire to succeed, the urge to reach your full potential… these are the keys that will unlock the door to personal excellence." - Confucius

The concept of "desiring" something and having the belief that you will attain it has been a formula for success long before Hill, however. This was written about in the Gospel of Mark in the second book of the New Testament of the Bible. "Therefore I say unto you, what things soever ye desire, when ye pray, believe that ye

---

2 "desire" - Merriam-Webster.com. 2012. http://www.merriam-webster.com
(14 December 2012).
3 Hill, Napoleon. *Think And Grow Rich*, Lexington, KY, Tribeca Books, November 2012.

receive them, and ye shall have them."[4]

Simply desiring something is not enough. But it is a start! When you truly desire something, it can be an incredibly strong motivator towards a specific goal. And let's face it - some people never have a desire to do anything. We see it in our society today. More and more people are content living off of government handouts. They have lost that drive, desire, and determination to use the loss of a job as motivation to learn a new career or trade. Instead of taking an entry-level position and working their way back up the ladder, they wait for the "higher rung" job to become available. Most people will say they want to succeed when all they really want is financial security without having to work for it. If you have a desire to succeed in this economic climate, chances are you are not the norm.

WHAT DO YOU TRULY DESIRE?

What is your consuming obsession? I'll tell you what it **should not** be - someone else's dreams or desires implanted on you. There is nothing worse than watching a person go through life pursuing a "dream" that someone had for them - instead of them choosing their own dream. You see it on so many different levels every day. It happens on the little league field, the kid who would rather be doing something else besides participating on a "travel baseball" team. The sport - which used to be for fun - now consumes two or three nights a week for practice, and then every weekend is on the road playing games. He is living out "daddy's dream" to try and play professional baseball. He can't quit because his dad will not let him, or he is afraid he will disappoint his hero if he tries to quit.

I see it on the faces of other attorneys too. They went to law school because that was what their parents wanted for them - to become a professional. They would hear it at an early age - "Be a lawyer - a doctor. I always wanted to do something like that but I never could. But now you can!" So the kid grows up, goes to college, gets into law school, graduates, passes the bar, and discov-

4 Mark 11:24.

ers he or she is stuck. The student loans are now in the $70,000 to $80,000 dollar range and they are in a profession they cannot stand. Quitting is not an option. This would be an admission that they are a failure. Even if they want to quit, most cannot afford to do so because their student loans are too high. So every day they wake up, they go to work at a job - not because they want to, but because they have to do it. How fortunate is the man or woman that can make a living doing what they love?

Once you find that dream - that burning desire (or desires) - then you must decide: Do you sit back and hope the dream becomes a reality? Or, do you take the necessary steps to put an action plan in place?

WHAT STEPS DO I NEED TO TAKE TO GET THAT WHICH I DESIRE?

Napoleon Hill describes for us: "The method by which DESIRE for riches can be transmuted into its financial equivalent" into "six definite, practical steps."[5]

First:
You must be **definite** about what you want. Specificity is the key. Pick an exact figure and focus on that amount. Though Hill uses "money" in his example, the "riches" one desires can be anything that can be a definite, specific goal. Clearly define what you want so you can focus on that goal.

Second:
Decide what you intend to give up to reach this goal. As Hill reminds us, there is no such thing as "something for nothing." It will cost you something. So just how bad do you want it? What are you willing to give up or to consistently do to achieve the goal?

Third:
When do you plan on reaching this goal? You need to set a firm date when you plan on acquiring the object of your desire. Circle

5 Hill, *Think And Grow Rich*, 24.

that date on the calendar. Put a sticky note with that date on your bathroom mirror to remind you of your target date.

Fourth:
Write out a specific, step by step plan, of how you will reach the goal you desire. It has often been said, "The devil is in the details." Create that list of things you need to do, and then prioritize the list. It will help you stay focused and on task. When a specific action is completed, mark it off so you can see your progress.

Fifth:
Hill tells us to "Write out a clear, concise statement of the amount of money you intend to acquire, name the time limit for its acquisition, state what you intend to give in return for the money, and describe clearly the plan through which you intend to accumulate it."[6] You are essentially memorializing your first four steps to a single sheet of paper. This is the contract you are making with yourself about your goal, the process, and the date you will achieve it.

Sixth:
Twice a day - in the morning, and then right before you go to bed, read your written statement out loud. This will help visualize your goal and reinforce it in your mind. Hill suggests "AS YOU READ - SEE AND FEEL AND BELIEVE YOURSELF ALREADY IN POSSESSION OF THE MONEY."[7] Hill suggests you truly desire something, and become so focused on having it that you CONVINCE yourself you will have it.

SO NOW WHAT?

You now have that burning desire. You are focused on YOUR goal, not someone else's. You have written out your goal, your steps for reaching that goal, and you have a fixed date for when you plan on achieving that goal.

---

6 Hill, *Think And Grow Rich*, 25.
7 Id.

What happens next?

I think you need to look in the mirror and ask that question of yourself. It all depends on you. And frankly, that is what will separate you from 99.9% of the population. Some people are just not motivated to do anything. Others fall into the trap of "getting ready to get ready." They will go out and buy into the latest "get rich quick program." Hours are spent reading the program, studying the plans, and researching the best way to get started. And then they come up with a reason(s) as to why it won't work, or why it can't work for them, and they put the program back into the closet . . . and they wait. They wait for the next big thing to come along and the cycle repeats itself. Some people never miss an opportunity to miss an opportunity!

Nike's advertising slogan sums it up best: "Just Do It!" Get your plan, believe in it, focus on it, repeat it twice a day, set your target date, and get started! If your target date is one year away from today, next year on this day, you will either be proud that you reached your goal, or you will be extremely disappointed you did not even get started. The choice is yours.

Everyone has heard of the classic childhood story - *The Little Engine That Could*.[8] A train was carrying a collection of toys, books, and special treats for boys and girls to the other side of the mountain. But the train stopped and it could not move another inch. Throughout the story, other engines come along, but none are willing to take up the load and pull it over the mountain... until a little blue engine comes along. When asked to carry the load over the mountain, the train started talking to herself "I think I can, I think I can, I think I can." And then she took action. She hitched herself to the little train, and she started tugging and pulling.

It was a slow start, but she kept on tugging and pulling. She kept telling herself "I think I can - I think I can - I think I can." Then she reached the top of the mountain and coasted to the valley

---

8 Piper, Watty. *The Little Engine That Could*, New York, New York, Penguin Group.

below. Her words changed from "I think I can" to "I thought I could. I thought I could." All of this success happened because of a positive belief - a burning desire to get over that mountain - coupled with action. She didn't run from the opportunity. She didn't stop when the tugging and pulling was slow. She kept telling herself "I think I can" until she did.

So I challenge you - transform yourself into the "Little Engine That Could" so you can become the successful "Little Engine That DID!" You will not regret it.

Now let's think back to our monkey sitting on the crates of bananas. Noah calls out for the monkeys to board the ark and you see two monkeys walking up the gangplank. What are YOU going to do?

I encourage you to find that inner desire!

Fight like you are the third monkey trying to get on the ark!

About Gary

Gary Martin Hays is not only a successful lawyer, but is a nationally recognized safety advocate who works tirelessly to educate our families and children on issues ranging from bullying to internet safety to abduction prevention. He currently serves on the Board of Directors of the Elizabeth Smart Foundation. Gary has been seen on countless television stations, including CNN Headline News, ABC, CBS, NBC and FOX affiliates. He has appeared on over 110 radio stations, including the Georgia News Network, discussing legal topics and providing safety tips to families. He hosts "Georgia Behind The Scenes" on the CW Atlanta TV Network and has been quoted in *USA Today, The Wall Street Journal,* and featured on over 250 online sites including *Morningstar.com,* CBS News's *MoneyWatch.com, The Boston Globe, The Miami Herald, The New York Daily News,* and *The Miami Herald.*

He is also co-author of seven (7) best-selling books *TRENDSETTERS, CHAMPIONS, SOLD, PROTECT AND DEFEND, THE SUCCESS SECRET, THE AUTHORITY ON TOUT,* and *THE AUTHORITY ON CHILD SAFETY* - all of which were released in the last two years.

Gary graduated from Emory University in 1986 with a B.A. degree in Political Science and a minor in Afro-American and African Studies. In 1989, he received his law degree from the Walter F. George School of Law of Mercer University, Macon, Georgia. His outstanding academic achievements landed him a position on Mercer's Law Review.

His legal accomplishments include being a member of the prestigious Multi Million Dollar Advocate's Forum, a society limited to those attorneys who have received a settlement or verdict of at least $2 million. He has been recognized in <u>Atlanta Magazine</u> as one of Georgia's top workers' compensation lawyers. Gary frequently lectures to other attorneys in Georgia on continuing education topics. He has been recognized as one of the Top 100 Trial Lawyers in Georgia since 2007 by the American Trial Lawyers Association, and recognized by Lawdragon as one of the leading Plaintiffs' Lawyers in America. His firm specializes in personal injury, wrongful death, workers' compensation, and pharmaceutical claims. Since 1993, his firm has helped over 27,000 victims and their families recover over $235 million.

In 2008, Gary started the non-profit organization Keep Georgia Safe with the mission to provide safety education and crime prevention training in Georgia. Keep Georgia Safe has trained over 80 state and local law enforcement officers in CART (Child Abduction Response Teams) so our first responders will know what to do in the event a child is abducted in Georgia. Gary has completed Child Abduction Response Team training with the National AMBER Alert program through the U.S. Department of Justice and Fox Valley Technical College. He is a certified instructor in the radKIDS curriculum. His law firm has given away 1,000 bicycle helmets and 14 college scholarships.

To learn more about Gary Martin Hays, visit: www.GaryMartinHays.com.
To find out more about Keep Georgia Safe, please visit: www.KeepGeorgiaSafe.org
or call (770) 934-8000.

CHAPTER 12

THE LINKS FROM DESIRE TO WEALTH – FAITH AND AUTO-SUGGESTION

BY JEFF COLON

Like the relationship between members of a successful Super Bowl team, the interplay between DESIRE, FAITH, and AUTO-SUGGESTION are important partners in the goal to attain WEALTH. Cultivation of this trio is crucial to what Napoleon Hill called the "money conscious" mindset. In the steps towards riches, the DESIRE to achieve your monetary goal has one route to reality. Implement the practices of FAITH and AUTO- SUGGESTION fully every day. Use these parameters for careful monitoring and input of the thoughts. This will translate into fulfilled desire in the form of money. Anyone can use this plan and achieve results when they follow the steps with passionate belief in the outcome. The process for obtaining the money you desire begins with seeds of burning DESIRE. This is the kind of desire that recognizes no such word as impossible and accepts no such reality as failure. This intense DESIRE becomes a real path toward your financial goal when FAITH propels it along and AUTO-SUGGESTION infuses each step of the process. These steps to riches find their footing in self-control of the mind and its thought processes. If you are willing to exercise self-control over your own mind, it is possible for you to follow the practical steps through DESIRE, FAITH, and AUTO-SUGGESTION and reach your financial goal.

THE PRACTICAL BEGINNING

Let's begin with the six practical steps for converting DESIRE for riches into CASH:

1. VISUALIZE THE CASH: firmly fix the exact amount of money you desire in your mind.

2. SELECT THE PRODUCT or SERVICE: determine exactly what you intend to give in return for the money you desire.

3. ESTABLISH A DEADLINE: establish a definite date when you intend to possess the money you desire.

4. CREATE AN ACTION PLAN: create a definite plan for carrying out your desire. Begin immediately, whether you are ready or not, to put this plan into action.

5. WRITE IT DOWN – write out a clear, simple statement of the first four steps.

   a. The amount of money you intend to acquire.

   b. The time limit for obtaining it.

   c. What you intend to give in exchange for the money.

   d. The plan through which you intend to accumulate the money.

6. READ YOUR WRITTEN PLAN: Read your written plan twice a day. As you do, see, feel, and believe yourself already in possession of the money.

There is the outline. It is where you begin the process of acquiring the money you desire. Yet you must realize that a sterile, unemotional application of this process won't lead to success. This is where FAITH comes into play.

THE ROLE OF FAITH IN GETTING RICH

FAITH is a state of mind.

You create faith by affirmation or repeated instructions to the subconscious mind. This is where the principle of auto-suggestion helps to develop faith. Hill called FAITH the head chemist of the mind. He elaborates: When FAITH is blended with the vibration of thought, the subconscious mind instantly picks up the vibration, translates it into its spiritual equivalent, and transmits it to Infinite Intelligence, as in the case of prayer.

The emotions of FAITH, LOVE, and SEX are the most powerful of all the major positive emotions. When the three are blended, they have the effect of "coloring" the vibration of thought in such a way that it instantly reaches the subconscious mind, where it is changed into its spiritual equivalent, the only form that induces a response from Infinite Intelligence.

The powerful role of these positive emotions, particularly FAITH, in achieving your monetary goals cannot be understated. The only known method to develop the emotion of faith is by repetition or affirmation of orders to your subconscious mind. Thoughts, which are formulated in your mind, become powerful agents - they translate into their physical equivalent - when they are attached to an emotion and mixed with faith.

INFLUENCING THE SUBCONSCIOUS MIND

The subconscious mind is your servant. Its inclination is to carry out the orders and ideas from your conscience thoughts that carry the weight of strong desire, expectant belief, and firm faith in the possibility of the outcome. This is where those who are successful in achieving their goals, be it financial or otherwise, make the crucial call. They actively influence their subconscious mind by controlling their thoughts and emotions. They grow and enlarge these for feeding the subconscious by means of AUTO-SUGGESTION. This is true for both negative and positive thoughts. Consider for example the mind of a criminal. If it is true that one may become a criminal by association with crime, it is equally true that one may develop faith by voluntary suggestion to the subconscious mind that one has faith. The influences which dominate the mind are the ones that capture it.

21ST CENTURY CHALLENGES TO AUTO-SUGGESTION

The digital age of the 21st century has brought exceptional challenges to the process of feeding the subconscious mind. Because information, entertainment, and diversion are so readily accessible even in the private spaces and times of our daily living, Hill's steps are a cautionary tale. His insistence that getting rich is born in the mind of an individual becomes an even more important idea.

Consider a modern day example such as Steve Jobs. A man of energy and imagination, he focused not just on making money, but also on making life better for millions of people. Contrast that to other computer "geniuses" who wreak havoc around the world via their skill at hacking and disrupting business. You can tap into the positive aspects of today's richness of information and thought-inducers by monitoring the thoughts you feed and enlarge on in your mind. Then feed your subconscious with the resulting positive beliefs, ideas, and energy. Hill was very adamant that integrity guides all paths toward wealth. His teachings always projected that positive message; that achieving your own wealth should be a benefit to the world at large, and not be achieved at another's expense.

DEVELOPING FAITH

A mind dominated by positive emotions is a fertile place where faith can take up residence. You attain this state of mind, this emotion of FAITH through AUTO- SUGGESTION. Amazingly, FAITH can be developed where it does not already exist. The object of FAITH is two-way: have faith in yourself; have faith in the Infinite. The power of FAITH gives life and action to the impulse of thought. In the path toward reaching your financial goal, faith is your loyal partner.

FAITH is:

- The starting point for the accumulation of riches.
- The basis of all miracles and mysteries, which cannot be explained by science.
- The only antidote for failure.
- The only element which when mixed with prayer gives one direct communication with the Infinite Intelligence.
- The element which transforms ordinary vibration of thought
  in the finite mind of man into the spiritual equivalent.
- The only agency through which the cosmic force of Infinite Intelligence can be harnessed and used by people.

THE ROLE OF EMOTIONS

Emotions are the feeling portion of thoughts. They are the factors which give thoughts their vitality, life, and actions. Thought impulses mixed with any of the positive emotions (or any of the negative emotions), may reach, and influence the subconscious mind. The subconscious mind translates thoughts into their physical equivalent.

For this reason, the positive emotion of FAITH is a primary one to develop and infuse into your thinking process toward your monetary goal. Millions of people believe (have faith) that they are doomed to poverty, that they have no control over their lives, and this negative belief plays out in a self-fulfilling prophecy. However, the opposite can be true when you believe (have faith) that riches are within your reach. There is an element of deceit (in a positive sense) in this. You convince your subconscious to proceed toward the physical equivalent of your desire for money when you repeatedly conduct yourself as if you were already in possession of the material things you are demanding.

Through experimentation and repeated practice, you acquire the ability to mix FAITH with any given order to the subconscious mind. Perfection will come through practice. It cannot come by merely reading instructions. It is essential to encourage the positive emotions as dominating forces in your mind and discourage - and eliminate - negative emotions. When your positive emotions dominate your mind, it becomes a favorable place for faith to develop. In this state of mind, dominance by faith-auto-suggestion becomes a natural positive agent for change.

REPETITION AND THOUGHT INVENTORY

We are what we are because the thoughts that register in our minds are invited to stay, and are fed. An original seed of an idea, plan, or purpose is planted in the mind through external stimuli, or vibrations in the unseen ether surrounding us. Through repetition of positive thought, the original thought-seed sprouts and bears fruit. This is why writing down your major purpose and regularly reviewing it is so important. The mind grows what it feeds.

The practice of AUTO-SUGGESTION will help you sort through your thoughts, as you read and repeat your major purpose (to make a definite amount of money). Resolve to discard any negative thoughts that come to mind via any unfortunate environment. Continually take an inventory of your mental assets and liabilities. Apply this principle by capturing positive thought-impulses in writing. Memorize and repeat them until they become a part of the working environment of your subconscious mind.

THE SELF-CONFIDENCE FORMULA

A powerful AUTO-SUGGESTION for keeping you on track toward your monetary goal follows in the five-part formula for self-confidence. Repeat it with faith in yourself, to yourself until it becomes part of your subconscious mindset.

1. KNOW & DEMAND: I know that I have the ability to

achieve my goal, therefore, I promise to demand of myself persistent, continuous action towards it.

2. 30-MINUTE THOUGHT EXERCISE: I know that what dominates my thinking will become my reality. Therefore, I will concentrate for 30 minutes daily on the person I intend to become, creating in my mind a clear mental picture of that person.

3. 10 MINUTES OF CONFIDENCE: Since I know that the principle of auto-suggestion empowers my mind to bring about results, I will devote 10 minutes daily to the development of my self-confidence.

4. WRITTEN GOAL: With my clearly written description of my chief aim in life, I resolve to work toward it always until I have developed sufficient self-confidence for its achievement.

5. The law of nature behind this formula is what psychologists have named "auto-suggestion." All impulses of thought have a tendency to clothe themselves in their physical equivalent. A mind filled with doubt and fear will lead, through the law of auto-suggestion, to misery, poverty, and all sorts of distress.

On the other hand, a mind that steadily and continually feeds on courage or faith, results in the attainment of a rich life of goals achieved and others who benefit as well as oneself. Arouse the genius that lies asleep in your brain. It will cause you to soar upward to whatever goal you may wish to achieve.

A POWERFUL EXAMPLE

The possibilities wrought by FAITH are known the world over in the life of Mahatma Gandhi. Through his ability to transplant faith into the minds of two hundred million people he accomplished what no other world leader could despite his lack of money, battleships, soldiers, and other materials of warfare. Committed to non-violence, his power came through his understanding of the principle of faith. His quest to lead India to independence from British rule was not only successful; it inspired movements for non-violence, civil rights, and freedom across the world.

Leadership and success like that is born in the quiet recesses of the mind. It is there where one commits to pursuing a goal with extraordinary faith in the possibilities and in their own role to influence the outcome.

THE GATEKEEPER MIND AND AUTO-SUGGESTION

All environmental suggestions and all self-administered stimuli, which reach one's mind through the five senses, are what we call auto-suggestion. The conscious mind is the outer-guard to the subconscious. All stimuli which come into the mind are stopped at the gate of the conscious mind and either rejected or permitted to pass on to the subconscious mind.

You have absolute control over this process. Yet not everybody exercises that control. In a great majority of instances, people do not exercise this privilege of control – this explains why so many people go through life in poverty. The instruction to read your written statement of your desire for money aloud two times daily is a practical way to exercise this control over your thoughts (see the six-step plan at the beginning of this chapter). Remember this must be accompanied by the act of seeing and feeling yourself already in possession of the money.

EMOTION AND MONEY CONSCIOUSNESS

These six steps for converting DESIRE into money are so crucial to your success, that they must be read and re-read. You are endeavoring in this exercise to develop a "money consciousness." Be sure to combine this with emotion - FAITH in yourself and the outcome. Your subconscious mind will only act upon thoughts which it receives that are supported by emotion or feeling.

This fact bears repeating — you will not get the desirable results from the practice of AUTO-SUGGESTION unless your thought repetitions are accompanied by the energy and conviction of the positive emotion of FAITH. You must believe in your own capacity to reach your goal.

Discouragement might confront you if you have a hard time controlling and directing your emotions. Remember that the ability to reach your goal comes with a price, and you must be willing to pay that price. Be persistent in applying these principles. You are the only one who must decide whether or not the reward of your striving (the "money consciousness") is worth the price you must pay in effort.

THE CAPACITY TO CONCENTRATE

Your ability to use the principle of AUTO-SUGGESTION will depend upon your capacity to concentrate upon a given desire. You must concentrate until desire becomes a burning obsession.

Effective use of concentration begins with visualization. Fix in your mind the exact amount of money you desire. Hold your thoughts on that amount of money, with your eyes closed, until you can actually see the physical appearance of the money. Remember, do this at least once each day.

The subconscious mind will take orders from you when given in a spirit of absolute FAITH. It interprets and acts on orders presented to it repeatedly. By believing yourself to be in possession of this money, the subconscious mind will hand over to you practical plans for acquiring the money, which is yours.

Your DESIRE for money will ignite your imagination to meet that demand and expectation. Soon it will present you with plans for acquiring money through an exchange of goods or services. This plan will probably flash into your mind through the sixth sense. Treat it with respect and put the plan into action immediately.

In step four above, you created a definite plan. When you visualize the end goal of this plan, couple it with FAITH, and call your imagination into play; and add one more thing. Close your eyes and see yourself rendering the service or delivering the merchandise you intend to give for this money.

SUMMARY

You can become the master of yourself and thereby reach your monetary goal because you have the power to influence your subconscious mind. The transformation of DESIRE into money becomes possible with the use of AUTO-SUGGESTION as a means by which you may reach and influence the subconscious mind. This positive, faith-filled influence on the subconscious mind is the key that unlocks your imagination, your ideas, your energy, and the cooperation of the Infinite Intelligence; and that leads to financial success.

Always implement these tools as though you were a small child. Act in faith. Be persistent. Involve your emotions in an honest manner. You can think and grow rich today. When DESIRE to reach your monetary goal is carried along by FAITH; when the concrete and proven practices of AUTO-SUGGESTION engage your mind and sub-conscious, your success in reaching your monetary goal is possible, certain, and near at hand.

About Jeff

Jeff Colon is the Director of the Jeff Colon Group, a Real Estate Luxury Home Brokerage firm in Danville, California that has been in business for ten years. Jeff, a native of the East Bay area, studied at the Mike Ferry Organization, the number one real estate training company in the nation. Although already very successful, he constantly strives to bring his career to the next level.

Jeff never settles for complacency. He has completed many intensive training programs relating to business strategies, real estate, sales, coaching and marketing. There is never a day that goes by when he is not studying and learning something new about the real estate industry so that he can inform his clients about the most current market information. He constantly keeps an eye on defining new trends and rooting out worthwhile investments.

Ranked in the top one percent nationally for professional realtors, Jeff has participated in thousands of transactions. Employing a full-time staff to meet the demands of his clients, he is known for his ability to sell a client's home quickly once it has been listed.

"I embrace the needs of my clients. If they are coming to me to help them purchase or sell a home, they are putting their trust in me. It is my responsibility to get them fast and secure results."

Unique Specialties

Jeff's brokerage firm focuses on single family homes in Danville, San Ramon, Alamo, Hayward and other Bay City areas.

Although Jeff doesn't subscribe to limiting the properties he sells, his specialties include fine homes, estate sales, probate and relocation services.

He has developed a unique home selling structure that has built customer loyalty and trust. Because he works with many high profile clients who wish to maintain their privacy, the VIP confidential executive services he offers are greatly appreciated.

Professionalism, Guidance and No Surprises

His clients and peers alike all lavish praise upon him because of the level of personal attention he gives them. He is not your average salesperson -- his clients truly appreciate his knowledge and his caring. His top priority is to listen to and understand his clients' needs and objectives – from the time they list to the time they move. Jeff believes his clients deserve the highest level of service, professionalism and guidance throughout the entire process.

"Representing buyers and sellers in the real estate business, I put an emphasis on communicating effectively and frequently with them so that there are no surprises suddenly popping up during the process. If you don't pay attention to a client's needs, a transaction can be delayed unnecessarily or even fall through."

Helping to Make Informed Decisions

Jeff doesn't hesitate to tell a client if he sees something wrong with a particular property and always explains why. The thanks he has received attest to his knowledge and professional services, all stating the confidence they felt in making the right decision because of all the attention and information he provided.

Seller Phillip B. says it well:

"Jeff was terrific in answering all of my questions, providing me with photos and information that I needed to make an informed investment."

When Jeff is not taking care of his business and clients, he loves to spend time with his wife and two daughters – 2-year-old Jasmine and 6-month-old Juliana. He loves golf and is an avid car collector.

Jeff can be contacted at the Jeff Colon Group located at 760 Camino Ramon, Danville, CA 94526; (925) 406-4259.

CHAPTER 13

CAN SELF-SUGGESTIONS MAKE YOU RICH?

BY JOSE GOMEZ, MD

When I was 10 years old, something happened to me that changed my life completely.

I was born in the Dominican Republic, a beautiful island in the Caribbean. I had a very financially comfortable childhood. Just to give you an idea of how I lived in my early years, I will mention that I used to live in a very nice neighborhood, in a big house with 8 bedrooms, and attended one of the best private schools in my hometown. My father owned the first Chevrolet convertible that entered the country, and we always had 3-4 full time live-in maids, and also at one point, a nurse taking care of my sick grandmother.

My family was not only wealthy, but also had powerful social and political influence in the country, since there were famous writers, historians, generals and politicians in my family. There were two Presidents of the country in my immediate family. Actually, I was named Jose Maria after my mother's grandfather, who was one the two Presidents of the Dominican Republic.

So, my childhood was really a nice one; surrounded with love from my family and an enjoyable life style. But, one day when I was 10 years old, everything changed. Early that day my mother called me and my two other brothers and said to us: "Children, soon we are going to be moving to a small apartment in a not very nice neighborhood… You all are going to start attending a public school… and your father is going to sell our car to pay some debts that we have."

My brothers and I were in shock and confused. "Why all of these changes mom?" – I asked my mother with a trembling voice; and she quietly replied in a soft and loving voice: "Jose, now you are not old enough to understand, but when you grow older I will explain everything to you."

I waited for four long years trusting that my parents knew what they were doing and that they were doing the right thing. But at age fourteen, which is often the time when most adolescents discover that they know more about life than their parents, I went to my mother and asked her again for the reason for the big changes which took place in our family life style four years back. And with tears in her eyes she said to me:

"Jose, your father is a good man, but he suffers from an illness called gambling; and he has gambled away all of our fortune. We are now very poor."

Then, she proceeded to introduce me for the first time in my life to seven very important self-suggestions for success, which can be implemented by anyone to think and grow rich today. The principle of self-suggestions is related to the way that we can condition our subconscious mind to truly believe that something is absolutely real, possible and attainable, as long as we continue to repeat it to ourselves on regular basis. By doing self-suggestions, I went from been financially broke as a young adult to a very successful physician living in the United States of America, who could enjoy from an early age most of the material things and life's comforts that this great country could provide to anyone.

So, here are those seven self-suggestions explained to me by my mother, at a time when probably she had not even heard of terms such as success principles, as taught by one of my mentors Jack Canfield, who is a best-selling author and co-creator of the "Chicken Soup For The Soul" books; or about the concept of how self-suggestions can powerfully impact our lives in order to achieve whatever we want. Likewise, the world's famous book: "Think and Grow Rich" by Napoleon Hill, still needed to be written.

I. SELF-SUGGESTION NUMBER ONE:

"Be clear what your current financial situation is and where you want to be in the future."

These are the three basic steps to "think and grow rich today." You have to first make an assessment and clearly find out what are your current financial assets and liabilities. Then, you have to decide where you want to be financially in the future. And finally, you need to have a system to get you from where you are now, to where you want to be in the future. Part of the system to get financial independence consists of repeatedly impacting your subconscious mind with constant reminders given as positive and effective self-suggestions such as: *"All the richness of the universe is available to me, right here and now, and I am constantly receiving it because I deserve to enjoy it."*

II. SELF-SUGGESTION NUMBER TWO:

"Assume one hundred percent responsibility for your life."

The way things happen in your life invariably follow a three-step process. First, there is an event when something happens to you. Second, there is your response to that event. And third, there is an outcome, desirable or undesirable, good or bad, painful or joyful, to that event and to your response to the same. This three-step process could be represented in this simple mathematical formula: **EVENT + RESPONSE = OUTCOME.**

You have to realize that most of the time you have very little or no control over the events happening in your life. If you want to change the outcome, the only thing that you can change is your response to the event. By changing your response to any given event, you can change the outcome of whatever happened to you.

One simple way to assume full responsibility for your life is by **practicing** the following self-suggestion: You can constantly think and mentally repeat to yourself positive self-suggestions such as: *"I will change my financial situation because I am powerful and capable of reacting in a very positive, effective and successful way to this financial challenge that I am facing now."*

You should constantly repeat this self-suggestion with the same or similar words. You can also say it aloud when no one can hear you; or write it down on a piece of paper and read it several times a day in order to create a powerful influencing force in your subconscious mind that will bring into your life positive financial changes. However, the most important ingredient that you need to keep in mind is that you have to experience intense and vivid emotions of power, self-confidence, joy and success while repeating these self-suggestions.

III. SELF-SUGGESTION NUMBER THREE:

"Live your life as if you were already there."

Think, move, dress and speak, as if you were already a wealthy person. As much as you can afford it, frequent the places and spend most of your time with people who are at a financial level much higher than yours. Learn from them. Their company is priceless to you.

If you want to be successful in reaching your financial goals you have to mix with the winners and learn to think like a winner. Tell yourself every day and all of the time: *"I am a winner. Other people see the winner in me, because I speak, dress and move like a winner."*

IV. SELF-SUGGESTION NUMBER FOUR:

"Follow Your Passion."

It has been said so many times: ***Do what you love and money will follow.*** Nothing could be more truthful than this. When you follow your passion, you start living your life full of contagious enthusiasm, increased energy, great creativity and total commitment to your projects and work.

But first, you really have to find out what your passion truly is. One way to do it is by implementing the following method:

STEP 1:
List 10 things that you believe you would need to do or that you would need to be, which in your opinion will make you a wealthier person. Make sure that you use a verb-word ending in "ing", such as: "socializing more with successful people," "recognizing my wrong ways of spending money," "learning better ways of how to handle my finances," "having big dreams of financial success in my life," etc.

1. _____

2. _____

3. _____

4. _____

5. _____

6. _____

7. _____

8. _____

9. _____

10. _____

STEP 2:

List what you would consider your top five most important things, among the ten things you have listed above.

1. _____

2. _____

3. _____

4. _____

5. _____

STEP 3:

Rate each one of the top five things from the above list by giving it a number from 0 to 10, where 0 means that you don't think it will greatly improve your financial situation and 10 means it will substantially improve your financial situation:

RATE
(0 – 10)

1. _____   _____

2. _____   _____

3. _____   _____

4. _____   _____

5. _____   _____

STEP 4:

On a separate piece of paper, write another list with all the details, keeping in mind that the more details you write the better it will be, what those five things mean to you, and how they are going to impact your financial situation. Start with the things with the highest numbers first, and then continue with those with the lower numbers.

STEP 5:
Make another final list stating what important actions you are going to take to follow your passions and by when they will be accomplished.

STEP 6:
Read and imagine as if it is already happening – everything that you wrote on your list in step 4. Do this any time at least 3-4 times a week. Also, read and imagine as if it is already happening, everything that you wrote in your list of step 5. Do this every single day after you first wake up in the morning.

Remember that the most important ingredient that you need to keep in mind is that you have to experience intense and vivid positive emotions while reading and imagining whatever you wrote in those two lists.

V. SELF-SUGGESTION NUMBER FIVE:

"Be always ready to serve others."

Remember that: *"A hand close to give is also a hand close to receive.* By sharing the abundant wealth that you are now creating in your life, you are attracting even more richness into your financial assets. And this is so, because the feelings you experience when you are being generous in helping others, and the gratitude and joy that you see in those who are being helped, open new channels in your brain allowing you to live in a more creative state of mind, which ultimately will result in conceiving more ways of increasing your wealth. Keep affirming to yourself all of the time: *"The more I am giving, the more I am receiving; and I am very happy about it."*

VI. SELF-SUGGESTION NUMBER SIX:

"Focus on the solution, not on the problem."

Your mind will attract more of the same things that it is focusing on. When you are constantly focusing on all of the problems that you have, and which you think are preventing you from having more financial abundance, you are just inviting into your life more of the same kind of problems.

You can easily and effectively remedy this type of wrong and negative thinking going on in your mind by doing the following fun thing:

Create the Board of Your Dreams: Draw and/or cut and paste colorful pictures and images you will find in the Internet, magazines, flyers, newspapers, advertisements, etc. on the "Board of Your Dreams," showing the kind of car you want to drive, the house you want to live in, the vacation you want to enjoy, the clothes you want to wear, the job or profession you want to have, the health and fitness you want to achieve, the ideal spouse or partner you want to find, the church or school you want to attend, or any other important dream that you have and that you want to attract into your life.

Then, place that Board of Your Dreams in a strategic place in your home, where you can see it many times a day. When you get in front of it, just stop for a few seconds and look at it with interest and attention, while enjoying in your mind what you are looking at, as if you already had it. As if all of those things were already yours. By doing this you are creating self-suggestions that will bring to realization all of those things that are so important and dear to you.

VII. SELF-SUGGESTION NUMBER SEVEN:

"Expect To Succeed."

You get exactly what you expect will happen. Unless you raise your expectations about yourself and about how wealthy you want to be, you will never amount to anything in your personal finances.

Have you ever asked yourself if you are one those people who never seems to be successful at creating wealth, because everything that you try seems to always fail? If that is your case, I will help you to find out why that is happening; and I will also offer you a solution to that problem.

First, why is it that you might be always failing in creating wealth in your life? One of the possible answers might be: Because unknowingly you might be sabotaging your successful outcome. And why would anyone want to do that?

There are multiple answers to that question. It might possibly be that you do it because deep down in your mind you're feeling or believe that you are not "good enough." And because you are not good enough, therefore you don't deserve to be wealthy and enjoy all the good things in life that money can buy; or you might feel that "money" is something kind of bad or evil; or you were possibly told or heard many times in your home when you were growing up, that your family did not have much financial means and that was the way your life was always going to be; or because you dislike people who have money, due to the arrogant, rude and superior way they sometimes act and treat others, and you have subconsciously decided that you are not going to be or act like one of them; or you might be inadvertently just punishing yourself for something that you did wrong.

As I said before, there are many different reasons why people will not expect to be wealthy. What would be the solution then? This is the answer to that question: Set clearly written, well-defined goals, and review them every day at least twice a day. A good simple way to do this is to write your goals with all of the details with the time when you are going to accomplish them. For instance, you could write something like: ***"I am going to be earning $30,000 gross per month by April 30th at 6:00 PM."***

IN CLOSING:

"Every man is what he is because of the dominating thoughts that he permits to occupy his mind." ~ **Napoleon Hill**

About Jose

Awarded for the past four consecutive years the qualification of one of the top Psychiatrists in America, Dr. Gomez has been an extremely successful professional in helping people to enjoy happier and successful lives.

He is a brilliant teacher who has been a former professor of Psychiatry and Director of the Medical School at the Technological Institute of Santo Domingo in the Dominican Republic.

His extensive work in helping couples to live fulfilling marriages began over forty years ago when he was appointed Medical Director of a community mental health center in Louisville, Kentucky. Since that time he has developed his own coaching system called The Drivers, used to teach spouses how to learn to meet each other's needs in their marital relationships.

Dr. Gomez is the author of the book *MARRIAGE TIPS – To Enjoy A Happy Marriage,* and also the creator of an on-line 30-day course. He is a dynamic motivational speaker who had delivered many talks in the United States of America and other foreign countries, including India and the Caribbean.

He is a distinguished member of the Royal Society of Medicine in England and a Founding Fellow of the Institute for Coaching at the prestigious Harvard University Medical School. He is also a member of the Harvard Business Review Advisory Council.

Dr. Gomez can be contacted by accessing his web site at:
www.MarriageAcademy.us

CHAPTER 14

MENTAL MODELING TIPS: Marketing an Experience With Your Business Website

BY LINDSAY DICKS

Have you ever looked forward to something – let's say, a vacation at a fancy resort – and come back from it feeling disappointed? Like there was something missing?

It's very likely the words you used to communicate that disappointment to a friend or family member were, "It wasn't like I pictured it."

We all picture how we want things to be – and so do our customers and clients when they buy from us. When that experience *isn't* like they "pictured it" we run the risk of losing that customer – perhaps forever.

So the question to ask is - do you know what customers are picturing in their minds? You should – because the answer to that question is the key to sales success.

In *Think and Grow Rich,* Napoleon Hill again and again emphasizes the power of thought – as a matter of fact, three out of the last four chapters are devoted to aspects of how our brains can attract and create success, often without us even being aware of it happening. As he wrote, *"Think twice before you speak, because your words and influence will plant the seed of either success or failure in the mind of another."*

But there's another half to that equation; *your* customers' words and influence can also plant the seeds of *your* success, if you're willing to listen.

The fact is that, just because you think you have the perfect way to market your business, doesn't mean it's true. Your approach can only be effective *if it connects with what your potential customers want from you.* If you can, however, unlock the secrets of their most powerful "wants" – you have an amazing path to prosperity laid out in front of you.

It all starts with understanding "Mental Models" – and, in this chapter, I'll tell you how to do just that!

THE ORIGIN OF MENTAL MODELS

The theory of mental models was first put forth in 1943 by Scottish psychologist Kenneth Craik. He believed that everyone constructed "small-scale models" of reality in their minds in order to explain things, to anticipate things and, basically navigate life. In other words, mental models are what we create to represent real or imaginary situations in our head.

Think about it. Say you're planning a short outing to take care of a few errands: you construct a model of the order of stores you need to visit, you imagine what's going to happen at each store and think through how long it will probably take and when you might get back.

We all do this – which is why we get so upset when our mental models get disrupted.

For example, maybe there's a long line at the grocery store when you just need to buy a couple of things – this throws off your mental model of how long you were going to spend getting those items. Or, worse, maybe you walk out to our parked car and discover a flat tire – that *definitely* wasn't in your mental model and you *definitely* aren't happy!

On a wider scale, mental models can and do affect our whole economy. In late 2008, for instance, when the Wall Street meltdown took place, consumers suddenly had a different mental model of how they should approach spending – mainly, they thought they shouldn't. This caused anxious retailers to drop their prices – causing consumers to wait even longer to make necessary purchases because their mental model now told them that prices would continue to drop, so why not wait?

Overall, this mental model helped worsen the recession – because suddenly, everyone, even those with plenty of money, felt that they shouldn't spend. That just started a snowball effect – when people stopped buying, the economy kept creeping to a halt.

Of course, a few years prior to that, in 2005, the housing bubble was in full upswing – and everybody thought it was the time to buy, because they could flip properties and immediately cash in. The common mental model was that this upward spike in real estate prices would be endless – when the reality was that the crash was about to happen.

All of this illustrates three VERY important facts about mental models:

FACT #1:
MENTAL MODELS ARE JUST THAT – *MENTAL.*

Mental models are conjured up in our brains, based on how we think things are (or how we want them to be). That means they're not exactly real, but still based on what we believe to be true. As noted above, just because everyone might believe it's the time to buy real estate doesn't mean it's necessarily *true* – but, of course, because everyone is so anxious to make money, they might be more *willing* to believe it's true. Perceptions rule when it comes to mental models, which is always important to remember when you're marketing. Reality isn't always the biggest selling point!

FACT #2:
EVERYONE HAS THEIR OWN
UNIQUE MENTAL MODELS.

Because mental models are based on perceptions, different people have different mental models, even though those models may be of the same situation. Frequently, certain categories of people (political parties, religious organizations, different age groups, etc.) may *share* the same mental models of a situation, because they reinforce each other's perceptions. That's why niches are so powerful to market to – they frequently share identical mental models that you can tap into.

FACT #3:
MENTAL MODELS ARE CONSTANTLY
CHANGING AND EVOLVING.

Depending on what we hear, read and experience, we will change most of our existing mental models as life goes on. For example, when new technology first hits the marketplace, it tends to be pretty costly, but many are willing to pay in order to get their hands on the newest "big thing" – the typical mental model is that it's worth it. Later on, when that technology becomes part of our everyday lives, suddenly that mental model is adjusted – because if it's commonplace, we shouldn't have to pay a premium for it.

THE BUSINESS OF MENTAL MODELS

So – you might be thinking, this is all very interesting, but what does this have to do with my business?

Well, a lot – especially when it comes to your business website. When potential leads happen to click on a link to your site, it's not just because they're looking for whatever product or service that you might be selling. No, what they're really after is fulfilling their *mental model* of what the experience of buying that product or service should be.

Let's go back to the errand run I used earlier as an example. We all have certain places that we like to buy from – a favorite grocery store, a favorite wine store, a favorite gas station, and so forth. We have these preferences because the businesses in question most fulfill our mental models of what we want from these experiences. Somebody who wants to buy primarily organic products in an upscale environment is going to shop at Whole Foods, while someone who wants fresh produce at a good price is going to shop at the local Farmer's Market.

It's the same thing when you go out to eat; you don't just stop at the first restaurant you see. Again, what you want is a certain *experience* – maybe, for example, you want Mexican food in a comfortable, well-established eatery where you can also order a margarita or two. Or maybe you want to go fast and cheap with a Big Mac from Mickey D's. It depends on the mental model you have in your head for what kind of eating experience you want to have.

So, unless you're the only one selling your particular product or service, you have to focus on your buyer's *experience* just as much as that product/service. And, since most of you are selling online rather than with a brick-and-mortar location, that focus should start with your business website – the virtual equivalent of your "store."

YOUR WEBSITE MODEL

Many businesses, to this day, think they can simply slap their logo on a webpage, add the necessary barebones information (About Us/Services/Contact Us), and they're done with their site. There's no thought really to creating the kind of experience that their target group might expect.

And yet, according to a 2012 Digital Influence study, the Internet is incredibly critical to consumers' buying decisions. In the U.S., it's almost equal in importance to recommendations from family and friends – and in countries like Canada, China and India, it's actually *more* important than personal recommendations!

That means your website is, more than ever, <u>THE </u>crucial factor as to whether a lead will buy from you or not. And that's why you must make sure your website creates an experience that matches up with your target group's mental model – as we do for our clients at CelebritySites.

How do you know what your target group's mental model is? There are a few ways you can understand what kind of experience they want to have buying from you:

- **Check out successful competitor's sites**
  Who in your field is the closest to what you want to be – and, at the same time, successful at it? Observe how their website markets their business and see what might work for yours.

- **Put yourself in your customers' shoes**
  What would *you* want to see on a website for your product and service? Try to visualize it through your target group's eyes – or, in other words, create what you think their mental model is for you!

- **Just *ASK* them!**
  Survey people in the target group you're after and pick their brains to get a glimpse inside their mental models. What needs and wants do they have? What's the best way to approach them? What *don't* they want to hear?

Once you have an idea of what kind of mental model you need to fulfill, you next have to apply that information to your site. With that in mind, here are a few important Mental "Modeling Tips" to help make sure your site is delivering the right experience:

MODELING TIP #1:
MAKE SURE IT LOOKS THE PART

Of course, an essential element of any mental model is *how something looks*. If you're going after a more affluent client base (say, NeimanMarcus.com), you want to make sure your site looks classy and elegant. If you're after a more "nuts-and-bolts" customer niche (say, Lowes.com), your site can appear to be more utilitarian. Whatever target group you're after, make sure that visually, you're appealing to that crowd's mental image of what they expect your site to look like – and try to *over*-deliver if possible (think of the power of the words, "It was *better* than I pictured it!").

MODELING TIP #2:
MAKE SURE IT SAYS THE RIGHT THINGS

No website should have typos or misspellings – but there are still plenty out there that have them! The worst cases are sites for doctors and lawyers who look like they flunked 3rd grade English – would you really put your life in these people's hands? That's why professional copy that's not only polished – but speaks *directly* to the desired mental models you want to attract – is critical. If you don't make the right statements about who you are and what you offer, a lead will be quick to pop over to a competing site that does.

MODELING TIP #3:
MAKE SURE IT HANGS OUT WITH
THE RIGHT PEOPLE

Testimonials and endorsements from people that match up with your lead's mental models can be critical to their decision to buy from you. There's a reason that products designed to appeal to men hire pro athletes as their pitchmen – and there's a reason that Cover Girl hires relatable women like Drew Barrymore and Ellen DeGeneres to sell their cosmetics: Their potential customers want to be like those people. Keep that in mind when choosing spokespeople and customers offering endorsements – make sure they're compatible with your leads' mental models of who they want to be like.

MODELING TIP #4:
MAKE SURE IT GIVES "FACE TIME"

At CelebritySites, we also suggest that the client put his or her face front and center on their websites. People like to buy from people, not nameless faceless businesses. Whether you use video or a large smiling portrait shot of yourself, make sure your customers can see who you are and feel as if you're a good person to do business with. That's a part of *everyone's* purchasing mental model, no matter what the venue or product category.

MODELING TIP #5:
MAKE SURE IT STAYS UP-TO-DATE

As noted, mental models evolve and change with the times: If you look like you're not keeping up with the latest trends, styles and services, you risk being perceived as outdated by your customers' mental models. Of course, some businesses have powerful retro images that are almost timeless – but, for the most part, we all need to be as modern as possible with our approach.

MODELING TIP #6:
DON'T BE *TOO* DIFFERENT

You want to stand out with your site – but if you do things too differently, you'll confuse your customers' mental modeling. For example, Netflix tested how their site was being used – and found that new subscribers had trouble understanding the company's "Queue" system for DVDs. Typically on an e-commerce site, when you add something to a shopping cart, nothing happens until you make the actual purchase. However, when you add a movie or TV show to the Netflix Queue on their site, it automatically will send that DVD out if the title is next in line. People tend to want things to work the same everywhere – studies show it's a huge part of their mental modeling.

MODELING TIP #7:
INNOVATE WHEN IT WORKS

This may seem to contradict the last Modeling Tip, but sometimes innovation *does* work out for all concerned. For example, once users got used to the Netflix system, they liked it because it made sense (possibly because they weren't actually buying something since Netflix is a flat-fee subscription service). When innovation provides an *easier* experience to the customer, that causes their preferred mental model to suddenly incorporate how you do things – and they'll be suddenly be disappointed when a competitor's systems aren't as good.

As my last Modeling Tip indicates, the best of all outcomes is when you become "the best of the best" – and your target group suddenly views *you* as the ultimate mental model for whatever you're selling. The trick is to first key into their mental models – and then find ways to improve on them without alienating them (about which Facebook is frequently guilty).

Your customers know what they want – and you should too. Remember, once you know what THEY think – YOU can grow rich!

About Lindsay

Lindsay Dicks helps her clients tell their stories in the online world. Being brought up around a family of marketers, but a product of Generation Y, Lindsay naturally gravitated to the new world of online marketing. Lindsay began freelance writing in 2000 and soon after launched her own PR firm that thrived by offering an in-your-face "Guaranteed PR" that was one of the first of its type in the nation.

Lindsay's new media career is centered on her philosophy that "people buy people." Her goal is to help her clients build a relationship with their prospects and customers. Once that relationship is built and they learn to trust them as the expert in their field, then they will do business with them. Lindsay also built a patent-pending process that utilizes social media marketing, content marketing and search engine optimization to create online "buzz" for her clients that helps them to convey their business and personal story. Lindsay's clientele span the entire business map and range from doctors and small business owners to Inc 500 CEOs.

Lindsay is a graduate of the University of Florida. She is the CEO of Celebrity-Sites™, an online marketing company specializing in social media and online personal branding. Lindsay is also a multi-best-selling author including the best-selling book "*Power Principles for Success*" which she co-authored with Brian Tracy. She was also selected as one of America's PremierExperts™ and has been quoted in *Newsweek, The Wall Street Journal, USA Today, Inc Magazine* as well as featured on NBC, ABC, and CBS television affiliates speaking on social media, search engine optimization and making more money online. Lindsay was also recently brought on FOX 35 News as their Online Marketing Expert.

Lindsay, a national speaker, has shared the stage with some of the top speakers in the world such as Brian Tracy, Lee Milteer, Ron LeGrand, Arielle Ford, David Bullock, Brian Horn, Peter Shankman and many others. Lindsay was also a Producer on the Emmy-nominated film Jacob's Turn.

You can connect with Lindsay at:
Lindsay@CelebritySites.com
www.twitter.com/LindsayMDicks
www.facebook.com/LindsayDicks

CHAPTER 15

ENJOY THE RICHES YOU DESIRE BY "GOING THE EXTRA MILE"

BY MARTY COATES

Even in the best of economic times, it is difficult for individuals and companies to envision amassing riches and success. Many profess to practice carefully planned strategies, but the fact is that far too few are willing to do what it takes to attain their desires. Those who do accomplish such goals do so by practicing a set of disciplines that requires unusual commitment and planning. Dr. Napoleon Hill, in his timeless classic, *Think and Grow Rich*, passionately teaches a philosophy that if embraced will yield financial and personal success.

The book's philosophy is based on the premise that how we think about the issues and circumstances we face will ultimately determine our success, and that to attain the success, riches, goals and dreams we desire, requires an attitude and way of thinking that goes beyond all the norms. We must overcome our natural fears, have faith in ourselves, our eternal source and take action towards our desires with purpose and passion. I liken it to the concept of "going the extra mile." Whether we desire to build a business, earn a college degree, or serve our customers, we will be successful if we commit to our purpose and work at it with passion and desire unparalleled by others.

GOING THE EXTRA MILE

Picture this! It's a beautiful Saturday morning in late August. College football season opens today and the family is packed in the SUV headed to the stadium for tailgating and the game. About forty-five minutes into the trip, I notice a light suddenly illuminate on the dash. I decide that since the car appears to be performing well, I will just keep driving.

A few minutes later, more lights pop up on the dashboard. At this point, I know something serious is happening, probably an electronic glitch. In a desperate attempt to keep moving towards the game, I decide to call Billy Threadgill, my car dealer friend, from whom I have bought all my cars in recent years, to see if he has any thoughts. All the while I am trying not to alert my family of the pending dilemma, because in South Carolina, besides church and hunting, not much gets in the way of college football, especially on opening day!

As I describe the symptoms to Billy, he immediately suggests that I might need an alternator. He recommends that I keep driving to the nearest exit and try to find an auto parts store. He goes on to say, "if you need me, just give me a call and I will come get you." Within minutes, the car shuts off. I coast off the interstate and into the parking lot of a convenience store. All the while, I am dialing Billy again.

Billy's immediate response confirms one of the reasons I do business with him. He says, "tell me exactly where you are and I will come get the car, bring you another car, and you can get to the ballgame." Remember to keep in mind that this is Saturday, and Billy's business is not even open on Saturday. Within an hour or so he is there and we are on our way.

This kind of service is indicative of the excellent customer service that Billy and his family provide to their customers. This practice began when Billy's father left a franchised car dealership to start his own independent car dealership. One customer at a time, one challenge at a time, his family has practiced "going the extra mile." As a result, their satisfied customers have afforded to them successful careers that span more than forty years, multiple profitable businesses, and national recognition in the industry. Billy, his family, and his team are driven by a passionate desire like that described by Dr. Hill.

For more than twenty-five years, I have worked as a speaker, consultant, author and trainer. Much of my ability to work in these capacities stems from my desire and passion to be successful. It started for me as a teenager when I began reading books and listening to tapes on personal development and self-improvement. Many noted works and authors have had a tremendous impact on shaping my desire to be successful as an entrepreneur. Books that I read include *You Can Become the Person You Want to be*, by Dr. Robert Schuller, and *See You at The Top*, by the late Zig Ziglar. I also read *Think and Grow Rich*. Two very important theories that Dr. Hill discusses are that you have to overcome various fears in order to achieve riches and you must have faith.

FACING FEAR - A NATURAL MOTIVATOR

It was in high school when I met the great motivator known as fear. My guidance counselor, in comparing me to the others in my small high school class, suggested she already knew my future. As an average academic student, she determined that I did not need to pursue four-year college. I went to her to request an application for the Scholastic Aptitude Test (SAT). She carved into my mental psyche a picture that could have derailed my dream to go to college. She said, "Marty, are you sure about this? Your grades indicate that you will not be successful in college. We have a terrific technical school in the county where you could learn a trade." I persisted and she reluctantly gave me the application. While the results of my score on the exam were less than perfect, and I did choose to attend a community college for my first year of college, she would be proven wrong. What she did not factor in to her vision, was my burning desire, passion, if you will, to attend college and to attain a life where the dreams of my youth would come true.

On many occasions during my undergraduate studies and graduate courses, this guidance counselor's words loomed in the back of my mind. When I was struggling and almost ready to quit, her piercing words of doubt would surface in my mind. What I know now is that my desire to succeed was stronger than my fear of failure. It was through the reading and internalization of the principles of Dr. Hill and others that I was able to achieve many of my dreams. "Whatever the mind of a man can conceive and believe, it can be achieved," Dr. Hill proclaimed (32).

FAITH IS INTEGRAL TO ATTAINING RICHES

In regards to having faith in order to achieve riches and success, I draw on my belief that giving first to Him who gives all riches is both a requirement for attaining my wishes and a pleasure. Whether or not you address faith in the same way as Dr. Hill is less important than the fact that we understand the theory. We must have faith in ourselves, our abilities, our plans, our talents, but I contend that we also must have faith in an eternal source. Jeremiah 29:11 says "For I know the thoughts that I think toward you, saith the Lord, thoughts of peace, and not of evil, to give you an expected end" (KJV). As I come to appreciate the successes of life, I realize that it is God who has given me my faith, my passion, and a plan for my business endeavors. I believe that it is only by following His plan for me that I can achieve true riches. Dr. Hill sites that "Faith is the starting point of all accumulation of riches!...Faith is the only known antidote for failure!" (52). Indeed, successful management theories and faith are not mutually exclusive but inter-related. This has certainly proven true in my own personal and professional life.

SEEK WISE COUNSEL FROM OTHERS
WHO PRACTICE "GOING THE EXTRA MILE"

Dr. Hill recommends that we "let great men shape your life" and that "the next best thing to being truly great is to emulate the great" (215). Along my career journey, I have had the opportunity to meet successful people that have demonstrated the principles of "going the extra mile" in order to attain riches. Early in my career, I was hired by Cotton States Insurance Company of Atlanta, Georgia, to manage the sales/operations in both North and South Carolina. Part of my initial training, was provided one-on-one, by Lennon Copeland, a long timer at the company and then Senior Vice-President of the division.

For a week, we travelled together meeting with customers. Lennon was a seasoned performer and a master at his trade. I knew of his legendary reputation, but I had no idea just how effective his dynamic personality was until I worked under his tutelage.

Amid various activities, Lennon demonstrated to me why he was legendary in our company. It was the result of his disciplined execution of principles and techniques. His focus was always on his customer. At every stop, customers complimented Mr. Copeland for his exemplary way of handling their issues. He worked tirelessly with great passion to meet their needs and wants. It seemed almost effortless to him. I found out that being great takes a lot of work, a definite purpose and an incredible commitment to accomplish your goals. I gained invaluable counsel from Mr. Copeland that week and continued to seek that kind of input from many other successful business, religious, and political mentors. Some of the tenets that defined his deliberate first-rate service to customers include:

1) Be accessible to your clients.

2) Respond promptly to their calls.

3) Listen intently to your customers' wants and needs.

4) Attend immediately to their needs.

5) Always do something to help.

6) Always accept responsibility for your actions and the actions of the company.

7) Always say "thank you," frequently writing notes to your customers.

On the final day of our time together, Lennon introduced me to a customer named Nancy. He told me that he had worked hard over the years to earn her business. While she had directed a portion of her business to Cotton States, we were not yet a primary player. He said, "I cannot figure out what I have to do to get her to give us more of her portfolio." After meeting Nancy, I, too, wondered how to do it. I closed our conversation with Nancy using a standard line that I had learned from Lennon saying, "While we may not get all of your business, what will it take for us to get more of it?" Quickly, without reservation and without cracking a smile, she said "buy me a Cadillac and I will give you more than you can write." I was admittedly a little naive at this point, so I responded "okay, what color do you want?" She smiled, gave me a hug, and said to Lennon, "He's going to be good." When we get back in the car, Mr. Copeland quickly says "you know we can't buy her a car. It is illegal to entice her in that way and the company would not likely stand for it." In his own kind way he told me to be observant, but also to be careful "not to let my mouth write a check that my pocketbook could not cover." If I did so, in most cases, the end result would be damaged relationships and lost business. He did, however, pose a challenge to me. He said "to date I have never been able to get her to give us more than $100k of business. If you ever figure out how to break her, you will be a big success in this business."

I took him back to the airport and headed to my home near Raleigh. The last visit of the week haunted me and I wondered, "How can I give Nancy what she wants? How can I convince her to trust us for more of her business?" I soon came upon a shopping mall and decided to go inside to the K&B Toy store. I perused the shelves to find a small "Mattel-like" car, a Cadillac, no doubt. Its doors opened and when you raised its tiny pink hood the headlights would come on. I purchased it, went home and boxed it up, and included a simple note to Nancy. It read:

Dear Nancy:

While the size of the car may be a bit different than you imagined, I am delighted to send to you, on behalf of our company, a Cadillac. Thank you for your continued business. I look forward to working with you to increase our service to you.

I sent the package via FEDEX and before 10:00 am the following morning I received a call from Nancy. She was crying and laughing at the same time as she said "When can you come by my office to discuss how we can increase our business?" I realized that morning that she had been joking about the car, that she was just pulling my leg. But I think this was the first time that anyone had taken the bait quite like me, and actually attempted to "go the extra mile" and meet her desires.

Before I left Cotton States a few years later, we were writing most of her business and our share had increased several times over the amount that Mr. Copeland said he was able to write while working on the account. Mr. Copeland would have been proud.

In this example, "going the extra mile" cost me less than $20.00 – but, the payoff was far greater than that for my company and me. What's more, I learned from the experience of riding with Mr. Copeland and from the relationship with Nancy, the simple truth of attaining riches by "going the extra mile" to help my customers.

CONCLUSION

Here are eight steps to move you toward your goals, dreams, desires and even riches. Let's recap:

1) Establish a definite purpose.

2) Commit to the purpose and work toward it with passion and desire.

3) Have faith in God and the abilities you possess.

4) Face your fears through confidence in your planned purpose.

5) Spend more time listening to your customers instead of talking.

6) Listen to your heart.

7) Take action.

8) Consistently deliver.

Finally, **go the extra mile** to give your customer what he/she is asking for (so long as it is ethical and legal). Zig Ziglar's famous quote "You can get everything in life you want if you will just help enough other people get what they want" is epic. Mastery of this principle will yield dividends greater than you can imagine. College degrees do not always produce this kind of success. Get-rich-quick schemes definitely do not deliver this kind of success. Only a person, company, or organization that completely immerses itself in a philosophy of doing whatever it takes to accomplish a goal or dream will enjoy the riches it desires.

Work Cited:

Hill, Napoleon. *Think and Grow Rich*. Northbrook: Napoleon Hill Foundation, 1963. Print.

About Marty

Marty W. Coates is a Waymaker! He has built his life and business as an unconventional speaker, author, consultant and trainer. As a passionate trainer and speaker, he energizes audiences with his humor and "preacher-like" approach and drives individuals and groups to get all they can out of life and work. In various consulting roles across the years, he has steered many organizations toward success.

Marty marches to the beat of a different drummer and his strategy is to help organizations look for different ways of doing things while remaining focused on their customers' needs. Marty passionately encourages, pushes and guides his clients to new horizons every year.

His work spans a number of areas including leadership, organizational development, marketing and continuous improvement.

Marty developed his skills as a salesman, manager, and executive in insurance, finance and healthcare. His leadership background also includes nearly fifteen years in the United States Army and Army Reserves as a field soldier, staff officer, and commander. He is a veteran of Desert Storm, where he was awarded a Bronze Star.

In 2000, he was elected to serve as a legislator in the South Carolina House of Representatives, a position he held until 2006 when he chose not to run for re-election. His reputation in politics is one of tackling the tough issues and standing firm on his principles.

His compassion is evident in his work and his mission relief efforts. Marty continually seeks ways to give back and help people all over the world.

He is the Co-Founder of Waymaker Learning Corporation, a company determined to develop and equip people to make a significant difference in this world.

He holds the position of President and Senior Consultant at Coates and Associates, Inc., a consulting and training firm he started more than twenty years ago.

Visit Marty's website at: www.coatesandassociatesinc.com or reach him by calling 843-229-3546.

Marty and his wife, Bridgette, have two children, Luke and Rachel. Marty enjoys splitting his office and work schedule via his primary residence in South Carolina and his hideaway home along the North Carolina coast.

CHAPTER 16

A CHANCE ENCOUNTER AT A CARWASH

BY MICHAEL LAWRENCE

Before I share the story of a chance encounter that completely changed the trajectory of my life, let me give you a quick peek into my upbringing. I grew up in Mesquite, TX, which is a small suburb of Dallas and home of the famous "Mesquite Rodeo." Yeehaw! My mother, Kathryn Lawrence, completed her Masters degree in Art History and nearly finished her Doctorate. She taught art in Richardson, TX for many years at both the primary and collegiate level until the end of her career when she shifted to teaching gifted and talented children. My father, Dale Lawrence, received his Doctorate in Education from the University of Texas. He began his career as a teacher/coach at Bishop Lynch High School in Dallas, was promoted to principal at Hyer Elementary, and finally Assistant Superintendent for Highland Park ISD. My mother is from upstate New York, and my father is from Texas, but I don't wear boots or a huge buckle, nor do I talk fast or order "pop."

My childhood was filled with some adversities. My parents divorced when I was four, and my father passed away from cancer when I was ten. My mother worked very hard to support us at times taking on multiple jobs. My father paid child support to help, but his battle with cancer limited our visits and involvement in our lives, especially towards the end. My mother, sister, and brother were role models for me, and the primary support system to get through these tough times.

NO CHEESE

One of the lessons I still remember from my early childhood (I think I was around 6 years old) came from my brother. We gathered the change that we could find and headed with some friends over to the Burger King that was at the end of our street. My brother's friend stepped up and ordered a couple of cheeseburgers and fries. I followed his example and ordered a cheeseburger and fries, but before the cashier could ring it up, my brother stopped me. It was 10 cents extra for cheese and he insisted that it was not worth the extra 10 cents. He then taught me a word I perhaps heard before, but didn't really understand at the time. The word was self-discipline. That was the first of many occasions where my brother would emphasize self-discipline, and it was firmly instilled in my mind.

With self-discipline most anything is possible
~ Theodore Roosevelt

EARN IT!

My mother taught me many valuable lessons such as "life is an adventure" with our annual trips and excursions that we made fun with a limited budget. She raised us with freedom to decide what we would do, but with an emphasis on getting an education and graduating from college. She also taught us the value of working for the things that we wanted. If we ever wanted something (bike, go-cart, drums, etc.), she cleverly attached a dollar figure for different chores and things to do around the house so we could earn the money. If we wanted to buy something, we would work until we saved enough to afford it.

One of the strange things about human beings is that they value only that which has a price. ~ Napoleon Hill

DRUMS!

After my father passed, my sister went off to college, and it was just my brother, mom and I. The following Christmas my mom and brother decided that drums might be a good outlet for both my brother and I, so we enrolled in lessons at the local music store. Shortly after, my brother and I put all of our money that we had saved over the years together and bought our first drum set. We both progressed quickly and I managed to learn most of Led Zeppelin's "Physical Graffiti" album at a fairly young age of 11. In spite of the lessons and progress, the band director who auditioned me for percussion in middle school didn't recognize the talent, and after a few pats on my legs and some claps with my hands, I did not get selected. He recommended trombone or saxophone, and I wasn't going for that.

The next year we got a new band director at the middle school. When it came time to choose electives, I decided to give it another shot for percussion. I reached out to the band director, but this time I was prepared. Rather than letting him decide how to audition me, I told him I would prepare a piece of music for him. A week later, I performed and was accepted into the band program. This event taught me a couple important lessons as a young man. Sometimes you have to change the rules of the game if you want to win, and although you may fail at first, with enough persistence you will succeed. My determination and persistence to get enrolled in the band program would end up paying huge dividends a few years later. I ended up getting a full music scholarship to Southern Methodist University in Dallas that was worth $120,000. Had I not gone back for a second attempt to be accepted as a percussionist in spite of the previous failure and the opinion of the first band director, I would not have achieved the success and scholarship that was to follow.

Failure will never overtake me if my determination to succeed is strong enough. ~ Og Mandino

THE PURSUIT

After an amazing 10 years of being in a rock and roll band, a dramatic break up left me shocked, and at age 26, I began to evaluate where my life was going. Even though I was making $40/hr. teaching lessons and gigging on the weekends, I only taught full-time during the school year, and gigs might account for an extra $500/month at best. I decided I needed to figure out a way to make more money, so I did what many people do who come to this point in life. I joined a network marketing company.

I remember coming back from a meeting and not being able to sleep because I was so excited about discovering a way to create the income and lifestyle that I desired. I SOLD OUT. I decided to pursue this opportunity with everything I had. I listened to all of the CDs and bought 3 copies of each for my future down-line. I attended every meeting and every conference. I spent my evenings meeting people to find recruits for the business and acquired over 1000 cold contacts in one year. I read 30 books including the Bible from cover to cover in 18 months. This is when I was first introduced to *Think and Grow Rich*.

I followed the "Six Ways to Turn Desires into Gold." I decided that I would be debt-free with $100,000 in the bank and I gave myself 1000 days to achieve that goal. I bought a couple rolls of white paper and covered the wall beside my bed. I used a yard-stick and a sharpie to divide the now paper covered wall into 1000 squares in which I would write what I had done each day to get me closer to my goal. I combined this goal with many others that covered all areas of life including health, relationships, character, spiritual growth, etc. I typed out all of these goals as if they were already in my possession (e.g., I am debt free with 100k in the bank) and read them every morning and evening.

Although I did not make a great deal of money in my network marketing endeavor, I have no regrets about the time and energy I spent pursuing my dream. All of the knowledge and insight that I gained along the way was shaping and preparing me for the next chapter in my journey.

Give me six hours to chop down a tree and I will spend the first four sharpening the axe. ~ Abraham Lincoln

THE GUY AT THE CARWASH

It was an ordinary 100 plus degree summer day in Austin, TX when I brought my seldom-washed Honda Accord to the car wash. I struck up conversation with a guy while we were waiting for our cars to go through the conveyer line. I asked him what sort of work he does, and he told me he sold cable for a local provider in Austin. I asked him how it was going and he said, "Well, the last two weeks I made about $4100." Although I was a little shocked, I could see he was clearly telling the truth. I responded, "Really... Are you guys hiring?" He said he would put me in touch with his manager and put a good word in for me. I was instructed to submit my resume online and wait to hear back for an interview. A couple of weeks went by, and I heard nothing.

About a month after the carwash encounter, I was driving with my girlfriend (now fiancé and the love of my life) Liana to her house, and I saw a guy walking down the street in a blue shirt. I immediately pulled over, got out of the car and walked towards him. I asked him, "What are you doing out here?" He replied, "Selling cable." I said, "Really... Are you guys hiring?" He replied, "Absolutely, I'm the hiring manager. Come in tomorrow for an interview."

I showed up the next day, resume in hand, and got the job. My first full week, I broke the company record by closing 20 sales, earned over $2,000 with bonuses and incentives, and quickly got the attention of the managers. After a few weeks of similar performance, the CEO called me and asked me what I wanted to do. By this time I had learned that the product we were selling was about to launch nationwide, and the biggest market was Chicago. So I told him, "I want to launch Chicago."

ON TOUR

After just a few months as a salesman, I made a bold move to go to Chicago and pursue this new opportunity. I continued to make over $2,000 a week, but I quickly learned that I did not agree with the way the company was being run. I decided I didn't want to be a part of an organization like this, so I teamed up with a colleague who felt the same way and found another company to work for in St. Louis.

This was a smaller company with an owner who was seldom seen. My business partner and I quickly put together a sales team and we were getting great results. About three weeks in, we were still waiting to get paid. As we were conducting a training class on the top of our downtown St. Louis loft building, a call came in from the mother of the owner of the company. She informed us that her son had died tragically in a car accident. We realized we weren't going to see any of the thousands of dollars we had earned over the last few weeks, and we were both out of work.

Shocked but determined, we found another company in St. Louis and set up an interview that same day and were able to negotiate a position to run a small office in Southern Illinois. After a couple of months, we had the opportunity to move to South Florida for a new market launch. The next 18 months we built some of the most successful offices in the country from Florida to California and I ended up making over $300,000 in that time frame.

Although my paper covered wall stayed in Austin when I left for Chicago to launch the first office, I figured out later that the goals I set out were achieved within the 1000 day time-frame that I was inspired to create from reading *Think and Grow Rich*.

When I decided to follow the 6 steps by determining exactly how much money I would make and exactly when I would attain it, the wheels were in motion. I used the process of auto-suggestion by writing out my goals as if they were already in my possession and reading them in the morning and evening. Then by creating the 1000 squares, I activated the plan with accountability to enforce action. Although the journey took many turns...Faith held the plan together.

Recall this powerful phrase Napoleon Hill delivered:

All thoughts which have been emotionalized (given feeling) and mixed with faith, begin immediately to translate themselves into their physical equivalent or counterpart.

THE DECISION

After 18 months of huge success and helping the company grow from 4 to 30 offices nationwide, I decided to fly myself to the company headquarters to negotiate a promotion. After presenting to the Vice-President and Owner a new position and vision to grow the company to the next level, to my amazement, there was essentially no response. It was then that I realized I had hit a ceiling. I only had two options. I could continue to travel across the country building offices feeling underappreciated without much hope of making progress, or I could take a leap of faith and start a new company from scratch. This would give me the opportunity to earn even more income, but it would come with a price and great risk.

I decided to take the risk. I negotiated a national contract with a Fortune 500 company, invested everything that I had, and launched my first office for my new company, Amp Marketing, Inc., in Chicago in 2011. With limited resources, there was very little room for error, but we made it through the first year and launched a second office in Florida. In 2012, two more offices were launched and the company grew 371%. The rapid growth has gotten the attention of Inc. Magazine for a feature entitled "The Next Big Thing."

I want to leave you with three nuggets that have helped me in my journey to success, and a fourth bonus nugget that is perhaps the most important.

Nugget #1 – Live by Faith

"Now faith is being sure of what we hope for and certain of what we do not see." - Hebrews 11:1

Nugget #2 – Practice Self-Discipline

Nothing great comes without a price. Do not listen to ANYONE that says there is an easy way to success. If you truly want to change your income and lifestyle, first ask yourself, "What am I willing to give up?" and "What price am I willing to pay?"

Nugget #3 – Never Give Up

Every adversity, every failure, every heartache carries with it the seed on an equal or greater benefit. ~ Napoleon Hill

NO ONE becomes successful without failures. As you learn from your failures, you make progress.

Bonus Nugget – Give Back

I once heard that if you want to see where your priorities truly are, look at what you do with your time and your money. I truly believe that perhaps the most significant impact on the success of my endeavors has been the reciprocation and blessings that come from giving.

"Bring the whole tithe into the storehouse, so that there may be food in My house, and test Me now in this," says the Lord of hosts, "if I will not open for you the windows of heaven and pour out for you a blessing until it overflows."
~ Malachi 3:10

I encourage you to approach life with certainty and faith.

- Be BOLD! Go for your dreams and don't listen to the naysayers. Understand that success comes with a price that most people are not willing to pay.

- Be willing to pay a price and delay certain gratifications NOW, so you can create your dream life LATER!

- Make a DECISION that no matter how tough things get, you will NEVER GIVE UP. Quitters never win and winners never quit.

- GIVE BACK. I am convinced that nothing brings more peace and joy in life than giving. Give generously with a grateful heart.

See you at the TOP!

About Michael

Mike Lawrence is an entrepreneur, speaker, business coach, author, and founder of Amp Marketing, Inc. Less than 5 years ago, Mike was a free-lance musician making less than $30,000 a year. Tired of just getting by, and concerned about being able to support his future family, Mike made a decision to find a way to make more income. Having no formal business education, Mike decided that network marketing was a safe place to give business ownership a shot. He spent two years completely "selling out." He read 30 books, made over 1000 cold contacts, devoured audio teachings, and attended every meeting and conference.

After two years and only mild success in network marketing, Mike finally ran into a stranger at a carwash that would change the trajectory of his life. Through this stranger, Mike would discover that the skills attained in the network marketing endeavor would prove to be valuable assets in sales, management, leadership, building relationships, and ultimately, running a business.

Over the next two years, Mike went from an entry level sales rep, to a sales manager, an office manager, a director overseeing nine offices, and finally - starting his own company. His company, Amp Marketing, has secured a national contract for marketing services with a Fortune 500 company, and increased revenues 371% in 2012. His rapid success has earned a feature in Inc. Magazine as "The Next Big Thing."

Now fueled with a passion to help others and give back, Mike has decided to share his message through media and books and serve as a coach/mentor for people who want to change their future financial situation.

CHAPTER 17

TAMING THE BRAIN:
A Journey to Enlightenment

BY TRISH MCCARTY

As I looked around the room of fourteen of the most extraordinary and accomplished women, my eyes rested on Gladys' gentle, but determined, ninety-three-year-old beaming face. We had gathered together for a luncheon in her honor to celebrate her birthday and to dedicate a community wellness center in her name. Dr. Gladys McGarey is a legend. She started the Holistic Healthcare Movement as a young, idealistic, third-generation medical doctor. Dr. McGarey was born in India to medical missionaries. She is internationally known for her pioneering work in holistic medicine, and natural birthing, including demanding that fathers be allowed in the delivery room.

Dr. Gladys (as she likes to be called) helped to co-found the American Holistic Medical Association in 1978, and is widely known as the "Mother of Holistic Medicine." Dr. Gladys has authored three books, *The Physician Within You, Born to Live,* and *Living Medicine* and soon will release a fourth, "The World Needs Old Women." She has beautiful silver hair, always neatly wound in circles on the crown of her head, giving her an almost celestial queen-look. Her eyes are bright and she laughs a lot.

The women in the room were asking her casual questions, as if we were all sitting around in comfortable living room chairs, just getting to know one another. I was consumed by this moment I was experiencing and thankful for being one of the lucky ones, one person in time able to listen to these priceless conversations of such significance.

We got into a deep conversation about what had caused each of our successes. I began to realize that all of these women had developed nearly exactly the same success habits. The youngest woman was in her early twenties and had just graduated from college. Her aspiration is to become an international attorney. Everyone else was over forty years old. They talked about time management, focus, showing up on time and always doing more than what is promised. We talked about the books that had impacted our success and nearly everyone had followed *Think and Grow Rich* at one time or another.

I began to talk about the fourteenth chapter of the original *Think and Grow Rich* and how much I had studied "The Sixth Sense." I'm not sure, until that moment, I had ever considered how closely my life had followed this one chapter. Without knowing it, I had started working on this "Sixth Sense" as a teenager when I learned about how to do Yoga exercises. I enjoyed learning about Yoga so much, it became a lifetime interest and hobby. I earned my certification as I continued to study and that certification required me to teach a class once a week, which led me to continue to learn and practice yoga. At the same time, I was developing my business skills and became an entrepreneur and executive in technology, banking and real estate and then K-12 education. For years it felt like I had a dual life; one required skills for the outside world, and one required skills for the inside world. Both were demanding and rigorous and each seemed opposed to the other.

The chapter in the original book said you had to master the

other twelve principles in order to master the thirteenth, the "sixth sense." As I reviewed the chapter to write this, a sentence jumped off of the page. "For this reason it is a mixture of both the mental and the spiritual." There it was. THE statement that described my dual life. I had been working, daily, on the mixture without realizing it. And at times, it seemed as if I was able to manifest incredible miracles. But they weren't miracles! These seeming miracles were actually being produced due to very specific actions taken on my part. Had I only known at the time that I could almost dictate when a miracle would occur due to my following specific practices, I would not have worried so much. I would have trusted more. I would have developed incredible certainty and faith. God always works. God sets the rules and we just need to pay attention.

When the tragedies of 9/11 occurred, I decided to attempt the greatest entrepreneurial venture of my life. You know what entrepreneurs do? They find a big problem and they solve it and then they make a bunch of money...they hope. Well I decided to use my acquired skills to completely change the way K-12 schools teach children to learn, or so I hope. I needed a demonstration site, so I opened my first charter school, StarShine Academy in September of 2002. And the thing I have learned the most about K-12 learning during the past eleven years is that our brain works in very specific ways. And our brains, hearts and body emit enormous energy patterns. When I started the first school, scientists said DNA doesn't change. It is whatever you are born with. Now, eleven years later, scientists have proven that DNA changes ALL THE TIME. And it changes when you change your thinking and it is affected by people's thoughts around you!

So you don't really have to master all the other principles before you get to use this one, you just have to practice very specific exercises for your brain so that it can connect with your body to help produce absolutely astounding results. First of all, if you haven't learned this one thing, you must now:

What you think about, you bring about. Concentrate on what you want...NOT what you don't want. "Whatsoever a man thinketh, so is he."

~ Proverbs 23:7

It isn't so easy to tame your brain. After all, your brain is not your friend. It is there to protect you from harm, to keep you alive. It constantly looks for something to go wrong. It constantly looks for fear, anger and aggravation because that is what it is wired to do. If you want your brain to help you to manifest things, you will have to be in charge...not your brain. It takes practice to train your brain. Prayer, meditation, physical exercise and hypnosis all help to train your brain to let you be in charge. Radio, television, advertising, energy-sucking, chaos-making people all make your brain go into panic and fear again, so pay attention to what you are letting into your brain. Your brain, and a child's brain, is one giant computer...viruses in, viruses rule.

One helpful thing I learned early into yoga was that breathing exercises combined with balancing on one foot, causes your brain to stop letting any other thought in. Here is how it goes. You breathe in as deep as possible for a count of six: one, two, three, four, five, six. You hold your breath for three: one, two, three. You let it out steady and slow for a count of six: one, two, three, four, five, and six. And then repeat this exercise as long as you can. While doing this exercise, you need to balance on one foot. The tighter you make your stomach, the stronger your balance will be, as your center of balance is just below your belly button. This incidentally, is about where you start to feel butterflies in your stomach begin to happen when you're scared or nervous. The more you practice this little exercise, the more automatically you will do this when you are trying to tame your brain from fear.

Napoleon Hill had a "cabinet" of imaginary "Invisible Counselors." Success gurus teach us today that we are an average of the five people we spend the most time with. So once again,

Napoleon Hill was far ahead of today's scientific evidence. He managed to develop his "Sixth Sense" whereby he was given information that caused him great success because he practiced continually keeping his brained tuned to what he wanted, not what he didn't want. Napoleon Hill chose a group of already deceased people to sit with him around his imaginary table, where he could ask for their advice. He practiced his routine daily and came to know these men almost as if they were real, giving him real advice to his questions and developing real personalities as he understood them to be. This was a truly brilliant way to practice harnessing pure human potential. Can you imagine if you really were best friends of some of the most powerful people ever to have lived? What would your life be like if you could actually hang out with these people, in your mind?

I actually became quite good at meeting with my imaginary experts when I was still a young executive at AT&T. At the time, there were few women executives and I had to really wrestle with feeling insecure or out of my league. So I made up a council in my head and imagined talking to them each evening before I went to bed. I asked them to size up my day, good and bad and to give me recommendations for the day coming up. I would discuss problems and potential solutions. I usually kept my imaginary council to five members, but sometimes I changed who they were. Some of the same people have always been on my council though, like Benjamin Franklin, one of my favorite. Believe it or not, many times I received incredible insight and new ideas I had never thought of. And it has been a common occurrence for me to wake up with a complete answer to a problem, as if it were "downloaded" to me while I slept. By the way, I have learned to get up immediately and write this information down because most likely I will not remember it in the morning. This pastime of imagining talking with amazing people has been something I quite enjoy. And it has made me keenly aware of times I am being bombarded by a person or persons of constant chaos or just bad energy. I rarely will allow myself to stay amidst people who are "energy sucks." It's not good for them and I am not going to allow someone by my choice, to steal my potential future.

In 1937, when Napoleon Hill first published *Think and Grow Rich*, little was really understood about the brain, energy or how to manifest success. Others, like Dale Carnegie, who also published in the same year, *How to Win Friends and Influence People*, had devised ideas of what causes success through researching, like Hill, those individuals who seemed to have attained it. But there were no huge computer databases to sift through material and few scientific discoveries that might link their research to actual outcomes. These two researchers wrote in faith from their own feelings about what caused success.

Today, there is no excuse, whatsoever, for not attaining success as you define it. Massive amounts of documentation and data have been sorted and combined to help anyone to become any amount of success they desire, if they seek it. We know about how the brain works, what energy it works with, and why negative creates negative and positive creates positive. Any person desiring success, need only to show up at any public library, sit down at a computer and Google "how to be successful" or "how to get success." There is even an article about what someone has discovered that all successful people do in the first hour they wake up. Apparently, most successful people begin their day by being grateful for at least ten minutes, combined with visualizing exactly what their life will "feel" like when their life is exactly how they want it. Amazing huh? This isn't rocket science. It is science that has existed since the beginning of time. Now, with our vast resources nearly at the end of the touch of our fingers, we all can obtain the information we need to be anything we want to be.

So, based on my life experiences and those I've gained from my gurus, imagined and real, here are the seven steps I believe automatically manifest success:

1. When you wake up, be thankful for ten minutes. Feel

what your life feels like, as if it is exactly the way you want it in every way. Smell it, taste it, enjoy it.

2. Drink a whole, clear glass of water without anything in it first to instantly energize your brain. (Water goes straight to your brain and avoids digestion when it is clear.) Next, drink a glass of water with ½ lemon fresh-squeezed juice. (It detoxes your liver from it working through the night.)

3. Decide to concentrate only on what you want. Don't listen to anything else. If you do have to be informed about something negative, say to yourself, "It is whatever it is, now I have to get back to work." Then immediately put your mind back to your wants and desires.

4. Breathe and Balance, now you know how. Do it as often as possible.

5. Be aware of what you put in your mouth; energy or poison?

6. Stay happy…listen to music, draw pictures, look at great magazines.

7. Go to bed and quietly imagine your expert counselors, your advisors, your mentors and ask them for an assessment of your day and help with tomorrow. If they answer, write it down or talk into a recorder next to your bed.

Napoleon Hill talked about developing your "God Sense." I believe it is a way to get rid of the clutter in your brain so that God and your angels can talk to you, help you, and develop you and your aspirations. You are here to manifest your dreams, live your highest calling, and develop your innermost desires. Because after all, who put those desires into your head in the first place?

About Trish

Trish McCarty is one of America's leading business strategy and education experts on developing peak performance in schools through school management technology and processes, shared brand marketing and cutting-edge student resources in brain-based training, self-discipline, self-esteem, motivation, and results. She has inspired thousands with her lectures, interviews, published articles and books. She has been an impassioned leader for K-12 education reinvention, alongside her corporate banking and technology backgrounds, serving on many children's' charity boards throughout her life. Trish McCarty helps education superstars and professionals have more power and income for reinventing K-12 education. She has democratized the best schools and brought innovation to an audience who traditionally found it difficult to get involved.

Ms. McCarty came into the world with a global view; born in Frankfurt, Germany, as a U.S. Air Force military "brat" and as a child in Tokyo, Japan, where she served on the United Nations Board of Children. She attended Fort Lewis College, in her family's home town of Durango, Colorado with a human biology and neuroscience major and was recruited from there as an executive for AT&T. After five years, she was recruited by the President of Mellon Bank to develop national banking centers. An avid entrepreneur, she subsequently started a bank that grew to $128M in five years and won awards and highlights in national news including INC. Magazine.

Her company opened her first charity charter school, STARSHINE ACADEMY INTERNATIONAL SCHOOLS in the fall of 2002 for K-12 high-risk children, on a crime-ridden street in Arizona. The highly acclaimed academic "School Eco-Village" is a replicable model for success based on the holistic education of a child in health, wealth, happiness, body, mind, and spirit. It integrates the environment and personal health with a community garden and the spirit with music, art sports and technology. All of the children participate in community service projects integrated into the curriculum to learn economic development and patriotism. She has created partnerships with the United Nations by hosting 11 Days of Peace & Sustainability each year from 9-11—21. The school prototype model integrates the best practices for human resource management, sustainability, professional development, data collection and business management. Ms. McCarty is a Lincoln Center Fellow for Arizona State University for Education Leadership and is a partner at ASU Skysong Innovation Center.

Yoga is an integral part of the StarShine student curriculum as Ms. McCarty has studied and taught yoga for nearly thirty years. She is a constant community activist for peace, women in leadership, and child advocacy. She is married to guitarist and platinum recording artist, Steve McCarty. Steve and Trish frequently combine their talents in workshops and lectures to spread their message of empowerment, love, harmony, and unity.

To contact Trish McCarty:
trish@eduresources.com
www.starshineacademy.org
www.eduresources.com

CHAPTER 18

THINK AND GROW RICH IN ALL AREAS OF YOUR LIFE

BY DR. REGGIE COCHRAN

Before I jump into the heart of things, let me start of by saying, Thank you Napoleon Hill! Thank you for dedicating your life to teaching us how to design, create and live the ultimate lifestyles of our choice. And a special thanks to everyone involved with the Napoleon Hill Foundation who are responsible for helping keep Napoleon's teaching alive today.

The lessons in *Think And Grow Rich* are just as effective and relevant today, as they were when the book was first published. People and governments change. Television shows and fashion styles change. Technology changes too quick for most people to keep up with. But the true basic keys and principals of success never change. And *Think And Grow Rich* shares several of those true basics with us. Today I will be sharing several of those keys with you in the same order I share them with my clients.

This book is not about me. So I will not go into all the ways *Think And Grow Rich* changed my life. But I will share this… they helped me to go from what people called "poor trailer trash" who was picked on as a kid for being fat and dropped out of high school… to become a world champion martial artist with advanced degrees in Christian counseling and clinical hypnotherapy. This led to a career as a mental skills / business coach to many internationally known celebrities, athletes and business professionals. Napoleon's teaching has further helped me in becoming a keynote speaker and Best-Selling author who has co-authored books with Bill Gates, Donald Trump, Brian Tracy, Jim Rohn and Zig Ziglar to name a few.

I mention these things not to brag, but to let you know that I am sharing with you from personal experience. These principals are working for me and I believe can work even better for you. This is very important to me. You see, as grateful as I am for what *Think And Grow Rich* has helped me accomplish, I am just as grateful for how it has helped my clients, friends and family. My prayer is that what my coauthors and I share in this book will help you become more successful too. So let's get started. :)

As a martial arts instructor, I teach my students that where the head goes, the body follows. In other words, if I grab your head or hair and pull you hard and fast enough in one direction, your body will start moving in that same direction as well. Being able to control the direction of my opponent can make the difference between winning a sport fight or protecting myself in a deadly street situation.

So my students will spend hours upon hours practicing many different techniques and drills learning how to take control of their opponents' head and body movement. The serious students will practice these techniques (and all other techniques they are taught) over and over, until they are second nature to them. If they are put into a situation of needing to use these techniques, their subconscious mind and body will take over and react without delay. The techniques are executed by reflex instead of a drawn-out thought process at the time of attack.

As a mental skills and business coach, I teach my clients that where their mind (thoughts, emotions, etc.) goes, their life follows. I show them how this is true in all areas of their lives including, physical, mental, emotional, financial and spiritual. I explain that their success starts in their own mind. I share that they can't always control every situation around them. Nor can they always control the actions (and reactions) of others in their lives. However, they can learn to control their own thoughts, actions, emotions and behaviors. And the first step in being able to do so is by taking full responsibility for all of their problems.

I go on to share with my clients that most of the successful people I know rarely play the "blame game" for their problems or setbacks. They realize that their success is not based on where they grew up, what color their skin is, who is ruling their country or what past education they have, or don't have. They don't spend time blaming others like their boss, employees, spouse, parents, kids, etc. They believe and practice that great old saying, "If it is to be, it is up to me."

Most people are willing to take credit and pat themselves on their own backs for their successes, but unfortunately, most people are not willing to take responsibility for their failures. If you are truly serious about being more successful, you must be willing to not only pat yourself on the back, but also kick yourself in the butt. (...figuratively speaking, lol.)

After interviewing my clients to find out what problem areas they are seeking help with, no matter what the problem is, or what area of the life it is in, I start digging with verbal questions and written assessments to find out what their real inner most secret thoughts and beliefs are concerning those trouble spots. Once this is accomplished, designing and creating a new success strategy is fairly simple, because I can start helping them right away change their thinking, attitudes and emotions that are holding them back.

Yes, this really is a simple process. No, not always easy, but yes, simple. So don't let those negative voices in your head tell you that the things I share with you will not work because they are too simple. Just like Napoleon's title says... allow yourself to "Think And Grow Rich." And not just financially, but in all areas of your life. These keys will also work for you physically, mentally, emotionally and spiritually. So please keep reading with an open mind.

Why do I start working with my clients thoughts and emotions first? Why do I make sure they are willing to take full responsibility for all their successes and failures? Because if they are not willing to make changes and take full responsibility, they will not benefit long term from anything Napoleon Hill, myself or anyone else teaches them. They are not coachable.

So let's keep moving forward. After I have a client that is coachable, we start focusing on details of what they want to accomplish or improve upon. Following the principals Napoleon lined out for us, I have my clients write down specific goals and specific time frames that they want to accomplish those goals.

Next I have them write down in as much detail as possible why they want to accomplish each goal. For example, if they write down they want to make $X in the next twelve months, I have them explain exactly what they are going to do with that money. I want them to write down how that money is going to benefit them. And why they need / want that amount of money in that amount of time. This step is important because it helps attach emotion to the goal. The more emotion attached to that goal, the greater chance of accomplishing it. I want them to be able to read "why" on a daily basis.

Then we work together to create, daily, weekly and monthly action steps. In most cases we stretch these action steps further into quarterly, semi-annual and annual plans. And many times as long as 5 to 10 years out. In this process, I also help my client determine what type of additional coaching and education they will need as well as where they are going to get it. Most people never take the time or money to hire a coach to help them become more successful. The successful people I know have several coaches to help them succeed. And they are always investing into new education.

I then have them plan a reward program for themselves. These rewards are things they are going to give themselves or do, when they stay on track with their activities for a predetermined period of time. These rewards could be as simple as a date night to the movies or an extra game of golf for a week of activity well done, to a vacation to (insert your dream location here) after accomplishing your annual goals.

The key is to reward yourself with things that you don't normally splurge on. Or in some cases, with things you splurge on, but won't feel guilty this time when you do it. For example, let's say you are working on losing a few 'pizza and wings' pounds that you put on during football season. A reward for sticking to your diet and following your written exercise routine for the week may be a small pizza and a few wings. Even professional body builders will allow a cheat day or meal. So you can too, and not feel guilty about it or blow your diet.

At this time, I have my clients go through what I call a daily lifestyle analysis to help uncover daily bad habits and bad activities that may keep them from following through with their daily action steps needed to accomplish their goals. This exercise also helps them become aware of what in their lives is / are holding them back in some way. When this exercise is done honestly, most clients have a very clear picture of how they can become a lot more successful – just by making a few minor daily changes.

For example... the average American watches almost 38 hours a week of television. No that's not a typo. Yes 38 hours, almost as many hours as working a full time job. So let's say that I am working with a business professional who thinks they don't have enough hours in the day to get everything done. And through this analysis we discover that this client is one of those average Americans spending on average 5+ hours a day watching

TV. My first goal is to get them to realize that every time we watch television, we are helping someone else accomplish and live their vision, not our vision. Then get them to commit to two things. First, take just one or two of those 5+ hours and work on an activity that is going to make them money. Second, take another one or two of those 5+ hours and multi-task while watching TV. This could something as simple as taking care of their social media marketing activities or updating their blogs, etc. I personally find this a great time to go through the hundreds of emails I receive on a daily basis. It's also a good time to do any search engine research I need to do. I rarely watch TV without working on a project that can be completed on my laptop.

If I have a client who has weight loss / fitness goals and spending too many hours watching television, I will get them to commit to three things. The first is to take at least 30 minutes away from their TV time to exercise. The second is to commit to limit the types and amount of food they are going to snack on while watching TV. The third is that every commercial, they get off their butt and move. This can include stretching, walking in place, set-ups, etc. I remind them that losing weight is a combination of eating less and moving more. The less they eat and the more they move, the quicker they will lose weight. Again, I am keeping it simple for them to visualize.

In both examples above, notice that I am not asking my client to make drastic changes. I want to help them create a plan of daily activity that they can stick to for a long time. I want them to learn that the most successful people we know of, have the same amount of time in each day, week, month, year as we do. They just have different habits of how they use their time.

After my client has completed their written goals, detailed action steps and reward system, I have them choose an accountability partner. This is someone that they are going to share their activities and results with on a regular basis. I personally recommend this be done on at least a weekly basis. Some people will need daily accountability to stay on track. Often times my clients choose me as their accountability partner. But in some cases due to the nature of their goals, geographical location, etc., this is not possible. So I have them choose someone else that they can trust to keep secrets and be supportive.

The last thing you want is a 'blabber mouth' who is going to Facebook your problems to the world. And you don't want someone who is going to kick you while you are down and give you 100 reasons why you are not going to accomplish your goals. So there has to be a lot of thought and consideration going into picking a great accountability partner.

I then meet with my client and go over everything they want to accomplish, how they are going to accomplish, who is going to help them accomplish and what rewards they are going to give themselves along the way. This is where I get them to commit to what I call, "See It, Say It, Be It!"

> **See It:** - I teach them how to visualize the outcome of their goals. To visually meditate in as much detail as possible their lifestyle – once they accomplish their goals.

> **Say It:** - I help them write down positive affirmations that they will see and say, several times a day. I even encourage them to record themselves reading those affirmations so they can listen to them as much as possible. Yes, I could do a recording for them in my voice and make more money for the service. But, without going into why, there is more power to your affirmations when you hear them in your own voice.

> **Be It:** - Then I have them commit in writing to me and to their accountability partner, that they are going to follow through with their plan, no matter what it takes, for as long as it takes. They are not going to stop "three feet from gold."

I want to clear up a big misconception among those who have not taken the time to read and truly understand what Napoleon has taught us in *Think And Grow Rich*. You must take action! Yes you must think about the results you want. You must believe that you will achieve the results you want. *But you must also work to achieve those results*. Napoleon's teachings are full of examples of hard-working believers who not only had positive thoughts, and great faith, but also had great work ethic. The most successful people are those who are willing to do what unsuccessful people are not willing to do. They know there is a high price to pay for achieving success. And they are willing to pay that price, because they know the price for failure is much greater.

In closing, I pray that God blesses you beyond your own wildest dreams and goals in everything good you do. And in return, I pray you become a blessing to others. You can start by sharing a copy of this book along with Napoleon's *Think And Grow Rich* with others. Remember, this is a We World, not a Me World.

And together we can help make the world we share a greater place to live!

About Reggie

Dr. Reggie Cochran is the project advisor / coordinator for Chuck Norris Enterprises. He is also a business partner with Chuck & Gena Norris. Reggie is an internationally known Consultant, Coach, Speaker, Best Selling Author & Martial Arts Champion. Reg has co-authored books with Bill Gates, Donald Trump, Brian Tracy, Dr. Wayne Dyer, Deepak Chopra, to name a few. His personal clients read like an International Who's Who directory filled with actors, entertainers, athletes and business professionals.

Reggie began his martial arts training in 1974. He has won many World Champion martial arts titles and has earned an 8th Degree Black Belt from his instructor, Mr. Chuck Norris. He is on the Board of Directors of the United Fighting Arts Federation. He is the co-founder of the International Federation Of Mixed Martial Artists along with Big John McCarthy and David Dunn. He is a multi-time martial arts Hall Of Fame member, Chuck Norris Man of The Year and recipient of the first Howard Jackson Memorial Award.

Dr. Reg is also the Founder of MentorsClub.com, an online private members only site created to help others achieve greater personal and business success. He is also involved in helping non profit foundations achieve their goals with new and refreshing fundraising ideas that also benefit the donors as well as the charities and their causes.

Reg invites you to connect with him at:
http://www.linkedin.com/pub/reggie-cochran/28/9a4/b0/
www.facebook.com/reggiecochran
To find out what others say about Dr. Reg, visit: www.reggiecochran.com

CHAPTER 19

THE SECRET OF SUCCESS:
Just Try Some Magic

BY STEFAN WISSENBACH

My brain is the key that sets me free. ~ Harry Houdini

Magic.

It can seem like a childish concept. We all know it doesn't truly exist, don't we?

Or do we?

The best-selling book series, as well as the highest-grossing film series of all time, both contain the same magical name: Harry Potter. And that name, of course, is all about magic.

The truth is we *want* magic to be real; we want something to lift us up from our everyday lives and allow fantastic things to happen. Fantastic *good* things, mind you – nobody wants a dragon to come breaking through the wall, spewing fire at the living room furniture (or, worse yet, at you!).

Well, I've got wonderful news for you: Magic is real. And it *does* create fantastic good things. With the help of Napoleon

Hill's four-score-old principles from *Think and Grow Rich*, I intend to show you how you can bring some real magic into your life in this very chapter.

And, believe me, there's nothing up my sleeve – except good wishes for your future.

A MAGICAL CHILDHOOD

When I was growing up, my family was not well off - far from it. It was my mother, my sister and I in a small apartment. At school, I was called "Lentil Boy" because my mother bought and soaked lentils to feed us as inexpensively as possible.

And yet, despite my economic disadvantages, I did believe magic was possible. But I already, perhaps, had a different idea of what magic was all about.

I became fascinated by magicians and their tricks. I studied them – and created my own illusions. The truth was that I knew magic wasn't about the supernatural – I knew it was about creating something amazing that *seemed* to be magic – I just had to understand how the professional magicians made these tricks happen. I learnt some tricks of my own: By simply planning things out the right way, in the right sequence with the right moves and the right props. When everything came together in the way I intended – it certainly *looked* like magic to my audience.

In the same way, I studied the lives of those around me. Some had hard lives, like my family. Some, however, had more than enough money, more than enough success, and more than enough resources. They had created a different kind of magic, and a much more powerful one. Still, I believed it was simply another trick that, once pulled apart and examined, I could successfully duplicate myself.

I was determined to do just that. I quit school early to make my own way - and placed no ceiling on my dreams. I wanted financial independence – that, for me, would be the ultimate "trick."

But I had help. I was very fortunate, in that, when I was in my teens, I was introduced to the world of personal development. I devoured books like *Think and Grow Rich*, and listened to many of the audio books from the self-improvement giant, Nightingale Conant. As I took in all this advice for success, I slowly began to see the magic within all this material. I learned what I should do, how I should do it, and I then did the most important thing any true magician should do – practice!

The result? Well, to the part of myself that still vividly recalls my childhood, my present-day circumstances are, indeed, truly magical.

I'm fortunate enough to enjoy a very comfortable lifestyle. I have a large country property—with staff—and travel all over the world with my fabulous wife and three delightful children. I've enjoyed staying in many fine hotels and have experienced several different cultures. I've learned to snowboard, fly helicopters, and indulge my passion for motor cars. In short, I've come a long way since the lentils.

To me, magic comes about whenever you put forth an organized effort to achieve a goal – and you stay dedicated to those efforts until that goal is met. When everything comes together as you intended, it may *seem* like some kind of instant and miraculous event – but it's really the result of the guiding principle behind Chapter 7 of Napoleon Hill's *Think and Grow Rich* – "Organized Planning."

True so-called "overnight successes" are extremely rare. As Hill notes, Thomas Edison failed over ten thousand times before he perfected the light bulb - and did not that invention seem like magic initially to those who beheld it? But it wasn't magic – it was hard work, dedication and constant working towards a goal.

Luck can be involved, to be sure – but more often, magical outcomes are merely the result of the right application of energies towards the needed *organized planning*.

MY MAGIC FORMULA FOR SUCCESS

"...everything man creates or acquires begins in the form of DE-SIRE, that desire is taken on the first lap of its journey, from the abstract to the concrete, into the workshop of the IMAGINATION, where PLANS for its transition are created and organized."

Those are the words of Napoleon Hill from the beginning of his "Organized Planning" chapter – and his main point is that, in order to succeed, <u>you must start with desire, imagine a successful outcome and then create a plan to make it happen.</u>

What I learned from my studies in personal development is that you can distill all its techniques and strategies into five separate elements. By addressing all five in your organized planning, you can begin to unlock the magic. That means you'll soon find that you're capable of slaying the dragons that stand in your way, as well as moving mountains to create significant change in your life.

Here, then, are the five elements of my Magic Formula:

#1: MOTIVATION

We grow hungry and we eat. We get tired and we sleep. These are physical conditions that *motivate* us to do what we need to do in order to survive.

But we're not talking about mere survival here. We're talking about quests that, frankly, most do not bother to undertake. Why? Because these quests are about achievement of a higher order – and they require *motivation* of a higher order. Many of the tasks required for these kinds of quests don't generate fast results or immediate gratification, which our society has conditioned us to expect – but they do bring long-lasting happiness and life satisfaction, if you're patient and committed to the effort.

For example, improving your health generally means you must exercise more and eat less. For most of us, that makes for an extremely unpleasant short-term result; long-term, however, you will end up looking better, feeling better and living longer – which are all extremely *magical* outcomes.

Great change requires great effort; reaching substantial goals requires substantial energy and enthusiasm; and the spark that lights a fire to this whole process is proper motivation. Without that motivation, your initial excitement on day one of tackling a difficult quest will soon dwindle to irritation and exhaustion – accompanied by a desire to slip back into old, easy, but ultimately self-destructive habits.

Make sure you feel *passion* for the great change you want to begin to accomplish – it will always bring you closer to your desired life. In the words of Napoleon Hill: *"everything man creates or requires begins in the form of desire."*

#2: APPLICATION

Of course, motivation is awesome – but you still have to actually *do* something to further your progress towards your goals.

In his best-selling book, *The War of Art: Break Through the Blocks and Win Your Inner Creative Battles*, author Steven Pressfield lays out the distance between motivation and action:

"Late at night, have you experienced a vision of the person you might become, the work you could accomplish, the realized being you were meant to be? Are you a writer who doesn't write, a painter who doesn't paint, an entrepreneur who never starts a venture? Then you know what Resistance is."

Resistance, according to Pressfield, is the gulf between the motivation to achieve something and the actual achievement of it; thus, the overcoming of Resistance is the singular objective in accomplishing any goal. We've all met people who are continually talking about what they're going to do, without actually doing it. No doubt we've all been guilty of it at some point in our lives. But the fact of the matter is that *successful people get things done.*

The law of inertia states that an object resists being moved; humans often aren't much different. So do something - but not just anything. *Apply* your motivation to *meaningful* action that will actually take you closer to your desired destination. Follow-through is imperative, so transfer the energy of your motivation, complete with all the energy, enthusiasm, desire and passion it contains, into unbridled application.

#3: GROWTH

When you're motivated and when you channel that energy into the right application of action, you begin to learn and, as a happy consequence, you begin to experience *growth*.

Or you *should* – it's really up to you!

Successful people take on board what works and what doesn't, and they discover through that process how to realize better results. Unsuccessful people, in contrast, don't learn from their mistakes and often misunderstand why something went right; they end up in unproductive loops and find progress to be difficult, if not unattainable.

We all have lives that are based around trial and error - and all experiences, good and bad, inform us and teach us. Those life lessons should spur us on to both expand our horizons and concentrate our focus. For that to happen, we must be open to new information, amenable to letting go of convictions that are proven wrong, and brave enough to embrace innovation and new perspectives.

Growth is the bedrock of the human experience itself, as well as all life. Even the most sedentary living thing is experiencing constant change. As human beings, however, we have the amazing gift to *direct* the course of our growth.

It's a shame to waste that gift – so don't!

#4: INDEPENDENCE

Why do we need motivation? Why do we put so much into application? Why do we do everything we can to drive our own personal growth?

Because we want *independence*.

All of us want the opportunity to chart our own courses for our lives. All of us want to experience the freedom to do what we wish. All throughout history – even to this day when I'm writing these words – people have fought and died for their chance at achieving independence.

Personal freedom is just the beginning, however. Financial freedom, even in small doses, magnifies that opportunity and multiplies our options in life; with it, we can truly choose what we want to do, and when we want to do it.

Do you want to take a luxury vacation or a rustic one, obtain an advanced degree or start a business, devote your time to non-profit causes or travel the world, pay off the car or start an emergency fund? Financial freedom allows you to make those choices and more. It brings with it not only the obvious consumer perks, but it also permits you to be in control, personally and professionally, of your time, your efforts…and your destiny!

#5: COMMUNITY

We all crave independence – but we all need *community.*

From the standpoint of a Brit, Americans have a fascination with individualism - the saddle-tramp cowboy conquering the West, the lone renegade cop seeking justice for the wronged and so forth. Though these caricatures often make great parts for movie stars, in truth, success is a more collaborative effort – and, over the years, it has been my observation that happy and successful people operate in positive communities.

Community also taps into a central concept of Napoleon Hill's success principles – that of the "Mastermind" group. To quote Hill, "No individual has sufficient experience, education, native ability and knowledge to ensure the accumulation of a great fortune, *without the cooperation of other people*" (italics mine). I totally agree.

The right community provides you with a network of supportive individuals you love and care about, with whom you can share your aspirations, goals, and achievements, and who provide feedback and encouragement on disappointments and setbacks—whether that community is blood-related or not.

I've been lucky enough to benefit from that kind of community and you can too. Life is meant to be shared, and not only is tackling any goal more difficult by yourself…it's just not as much fun!

So, those are the five elements of my Magic Formula. I don't know if you've noticed anything interesting about those five elements, but, if you take a moment and put together the first letter of each one of them…well, let me spell it out for you:

Motivation

Application

Growth

Independence

Community

Yes, if you put them all together, you end up with **MAGIC.**

And I sincerely believe from my experience, when you fully introduce these five elements into your life, you can create, from the outside, what will appear to be some amazing magic of your own.

YOUR MAGIC FUTURE

Like Napoleon Hill, I've studied many successful people over the years to discover their secrets. I've also spent the last two decades helping rich people get richer, and I currently work with a number of very wealthy private families, helping them to organize their affairs and realize the most from their resources – working in harmony with their goals. That means I've been (and am) responsible for literally hundreds of millions of dollars.

It's very rewarding work and I enjoy it – but I would very much like to see many others achieve their dreams the way I've achieved mine. I know there are many out there who could benefit from the advice of someone like me – but just don't have access to that kind of counsel.

That's why I've launched: magicfuture.com, a website which enables people to design the life they want to lead, and provides the tools they need to make their dreams come true. I believe it's a wonderful way to focus your "organized planning" in a very pro-active way.

My kind of magic is really all about mastery, not miracles or mystery - mastery of a way of thinking, of key actions and applications, and a process that will profoundly impact your life. In short, we all have the capacity to create what to the outside world looks like magic.

After all, isn't building a great life really the ultimate "trick?"

Here's hoping you pull yours off – to the applause of millions.

About Stefan

Stefan Wissenbach is an entrepreneur, author and speaker.

From a humble but happy childhood, he has built and sold several successful businesses and is an advisor to a number of leading business figures.

In 1994, he founded The Wissenbach Group, providing strategic advice to wealthy private individuals, helping them manage their affairs in harmony with their personal goals. Whilst developing his unique process, he created the concept of MagicNumber® – the amount of money or accumulated wealth needed to live your desired lifestyle where work is optional.

Having spent many years helping wealthy people, Stefan's mission is to now also help a wider audience. He is passionate about providing education and inspiration to enable others to fulfill their potential and bridge the gap between aspiration and achievement. His unique approach is to simplify the complex and provide a framework for people to take action, distilling a lifetime of learning into simple success strategies that anyone can master. In 2010, he formed and launched magicfuture.com to achieve this mission.

His revolutionary Magic Future corporate benefit programs have created thousands of successful, engaged and happy employees delivering greater value in the workplace.

Stefan has a lifelong commitment to personal development and travels to Chicago four times a year to meet with Dan Sullivan – one of the world's leading entrepreneurial coaches. Magicfuture.com takes the best practices from his lifetime of learning and applies his proven strategies in an easy-to-use, fun, inspirational online platform available to anyone with access to the web. Stefan's personal success is behind every feature of the tools.

His book, *Slaying Dragons & Moving Mountains, A beginners guide to a happy fulfilled life* and his audio program, *Your Magic Formula: The Life-Planning Solution for Making Work Optional,* both teach practical and timeless skills, techniques and knowledge that enable anyone to create greater levels of happiness and success.

Stefan is happily married with three children. He enjoys living life to the full, flying helicopters and travelling to new places. He is also the Founder of The Magic Future Foundation.

To learn more about Stefan Wissenbach visit: stefanwissenbach.com.

CHAPTER 20

SEVEN STEPS TO CREATING WEALTH AND PLANNING YOUR EXIT STRATEGY

BY MICHELLE SEILER-TUCKER

Many people have asked me, Michelle why did you write "Sell Your Business for More Than It's Worth" and why are you writing a chapter in *Think and Grow Rich*?

The truth of the matter is that I have wanted to write a book since I was 6 years old. When most little girls were playing with their dolls, I was interviewing people and taking extensive notes in a notebook I carried everywhere. I interviewed people as if I was reporting for CNN. My mother always thought and hoped I would become the next Barbra Walters. Following in Barbra's footsteps would have certainly been a nice career, however, I have always gravitated towards wanting to own my own businesses. I am extremely pleased with the path I have chosen to walk. I feel truly rewarded by the hundreds of sellers that I was able to assist in improving their business, increasing their cash flow, and selling their business for maximum value.

In addition, I am honored that I was able to help buyers from all walks of life buy the American Dream, create financial freedom, be their own boss, and obtain a better quality of life. Throughout my life, I have felt compelled towards a desire to help others. I love the thrill of the deal; most importantly I love to create wins for my clients. My clients have been a true inspiration and continue to enrich my life.

I attribute my success to two main principles. First and foremost, *persistence*; I am extremely persistent. My friends, family and customers refer to me as the Rottweiler that never lets go. I don't give up. Against all odds I will persevere, succeed and lead.

Second, I believe in *organized planning*. People don't plan to fail, they fail to plan. The biggest mistake business owners make is not planning their exit strategy. Most owners are so entrenched in working in their business, they do not think about selling their business until forced to sell due to an unexpected catastrophic event or retirement. The best time to sell your business is when your business is doing well, not when your business begins to decline and is losing profits. In addition, most business owners do not implement a strategic plan to create a sustainable business. Many owners find themselves with a job, rather than an actual business that works for them.

Currently, there are over 27,000,000 businesses in the United States. Approximately twenty-five percent will be up for sale at any given time. Eight out of ten businesses do not sell. Sellers either end up keeping their business, giving their business away, closing their business, or filing bankruptcy.

Millions of baby boomers are planning their exit strategy. They want to sell their nest egg, so they can finally relax and enjoy their retirement or begin the next phase of their life. Many of these businesses will not sell, leaving baby boomers with a serious problem. This generation will be left with very little to nothing to live on, if they do not successfully sell their business for maximum value. This is a huge crisis facing our baby boomers and must be addressed immediately. It is my passion and mission to reach out to as many of these owners as possible. This is one of my main objectives for writing "Sell Your Business for More Than It's Worth."

These are startling and grim statistics for the entrepreneurs that have poured their hearts and souls into their business for many decades. Baby boomers made enormous sacrifices over the years and are now faced with the most difficult challenge of all—selling their business!

In addition, many sellers do not implement an organized plan to sell their business. Sellers that attempt to sell their own business fail sixty percent of the time. Many sellers waste time, money and energy trying to sell their own business. Just when they think they are going to close on the sale of their business, the deal falls apart for any number of reasons. Most deals fall apart because the buyer was never financially qualified in the first place. In most cases, the seller never obtains the buyer's financials nor do they have the buyers sign the appropriate non-disclosure agreements and non-compete (if necessary).

Bottom line: Sellers do not properly qualify buyers, nor do they protect themselves. Most sellers provide proprietary documents and information to unqualified buyers that have not been disclosed. Therefore, the buyer is free to tell everyone they meet that the seller's business is up for sale, which will cause major problems for the seller's business. In addition, prospective buyers that have not signed NDA's will discuss the seller's proprietary information with strangers. Even worse, the prospective buyer could go out and directly compete with the seller. In my book, I offer valuable information and tips on how to sell your business and protect yourself in the interim.

As disheartening as the above statistics are, many business brokers also fail sixty percent of the time when attempting to sell businesses. It is imperative that you read, "The Top Twenty Questions to Ask When Choosing a Business Broker." (Go to: www.betterbusinesbrokers.com)

These statistics inspired me to assist business owners sell their most prized possession: their business. My peers consider me the leading authority in buying and in selling businesses. I dedicated my career to assisting sellers sell for the ultimate value so they can afford the lifestyle they have always dreamed of and deserve.

Most businesses do not sell for the value that the seller requires to build the next chapter of their life. Consequently, I work with each seller to identify the top mistakes they are making in their business in order to create a more profitable and sustainable business that will sell for top dollar. I have assisted hundreds of business owners improve their bottom line and create a business that works for them, rather than them working for their business.

Again, I am extremely passionate and dedicated to assisting business owners improve their business, plan their exit strategy and sell their business for more than it's worth. I love the thrill of the deal and obtaining the highest price for my clients. Most importantly, I love turning businesses around by assisting the seller in adding congruent revenue streams. There is nothing more exciting than successfully turning around a business that was in dire need, keeping families employed and continuing to service customers. Make no mistake about it—small businesses are the backbone of our economy. The more successful our small business owners are, the more successful our economy will be.

As mentioned above, you should always plan your exit strategy from day one of buying or starting a business. Below are the top SEVEN ACTION STEPS for creating a sustainable and desirable business that will exceed buyer's demands when it's time to sell:

ACTION STEP 1:
KNOW YOUR GOALS AND KNOW YOUR WHY.

Most business owners do not have a business plan, nor do they have goals. They also don't know their WHY? Why are they in business? What do they want to accomplish and what do they want on their tombstone? It becomes much easier to accomplish goals when you are clear and laser-focused on the WHY. Upon knowing your WHY, you can write and implement your goals. You cannot run a successful business without setting, reviewing and adjusting your goals— daily, monthly and quarterly. Your goals become an organized plan, the road map for your business. How do you know where you are going, if you do not have clear directions? Visualize and share your goals with your staff, community and network. The key elements to obtaining your goals are persistence and organized planning.

ACTION STEP 2:
BRAND YOURSELF AND MOST IMPORTANTLY, YOUR BUSINESS.

Ask yourself, is your business based upon brand loyalty or location loyalty?

Do your customers purchase your products/services because you have a convenient location? If you answered yes, it's time to work on building your name recognition and brand awareness. Over 95% of businesses are not branded. Not branding yourself and your business is one of the top mistakes that business owners make. In addition, if your business is based upon location loyalty then you need to own the real estate and or have a long-term lease with options to renew, along with favorable terms and conditions. On the other hand, if your clients are going out of their way to purchase your products/services, congratulations, you have built brand loyalty.

There are five levels of branding:

- Level 1 Brand Absence: 95% of businesses fall into this category.

- Level 2 Brand Awareness: certainly better than brand absence, at least consumers are aware of your products/services.

- <u>Level 3 Brand Preference</u>: customers prefer doing business with your company.

- <u>Level 4 Brand Loyalty</u>: clients purchase your goods/services exclusively.

- <u>Level 5 Brand Advocacy</u>: it is imperative to have tunnel vision and aim at this bulls-eye target. It is always better when someone recommends your product/service. This is the ultimate level at which money will come to you in droves. Apple and Coke are perfect examples and do this better than anyone. How many people have told you to buy an iPhone or iPad? Or how many times has someone said, "Have a coke?" Build your brand and have consumers insist on using your company. Many business owners have done a better job at building their personal brand versus their company brand. Personal brands are more difficult to sell than company brands. You remove the person and the brand disappears. Great businesses and entrepreneurs, brand both. Steve Jobs built his brand as the face, innovator and brain trust of Apple. However, Apple is also very well branded. A lack of company branding would have been detrimental for Apple.

ACTION STEP 3:
CREATE A SUSTAINABLE BUSINESS THAT WORKS FOR YOU RATHER THAN YOUR WORKING FOR IT.

Do you have a business or a job? Do you have employees? Are you the business? If so, then your business will be very difficult to sell. In many cases the owner is the business, and when the owner leaves, the clients leave. Most buyers are adamant about purchasing a business, not a job. It is imperative that you write an employee's training/operations manual. You must duplicate yourself, hire employees or independent contractors and create a management team. Business owners need to stop working in their business and start working on their business.

ACTION STEP 4:
CREATE CONGRUENT REVENUE STREAMS AND GROW YOUR BUSINESS VIA ACQUISITIONS.

Is your industry a dying breed or on the cutting edge? Is your industry desirable to buyers? It is necessary to continue to reinvent your business to keep up with consumer demands. Is your business based upon one profit center? What happens when that profit center in no longer viable? In today's economy, businesses must add multiple sources of income. They should not rely on one revenue stream. Businesses, now more than ever, need to provide a one-stop shop environment for their client's needs. Many of my buyers are strategic buyers; they look for businesses that grow their business by providing products/services to their existing client base. Listen to your clients. What are your customers asking for and what are their ultimate needs? It is imperative to fill your clients' void. If you don't, your competitors will.

ACTION STEP 5:
KEEP YOUR CURRENT CUSTOMERS AND INCREASE YOUR CLIENT BASE.

It is a known statistic that 80 percent of your business comes from 20 percent of your clients. Many of my clients' business come from 5-10 customers. Therefore, if they lose a customer it will become detrimental to their business. Many buyers will not buy a business without a healthy client base. It is prudent that you continue to expand your customer list. Don't just think outside the box, throw the box away. One of the best ways to obtain more clients is to network. Call five new people every day that you can build a mutually beneficial and prosperous relationship with. Expand your geographical area to reach more prospects. It is more cost effective to keep a customer than it is to replace one. Continue to provide excellent customer service and roll out the red carpet for your clients by creating WOW experiences for new and existing customers. Creating WOW experiences will set you apart from your competition.

In addition, your clients will brag about the tremendous treatment they received from your company, which will convert your customers to brand advocates. It is always better when someone else sells you rather than you selling yourself. Keep in mind, that a negative or un-WOW will have the opposite effect and could significantly damage your brand. Unfortunately, negative news tends to spread quicker than the positive news.

ACTION STEP 6:
MARKETING

Know your numbers. How much does it cost to obtain a lead? How many leads convert to a sale? How many sales convert to repeat sales? It is impossible to implement a marketing budget unless you know your numbers. Most companies do not reach their full potential. Almost all businesses fall short when it comes to marketing and branding. Many businesses will not invest in marketing nor do they even have a marketing plan. Some businesses only utilize one or two marketing channels. It is imperative to know and track your numbers.

Also, it is critical that you conduct market research studies to discover what your target market's number one problem is and solve their problem, ease their pain and your business will skyrocket. Don't just throw a bunch of marketing ideals and concepts against the wall in the hopes that something will stick. Create a marketing campaign based upon your market research results, using a multitude of different channels.

For example, I recommend that many of my clients test the following marketing avenues:

✓ SEO/Pay-per-Clicks

✓ Media Buys

✓ Auto Responders

✓ Social Networking

✓ Blogs/Newsletters

✓ Joint Ventures

✓ Email Blast

✓ Direct Mail

✓ Telemarketing

✓ Customer Referral programs

✓ Employees Incentive Programs

✓ Trade Shows/Publications

Above are just a few ideas. At the end of the day you need to implement at least five or more of these resources. Most importantly, you need to train your staff to track your marketing efforts. This is one of the biggest mistakes that my clients make. They spend a lot of money, energy and effort in organizing their campaign and then they do not track their results. Without tracking your results, you are throwing money down the drain and that's insane! Again, know your numbers, know your market, test your marketing campaigns and track your results. Also, you must inspect what you expect. Owners delegate, yet do not follow up to ensure quality.

ACTION STEP 7:
FINANCIAL HOUSEKEEPING

It's amazing to me how many businesses do not know their numbers and have no idea how much money they make. As mentioned above, there are over 27,000,000 businesses in the US, over 90% percent of them are small businesses. Most small business owners live out of their business via paying their personal expenses through their business. Most business owners keep very poor records and in many cases cannot prove their personal expenses. In addition, it is very difficult to obtain financing on a business that is showing minimal profits on their tax returns. Again, it is crucial to know your numbers and keep clean books and records. My company specializes in assisting business owners on cleaning their financial house so we can sell their business. On average, I obtain a 20-40 percent higher selling price for my client's business.

Obviously the above statistics and action steps are just the tip of the iceberg. This might seem like common sense, however, common sense is not as common as it once was. I specialize in evaluating my clients business by identifying the top NINE mistakes business owners make in order to get their businesses in LINE, increase profits, cut costs and run efficiently. A PRO is never out of school! The more you learn, the more you earn. In addition to learning, the key factor to success is speed of implementation. Utilize the brain trust of the authorities, implement an organized plan immediately and above all be persistent.

About Michelle

Leading Authority on Buying and Selling Businesses

Michelle Seiler-Tucker is Founder/President of Capital Business Solutions, Better Business Brokers, founding partner of Capital Business Solutions Franchise, and Founder/President of The Business Doctors and Advanced Medical Rehab. Ms. Tucker has (and continues to have) an amazing entrepreneurial career; to date she has owned and operated several successful businesses.

Michelle Seiler-Tucker is the leading authority on buying, selling and improving businesses, as well as increasing a business's revenue streams. Michelle has sold several hundred businesses and franchises. She has helped buyers from all walks of life buy the American Dream, create financial freedom, be their own boss and obtain a better quality of life.

What makes Michelle a formidable force in her industry is that she closes nearly 98 percent of all offers she writes, and on average obtains a 20 to 40 percent higher selling price for her clients! Her remarkable track record proves her dedication and persistence; Michelle makes sure the job gets done the right way, the profitable way. While Michelle's numbers are impressive, it's her ability to create win-win situations for her buyers and sellers that guarantee her continued success. Michelle's mission is to always deliver more than is expected. She sees opportunity when many are discouraged and give up. Michelle does not give up; she identifies and corrects the top mistakes business owners make. Michelle will fine-tune businesses into a "well-oiled machine" with the primary objective to sell it for the ultimate value; therefore you can afford the lifestyle you have always dreamed of and most importantly deserve!

In addition, Michelle is the award-winning author of *Sell Your Business For More Than It's Worth*. This book details how to enhance the value of your business to obtain the optimal selling price.

Michelle is passionate about sharing her considerable knowledge and experience with others through her mentoring and training programs. This program has helped many individuals become successful business brokers. Michelle Seiler-Tucker is considered by her peers to be the preeminent specialist in buying and selling businesses. Her mission is and will continue to always under promise and over deliver. And those she has helped will testify to that!

Michelle is truly one of a kind!

Services offered by Michelle's office include: buying businesses, business consulting, business brokerage, business valuations, business and franchise consulting, sales, and development.

Call Michelle today for your FREE Business Evaluation:
(877) 853-4227
www.betterbusinessbrokers.com
www.sellyourbusinessformorethanitsworth.com

CHAPTER 21

THINK AND GROW HEALTHY:
An Alternative Reading of the Financial Classic

BY DANY BLANCHET

In the last five years, I've lost a lot of weight, upwards of 30 pounds, most of it within 3 months after deciding to improve my health.

My cholesterol dropped to a healthy level for the first time since my 20s, and my resting heart rate now keeps my doctor at ease – something I feel great about.

Prior to that, I was drifting, falling into hypnotic rhythm as Napoleon Hill described in "Outwitting the Devil." Only something that would scare me enough would be able to wake me up. In my case, it was shingles and arthritic pain.

There were many other undesirable health symptoms present, but ignored. They eventually disappeared with the weight and pain.

Now, I am proud to say that I haven't taken any drugs, including over the counter medication, for more than five years. What's even better is that I haven't regained any of the weight like I previously used to when engaging in unhealthy yo-yo diets.

The health concerns I faced pushed me into intense research about natural healing, which I am now confident to teach others about. We can reverse the hypnotic rhythm by shifting to a positive mindset starting with good friends, positive readings, inspiring music, and so on, while eliminating or mitigating negative influences, such as TV, radio, negative friends and co-workers. This will eventually help you fall into the positive side of hypnotic rhythm and turn your life around.

In the decades before my newfound health consciousness, I gained a lot of weight while I tried to make money to stay afloat, only to indulge in things bringing me temporary joy such as food, TV, and movies.

I would stop by a drive-thru to save time. I would grab a soda without thinking. I would work late, repeatedly skipping the gym. I kept saying, I'll eat better tomorrow, I'll be better tomorrow. It's funny how much you learn when you try to do too much.

I want to help you to become a more well-rounded, happier person. For much of my life I, like most, have strived to become better – a better businessman, a better friend, a healthier person. And for much of my life, I was very successful in many things. I've led a successful business. I have a wonderful circle of friends and a caring family. But I wasn't a success at everything.

Now, I feel much better off than when I was fighting to save every minute I could, often choosing to eat processed or junk foods and working long days over a breath of fresh air and an hour off to recharge. One thing I've learned, over and over again, is the one thing I want to communicate to you here: when you strive to do something, make *every step* with dedication and make sure it's not just a mere wish, but rather a burning desire that you will do everything you have to do to achieve it.

There are no shortcuts and no room to trim off the non-essentials. It's all essential if you want to be well-balanced. One caveat, though: don't expect it to be easy. I spent much of my life trying to do things the easy way, and that won't work when what you're working on is yourself.

To get ahead in some parts of my life, I often neglected other things. To get ahead in my business, I felt that if I pushed the non-essentials, such as exercise aside, I'd save time and, as a result, money. I even took my kids to fast food joints to save time, energy and even money.

I remember when I first began working longer hours, and bringing my work mentally home with me. I began sleeping irregularly. I'd lie awake at night. Then, in the morning, I repeated what I'd done the day before. The same unhealthy breakfast, lunch and dinner. Sometimes I ate late at night. I thought I could "power through" anything.

Well, bad habits have a tendency to catch up with you. By the time my ex-wife and our children moved out of state, I felt the years of neglect weighing me down. I was diagnosed with shingles. From my stressful work life to my poor diet and lack of exercise, I had literally made myself sick and shut down my immune system.

Of course I eventually recovered, and in my recovery I realized something about myself that I believe changed me forever. Never neglect one thing for another; never try to save time by sacrificing your health, relationships or wellbeing. You might make more money, but this plan is far from sustainable. I was going about it the wrong way. I was addicted to what felt good rather than what needed to be done.

Eventually, you'll crash.

But that's not the worst part about it. Long before you ever crash, something else starts to wear you down. See, I always looked to save time. If there were ten steps to completing something, I tried to do it in four or just something else if it was too hard or pushing me outside of my comfort zone. I thought that as long as I trimmed the non-essentials away, I'd become more efficient.

That's the wrong way to go about it.

By repeatedly throwing out the activities that used to make me a healthy person – exercise, healthy food, sunshine, sleep – I figured I had more hours in the day to focus on business. But I could do less and less with those extra hours as my energy and mental clarity dropped from ignoring my health.

I learned to take care of myself the hard way: by examining my life from bed, sick with shingles. By the time I was fully recovered, I was on a detox program and I had promised myself to never avoid the things that make me strong and healthy.

Life is all about doing things in a complete way – never cutting corners. That is the type of philosophy you need to apply to reading a masterpiece like *Think and Grow Rich*, or just being a healthier person.

Think and Grow Rich will also help you prevent drifting (like 98% of the population does to a certain degree) by keeping you focused on your goals and dreams, as well as giving you the persistence and confidence necessary to overcome distractions, negative self-talk, and naysayers surfacing in your mind.

HOW *THINK AND GROW RICH* CHANGED MY LIFE

I've read "Think and Grow Rich" over and over. I didn't get it the first time, but a few years later I read it again and it changed my life.

I had many limiting beliefs restricting the flow of financial abundance in my life, even if I always had enough for basics. I have to admit that I had to be very creative at times. Personal bankruptcy became inevitable and this book helped me overcome the negative feelings with bankruptcy and to see it as a necessary step in my life, for which I promised myself to give more than its equivalent to humanity. This really helped me find the strength and persistence to continue working toward my dreams.

I believe that this book's lessons are as applicable to one's philosophies and lifestyle as they are to financial planning, entrepreneurship, happiness and more. I read it the first time and wrote down some steps I wanted to follow. *This is it*, I told myself. I was going to follow a few tricks and finally be able to move closer to my kids the following year. Of course that's not what happened at the time.

I finally moved a few minutes away from my children last December, largely due to the increased self-confidence I acquired while applying the entire approach.

Now, I see that the only way to reap the benefits of that wonderful book is to follow its steps in the way they are meant to be followed: thoroughly and with honesty. ***No shortcuts.*** Being thorough, of course, isn't a business-only virtue. If you're thorough, you won't leave half the dishes in the sink when its time to clean the kitchen. You won't leave things undone, whether they're messes in your home or your emotional life.

Definiteness of purpose, combined with a burning desire and faith, will provide the necessary persistence to go through the challenges. Of course, the support of a mastermind group, or at least a few positive and supportive friends, mentors and/or coaches, will make your growth and results happen much faster. I have worked with several of them in the past 7 years.

You must be thorough and complete things you start, from top to bottom and from step 1 to 13. I occasionally skip a day, sometimes more, and quickly notice the difference. It is definitely worth the time.

WHY I CHOSE TO BE HEALTHIER

I never want to live in a nursing home and become a burden or lose my flame. Initially, that was one of my chief reason for becoming a healthier person after I got sick. I truly felt that's where I was heading, the same place where I have spent 19 years working as an Occupational Therapist.

Note: it wasn't because I wanted to look great on the beach. I wasn't out to get dates (even though those can be healthy too). I started and kept at it because I wanted to be vibrant throughout life and into my old age, and most importantly, be able to pursue my mission and be a source of inspiration for my children, friends, family and any human being I have the chance to come in contact with.

Most people are more motivated by avoiding painful experiences rather than taking the necessary risks to improve oneself and become happier and successful. I finally realized that being healthy now is crucial to living the life that I really want. All the wealth and success cannot be fully appreciated without good health.

The more reasons (whys) you have and the more emotionally charged they are, the better equipped you are to stay focused and motivated. I recommend you make sure they are worded in a positive manner and in the present tense – "I AM healthy", "I AM at my ideal weight," or "I AM better and better every day" rather than just, "I want to lose weight." Then just add the emotionally-charged portion such as: … so that I can fully enjoy my grandkids, travel around the world … and fulfill my mission so that I have made a difference without any regrets when my time is up.

I attribute reasons to results. And my reasons were reasons enough for me to eliminate the weight, and be healthy of mind and body.

People often think that wanting something is enough to keep their spirits up through the challenges along the way. That's simply untrue. As the book says, you need to be clear on what you want and why you want it, because if it's worth getting, it will test your persistence and ability to take meaningful action.

Nothing worth gaining was ever gained without effort.

~ Teddy Roosevelt.

A healthy, well-balanced lifestyle definitely doesn't come easy to anyone used to a life of junk food and convenience. Time is the key to positive changes. As it took a lot of time and negative behaviors to move my health and finances into a negative rhythm, reversing it also takes time.

Think about health as a lifestyle and seek progressive changes, not something that you focus on once in a while when you don't feel good or don't like what you see in the mirror. That's what diets are, and that's why people spend so much time, money and energy on them, while experiencing frustrations and decreased self-esteem by failing every time to keep the weight off.

One product taken for one month or even every day for the rest of your life will not keep you healthy forever!!! Health is a result of many components including the most important - the mind. And that's why *Think and Grow Rich* applied to your health can do wonders. Our mind is responsible for most stress in our lives, and negative stress is the most damaging element for the body, affecting our hormones, immune system and so many other elements.

Simply wanting to look good with your shirt off will give you more confidence, but probably won't be enough to see you through the temptations and other triggers potentially sabotaging your efforts. One good decision leads to another, and the same can be said for bad decisions. If you don't have this 'burning desire' beyond looking better at the beach, these disempowering choices will drown your motivation eventually.

Similarly, everyone wants more money. But why? Imagining a stack of cash won't get you up early every morning or keep you away from the Internet or the TV rather than spending time developing and following a life changing plan of action. A plan for the future, including more freedom of doing what you want, when you want, with whom you want, however, will.

So set goals, visualize yourself meeting the goals, believe it can be done, and take actions no matter how small – in the right direction. Don't worry so much about the plan. Focus on the goal; the real emotionally-charged reasons why you want to achieve it. Connect to Infinite Intelligence and trust that the specialized knowledge and resources needed to help you improve your life will show up when you need them.

A mere wish is never enough.

I want to help people find the subconscious and conscious affirmations that will keep them going when times get hard. I want to help you become persistent. Persistence is crucial to push through obstacles, as I'm sure you know. But it's also one of the hardest things to do, day in and day out.

But it's made easier with a goal – a reason for being, for growing into the person you need to be to do what is necessary to have the life you deserve.

KEYS TO THINKING YOURSELF TO HEALTH

Developing a healthy body really starts in your mind. You want to be toned, healthy and vibrant? Don't we all. But unless you make it a priority and develop persistence, you are highly unlikely to get there, and even less likely to remain at your ideal state of health. Remember, *Think and Grow Rich* is about a burning desire, and I want everyone to have that. Once you learn it, you can apply it to any areas of your life: health, wealth, happiness, and relationships. But if you have a desire to be better, which I'm sure you do, aim it at something worth fighting for and your chances will double – I promise.

Having a sincere intention to give back, as recommended in the book, will multiply your odds of getting what you want. As Zig Ziglar said, "You can have everything in life if you will help other people get what they want." He is also the one who said that as bathing doesn't last forever, same goes for motivation, that's why it is recommended daily. Following the steps will give you that daily dose of motivation, confidence and focus.

Most of us are looking for quick fixes. They may exist, but will just not last and many can actually harm you and your family. And when you realize that, you better really want what you're trying to get because it won't be easy. There will be hard times, and you'll be tried by your inner demons, but if you come from a place of true desire for improvement, one step in the right direction will lead to another, and another.

One thing the book reminds us of is that if we try one thing that scares us, the next step won't be as scary. Put those fears in their place! Identify them as they are your greatest teachers, and realize that most of them are just self-created in your mind. I strongly suggest you read *Outwitting the Devil* as a complement to *Think and Grow Rich* to get clear on the concept of drifting, time and hypnotic rhythm. That book will help melt away any remaining fears you might have.

I know it's hard, but I've been through it and I can tell you: the other side is very sweet. I've learned such a great deal from this book that it's now as pleasurable to talk about it as it is to use what I have learned. I've built my business around its tenets and I live to help others approach their better, more fulfilling life with a promise of better things to come.

Nothing that's worth it is ever easily obtained, but if you take the time to do your work and live your life with respect to yourself and your loved ones, you'll make it to where you so desperately want to be.

I will leave you with Mr. Hill's hallmark quote:

"What the mind of man can conceive and believe, it can achieve."

About Dany Blanchet

Dany Blanchet struggled with health, relationship and finances into his mid-thirties.

Through self-awareness, study and dedication, he has
created a purposeful life filled with joy and happiness
simply by focusing on acquiring a more positive mindset, thus eliminating
most sources of internal pain and suffering.

To share these gifts, Dany founded the Abundance Health and Happiness
Academy (AHHA), a company with a mission to inspire people to take charge
of their own lives and obtain optimal health, abundance and happiness, using an approach strongly influenced by the principles taught in *Think and
Grow Rich* and *Outwitting the Devil,* both by Napoleon Hill, a pioneer in personal development and creator of the Philosophy of Achievement.

Dany has worked and studied with top people in each area of natural health
and personal development. He is certified as a Happiness Generator and
Love Ambassador by International best-selling author Marci Shimoff. He also
worked as an Occupational Therapist for over 19 years, mostly in long-term
care and hospitals.

He likes golf, yoga, hockey, football, and mostly spending time with his two
children, friends and family.

To learn more about Dany and how you can receive a Free Training Video and
report, visit: www.YourAHHA.com or email: dany@yourahha.com.

CHAPTER 22

A COLLEGE EDUCATION – A DEFINITENESS OF PURPOSE

BY DAVE SMITH

Napoleon Hill's Principal One – Definiteness of purpose is the starting point of all achievement.

One would have to agree that getting a relevant college education is a worthy achievement. Getting that college degree without going into debt makes it an even greater achievement. In order to achieve that, one has to have a definiteness of purpose. How does one make that happen in a time when:

Average Cost of Attendance (COA)   – $40,000+
Average Time to Graduate (Undergrad) – 5.8 years
Average Cost—Undergrad Degree   – $232,000
Average Student Loan Debt approx.   – $ 30,000+

THE S-A-F-E WAY

We have developed a process that helps parents and their children, working in concert to obtain the best, most relevant education possible with the minimum out of pocket expense as possible. By following our guide to Selection, Acceptance, Funding, and Execution you will be well on your way to obtaining the relevant education necessary to be successful in today's world.

I. SELECTION

The first critical step is to align your student's unique talents and abilities with an elite, selective, or competitive school that will offer attractive admissions and financial aid packages. There are approximately 2,000 non-profit institutions in the U.S. College and University system. There is a specific breakdown of how schools are ranked. Schools such as Stanford, Harvard, MIT, Duke, Vanderbilt, Yale, and Pomona are some of the 50 "Elite" schools. Next are "Selective" schools made up of roughly 150 institutions including USC, Cal, UCLA, Santa Clara, Cal Tech, and Pitzer. The third category is made up of approximately 250 "Competitive" colleges such as Pepperdine, USD, Occidental, LMU and UC Davis. The remaining 1,750 are basic, standard colleges such as state schools and universities.

The sheer number of students following the herd mentality of attending state and local colleges reduces the amount of merit based and academic awards available there. Elite, Selective, and Competitive colleges typically perceived as too expensive or exclusive have ample means of discounting their tuition for those students deemed as desirable. Merit-based aid has no income requirement or limitations; it's the school's subjective decision. The more valuable your student is to them, the more they will discount their services in order to secure their attendance.

Selecting the right college requires a thorough analysis of multiple factors that are unique to your student's career objectives and lifestyle. Using their time in high school to develop interests and to make connections to a possible career path is one of the most effective ways for your student to fine-tune their decision-making process. Rather than arbitrarily deciding to be a doctor or a lawyer, this process helps them gain a better perspective of what they are truly interested in. It allows them to gain an understanding of what their career path entails and the options that are available within it.

No other decision has such lasting academic and financial impact as the choice of the college your student attends. Most families use emotional criteria such as a school's proximity to home, school reputation or even the best football team in order pick a school and just assume that the student will fit in. They are not aware that there are schools out there that will be a good fit based on class size, major offerings, environment, and overall attitude.

Here is a quick review of what needs to happen before your student begins to fill out an application form:

- Set the expectation – In families where college is an expectation from an early age, students rise to the challenge and select colleges, majors, and careers and usually finish college in four years.

- Fit, Fit, Fit – An education that fits your student's goals, aspirations, talents, and personality is priceless. This leads to happiness, contentment, higher productivity, and eventually to just the right career. Keep your eyes open for the clues.

- "Why" is more important than "How" – Your student needs to answer; Why am I going to college; why should I put forth the effort; why is it important? This helps provide the motivation necessary for a successful college experience.

- Utilize all of the available tools – Science-based selection programs, Internet searches, volunteer activities, and job shadowing. Thorough preparation helps guarantee success.

II. ACCEPTANCE

Although the institution makes the final decision regarding acceptance or rejection of the admission applications, knowing and then utilizing some of the selection criteria can put your student at the top of the list.

Let's change the paradigm. It's vital to replace the common mindset of "How can my student compete?" with "Which colleges are willing to compete for my student?"

While a central part of the admission process is to know which colleges your student prefers, you can take it a step further and apply to colleges of equal quality that compete for the same students. Research can uncover these "unknown" colleges that will provide award letters that your student can use as leverage. Test scores and GPAs are just starting points or the common denominator among applicants. Tagging, legacies, and demonstrable interest play an important role in the acceptance process.

Tagging

A "Tag" is a positive mark added to a student's admissions application that indicates that he or she is of special interest to the college. Children of alumni get tags known as "legacies," the size of the tag or size of their advantage is usually measured by the depth of the parent's generosity to the school. Students with special talents also get tagged. Students with outstanding academic qualities, athletic qualities, or musically/artistically-inclined students are of special interest to the colleges.

Your student's intended school may need three tuba players for the marching band and have a glut of saxophone players. This may not help your saxophone-playing student, but be aware that sometimes it's enough of an advantage to help them get in at competing, equally attractive institutions. Having more than one school choice gives your student an edge because the other school just may need another saxophone player.

Under-represented minorities, sexes, and students from under-represented states receive tags. Based on federal funding requirements your student may receive a tag if they are from a certain state, female, male, etc.

Once an application is tagged, the individual is removed from the common pool of applicants and moved to an entirely new level for special consideration. An applicant that normally may not have been looked at twice may find that being tagged opens many doors. It's vitally important to know in advance which colleges give extra attention to specific tags.

Packaging

Imagine looking out over a cornfield. There are thousands of stalks of corn all planted in neat, evenly spaced rows. Now imagine that several of these stalks are three feet taller than the rest. Help your student stand out like those taller stalks amid all of the remaining freshman applicants and you make it easier for the admissions officer to find them.

College is big business loaded with rules and procedures geared to help fill their classrooms with students that have a high probability of success. The key to making your student one of the desirable ones is by promoting their value to each school. Make it obvious to the school that your child is the one that they have been looking for.

You must "Package & Position" your student based on the College Acceptance Profile (CAP) that is unique to each school. The students with the highest CAP scores are most attractive to colleges and are eligible for the best financial aid packages. These students receive more grants and free money versus them having to obtain student loans and participate in work-study programs.

The CAP criteria used by selective and elite institutions includes:

- Awards – National, Regional, State, County, and School
- Academics – Standard Test Scores
- Activities – School and Outside (Leadership is important)
- Community Service – Volunteerism, Helping Others
- Character Traits – Teacher/Counselor Ratings

Admissions committees rely on CAP to objectively review each applicant and then compare them to the established selection criteria for the school. In a survey by the National Association of College Admission Counselors, 54% of the colleges that responded said that they use preferential packaging.

III. FUNDING

Financial aid can be made up of these sources:

- Need-Based
- Merit-Based
- Scholarships
- Endowments

College costs money…whether it's your money, the government's money, or the school's money depends on smart strategy and a winning formula. Since the goal is for your student to attend a great school without student loans, the first step is to understand Need-Based Financial Aid. Applying for Need-Based aid is essential even if you don't think that you're eligible because many schools won't even consider your student for "non-need" based aid if you don't apply. This is done through the Free Application for Federal Student Aid (FAFSA) which is available online at: www.fafsa.ed.gov.

The Higher Education Act of 1965 states that it is the parents' responsibility to educate their children beyond the 12th grade. The law states that if a family can demonstrate "Need" the government will assist in paying for the education. The good news is "Need" is not subjective but is based on a formula and you can estimate your contribution much easier by understanding the calculation.

The financial aid administrator at each school develops the average Cost of Attendance (COA) for all categories of students. The COA = Tuition & Fees + Room & Books + Transportation + Miscellaneous Expenses. The law also provides limited allowances for computer expenses, dependent care, and expenses for handicapped students. The COA can vary for each student at the same school but students in the same situation must have the same COA.

The next part of the formula is the Expected Family Contribution (EFC), which is the amount you as a family are expected to contribute toward your student's education expenses, and is recalculated each academic year during the FAFSA process.

After subtracting your EFC from the college's COA, the remainder is need. Your EFC is the same at every college, but your need at each college will vary according to the college's COA. If your EFC is $10,000 and the COA at college A is $13,000 and college B, which happens to be an elite school is $43,000 it may make perfect sense to choose college B. FAFSA is just the first step of the funding process however.

Once your student has filed the FAFSA, you are able to explore various financial aid opportunities that can make the difference between affording your student's first choice school and having to settle for less. It has been estimated that an excess of $60 billion is available every year that goes untouched by students.

In many cases parents assume that Scholarships, monies distributed by entities such as civic organizations or corporations, are the key to making up the difference for them financially. These funds are paid directly to the student to offset the cost of college, but they represent less than three percent of the total money available for education. A college plan that counts on scholarships to pay the majority of costs is an ill-fated strategy that will have disastrous results for most families.

Merit-Based aid is an incentive to attract students considered valuable to the institution in the "subjective" areas of academics, arts, athletics, or outside activities. Merit awards are distributed by the Admissions Office of each school in the form of distributional discounts and loans subsidized by endowment funds. Colleges control over $150 billion in endowment funds, the 2nd largest pool of money behind Federal Aid, meaning they are choosing who gets this money. Properly positioning and demonstrating the value of your student is not just a good idea, but imperative if you want to make college affordable today.

Generally private schools exhibit the highest COA and many families eliminate them believing that they cannot afford the high expense. While this thinking seems reasonable, it is faulty thinking. Private institutions have the largest endowment funds available and therefore offer the largest awards to students that meet or exceed the school's criteria.

Accessing this additional money at selective and elite schools may require more effort, but is certainly worth it. The keys to properly position your student includes them (a) having achieved strong scores on the SAT or ACT, (b) maintaining contact with the Department Chairman at their selected schools, and (c) demonstrating their direction and focus along with the other qualities potential schools are searching for.

IV. EXECUTION

Now that you have an inside look at how desirable schools will compete for your student, it's time to use that information to your student's best advantage. It's time to implement the plan that hopefully has been in place since your student's sophomore year in high school.

Applying early is a form of demonstrable interest and typically results in a favorable review from admissions. It is a great strategy and can be used as leverage against other schools with attractive offers. In essence, the longer your student waits to apply, the fiercer the competition becomes for the remaining seats. With an admissions process that is both objective and subjective in a highly competitive environment, the odds of success increase dramatically as your student ferrets out the ideal fit from the good fits that we discussed in the Selection section.

Working ahead of schedule allows your student time to fine tune the applications and get valuable unhurried input from counselors or professionals. Requesting high school transcripts, letters of recommendation, and SAT/ACT scores all take time to coordinate. Exceeding deadlines can work wonders in getting a school's attention and it also takes the last minute pressure off you and your student.

Timeline:

- Freshman & Sophomore Year – Focus on SAT/ACT preparation and fine tune career interests.

- Junior Year – Continue preparation for SAT/ACT. Participate in volunteer and extracurricular activities that will strengthen their overall profile.

  o January through May – Refine list of schools to apply to and ensure a good fit.

  o Summer – Obtain requirements plus all admission applications and begin to complete them and work on the required essays.

- Senior Year – Continue participation in volunteer and extracurricular activities.

  o September – Fine tune applications and request letters of recommendation from teachers, counselors, coaches, and mentors.

  o October – Submit applications and begin applications for financial aid.

  o November and December – Contact potential schools and arrange for personal visits and interviews.

  o January – Submit the FAFSA and CSS profile.

  o February and March – Follow up with potential schools and schedule personal visits with additional schools if desired.

  o March – Acceptance/Waiting List/Denial letters will start arriving.

  o April – Student Aid Report (SAR) awards and offers of acceptance from individual schools will begin to arrive. Review each SAR for accuracy and notify the school's department of admission prior to end of month.

  o May – Commit to the school of choice.

Through the S-A-F-E process you and your student will exercise due diligence, carefully consider what constitutes a good fit, apply with confidence, and then have the opportunity to choose between attractive offers made by your collection of ideal schools.

Getting the right education is not merely a four-year decision, but a decision that will help guarantee a lifetime of success!

For more information and to let us know how helpful this information has been please visit us and give us your feedback at: www.safe-steps.com

ABOUT DAVE

D.A. "Dave" Smith has been tagged by his clients as "The College Strategist" – a moniker he is very proud of earning by helping students attend the best colleges in the USA. Additionally, his proprietary process saves an average of $21,783 annually for the parents of undergraduates. Proving this fact by working with over 500 families, he has saved his clients over $53 million in the last four years. All the students graduated without any student debt in five years or less.

A resident of San Diego, California, he has established himself as a subject matter expert for college-related topics, and can be regularly seen on the most watched television show in the county, "Good Morning San Diego" – KUSI TV channel 51. He provides 5-6 educational workshops per month to educate the community on the always-changing landscape for higher education.

Dave's expertise comes from his research and then application of the insights college administrators gave him as he sought the answers that would allow a student to attend college, receive a Bachelor's degree, and move on to a career without the burden of being in debt. He is neither an educator nor a parent, just a son striving to fulfill his commitment to his mother who passed away from the complications of breast cancer. His motivation is from the great saying by Zig Ziglar, "You will get everything you want out of life, IF you help enough people get what they want."

Today he is documenting his successes and expanding the scope of his message to families across the United States. Dave does not believe that the $1 trillion student loan bubble should exist, and he is standing up and educating families about the educational opportunities available today and seldom used by college bound students.

He is proud of each family that works with him, because he is changing lives one family at a time. Please review the video testimonials by families touched by Dave and his team at: www.safe-steps.com.

CHAPTER 23

IMMIGRANT TO MILLIONAIRE – A JOURNEY OF SEVEN STEPS

BY EVAN KLASSEN

If you could interview the 1,000 most successful people in the world, you would probably find out that nearly all of them had one thing in common that made them that way. Deep within, they had an impelling *reason* for doing what they did that led them to riches, fame or satisfaction in life. I call it their *"desperate why."*

It's the same driving force that will, for example, make a father display what amounts to miraculous strength that he doesn't possess under normal circumstances to lift the bumper of a 4,000-pound car to free his trapped child. It is the ingredient of the soul that drives you to go far beyond your comfort zone to accomplish a task. It is what gives you the courage to pick yourself up once you have fallen down and get back into the race.

For many of us, our *"desperate why"* begins forming early on in our lives. I was born in 1984 in Dushanbe, Tajikistan, the son of a German father and a Ukrainian mother, and one of nine children, all of whom my father supported by keeping bees. We were happy and our family was getting by until the early 1990s when civil war broke out. Food became scarce. On some days, army trucks would roll into town carrying bread. Lines would form and soldiers with machine guns were forced to fire in the air to control the crowd. Some were even trampled to death. It was not a pleasant time for an eight-year-old boy who only wanted to play and go to school.

When the fighting intensified in 1992, my father began making plans for our escape. He risked his life to drive into the country-side in search of clean water. Upon his return he recounted hearing gunshots. We drank appreciatively and bathed sparingly. He filled out the necessary paperwork to move us back to Germany A trip over land was impossible, as the borders were dangerous. After selling all we owned, we had just enough for airfare.

Modern West Germany was a paradise compared to Tajikistan. The day after our plane touched down in the free world, my father, who had only $120 in his pocket and a family of nine to support, bought me a chocolate bar. I carefully carved thin slices from the bar and ate them with bread so as to prolong the experience. It was not easy for us to assimilate into our new surroundings. We slept on cots in a large warehouse with public bathrooms. Thanks to the generosity of others and by the grace of God, we had food, shelter and clothing... and little else. But it was enough. I would never again take such basic things for granted.

An electrical engineer by trade, my father soon found work and we moved into a small house in Minden, Germany. By the time I was 11, I was itching to get a job. I figured since my age was now two digits and not one, that I was adult enough to join the workforce. I learned of a large publishing firm that sold maga-zines and paid to have them delivered. I owned a bicycle. I could ride like the wind. But my heart sank when I discovered that I was considered two years too young for the job. My *"desperate why"* pushed me forward. My sister was 13. She could get the job and I could do the work. Filling my saddlebags with magazines, I set out to find the subscribers, riding for miles until the job was done. Earning money was a thrill. I arose at 6:00 a.m. every morning and rode my bike three miles to school. While the other kids stood in line for the slow school buses to take them home after classes, I was on my bike and halfway to work. I even asked for extra work and got it. I was soon earning extra money placing the magazines into packages. Then I was performing all three tasks associated with my job. I had taken on a second route. It was not unusual for me to arrive home at 11:30 p.m., get up the next morning at 6:00 a.m. to do my homework and leave for school. There I was, at the tender age of 13, earning almost as much as a grown man.

When I was 14, I learned that my 16-year-old cousin was working at a chair factory assembling arms for $10 an hour. I did the math and applied for the job. "You must be 16 to work here," said the boss. "Just let me do it one day and you will see. I will be the best assembler ever," I convinced him. It worked again. My *"desperate why"* was my secret weapon. By the time I was 20, I was burning the candle at both ends and would have lit a third end if there had been one. But my life wasn't balanced, and this eventually took its toll.

For no reason that was clear to me at the time, I experienced a period of depression. I even contemplated taking my own life. List any negative emotion you like and I felt it. The flame of my *"desperate why"* wasn't extinguished, but it was flickering. Yet what seemed like a curse actually turned into a blessing. Although it lasted only 90 days, my fight with depression created a hunger within me to live up to an unrealized potential that I knew lay-within me.

I traveled to America to visit friends, and as is often the case, when one door closed for me, another door opened. At the age of 21, I met a beautiful girl named Ella who, down the road, I ended up marrying and that changed my life immeasurably. Three months after my visit, I was on a plane headed back to America, this time for good. Just before I left Germany, I had the good fortune of attending a business meeting where a friend gave me a copy of a book entitled, *Think and Grow Rich* by Napoleon Hill. The title struck me immediately. Only six months earlier, I had been thinking of ending what I perceived to be a worthless life, but the clear message of the book lifted me like the wings of an eagle. My *"desperate why"* was reignited and propelled me toward what I knew would be great things.

America is the land of opportunity. I could stand on a street corner in Portland, Oregon and feel the surging, electrical current of this exciting country. In Germany, I had a taste of entrepreneurship and I vowed I would never work for anyone else again. I went to school to polish up my English and I studied for my real estate license. It was 2007, which, according to the "experts," was the worst year possible, to have entered the real estate business. The housing bubble had burst, the stock markets crashed, the banks tightened up their lending policies, and people who had been in the real estate business for 20 years were leaving the industry. After six months, I had still not made a dime but my resolve to succeed was intact. Following the suggestions of personal development coaches, I wrote myself a check for $100,000, posted it on the refrigerator, and gave myself a year to make it good.

I was still full of hope, even as I was borrowing money to pay the bills. I was behind the wheel of the two-year-old Toyota my wife had received as a wedding present from her parents, driving around Portland, looking for "for sale by owner" signs in the rain when a car stopped suddenly in front of me. The ensuing collision left the car crumpled, but drivable, and my *"desperate why"* kept me pressing forward. I was convinced that my first listing was on its way. On my last try for the day, having parked my car around the corner so they wouldn't see it, I met a couple who, like me, spoke Russian. In my best Russian, I told them that I would fight for the sale of their house with all my being… and I meant it. It was an interesting time in the real estate business. I learned to do short sales. I learned how to work with banks. My timing was awful, some said. But I had been turning lemons into lemonade all my life. This was nothing new. Soon, I had so many listings that I had to hire two other realtors to handle the workload. At a time when others were leaving the business, I had built my enterprise in 4.5 years to over $22 million in sales. Oh yes! The check I had written myself for $100,000 and had given myself a year to make it happen? My first year, I earned exactly $102,000.

In 2008, I was re-introduced to the profession of network marketing. While I was still operating my real estate business, I built an organization of 14,000 people in 18 months. I found that I loved relationship-building and helping people improve their lives. In 2011, I decided to leave real estate and pursue my dream of building entrepreneurs all over the world through personal development. Between two separate companies, over a period of three and a half years, I was able to build two organizations with a combined 20,000 customers and distributors in 23 countries with total sales of over $10 million. From 2007 to 2012, I achieved my personal goal of earning $1 million as an entrepreneur. That's my "first million" and I look forward to many more. My latest project is a new TV show, *Immigrant-2millionaire,* which showcases the lives of others who have discovered the keys to massive success and who went from being nowhere to millionaires.

In the book *Think and Grow Rich,* by Napoleon Hill, there are 14 principles expressed that changed my life. Distilled from my life experience, I offer you these seven keys to success that reflect those original 14 principles:

Key # 1. Possess a Hunger Fueled by Your "Desperate Why" - This is the engine that powers the soul. Without that burning desire to accomplish a meaningful objective, we become commonplace in the world.

Key #2. Have Clear, Written Goals - Make them so real that you can see yourself reaching them. Make sure that your goals are (1) Specific (2) Attainable (3) Measurable, and (4) Time-Specific. Goals give your subconscious mind something to aim for. Make certain your goals challenge you to grow.

Key #3. Commitment - You must be committed to your goals and decisions. There is a great saying that goes "There's a difference between interest and commitment. When you're interested in doing something, you do it only when circumstances permit. When you're committed to something, you accept no excuses, only results." You know when a person is committed. They don't have to tell you. You know that they will either accomplish a goal or die trying. I was in a seminar with 17,000 people and Daren Hardy the speaker asked the crowd if anybody was ever bitten by an elephant. No hands went up. He then asked if anyone had ever been bitten by a mosquito. Every hand went up. "In life," he said, "it's the little things that come and bite you." It's important to make a big commitment to the little things and practice that disciple daily. This will allow you be great in the big things in life. Most people give up right before they achieve greatness just because the going got tough.

Key # 4. Attitude - I have traveled to 20 countries and lived on three continents and met tens of thousands of people both rich and poor, healthy and sick, at peace and at war, and I have come to the conclusion that *attitude* is the most important factor in a happy and fulfilled life. What happens to you will only determine 10% of your outcome. What happens *in* you, on the other hand, will determine 90% of your outcome. Too many people hold on to negative experiences in their life. If you can't change the past, please let go of it.

Key # 5. Unwavering Belief - The world will move aside for someone who knows where he or she is going and has no doubt at all that his or her destination will be realized. Youth is no obstacle. William Wallace was in his early 20s when he challenged the most powerful country in the world and chased them out of his back yard with some stick-wielding, angry Scotsmen. Create a cause for your life that you believe in wholeheartedly and never give up, regardless of any obstacles that may be in your way.

Key #6. Take Massive, Consistent Action - Once you have identified your *"desperate why,"* set your goals, build your belief powered by a great attitude and made a commitment, you have set your foundation. Now build a high-rise on it. Start doing something immediately toward your goals and keep doing it. Many people set themselves up for great success but, like a rocket left on the launching pad, they never take off. They create an illusion of success but they never experience the new heights of which they are capable. They go through life dreaming that they are flying when they are, in reality, still on the ground. Know that 20% of your activity will produce 80% of your results. Find out what that activity is and direct 80% of your energy to it. Simple, consistent discipline, compounded over time, will produce massive results. If you feel like giving up, simply go back to your *"desperate why"* and recharge your battery.

Key # 7. Personal Growth - Personal Development will allow you to tap into the human capital you possess that will allow you to build anything in life that you want. Jim Rohm said it best: "You've got to work harder on yourself than on your business." Personal growth has made a significant impact on my life. Over a period of six years I have invested over $100,000 into personal growth. For every dollar you invest into personal de-velopment you will get $100 back. Make a conscious commitment to lifelong learning. Massive action will get your rocket ship off the ground. Your *"desperate why"* will be the fuel to keep you going. Personal development will be the navigation that will guide you. Abraham Lin-coln said, "Give me 6 hours to chop down a tree, and I will spend the first 4 sharpening my axe." Committing to

daily growth can be the best decision to empower you to
live life to the fullest.

About Evan

Evan Klassen is an author, speaker, and entrepreneur whose "rags-to-riches" story, from extreme poverty in war-torn Central Asia to becoming an American entrepreneur, inspires all who meet him. You might have also seen Evan as host of the TV show "Immigrant 2 Millionaire," which was created to bring to light incredible stories of success. Currently, Evan is leading the creation of a revolutionary organization with the purpose of inspiring people to grow and reach their maximum potential in life through entrepreneurship and personal development.

Evan was born in the mid 1980s in a life of war and poverty where having food and clean water was considered a "good day." Being one of nine children in a blue-collar working family taught him to work hard for everything in life. After moving to Germany as a child, Evan began working for himself at age 11 and began developing his skills in entrepreneurship and music. At age 21, he was introduced to personal growth. To date, Evan has invested well over $100K into books, seminars, events, audio trainings and personal coaching. He believes that the best investment you can make is an investment in yourself.

In 2006, he moved to the United States where a year later he started a real estate business. Through many struggles and persistence he grew his business from 0 to over $22 million in revenue in a period of 4.5 years. His passion for music and business gave Evan the opportunity to travel to over 20 different countries and has allowed him to touch tens of thousands of lives. His excitement and love for people brought him back into the network marketing profession in mid 2008. Since then he has built two sales organizations with over 20,000 customers and distributors in 23 countries, and over $10 million in revenue, as well as a combined income, as an Entrepreneur between 2007 - 2012, in excess of 1 million dollars.

Evan Klassen is a true star in the field of personal development, having battled with depression and suicide at one point, and coming out victorious to share his story of failure and success to inspire people all over the world. Evan gives glory to his creator for all of his achievements.

Click the link below to stay tuned and get instant access to FREE Training and a Special Gift.

→ Click here: www.EvanKlassen.com
Follow Evan at: Facebook.com/EvanKlassenVIP
twitter.com/EvanKlassenVIP
4 his TV Show go2: www.Immigrant2Millionaire.com
ONE STOP Connect go2: www.ConnectWithEvan.com

Special Acknowledgement from Evan Klassen:

My beautiful girl Ella Klassen, my Parents Johann and Tanya Klassen, my brother Sergej Klassen, my Mentors:
John C Maxwell, Anthony Robbins, Ryan Blair, Blake Mallen, Tanis MacDonald & Lorn Humany, Darren Hardy, Luba Winter, rt Jonak, Sven Goebel, Nick Sarnicola, Ted Nuyten, Eric Worre, Troy Dooly, Josephine Gross, The Amazing Production Team at CelebrityPress™ and many others who have inspired me to grow.

I love and appreciate you all. It's a great life.

CHAPTER 24

HOW TO HAVE FINANCIAL FREEDOM DURING RETIREMENT

BY TAD HILL

Hi, my name is Tad Hill and I'm a Chartered Retirement Planning Counselor. Now, that means a lot of things in terms of what I help my clients accomplish, but the focus of this discussion is going to be on how to have financial freedom. This isn't a new topic, by any means. I'm sure you've read or heard a thing or two on this before. My desire is to bring a fresh perspective to the topic and hopefully have you gain an insight or two that will really make a difference in your life financially. You may have noticed that I said "an insight or two that will really make a difference," NOT "Give you the silver bullet that with little or no effort will make all of your dreams come true!" You see, I consider myself to be a lifelong learner, and one of the things I've learned is that if something really matters, it takes focus and effort to master it. My hope is that by reading this chapter you will have a good blueprint on how to do that for yourself as it relates to having financial freedom. But before I dive into the specific steps that I believe are critical to accomplishing this goal that seems to be so elusive for people, I'd like to tell you a story. I call this story ……..

A TALE OF TWO WIDOWS

This is a true story where only the names have been changed. I live in Birmingham, Alabama, and as a Chartered Retirement Planning Counselor I have the opportunity to meet with dozens of people every year who would like me to help them protect their retirement from the risks that can cause their golden years to go from fulfilling to frightening. Depending on the circumstances, and whether I think that we are a fit, some of them I will take on as clients, and some I won't. In either case, before coming to see me, most folks have seen my television show, have been referred by an existing client, or have listened to one of my radio shows – all of which are designed to educate them on what these risks are and how to eliminate or at least reduce them.

This was the case with Mary Sue and Barbara. Both of them were callers to my radio show and asked to meet with me – to see if I could help them create a plan to protect their retirement years from the aforementioned risks. They are both widows and, prior to the deaths of their husbands, neither of them had much direct involvement with managing the family finances. But the similarities stopped there. You see, Mary Sue and Barbara are in VERY different positions financially. Their situations differ both from a dollars-and-cents standpoint, as well as a mental and emotional standpoint. Barbara has well over $2 million in savings and investments, lives in a paid for 5,000 square foot house in the nicest area of town, and drives a Mercedes. Mary Sue, on the other hand, has a little less than $500,000 in savings, still owes some on her home, and drives a 10-year old Ford. Now let me ask you. Which person would you prefer to be? Before you answer, let's dig a little deeper.

Upon first meeting these two women, I realized that Barbara is absolutely terrified about her situation, while Mary Sue exudes an aura of contentment like that of a Tibetan monk (not that I know any Tibetan monks, but in my imagination they would act a lot like Mary Sue!). This illustrates what I've consistently found to be true. How much money you have has very little to do with your sense of security. In my experience, a sense of security comes from feeling that you have control of your circumstances, OR the belief that the person in control of your financial affairs is trustworthy, competent and has your best interests at heart. You see, Barbara had previously refused to learn anything about financial matters. In fact, she was intimidated by the topic and wasn't encouraged to do so by her late husband, or her parents before him, to think otherwise. Worse than that, she felt like she was all alone with this huge burden on her shoulders, and no idea how to carry it. Mary Sue on the other hand, while never directly managing the family finances, was taught at an early age to pay attention to her money. She had always been aware of her finances and the decisions they involved. But even those things aren't the difference maker here. The big difference is that Mary Sue doesn't feel like she is alone.

At the risk of being politically incorrect, I'm going to tell you the most common difference between the people with whom I meet that are worried and anxious, and the people like Mary Sue, who are calm and secure. Mary Sue has a deep and abiding faith in the Lord. She knows that the person in control is trustworthy, competent and has her best interest at heart. I've watched this play out over and over again. No amount of money is going to give you security, but having true and lasting faith will. Now does that mean that Mary Sue doesn't want to be a good steward of what she's been given, and to have a plan for doing that? Absolutely not! And that's where good retirement planning comes in. So let's continue examining their situations.

Barbara's husband had chosen a 0% spousal benefit on his pension because it paid more while he was living. He felt that Barbara wouldn't need as much if he wasn't around. She also lost one of their Social Security payments at his death. Added together, this reduced her income by over 75%. She has an adult daughter with two children who is divorced, and Barbara and her husband have been helping the daughter financially for quite some time. As I got to know Barbara better, I found out that she was poor growing up. The attitude she had picked up from her parents was that if they only had "more" they would be happy. They believed that what was creating the unhappiness in their home was a lack of financial resources. Her earliest memories were focused on a lack of material possessions. As a result, when she began to get some money, she used it to buy "happiness," thus creating a lifelong habit of overspending.

When we analyzed her income plan it became clear that in order to sustain her current lifestyle we were going to need to withdraw almost 6% of her savings every year. This is a very risky withdrawal rate. In contrast, Mary Sue has a pension from being a teacher, which, when combined with her Social Security , gives her $1,000 a month more than what she spends. What she learned from her parents was to be grateful for everything they had and to treat money with respect. While she too was poor growing up, her earliest memories were of her parents putting money aside every month for savings. She picked up from them that happiness doesn't come from "stuff." She learned that money is important; we need it to live on. But it should not be the focus of our lives. Therefore, her spending habits reflect this. She enjoys her life and spends money on what she needs and wants, but lives below her means.

The good news is that with the proper retirement planning process, we have been able to create a sustainable retirement plan for Barbara that enables her to feel more in control. For Mary Sue, we've designed a strategy to grow her money conservatively while still protecting her life savings from excessive risk. We also have a plan to maximize what she will leave to her three children. This is very important to her. The moral of the story is this: Financial Freedom is created as much by your state of mind and what you believe in as it is your net worth, and EVERY person's situation is different. You can't just look at the surface and expect to make good retirement planning and investment decisions. You must have a process designed to help you dig deep and make the best decisions possible, which leads me to......

THE 4 KEYS TO CREATING FINANCIAL FREEDOM IN YOUR LIFE

Key #1- Learn to dwell on all of the things you are grateful for

I have found that people that have an "attitude of gratitude" are not only more happy and fulfilled, but have more financial abundance in their life. While these two things may not seem related, I can tell you that the empirical evidence I see everyday links them inextricably. I need to explain that what I mean by financial abundance isn't necessarily about how much money or "stuff" someone has. One thing you learn very quickly in the discipline of retirement planning is that financial abundance means that you have more coming in than you have going out every year. It's not about your net worth, it's about positive cash flow. I define retirement as "20-30 years of unemployment." So the most important thing during this time in your life is to replace your paycheck in a predictable way. That equation is all about sustainable cash flow and those individuals who focus on what they are grateful for and who have many traits that impact this.

For one, if you are focused on what you do have instead of what you don't, you are less likely to overspend. This is huge. The contrast between Barbara and Mary Sue is a perfect example of this dynamic. Mary Sue has significantly less money than Barbara, but is in a much more secure position in terms of sustaining her lifestyle during her golden years. When I first learned the power of this, I turned this knowledge into a habit by writing down 8-10 things I was grateful for and taping it to my bathroom mirror. That way, I started and ended every day focusing on those things. It has now become such a habit that it's as involuntary as breathing. But at first I had to really train myself to think like that. That leads us to the next key.

Key #2- Knowledge isn't enough. You must take action

The old saying that knowledge is power is only part of the equation. *Applied* knowledge is the key. It is not enough to know what needs to be done. You have to DO IT. If you know you need to pay more attention to your finances, or if there is a specific concern you have, the only way to solve for that is to ACT. The challenge for most folks is that change is scary. Or, looking at it another way, it's comfortable to just do things the way we've always done them. This is the point where I have to take off the gloves and tell you a cold, hard fact. If you look at your retirement plan this way, there is a very good chance you will live to regret it.

Most people think of getting to retirement as the goal. I can tell you with certainty that protecting your retirement years once you get there makes getting there in the first place look like a Sunday stroll. A financial mistake in your 30s can be overcome. Make a serious error in judgment about what you need, or how to get it, *in retirement...* and that can be a disaster. Here's something else to chew on. The best plan for *getting* you there could be the very approach that causes the disaster once you *are* there. This fact alone demands that you think long and hard about changing your approach once you are near or in retirement. No matter how scary change can be, or how comfortable you are with the status quo, it is critical that you educate yourself on the things that must be done to protect your retirement and put a plan in place to accomplish them. Then, EXECUTE THE PLAN.

Key #3- Have the right plan

You may think I've got #2 and #3 in the wrong order. Shouldn't we create the plan and then talk about action?.. Nope. It's the commitment to taking action that comes before the plan ever gets created. Trust me on this; I've seen it over and over. OK, you're committed to action, what now? The key to a good plan is to first *ask the right questions.* I can't overstress this point. When it comes to financial matters, one of the most common mistakes that people make is getting answers to the wrong questions. Let me illustrate this for you. Let's say I have an infection in my foot and I ask the doctor, "Hey doc, what's the fastest way to get rid of this infection?" He could very truthfully say "well, the fastest way would be to cut off your foot!" Now if I said, "Hey doc, what's the best and safest way to get rid of this infection?" do you think I might get a different answer? This may seem like an extreme example but I can't tell you how often I get asked, "Hey Tad, what's the best way to grow my money?" WRONG QUESTION ALERT! Because the right answer to that question would be to invest in a way that could cause you to lose half of your life savings in a market crash. The right question for retirement planning is, "Hey Tad, what's the best way to structure my investments so that my money lasts as long as I do, and I'm not taking too much risk to accomplish that?" So here is a list of great questions we should be asking and answering BEFORE we make investment decisions:

1. How much exactly are we going to need from our savings each year?

2. What happens to that need when one of you passes away first?

3. Is the need going to change due to changes in expenses or income during retirement? (maybe your house gets paid off, or an income stream disappears at some point).

4. What spousal options should you chose on your pension and when should you take social security?

5. How should you structure your investments to replace your pay check without taking too much risk?

These are just a few of the most important ones. And while I would love to give you all the answers, the truth is that the answers are different for every single person. There is no "right" way to do this for everyone. The only things that stay constant are the questions themselves. Answering these questions is how you create the right plan. Which leads me to the last Key.

Key #4- Make sure you are working with the right advisor

I have written on this topic before. The key here is to make sure that your advisor is a *fiduciary*. That means that he or she has a requirement, based upon the license they hold, to do what is in your best interest, NOT what is best for their pocketbook.

Another qualifying test is to ask if they are willing to operate as a *fee-only advisor*. A fee-only advisor means they are licensed to do financial planning and are willing to put a plan together for a fee, that does not include them implementing any piece of the plan. This is different than a *fee-based advisor*, or a *commission-based broker*. A *fee-based advisor* will manage your investment assets for a fee, usually a percentage of the amount they are managing. A *commission-based broker* gets paid commission every time they buy or sell an investment for you. With a *fee-only advisor* you know they aren't trying to sell you some investment that isn't in your best interest, because they aren't getting paid on the investments you use. It also hopefully means they have a planning process designed to answer the questions I listed in key #3. Now many fee-only advisors will do the implementation for you if you want them to, but will (or should) be willing to disclose to you how they get compensated for doing so.

Most of my clients don't just want a plan; they want help with the implementation as well. I'm happy to do this and I always explain how I get paid in that scenario. But I'm also just as happy to put the plan in place and let them execute it themselves, if that's what they desire.

I sincerely hope this discussion has helped clarify the keys to having financial freedom in retirement. One thing it has done for me is to make me aware of the fact that there is so much more that needs to be said and explained on this topic. Soon, I will be writing a full book on how to create the right plan for your retirement. Stay Tuned and God Bless!

About Tad

Tad Hill is the President of Freedom Financial Group. He founded Freedom Financial Group with his wife and business partner, Toni; in order to fill a niche they felt was not being addressed properly in the retirement planning environment—helping retirees and pre-retirees in Alabama find answers to issues that may affect their quality of life during retirement. They believe each investor is unique and no single strategy is right for everyone. In fact, the defining point that separates their process from other firms is that they carefully identify all of the "must-know facts" that are critical to the individual client's retirement success BEFORE they make investment decisions. This goes far beyond a "risk tolerance" questionnaire that is employed by typical firms. Eliminating potential risks for their clients' retirement success is done through a four-step process, including: Income Planning, Investment Planning, Legacy Planning and Tax Planning. This approach requires more effort on the part of Freedom Financial, but results in a roadmap that creates a greater sense of security for their clients.

Tad is a Chartered Retirement Planning Counselor (CRPC®), a Registered Financial Consultant (RFC) and holds a Series 65 License. He is an Investment Advisor Representative, offering advisory services through Global Financial Private Capital, LLC, an SEC Registered Investment Advisor, and he also holds insurance licenses in the state of Alabama. Tad is honored to be the co-host of the nationally-syndicated television show Retiring Well. He is also a frequent financial commentator on ABC's *Talk of Alabama*, and Fox 6's *Good Day Alabama*. You can also hear him weekly as the co-host of the Financial Safari Radio Show on 105.5 WERC, 101.5 WAPI, and 100.5 The Source. He was recently recognized in *Newsweek* as one of the nations "Financial Trendsetters" and has co-authored two books. The first book is *Think and Grow Rich Today,* an updated version of the Napoleon Hill classic, *Think and Grow Rich,* and the second is the *Ultimate Success Guide* with Brian Tracy.

Tad is a member of the Better Business Bureau, the National Ethics Bureau and the International Association of Registered Financial Consultants. He was awarded the Global Financial Award for Fiduciary Excellence in 2011 & 2013, and he was featured on the cover of Advisors Excel's AE Insider magazine in 2012 as the leader of one of the fastest growing financial planning firms in the country. He and Toni are graduates of Auburn University and reside in Indian Springs with their three daughters: Peyton, Tyler and Shannon.

To schedule a time to discuss your financial future, contact us at:
TadHill@freedomfingroup.com
Or call us at 205-988-0006 today!

CHAPTER 25

MOVING FROM DESIRE TO RESULTS

BY GREG ROLLETT

Desire is a funny thing. We all inherently desire things. It might be cars, money, love, a certain food or a profession. Others have a desire to make an impact, ...to change the world, ...or to change their world. If you listen to the world around you, people talk a lot about desire. They talk about how they desire more from their life, ...for better health, ...for a better relationship or job.

I was having a conversation with an expert friend of mine recently and we were both talking about our inners desires and ambitions. We had previously started a few businesses together that had not succeeded, and were now in more prosperous ventures. Neither of us had ever considered taking a "regular job" at any time during this stretch, no matter how tough or financially strapped we became.

We had a desire to make it.

We hear these stories much more often in the sports world than in the business world. A child with no resources, no supporting loved ones and more opportunities to get into trouble than to get an athletic scholarship and excel. These stories flurry into ESPN on the weekends and bring tears to even the most barbaric of sports fans.

Reading a recent issue of Forbes Magazine, it was revealed that 279 of the 400 richest people in America claimed to be self-made – not given their fortunes in Trust Funds or from their parent's business ventures. They embody desire and ambition. They have built businesses, created jobs, changed lives, gifted charitable donations and keep the economy moving. All from their own desires to excel.

My own desire came from a young age as well. Growing up I knew we didn't have much, but we always had enough. We never missed signups for a sports league or went on a field trip without lunch money.

By the time high school rolled around, this hunger for more was starting to brew up inside of me. From the other students around me in nicer cars and clothes, to the ones taking the popular girls to the movies on the weekend, to the athletes that spent a few more hours working on their craft than I did, I knew I needed to do more to excel in my life.

FINDING YOUR INNER DESIRE

It wasn't enough to just want to be a part of a certain social or peer group. That doesn't create a deep desire that inspires action. For me, that desire came when I made the decision to create my own destiny. A decision to take responsibility for my life and the experiences that I knew I could create for myself.

I couldn't wait for my parents to give it to me, or my teachers to hand it to me or for my coaches to draw up a magical play. I had to do it for myself and accept full responsibility. I had to wake up early to get into the gym and onto the track no matter how tired I was or how special the party was the night before.

I had to study hard, learn insights and ask questions that would move me further towards the success I desired. These traits still live with me today as I awake at 5am to get into the CrossFit gym and stay at the office well past last call to help my clients get everything they need to live a better life.

But as you grow throughout life, your desires, ambitions and motivations change. They evolve into things you could have never dreamt up before you experienced life. For me, this came when my first son was born.

My perspective changed in the blink of an eye. I was no longer taking responsibility for my own life, but for the lives of my new family. The inner desires began to burn even deeper to create a life, and a lifestyle, that allows my wife, my son and I to all be able to do everything we want to do, with no limits or reservations.

Your mindset plays a critical role in creating this reality for yourself. As Napoleon Hill wrote in the original *Think And Grow Rich* –

"Desire is the starting point of all achievement, not a hope, not a wish, but a keen pulsating desire which transcends everything."

Many people fail to ever find the thing that radiates within them every morning when the sun comes up. They coast through their life, living for weekends, the snooze button and an escape from their reality.

GETTING OUT OF THE DESIRE TRAP

Living without desire is detrimental to your health. It gives you nothing to wake up for, nothing to work for or constantly learn from to improve your life. With no desires we become complacent, begin to eat poorly, stop educating ourselves and stop dreaming about what is possible.

I see it in the eyes of people everyday in line at lunch waiting for their fast food, at gas stations buying 2 for 1 energy drinks and at happy hour, just killing time before you have to "do it again."

What I understood at a young age is that you cannot hope to have a great life, you have to create it. Much like the coaches who weren't going to draw up the magical play, it's the hard work that you put yourself through that allows you to experience the fruits of your labor. A winning Super Bowl team might credit the play call that won the game at the last second, but it was their work throughout their entire careers that gave them an opportunity to make that play when it counted. They didn't just show up, put on a uniform and execute.

I remember the moment I knew that everything I had been working towards was finally realized. I was walking into the Staples Center in Los Angeles, CA. My wife was wearing a stunning Badgley Mischka dress with her hair styled like it was our wedding day. I was in a tailored tuxedo held together with a brand new tie clip.

As we walked our way up the terrace levels and into the Luxury Box, I could not hold back the grin that was quickly forming on my face. ...To come this far. ...To work this hard. ...To celebrate at the Grammy Awards. This was my Summit, my mountain peak.

But before you can get to the mountaintop, you need to put it out and into the world that you have a desire to get there. You must define that mountaintop.

And even though you think about the peak, the summit of all summits, creating that reality does not come from thinking alone. Nor just desire.

Like I mentioned earlier, everyone has desires - good and bad, right and wrong, possible and far reaching. But most never get there. And this is the missing piece to the puzzle.

THE ACTION!

How are you going to get there? How was I going to get into the Luxury Box to watch McCartney, Springsteen and Coldplay on music's biggest stage? Honestly I had no idea how I was going to get to the Grammy Awards 10 years ago, but I did know how I was going to get myself into a position to do everything I ever wanted. ...To be excellent.

It started with desire and ambition and led to a lot of early mornings and long nights. There was stress and there were dog fights. There were good days and there were really bad days. But everyday had a purpose. Everyday there was fire in my eyes and a mission on my mind.

GOING FROM DESIRE TO RESULTS

Today I walk my clients through a simple exercise that makes everything easier for them to understand. And more importantly, to find their core desires and develop a plan to get there. It's an exercise I went through myself when I was on the road to success.

First, I ask where they want to be. Where do they want to live, how much do they want to earn and what activities do they want to be doing? I go into the work they despise and the tasks that bring stress into their lives. I ask them what worries them and keeps them up at night. I learn what makes them jump out of bed and what keeps them cuddled under the sheets.

These questions paint the picture of your inner desires. Knowing what you want from life can be simplified just by spending time consciously thinking these things through, which is another important principle Napoleon Hill uncovered.

From all my clients, only a very small handful had ever taken the time to ask and answer these questions – to put goals and ambitions down on paper. It took me 27 years to ask and answer these questions. But when I did, the world began to open up. I saw opportunities, paths and trails. One door led to another and soon enough, I had created my own version of the Matrix.

After answering these questions, my clients had the same realization. But they still had to put in the work. They still had to hit the pavement, grab a shovel and start digging. But with the end path in their sights, it made digging much easier.

Let's take an income goal for example. If you want to make

$100,000 in a year, you need to bring in a little more than $8,000 per month. How do you bring in $8,000 per month? You can start by finding a skill or talent for which 8 people will pay $1,000 per month. ...Or 16 people $500 per month. The math becomes simple when you know the solution. Then your desire and ambition kicks in to get you there.

Other clients want to travel a good portion of the year. So we work backwards to make it happen. If you want to live in Chang Mai for 6 months what does it cost to get there? What will it cost to rent an apartment for 6 months and what other expenses do you need to cover?

Then you book the ticket. You put it in your calendar and you prepare to go.

You take charge of your life. You live out your desires.

CREATING A LIFE FILLED WITH PURPOSE

I used to think a lot about lifestyle design. The thought of designing your life in such a way that you only did the things you want, at the times you want and with the people you want.

What it led to was more thinking and less doing. I was stuck. I had no purpose, a very important piece of Napoleon Hill's work. In it he mentions that –

"Without a purpose and a plan, people drift aimlessly through life."

And that's where many people spend their life. Waiting for the money to come in. Waiting for the business to take off. Not living with urgency and a purpose.

As you go through these pages today, in the updated version of one of the most important books of all time, I urge you to find purpose. It will lead to the right kind of desires and give you the ambition you need to not just find success, which is temporary, but to become excellent. ...To become a leader. ...To be someone that people look up to and admire.

You know, desire is a funny thing. We can desire more money or faster cars. We can desire a better home or a more exotic meal. But what happens when you desire to be excellent? When you desire to do something that doesn't start and stop tomorrow, but creates a legacy as Napoleon Hill has done with his life's work?

It is an incredible world of opportunity out there. I see it every-day. Everyone is my office dreams. They are filled with desire and ambition for more. We want to help the most people help the most people. It is that drive that keeps us alive. That wakes us up before the alarm goes off. That builds the fire in our eyes.

That kind of desire will build you whatever life you want. And I for one am glad I have it.

About Greg

Greg Rollett, the ProductPro, is a best-selling author and online marketing expert who works with authors, experts, entertainers, entrepreneurs and business owners all over the world to help them share their knowledge and change the lives and businesses of others. After creating a successful string of his own educational products, Greg began helping others in the production and marketing of their own products.

Greg is a front-runner in utilizing the power of social media, direct response marketing and customer education to drive new leads and convert those leads into long-standing customers and advocates.

Previous clients include Coca-Cola, Miller Lite, Warner Bros and Cash Money Records, as well as hundreds of entrepreneurs and small-business owners. Greg's work has been featured on FOX News, ABC, and the Daily Buzz. Greg has written for Mashable, the Huffington Post, AOL, AMEX's Open Forum and more.

Greg loves to challenge the current business environments that constrain people to working 12-hour days during the best portions of their lives. By teaching them to leverage technology and the power of information, Greg loves helping others create freedom businesses that allow them to generate income, make the world a better place and live a radically ambitious lifestyle in the process.

A former touring musician, Greg is highly sought after as a speaker, having appeared on stages with former Florida Gov. Charlie Crist, best-selling authors Chris Brogan and Nick Nanton, as well as at events such as Affiliate Summit.

If you would like to learn more about Greg and how he can help your business, please contact him directly at greg@productprosystems.com or by calling his office at 877.897.4611.

You can also download a free report on how to create your own educational products at www.productprosystems.com.

The classic Napoleon Hill book

Think and Grow Rich

follows for reference, research
or analysis by the reader…

THINK AND GROW RICH

Teaching, for the first time, the famous Andrew
Carnegie formula for money-making, based upon the THIRTEEN PROVEN STEPS TO RICHES.

★　　★　　★　　★　　★

ORGANIZED THROUGH 25 YEARS OF RESEARCH,
IN COLLABORATION WITH MORE THAN 500
DISTINGUISHED MEN OF GREAT WEALTH, WHO
PROVED BY THEIR OWN ACHIEVEMENTS THAT
THIS PHILOSOPHY IS PRACTICAL.

★　　★　　★

By
NAPOLEON HILL
Author of
THE LAW OF SUCCESS
Philosophy

★

1937

Published by **THE RALSTON SOCIETY,** Meriden, Conn.

WHAT DO YOU WANT MOST?

Is It Money, Fame, Power,
Contentment, Personality,
Peace of Mind, Happiness?

The Thirteen Steps to Riches described in this book offer the shortest dependable philosophy of individual achievement ever presented for the benefit of the man or woman who is searching for a definite goal in life.

Before beginning the book you will profit greatly if you recognize the fact that *the book was not written to entertain.* You cannot digest the contents properly in a week or a month.

After reading the book thoroughly, Dr. Miller Reese Hutchison, nationally known Consulting Engineer and long-time associate of Thomas A. Edison, said—

"This is not a novel. It is a textbook on individual achievement that came directly from the experiences of hundreds of America's most successful men. It should be *studied, digested,* and meditated upon. No more than one chapter should be read in a single night. The reader should underline the sentences which impress him most. Later, he should go back to these marked lines and read them again. *A real student will not merely read this book,* he will absorb its contents and make them his own. The book should be adopted by all high schools and no boy or girl should be permitted to graduate without having satisfactorily passed an examination on it. This philosophy will not take the place of the subjects taught in schools, but it will enable one to *organize and apply* the knowledge acquired, and convert it into useful service and adequate compensation without waste of time."

Dr. John R. Turner, Dean of the College of The City of New York, after having read the book, said—

"The very best example of the soundness of this philosophy is your own son, Blair, whose dramatic story you have outlined in the chapter on Desire."

Dr. Turner had reference to the author's son, who, born without normal hearing capacity, not only avoided becoming a deaf mute, but actually converted his handicap into a priceless asset by applying the philosophy here described. After

THE MOST PROFITABLE WAY TO USE THIS BOOK

reading the story (starting on page 52), you will realize that you are about to come into possession of a philosophy which can be transmuted into material wealth, or serve as readily to bring you peace of mind, understanding, spiritual harmony, and in some instances, as in the case of the author's son, it can help you master physical affliction.

The author discovered, through personally analyzing hundreds of successful men, that *all* of them followed the habit of exchanging ideas, through what is commonly called *conferences.* When they had problems to be solved they sat down together and talked freely until they discovered, from their joint contribution of ideas, a plan that would serve their purpose.

You, who read this book, will get most out of it by putting into practice the Master Mind principle described in the book. This you can do (as others are doing so successfully) by forming a study club, consisting of any desired number of people who are friendly and harmonious. The club should have a meeting at regular periods, as often as once each week. The procedure should consist of reading one chapter of the book at each meeting, after which the contents of the chapter should be freely discussed by all members. Each member should make notes, putting down *ALL IDEAS OF HIS OWN* inspired by the discussion. Each member should carefully read and analyze each chapter several days prior to its open reading and joint discussion in the club. The reading at the club should be done by someone who reads well and understands how to put color and feeling into the lines.

By following this plan every reader will get from its pages, not only the sum total of the best knowledge organized from the experiences of hundreds of successful men, but more important by far, *he will tap new sources of knowledge in his own mind as well as acquire knowledge of priceless value FROM EVERY OTHER PERSON PRESENT.*

If you follow this plan *persistently* you will be almost certain to uncover and appropriate the secret formula by which Andrew Carnegie acquired his huge fortune, as referred to in the author's introduction.

TRIBUTES TO THE AUTHOR
From Great American Leaders

"THINK AND GROW RICH" was 25 years in the making. It is Napoleon Hill's newest book, based upon his famous Law of Success Philosophy. His work and writings have been praised by great leaders in Finance, Education, Politics, Government.

Supreme Court of the United States
Washington, D.C.

Dear Mr. Hill:—

I have now had an opportunity to finish reading your Law of Success text-books and I wish to express my appreciation of the splendid work you have done in the organization of this philosophy.

It would be helpful if every politician in the country would assimilate and apply the 17 principles upon which your lessons are based. It contains some very fine material which every leader in every walk of life should understand.

I am happy to have had the privilege of rendering you some slight measure of help in the organization of this splendid course of "common sense" philosophy.

Sincerely yours

(Former President and former Chief Justice of the United States)

KING OF THE 5 AND 10 CENT STORES

"By applying many of the 17 fundamentals of the Law of Success philosophy we have built a great chain of successful stores. I presume it would be no exaggeration of fact if I said that the Woolworth Building might properly be called a monument to the soundness of these principles."

F. W. WOOLWORTH

A GREAT STEAMSHIP MAGNATE

"I feel greatly indebted for the privilege of reading your Law of Success. If I had had this philosophy fifty years ago, I suppose I could have accomplished all that I have done in less than half the time. I sincerely hope the world will discover and reward you."

ROBERT DOLLAR

FAMOUS AMERICAN LABOR LEADER

"Mastery of the Law of Success philosophy is the equivalent of an insurance policy against failure."

SAMUEL GOMPERS

A FORMER PRESIDENT OF THE UNITED STATES

"May I not congratulate you on your persistence. Any man who devotes that much time...must of necessity make discoveries of great value to others. I am deeply impressed by your interpretation of the 'Master Mind' principles which you have so clearly described."

WOODROW WILSON

A MERCHANT PRINCE

"I know that your 17 fundamentals of success are sound because I have been applying them in my business for more than 30 years."

JOHN WANAMAKER

WORLD'S LARGEST MAKER OF CAMERAS

"I know that you are doing a world of good with your Law of Success. I would not care to set a monetary value on this training because it brings to the student qualities which cannot be measured by money, alone."

GEORGE EASTMAN

A NATIONALLY KNOWN BUSINESS CHIEF

"Whatever success I may have attained I owe, entirely, to the application of your 17 fundamental principles of the Law of Success. I believe I have the honor of being your first student."

WM. WRIGLEY, JR.

CONTENTS

** Pls. note: The page numbers shown here fit the numbering
sequence for this complete book. They are not the numbers
used in the original publication of Napoleon Hill's book.*

PUBLISHER'S PREFACE

THIS book conveys the experience of more than 500 men of great wealth, who began at scratch, with nothing to give in return for riches except THOUGHTS, IDEAS, and ORGANIZED PLANS.

Here you have the entire philosophy of money-making, just as it was organized from the actual achievements of the most successful men known to the American people during the past fifty years. It describes WHAT TO DO, also, HOW TO DO IT!

It presents complete instructions on HOW TO SELL YOUR PERSONAL SERVICES.

It provides you with a perfect system of self-analysis that will readily disclose what has been standing between you and "the big money" in the past.

It describes the famous Andrew Carnegie formula of personal achievement by which he accumulated hundreds of millions of dollars for himself and made no fewer than a score of millionaires of men to whom he taught his secret.

Perhaps you do not need all that is to be found in the book—no one of the 500 men from whose experiences it was written did—but you may need ONE IDEA, PLAN OR SUGGESTION to start you toward your goal. Somewhere in the book you will find this needed stimulus.

The book was inspired by Andrew Carnegie, after he had made his millions and retired. It was written by the man to whom Carnegie disclosed the astounding secret of his riches—the same man to whom the 500 wealthy men revealed the source of their riches.

In this volume will be found the thirteen principles of money-making essential to every person who accumulates sufficient money to guarantee financial independence. It is estimated that the research which went into the preparation, before the book was written, or could be written—research covering more than twenty-five years of continuous effort—could not be duplicated at a cost of less than $100,000.00.

Moreover, the knowledge contained in the book never can be duplicated, at any cost, for the reason that more than half of the 500 men who supplied the information it brings have passed on.

Riches cannot always be measured in money!

Money and material things are essential for freedom of body and mind, but there are some who will feel that the greatest of all riches can be evaluated only in terms of lasting friendships, harmonious family relationships, sympathy and understanding between business associates, and introspective harmony which brings one peace of mind measurable only in spiritual values!

All who read, understand and apply this philosophy will be better prepared to attract and enjoy these higher estates which always have been and always will be denied to all except *those who are ready for them.*

Be prepared, therefore, when you expose yourself to the influence of this philosophy, to experience a CHANGED LIFE which may help you not only to negotiate your way through life with harmony and understanding, but also to prepare you for the accumulation of material riches in abundance.

THE PUBLISHER

AUTHOR'S PREFACE

IN EVERY chapter of this book, mention has been made of the money-making secret which has made fortunes for more than five hundred exceedingly wealthy men whom I have carefully analyzed over a long period of years.

The secret was brought to my attention by Andrew Carnegie, more than a quarter of a century ago. The canny, lovable old Scotsman carelessly tossed it into my mind, when I was but a boy. Then he sat back in his chair, with a merry twinkle in his eyes, and watched carefully to see if I had brains enough to understand the full significance of what he had said to me.

When he saw that I had grasped the idea, he asked if I would be willing to spend twenty years or more, preparing myself to take it to the world, to men and women who, without the secret, might go through life as failures. I said I would, and with Mr. Carnegie's cooperation, I have kept my promise.

This book contains the secret, after having been put to a practical test by thousands of people, in almost every walk of life. It was Mr. Carnegie's idea that the magic formula, which gave him a stupendous fortune, ought to be placed within reach of people who do not have time to investigate how men make money, and it was his hope that I might test and demonstrate the soundness of the formula through the experience of men and women in every calling. He believed the formula should be taught in all public schools and colleges, and expressed the opinion that if it were properly taught it would so revolutionize the entire educational system that the time spent in school could be reduced to less than half.

His experience with Charles M. Schwab, and other young men of Mr. Schwab's type, convinced Mr. Carnegie that much of that which is taught in the schools is of no value whatsoever in connection with the business of earning a living or accumulating riches. He had arrived at this decision, because he had taken into his business one young man after another, many of them with but little schooling, and by coaching them in the use of this formula, developed in them rare leadership. Moreover, *his coaching made fortunes for everyone of them who followed his instructions.*

In the chapter on Faith, you will read the astounding story of the organization of the giant United States Steel Corporation, as it was conceived and carried out by one of the young men through whom Mr. Carnegie proved that his formula will work *for all who are ready for it.* This single application of the secret, by that young man—Charles M. Schwab—made him a huge fortune in both money and OPPORTUNITY. Roughly speaking, this particular application of the formula was worth *six hundred million dollars.*

These facts—and they are facts well known to almost everyone who knew Mr. Carnegie—give you a fair idea of what the reading of this book may bring to you, provided you KNOW WHAT IT IS THAT YOU WANT.

Even before it had undergone twenty years of

practical testing, the secret was passed on to more than one hundred thousand men and women who have used it for their personal benefit, as Mr. Carnegie planned that they should. Some have made fortunes with it. Others have used it successfully in creating harmony in their homes. A clergyman used it so effectively that it brought him an income of upwards of $75,000.00 a year.

Arthur Nash, a Cincinnati tailor, used his near-bankrupt business as a "guinea pig" on which to test the formula. The business came to life and made a fortune for its owners. It is still thriving, although Mr. Nash has gone. The experiment was so unique that newspapers and magazines, gave it more than a million dollars' worth of laudatory publicity.

The secret was passed on to Stuart Austin Wier, of Dallas, Texas. He was ready for it—so ready that he gave up his profession and studied law. Did he succeed? That story is told too.

I gave the secret to Jennings Randolph, the day he graduated from College, and he has used it so successfully that he is now serving his third term as a Member of Congress, with an excellent opportunity to keep on using it until it carries him to the White House.

While serving as Advertising Manager of the LaSalle Extension University, when it was little more than a name, I had the privilege of seeing J. G. Chapline, President of the University, use the formula so effectively that he has since made the LaSalle one of the great extension schools of the country.

The secret to which I refer has been mentioned no fewer than a hundred times, throughout this book. It has not been directly named, for it seems to work more successfully when it is merely uncovered and left in sight, where THOSE WHO ARE READY, and SEARCHING FOR IT, may pick it up. That is why Mr. Carnegie tossed it to me so quietly, without giving me its specific name.

If you are READY to put it to use, you will recognize this secret at least once in every chapter. I wish I might feel privileged to tell you how you will know if you are ready, but that would deprive you of much of the benefit you will receive when you make the discovery in your own way.

While this book was being written, my own son, who was then finishing the last year of his college work, picked up the manuscript of chapter two, read it, and discovered the secret for himself. He used the information so effectively that he went directly into a responsible position at a beginning salary greater than the average man ever earns. His story has been briefly described in chapter two. When you read it, perhaps you will dismiss any feeling you may have had, at the beginning of the book, that it promised too much. And, too, if you have ever been discouraged, if you have had difficulties to surmount which took the very soul out of you, if you have tried and failed, if you were ever handicapped by illness or physical affliction, this story of my son's discovery and use of the Carnegie formula may prove to be the oasis in the Desert of Lost Hope, for which you have been searching.

This secret was extensively used by President

Woodrow Wilson, during the World War. It was passed on to every soldier who fought in the war, carefully wrapped in the training received before going to the front. President Wilson told me it was a strong factor in raising the funds needed for the war.

More than twenty years ago, Hon. Manuel L. Quezon (then Resident Commissioner of the Philippine Islands), was inspired by the secret to gain freedom for his people. He has gained freedom for the Philippines, and is the first President of the free state.

A peculiar thing about this secret is that those who once acquire it and use it, find themselves literally swept on to success, with but little effort, and they never again submit to failure! If you doubt this, study the names of those who have used it, wherever they have been mentioned, check their records for yourself, and be convinced.

There is no such thing as SOMETHING FOR NOTHING!

The secret to which I refer cannot be had without a price, although the price is far less than its value. It cannot be had at any price by those who are not intentionally searching for it. It cannot be given away, it cannot be purchased for money, for the reason that it comes in two parts. One part is already in possession of those who are ready for it.

The secret serves equally well, all who are ready for it. Education has nothing to do with it. Long before I was born, the secret had found its way into the possession of Thomas A. Edison, and he used it so intelligently that he became the world's leading inventor, although he had but three months of schooling.

The secret was passed on to a business associate of Mr. Edison. He used it so effectively that, although he was then making only $12,000 a year, he accumulated a great fortune, and retired from active business while still a young man. You will find his story at the beginning of the first chapter. It should convince you that riches are not beyond your reach, that you can still be what you wish to be, that money, fame, recognition and happiness can be had by all who are ready and determined to have these blessings.

How do I know these things? You should have the answer before you finish this book. You may find it in the very first chapter, or on the last page.

While I was performing the twenty year task of research, which I had undertaken at Mr. Carnegie's request, I analyzed hundreds of well known men, many of whom admitted that they had accumulated their vast fortunes through the aid of the Carnegie secret; among these men were:—

HENRY FORD
WILLIAM WRIGLEY JR.
JOHN WANAMAKER
JAMES J. HILL
GEORGE S. PARKER
E. M. STATLER
HENRY L. DOHERTY
CYRUS H. K. CURTIS
GEORGE EASTMAN

THEODORE ROOSEVELT
JOHN W. DAVIS
ELBERT HUBBARD
WILBUR WRIGHT
WILLIAM JENNINGS
  BRYAN
DR. DAVID STARR
  JORDAN
J. ODGEN ARMOUR

CHARLES M. SCHWAB

HARRIS F. WILLIAMS

DR. FRANK GUNSAULUS

DANIEL WILLARD

KING GILLETTE

RALPH A. WEEKS

JUDGE DANIEL T. WRIGHT

JOHN D. ROCKEFELLER

THOMAS A. EDISON

FRANK A. VANDERLIP

F. W. WOOLWORTH

COL. ROBERT A. DOLLAR

EDWARD A. FILENE

EDWIN C. BARNES

HON. JENNINGS
    RANDOLPH

ARTHUR NASH

ARTHUR BRISBANE

WOODROW WILSON

WM. HOWARD TAFT

LUTHER BURBANK

EDWARD W. BOK

FRANK A. MUNSEY

ELBERT H. GARY

DR. ALEXANDER
    GRAHAM BELL

JOHN H. PATTERSON

JULIUS ROSENWALD

STUART AUSTIN WIER

DR. FRANK CRANE

GEORGE M.
    ALEXANDER

J. G. CHAPLINE

CLARENCE DARROW

These names represent but a small fraction of the hundreds of well known Americans whose achievements, financially and otherwise, prove that those who understand and apply the Carnegie secret, reach high stations in life. I have never known anyone who was inspired to use the secret, who did not achieve noteworthy success in his chosen calling. I have never known any person to distinguish himself, or to accumulate riches of any consequence, without possession of the secret. From these two facts I draw the conclusion that the secret is more important, as a part of the knowledge essential for self-determination, than any which one receives through what is popularly known as "education."

What is EDUCATION, anyway? This has been answered in full detail.

As far as schooling is concerned, many of these men had very little. John Wanamaker once told me that what little schooling he had, he acquired in very much the same manner as a modern locomotive takes on water, by "scooping it up as it runs." Henry Ford never reached high school, let alone college. I am not attempting to minimize the value of schooling, but I am trying to express my earnest belief that those who master and apply the secret will reach high stations, accumulate riches, and bargain with life on their own terms, even if their schooling has been meager.

Somewhere, as you read, the secret to which I refer will jump from the page and stand boldly before you, IF YOU ARE READY FOR IT! When it appears, you will recognize it. Whether you receive the sign in the first or the last chapter, stop for a moment when it presents itself, and turn down a glass, for that occasion will mark the most important turning-point of your life.

We pass now, to Chapter One, and to the story of my very dear friend, who has generously acknowledged having seen the mystic sign, and whose business achievements are evidence enough that he turned down a glass. As you read his story, and the others, remember that they deal with the important problems of life, such as all men experience.

The problems arising from one's endeavor to earn a living, to find hope, courage, contentment and peace of mind; to accumulate riches and to enjoy freedom of body and spirit.

Remember, too, as you go through the book, that it deals with facts and not with fiction, its purpose being to convey a great universal truth through which all who are READY may learn, not only *WHAT TO DO, BUT ALSO HOW TO DO IT!* and receive, as well, THE NEEDED STIMULUS TO MAKE A START.

As a final word of preparation, before you begin the first chapter, may I offer one brief suggestion which may provide a clue by which the Carnegie secret may be recognized? It is this—*ALL ACHIEVEMENT, ALL EARNED RICHES, HAVE THEIR BEGINNING IN AN IDEA!* If you are ready for the secret, you already possess one half of it, therefore, you will readily recognize the other half the moment it reaches your mind.

THE AUTHOR

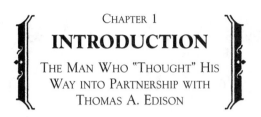

CHAPTER 1

INTRODUCTION

THE MAN WHO "THOUGHT" HIS
WAY INTO PARTNERSHIP WITH
THOMAS A. EDISON

TRULY, "thoughts are things," and powerful things at that, when they are mixed with definiteness of purpose, persistence, and a BURNING DESIRE for their translation into riches, or other material objects.

A little more than thirty years ago, Edwin C. Barnes discovered how true it is that men really do THINK AND GROW RICH. His discovery did not come about at one sitting. It came little by little, beginning with a BURNING DESIRE to become a business associate of the great Edison.

One of the chief characteristics of Barnes' Desire was that it was *definite*. He wanted to work *with* Edison, not *for* him. Observe, carefully, the description of how he went about translating his DESIRE into reality, and you will have a better understanding of the thirteen principles which lead to riches.

When this DESIRE, or impulse of thought, first flashed into his mind he was in no position to act upon it. Two difficulties stood in his way. He did not know Mr. Edison, and he did not have enough money to pay his railroad fare to Orange, New Jersey.

These difficulties were sufficient to have discouraged the majority of men from making any attempt to carry out the desire. But his was no ordinary desire! He was so determined to find a way to carry out his desire that he finally decided to travel by "blind baggage," rather than be defeated. (To the uninitiated, this means that he went to East Orange on a freight train).

He presented himself at Mr. Edison's laboratory, and announced he had come to go into business with the inventor. In speaking of the first meeting between Barnes and Edison, years later, Mr. Edison said, "He stood there before me, looking like an ordinary tramp, *but there was something in the expression of his face which conveyed the impression that he was determined to get what he had come after.* I had learned, from years of experience with men, that when a man really DESIRES a thing so deeply that he is willing to stake his entire future on a single turn of the wheel in order to get it, he is sure to win. I gave him the opportunity he asked for, *because I saw he had made up his mind to stand by until he succeeded.* Subsequent events proved that no mistake was made."

Just what young Barnes said to Mr. Edison on that occasion was far less important than *that which he thought.* Edison, himself, said so! It could not have been the young man's appearance which got him his start in the Edison office, for that was definitely against him. It was what he THOUGHT that counted.

If the significance of this statement could be conveyed to every person who reads it, there would be no need for the remainder of this book.

Barnes did not get his partnership with Edison on his first interview. He did get a chance to work in the Edison offices, at a very nominal wage, doing work that was unimportant to Edison, but most important to Barnes, because it gave him an opportunity to display his "merchandise" where his intended "partner" could see it.

Months went by. Apparently nothing happened to bring the coveted goal which Barnes had set up in his mind as his DEFINITE MAJOR PURPOSE. But something important was happening in Barnes' mind. He was constantly intensifying his DESIRE to become the business associate of Edison.

Psychologists have correctly said that "when one is truly ready for a thing, it puts in its appearance." Barnes was ready for a business association with Edison, moreover, he was DETERMINED TO REMAIN READY UNTIL HE GOT THAT WHICH HE WAS SEEKING.

He did not say to himself, "Ah well, what's the use? I guess I'll change my mind and try for a salesman's job." But, he did say, "I came here to go into business with Edison, and I'll accomplish this end if it takes the remainder of my life." *He meant it!* What a different story men would have to tell if only they would adopt a DEFINITE PURPOSE, and stand by that purpose until it had time to become an all-consuming obsession!

Maybe young Barnes did not know it at the time, but his bulldog determination, his persistence in standing back of a single DESIRE, was destined to mow down all opposition, and bring him the opportunity he was seeking.

When the opportunity came, it appeared in a different form, and from a different direction than Barnes had expected. That is one of the tricks of opportunity. It has a sly habit of slipping in by the back door, and often it comes disguised in the form of misfortune, or temporary defeat. Perhaps this is why so many fail to recognize opportunity.

Mr. Edison had just perfected a new office device, known at that time, as the Edison Dictating Machine (now the Ediphone). His salesmen were not enthusiastic over the machine. They did not believe it could be sold without great effort. Barnes saw his opportunity. It had crawled in quietly, hidden in a queer looking machine which interested no one but Barnes and the inventor.

Barnes knew he could sell the Edison Dictating Machine. He suggested this to Edison, and promptly got his chance. He did sell the machine. In fact, he sold it so successfully that Edison gave him a contract to distribute and market it all over the nation. Out of that business association grew the slogan, "Made by Edison and installed by Barnes."

The business alliance has been in operation for more than thirty years. Out of it Barnes has made himself rich in money, but he has done something infinitely greater, he has proved that one really may "Think and Grow Rich."

How much actual cash that original DESIRE of Barnes' has been worth to him, I have no way of knowing. Perhaps it has brought him two or three million dollars, but the amount, whatever it is, becomes insignificant when compared with the greater asset he acquired in the form of definite knowledge that *an intangible impulse of thought can be transmuted into its physical counterpart* by the application of known principles.

Barnes literally *thought* himself into a partnership with the great Edison! He thought himself into a fortune. He had nothing to start with, except the capacity to KNOW WHAT HE WANTED, AND THE DETERMINATION TO STAND BY THAT DESIRE UNTIL HE REALIZED IT.

He had no money to begin with. He had but little education. He had no influence. But he did have initiative, faith, and the will to win. With these intangible forces he *made himself* number one man with the greatest inventor who ever lived.

Now, let us look at a different situation, and study a man who had plenty of tangible evidence of riches, but lost it, *because he stopped* three feet short of the goal he was seeking.

THREE FEET FROM GOLD

One of the most common causes of failure is the habit of quitting when one is overtaken by *temporary defeat.* Every person is guilty of this mistake at one time or another.

An uncle of R.U. Darby was caught by the "gold fever" in the gold-rush days, and went west to DIG AND GROW RICH. He had never heard that *more gold has been mined from the brains of men than has ever been taken from the earth.* He staked a claim and went to work with pick and shovel. The going was hard, but his lust for gold was definite.

After weeks of labor, he was rewarded by the

discovery of the shining ore. He needed machinery to bring the ore to the surface. Quietly, he covered up the mine, retraced his footsteps to his home in Williamsburg, Maryland, told his relatives and a few neighbors of the "strike." They got together money for the needed machinery, had it shipped. The uncle and Darby went back to work the mine.

The first car of ore was mined, and shipped to a smelter. The returns proved they had one of the richest mines in Colorado! A few more cars of that ore would clear the debts. Then would come the big killing in profits.

Down went the drills! Up went the hopes of Darby and Uncle! Then something happened! The vein of gold ore disappeared! They had come to the end of the rainbow, and the pot of gold was no longer there! They drilled on, desperately trying to pick up the vein again—all to no avail.

Finally, they decided to QUIT.

They sold the machinery to a junk man for a few hundred dollars, and took the train back home. Some "junk" men are dumb, but not this one! He called in a mining engineer to look at the mine and do a little calculating. The engineer advised that the project had failed, because the owners were not familiar with "fault lines." His calculations showed that the vein would be found JUST THREE FEET FROM WHERE THE DARBYS HAD STOPPED DRILLING! That is exactly where it was found!

The "Junk" man took millions of dollars in ore from the mine, because he knew enough to seek expert counsel before giving up.

Most of the money which went into the machinery

was procured through the efforts of R.U. Darby, who was then a very young man. The money came from his relatives and neighbors, because of their faith in him. He paid back every dollar of it, although he was years in doing so.

Long afterward, Mr. Darby recouped his loss many times over, *when he made the discovery* that DESIRE can be transmuted into gold. The discovery came after he went into the business of selling life insurance.

Remembering that he lost a huge fortune, because he STOPPED three feet from gold, Darby profited by the experience in his chosen work, by the simple method of saying to himself, "I stopped three feet from gold, but I will never stop *because men say 'no'* when I ask them to buy insurance."

Darby is one of a small group of fewer than fifty men who sell more than a million dollars in life insurance annually. He owes his "stickability" to the lesson he learned from his "quitability" in the gold mining business.

Before success comes in any man's life, he is sure to meet with much temporary defeat, and, perhaps, some failure. When defeat overtakes a man, the easiest and most logical thing to do is to QUIT. That is exactly what the majority of men do.

More than five hundred of the most successful men this country has ever known, told the author their greatest success came just one step *beyond* the point at which defeat had overtaken them. Failure is a trickster with a keen sense of irony and cunning. It takes great delight in tripping one when success is almost within reach.

A Fifty Cent Lesson in Persistence

Shortly after Mr. Darby received his degree from the "University of Hard Knocks," and had decided to profit by his experience in the gold mining business, he had the good fortune to be present on an occasion that proved to him that "No" does not necessarily mean no.

One afternoon he was helping his uncle grind wheat in an old fashioned mill. The uncle operated a large farm on which a number of colored sharecrop farmers lived. Quietly, the door was opened, and a small colored child, the daughter of a tenant, walked in and took her place near the door.

The uncle looked up, saw the child, and barked at her roughly, "what do you want?"

Meekly, the child replied, "My mammy say send her fifty cents."

"I'll not do it," the uncle retorted, "Now you run on home."

"Yas sah," the child replied. *But she did not move.*

The uncle went ahead with his work, so busily engaged that he did not pay enough attention to the child to observe that she did not leave. When he looked up and saw her still standing there, he yelled at her, "I told you to go on home! Now go, or I'll take a switch to you."

The little girl said "yas sah," *but she did not budge an inch.*

The uncle dropped a sack of grain he was about to pour into the mill hopper, picked up a barrel stave, and started toward the child with an expression on his face that indicated trouble.

Darby held his breath. He was certain he was about to witness a murder. He knew his uncle had a fierce temper. He knew that colored children were not supposed to defy white people in that part of the country.

When the uncle reached the spot where the child was standing, she quickly stepped forward one step, looked up into his eyes, and screamed at the top of her shrill voice, "MY MAMMY'S GOTTA HAVE THAT FIFTY CENTS!"

The uncle stopped, looked at her for a minute, then slowly laid the barrel stave on the floor, put his hand in his pocket, took out half a dollar, and gave it to her.

The child took the money and slowly backed toward the door, never taking her eyes off the man *whom she had just conquered.* After she had gone, the uncle sat down on a box and looked out the window into space for more than ten minutes. He was pondering, with awe, over the whipping he had just taken.

Mr. Darby, too, was doing some thinking. That was the first time in all his experience that he had seen a colored child deliberately *master* an adult white person. How did she do it. What happened to his uncle that caused him to lose his fierceness and become as docile as a lamb? What strange power did this child use that made her master over her superior? These and other similar questions flashed into Darby's mind, but he did not find the answer until years later, when he told me the story.

Strangely, the story of this unusual experience was told to the author in the old mill, on the very spot where the uncle took his whipping. Strangely, too, I had devoted nearly a quarter of a century to the study of the power which enabled an ignorant, illiterate colored child to conquer an intelligent man.

As we stood there in that musty old mill, Mr. Darby repeated the story of the unusual conquest, and finished by asking, "What can you make of it? What strange power did that child use, that so completely whipped my uncle?"

The answer to his question will be found in the principles described in this book. The answer is full and complete. It contains details and instructions sufficient to enable anyone to understand, and apply the same force which the little child accidentally stumbled upon.

Keep your mind alert, and you will observe exactly what strange power came to the rescue of the child, you will catch a glimpse of this power in the next chapter. Somewhere in the book you will find an idea that will quicken your receptive powers, and place at your command, for your own benefit, this same irresistible power. The awareness of this power may come to you in the first chapter, or it may flash into your mind in some subsequent chapter. It may come in the form of a single idea. Or, it may come in the nature of a plan, or a purpose. Again, it may cause you to go back into your past experiences of failure or defeat, and bring to the surface some lesson by which you can regain all that you lost through defeat.

After I had described to Mr. Darby the power unwittingly used by the little colored child, he quickly retraced his thirty years of experience as a life insurance salesman, and frankly acknowledged that his success in that field was due, in no small degree, to the lesson he had learned from the child.

Mr. Darby pointed out: "every time a prospect tried to bow me out, without buying, I saw that child standing there in the old mill, her big eyes glaring in defiance, and I said to myself, 'I've gotta make this sale.' The better portion of all sales I have made, were made after people had said 'NO'."

He recalled, too, his mistake in having stopped only three feet from gold, "but," he said, "that experience was a blessing in disguise. It taught me to *keep on keeping on*, no matter how hard the going may be, a lesson I needed to learn before I could succeed in anything."

This story of Mr. Darby and his uncle, the colored child and the gold mine, doubtless will be read by hundreds of men who make their living by selling life insurance, and to all of these, the author wishes to offer the suggestion that Darby owes to these two experiences his ability to sell more than a million dollars of life insurance every year.

Life is strange, and often imponderable! Both the successes and the failures have their roots in simple experiences. Mr. Darby's experiences were commonplace and simple enough, yet they held the answer to his destiny in life, therefore they were as important (to him) as life itself. He profited by these two dramatic experiences, because *he analyzed them*, and found the lesson they taught. But what of the man who has neither the time, nor the inclination to study failure in search of knowledge that may lead to success? Where, and how is he to learn the art of converting defeat into stepping stones to opportunity?

In answer to these questions, this book was written.

The answer called for a description of thirteen principles, but remember, as you read, the answer *you* may be seeking, to the questions which have caused you to ponder over the strangeness of life, may be found *in your own mind*, through some idea, plan, or purpose which may spring into your mind as you read.

One sound idea is all that one needs to achieve success. The principles described in this book, contain the best, and the most practical of all that is known, concerning ways and means of creating useful ideas.

Before we go any further in our approach to the description of these principles, we believe you are entitled to receive this important suggestion...WHEN RICHES BEGIN TO COME THEY COME SO QUICKLY, IN SUCH GREAT ABUNDANCE, THAT ONE WONDERS WHERE THEY HAVE BEEN HIDING DURING ALL THOSE LEAN YEARS. This is an astounding statement, and all the more so, when we take into consideration the popular belief, that riches come only to those who work hard and long.

When you begin to THINK AND GROW RICH, you will observe that riches begin with a state of mind, with definiteness of purpose, with little or no hard work. You, and every other person, ought to be interested in knowing how to acquire that state of mind which will attract riches. I spent twenty-five years in research, analyzing more than 25,000 people, because I, too, wanted to know "how wealthy men become that way."

Without that research, this book could not have been written.

Here take notice of a very significant truth, viz: The business depression started in 1929, and continued on to an all time record of destruction, until sometime after President Roosevelt entered office. Then the depression began to fade into nothingness. Just as an electrician in a theatre raises the lights so gradually that darkness is transmuted into light before you realize it, so did the spell of fear in the minds of the people gradually fade away and become faith.

Observe very closely, as soon as you master the principles of this philosophy, and begin to follow the instructions for applying those principles, your financial status will begin to improve, and everything you touch will begin to transmute itself into an asset for your benefit. Impossible? Not at all!

One of the main weaknesses of mankind is the average man's familiarity with the word "impossible." He knows all the rules which will NOT work. He knows all the things which CANNOT be done. This book was written for those who seek the rules which have made others successful, and are willing to *stake everything* on those rules.

A great many years ago I purchased a fine dictionary. The first thing I did with it was to turn to the word "impossible," and neatly clip it out of the book. That would not be an unwise thing for you to do.

Success comes to those who become SUCCESS CONSCIOUS.

Failure comes to those who indifferently allow themselves to become FAILURE CONSCIOUS.

The object of this book is to help all who seek it, to learn the art of changing their minds from FAILURE CONSCIOUSNESS to SUCCESS CONSCIOUSNESS.

Another weakness found in altogether too many people, is the habit of measuring everything and everyone, by *their own* impressions and beliefs. Some who will read this, will believe that no one can THINK AND GROW RICH. They cannot think in terms of riches, because their thought habits have been steeped in poverty, want, misery, failure, and defeat.

These unfortunate people remind me of a prominent Chinese, who came to America to be educated in American ways. He attended the University of Chicago. One day President Harper met this young Oriental on the campus, stopped to chat with him for a few minutes, and asked what had impressed him as being the most noticeable characteristic of the American people.

"Why," the Chinaman exclaimed, "the queer slant of your eyes. Your eyes are off slant!"

What do we say about the Chinese?

We refuse to believe that which we do not understand. We foolishly believe that our own limitations are the proper measure of limitations. Sure, the other fellow's eyes are "off slant," BECAUSE THEY ARE NOT THE SAME AS OUR OWN.

Millions of people look at the achievements of

Henry Ford, after he has arrived, and envy him, because of his good fortune, or luck, or genius, or whatever it is that they credit for Ford's fortune. Perhaps one person in every hundred thousand knows the secret of Ford's success, and those who do know are too modest, or too reluctant, to speak of it, *because of its simplicity*. A single transaction will illustrate the "secret" perfectly.

A few years back, Ford decided to produce his now famous V-8 motor. He chose to build an engine with the entire eight cylinders cast in one block, and instructed his engineers to produce a design for the engine. The design was placed on paper, but the engineers agreed, to a man, that it was simply *impossible* to cast an eight cylinder gas engine block in one piece.

Ford said, "Produce it anyway."

"But," they replied, "it's impossible!"

"Go ahead," Ford commanded, "and stay on the job until you succeed no matter how much time is required."

The engineers went ahead. There was nothing else for them to do, if they were to remain on the Ford staff. Six months went by, nothing happened. Another six months passed, and still nothing happened. The engineers tried every conceivable plan to carry out the orders, but the thing seemed out of the question; *"impossible!"*

At the end of the year Ford checked with his engineers, and again they informed him they had found no way to carry out his orders.

"Go right ahead," said Ford, "I want it, and I'll have it."

They went ahead, and then, as if by a stroke of magic, the secret was discovered.

The Ford DETERMINATION had won once more!

This story may not be described with minute accuracy, but the sum and substance of it is correct. Deduce from it, you who wish to THINK AND GROW RICH, the secret of the Ford millions, if you can. You'll not have to look very far.

Henry Ford is a success, because he understands, and *applies* the principles of success. One of these is DESIRE: knowing what one wants. Remember this Ford story as you read, and pick out the lines in which the secret of his stupendous achievement have been described. If you can do this, if you can lay your finger on the particular group of principles which made Henry Ford rich, you can equal his achievements in almost any calling for which you are suited.

You Are "the Master of Your Fate, the Captain of Your Soul," because . . .

When Henley wrote the prophetic lines, "I am the Master of my Fate, I am the Captain of my Soul," he should have informed us that we are the Masters of our Fate, the Captains of our Souls, *because* we have the power to control our thoughts.

He should have told us that the ether in which this little earth floats, in which we move and have our being, is a form of energy moving at an inconceivably high rate of vibration, and that the ether is filled with a form of universal power which ADAPTS itself to the nature of the thoughts we hold in our minds; and INFLUENCES us, in natural ways, to transmute our thoughts into their physical equivalent.

If the poet had told us of this great truth, we would know WHY IT IS that we are the Masters of our FATE, the Captains of our Souls. He should have told us, with great emphasis, that this power makes no attempt to discriminate between destructive thoughts and constructive thoughts, that it will urge us to translate into physical reality thoughts of poverty, just as quickly as it will influence us to act upon thoughts of riches.

He should have told us, too, that our brains become magnetized with the dominating thoughts which we hold in our minds, and, by means with which no man is familiar, these "magnets" attract to us the forces, the people, the circumstances of life which harmonize with the nature of our *dominating* thoughts.

He should have told us, that before we can accumulate riches in great abundance, we must magnetize our minds with intense DESIRE for riches, that we must become "money conscious" until the DESIRE for money drives us to create definite plans for acquiring it.

But, being a poet, and not a philosopher, Henley contented himself by stating a great truth in poetic form, leaving those who followed him to interpret the philosophical meaning of his lines.

Little by little, the truth has unfolded itself, until it now appears certain that the principles described in this book, hold the secret of mastery over our economic fate.

We are now ready to examine the first of these principles. Maintain a spirit of open-mindedness, and
remember as your read, they are the invention of no
one man. The principles were gathered from the life
experiences of more than 500 men who actually
accumulated riches in huge amounts; men who
began in poverty, with but little education, without
influence. The principles worked for these men. You
can put them to work for your own enduring benefit.

You will find it easy, not hard, to do.

Before you read the next chapter, I want you to
know that it conveys factual information which
might easily change your entire financial destiny, as
it has so definitely brought changes of stupendous
proportions to two people described.

I want you to know, also, that the relationship
between these two men and myself, is such that I
could have taken no liberties with the facts, even if I
had wished to do so. One of them has been my
closest personal friend for almost twenty-five years,
the other is my own son. The unusual success of
these two men, success which they generously
accredit to the principle described in the next
chapter, more than justifies this personal reference as
a means of emphasizing the far-flung power of this
principle.

Almost fifteen years ago, I delivered the
Commencement Address at Salem College, Salem,
West Virginia. I emphasized the principle described
in the next chapter, with so much intensity that one
of the members of the graduating class definitely
appropriated it, and made it a part of his own philosophy. The young man is now a Member of Congress,

and an important factor in the present administration. Just before this book went to the publisher, he wrote me a letter in which he so clearly stated his opinion of the principle outlined in the next chapter, that I have chosen to publish his letter as an introduction to that chapter.

It gives you an idea of the rewards to come.

"My dear Napoleon:

"My service as a Member of Congress having given me an insight into the problems of men and women, I am writing to offer a suggestion which may become helpful to thousands of worthy people.

"With apologies, I must state that the suggestion, if acted upon, will mean several years of labor and responsibility for you, but I am enheartened to make the suggestion, because I know your great love for rendering useful service.

"In 1922, you delivered the Commencement address at Salem College, when I was a member of the graduating class. In that address, you planted in my mind an idea which has been responsible for the opportunity I now have to serve the people of my State, and will be responsible, in a very large measure, for whatever success I may have in the future.

"The suggestion I have in mind is, that you put into a book the sum and substance of the address you delivered at Salem College, and in that way give the people of America an opportunity to profit by your many years of experience and association with the men who, by their greatness, have made America the richest nation on earth.

"I recall, as though it were yesterday, the marvelous description you gave of the method by which Henry Ford, with but little schooling, without a dollar, with no influential friends, rose to great heights. I made up my mind then, even before you had finished your speech, that I would make a place for myself, no matter how many difficulties I had to surmount.

"Thousands of young people will finish their schooling this year, and within the next few years. Every one of them will be seeking just such a message of practical encouragement as the one I received from you. They will want to know where to turn, what to do, to get started in life. You can tell them, because you have helped to solve the problems of so many, many people.

"If there is any possible way that you can afford to render so great a service, may I offer the suggestion that you include with every book, one of your Personal Analysis Charts, in order that the purchaser of the book may have the benefit of a complete self-inventory, indicating, as you indicated to me years ago, exactly what is standing in the way of success.

"Such a service as this, providing the readers of your book with a complete, unbiased picture of their faults and their virtues, would mean to them the difference between success and failure. The service would be priceless.

"Millions of people are now facing the problem of staging a come-back, because of the depression, and I speak from personal experience when I say, I know these earnest people would welcome the opportunity to tell you their problems, and to receive your suggestions for the solution.

"You know the problems of those who face the necessity of beginning all over again. There are thousands of people in America today who would like to know how they can convert ideas into money, people who must start at scratch, without finances, and recoup their losses. If anyone can help them, you can.

"If you publish the book, I would like to own the first copy that comes from the press, personally autographed by you.

"With best wishes, believe me,

"Cordially yours,

"JENNINGS RANDOLPH"

CHAPTER 2

DESIRE

THE STARTING POINT OF
ALL ACHIEVEMENT
The First Step toward Riches

WHEN Edwin C. Barnes climbed down from the freight train in Orange, N. J., more than thirty years ago, he may have resembled a tramp, but his *thoughts* were those of a king!

As he made his way from the railroad tracks to Thomas A. Edison's office, his mind was at work. He saw himself *standing in Edison's presence*. He heard himself asking Mr. Edison for an opportunity to carry out the one CONSUMING OBSESSION OF HIS LIFE, a BURNING DESIRE to become the business associate of the great inventor.

Barnes' desire was not a *hope!* It was not a *wish!* It was a keen, pulsating DESIRE, which transcended everything else. It was DEFINITE.

The desire was not new when he approached Edison. It had been Barnes' *dominating desire* for a long time. In the beginning, when the desire first appeared in his mind, it may have been, probably was, only a wish, but it was no mere wish when he appeared before Edison with it.

A few years later, Edwin C. Barnes again stood before Edison, in the same office where he first met the inventor. This time his DESIRE had been translated into reality. *He was in business with Edison.* The dominating DREAM OF HIS LIFE had become a reality. Today, people who know

Barnes envy him, because of the "break" life yielded him. They see him in the days of his triumph, without taking the trouble to investigate the *cause* of his success.

Barnes succeeded because he chose a definite goal, placed all his energy, all his will power, all his effort, everything back of that goal. He did not become the partner of Edison the day he arrived. He was content to start in the most menial work, as long as it provided an opportunity to take even one step toward his cherished goal.

Five years passed before the chance he had been seeking made its appearance. During all those years not one ray of hope, not one promise of attainment of his DESIRE had been held out to him. To everyone, except himself, he appeared only another cog in the Edison business wheel, but in his own mind, HE WAS THE PARTNER OF EDISON EVERY MINUTE OF THE TIME, from the very day that he first went to work there.

It is a remarkable illustration of the power of a DEFINITE DESIRE. Barnes won his goal, because he wanted to be a business associate of Mr. Edison, more than he wanted anything else. He created a plan by which to attain that purpose. But he BURNED ALL BRIDGES BEHIND HIM. He stood by his DESIRE until it became the dominating obsession of his life— and—finally, a fact.

When he went to Orange, he did not say to himself, "I will try to induce Edison to give me a job of some sort." He said, "I will see Edison, and put him on notice that I have come to go into business with him."

He did not say, "I will work there for a few months, and if I get no encouragement, I will quit and get a job somewhere else." He did say, "I will start anywhere. I will do anything Edison tells me to do, but *before I am through,* I will be his associate."

He did not say, "I will keep my eyes open for another opportunity, in case I fail to get what I want in the Edison organization." He said, "There is but ONE thing in this world that I am determined to have, and that is a business association with Thomas A. Edison. I will burn all bridges behind me, and stake my ENTIRE FUTURE on my ability to get what I want."

He left himself no possible way of retreat. He had to win or perish!

That is all there is to the Barnes story of success!

A long while ago, a great warrior faced a situation which made it necessary for him to make a decision which insured his success on the battlefield. He was about to send his armies against a powerful foe, whose men outnumbered his own. He loaded his soldiers into boats, sailed to the enemy's country, unloaded soldiers and equipment, then gave the order to burn the ships that had carried them. Addressing his men before the first battle, he said, "You see the boats going up in smoke. That means we cannot leave these shores alive unless we win! We now have no choice—*we win—or we perish!* They won.

Every person who wins in any undertaking must be willing to burn his ships and cut all sources of retreat. Only by so doing can one be sure of maintaining the state of mind known as a BURNING DESIRE TO WIN, essential to success.

The morning after the great Chicago fire, a group of merchants stood on State Street, looking at the smoking remains of what had been their stores. They went into a conference to decide if they would try to rebuild, or leave Chicago and start over in a more promising section of the country. They reached a decision—all except one—to leave Chicago.

The merchant who decided to stay and rebuild pointed a finger at the remains of his store, and said, "Gentlemen, on that very spot I will build the world's greatest store, no matter how many times it may burn down."

That was more than fifty years ago. The store was built. It stands there today, a towering monument to the power of that state of mind known as a BURNING DESIRE. The easy thing for Marshal Field to have done, would have been exactly what his fellow merchants did. When the going was hard, and the future looked dismal, they pulled up and went where the going seemed easier.

Mark well this difference between Marshal Field and the other merchants, because it is the same difference which distinguishes Edwin C. Barnes from thousands of other young men who have worked in the Edison organization. It is the same difference which distinguishes practically all who succeed from those who fail.

Every human being who reaches the age of understanding of the purpose of money, wishes for it. *Wishing* will not bring riches. But *desiring* riches with a state of mind that becomes an obsession, then planning definite ways and means to acquire riches, and backing those plans with persistence which *does not recognize failure*, will bring riches.

The method by which DESIRE for riches can be transmuted into its financial equivalent, consists of six definite, practical steps, viz:

First. Fix in your mind the *exact* amount of money you desire. It is not sufficient merely to say "I want plenty of money." Be definite as to the amount. (There is a psychological reason for definiteness which will be described in a subsequent chapter).

Second. Determine exactly what you intend to give in return for the money you desire. (There is no such reality as "something for nothing.)

Third. Establish a definite date when you intend to *possess* the money you desire.

Fourth. Create a definite plan for carrying out your desire, and begin *at once*, whether you are ready or not, to put this plan into *action*.

Fifth. Write out a clear, concise statement of the amount of money you intend to acquire, name the time limit for its acquisition, state what you intend to give in return for the money, and describe clearly the plan through which you intend to accumulate it.

Sixth. Read your written statement aloud, twice daily, once just before retiring at night, and once after arising in the morning. AS YOU

READ—SEE AND FEEL AND BELIEVE YOUR-
SELF ALREADY IN POSSESSION OF THE
MONEY.

It is important that you follow the instructions
described in these six steps. It is especially important that you observe, and follow the instructions
in the sixth paragraph. You may complain that is
impossible for you to "see yourself in possession of
money" before you actually have it. Here is where
a BURNING DESIRE will come to your aid. If you
truly DESIRE money so keenly that your desire is
an obsession, you will have no difficulty in
convincing yourself that you will acquire it. The
object is to want money, and to become so determined to have it that you CONVINCE yourself you
will have it.

Only those who become "money conscious" ever
accumulate great riches. "Money consciousness"
means that the mind has become so thoroughly satu-
rated with the DESIRE for money, that one can see
one's self already in possession of it.

To the uninitiated, who has not been schooled in
the working principles of the human mind, these
instructions may appear impractical. It may be
helpful, to all who fail to recognize the soundness of
the six steps, to know that the information they
convey, was received from Andrew Carnegie, who
began as an ordinary laborer in the steel mills, but
managed, despite his humble beginning, to make
these principles yield him a fortune of considerably
more than one hundred million dollars.

It may be of further help to know that the six

steps here recommended were carefully scrutinized by the late Thomas A. Edison, who placed his stamp of approval upon them as being, not only the steps essential for the accumulation of money, but necessary for the attainment of *any definite goal.*

The steps call for no "hard labor." They call for no sacrifice. They do not require one to become ridiculous, or credulous. To apply them calls for no great amount of education. But the successful application of these six steps does call for sufficient *imagination* to enable one to see, and to understand, that accumulation of money cannot be left to chance, good fortune, and luck. One must realize that all who have accumulated great fortunes, first did a certain amount of dreaming, hoping, wishing, DESIRING, and PLANNING *before* they acquired money.

You may as well know, right here, that you can never have riches in great quantities, UNLESS you can work yourself into a white heat of DESIRE for money, and actually BELIEVE you will possess it.

You may as well know, also that every great leader, from the dawn of civilization down to the present, was a dreamer. Christianity is the greatest potential power in the world today, because its founder was an intense dreamer who had the vision and the imagination to see realities in their mental and spiritual form before they had been transmuted into physical form.

If you do not see great riches in your imagination, you will never see them in your bank balance.

Never, in the history of America has there been

so great an opportunity for practical dreamers as now exists. The six year economic collapse has reduced all men, substantially, to the same level. A new race is about to be run. The stakes represent huge fortunes which will be accumulated within the next ten years. The rules of the race have changed, because we now live in a CHANGED WORLD that definitely favors the masses, those who had but little or no opportunity to win under the conditions existing during the depression, when fear paralyzed growth and development.

We who are in this race for riches, should be encouraged to know that this changed world in which we live is demanding new ideas, new ways of doing things, new leaders, new inventions, new methods of teaching, new methods of marketing, new books, new literature, new features for the radio, new ideas for moving pictures. Back of all this demand for new and better things, there is one quality which one must possess to win, and that is DEFINITENESS OF PURPOSE, the knowledge of what one wants, and a burning DESIRE to possess it.

The business depression marked the death of one age, and the birth of another. This changed world requires practical dreamers who can, *and will* put their dreams into action. The practical dreamers have always been, and always will be the pattern makers of civilization.

We who desire to accumulate riches, should remember the real leaders of the world always have been men who harnessed, and put into practical use, the intangible, unseen forces of unborn opportunity, and have converted those forces, (or impulses of thought), into sky-scrapers, cities, factories, airplanes, automobiles, and every form of convenience that makes life more pleasant.

Tolerance, and an open mind are practical necessities of the dreamer of today. Those who are afraid of new ideas are doomed before they start. Never has there been a time more favorable to pioneers than the present. True, there is no wild and woolly west to be conquered, as in the days of the Covered Wagon; but there is a vast business, financial, and industrial world to be remoulded and redirected along new and better lines.

In planning to acquire your share of the riches, let no one influence you to scorn the dreamer. To win the big stakes in this changed world, you must catch the spirit of the great pioneers of the past, whose dreams have given to civilization all that it has of value, the spirit which serves as the life-blood of our own country—your opportunity and mine, to develop and market our talents.

Let us not forget, Columbus dreamed of an Unknown world, staked his life on the existence of such a world, and discovered it!

Copernicus, the great astronomer, dreamed of a multiplicity of worlds, and revealed them! No one denounced him as "impractical" *after* he had triumphed. Instead, the world worshipped at his shrine, thus proving once more that "SUCCESS REQUIRES NO APOLOGIES, FAILURE PERMITS NO ALIBIS."

If the thing you wish to do is right, and *you believe in it*, go ahead and do it! Put your dream across, and never mind what "they" say if you meet with temporary defeat, for "they," perhaps, do not know that EVERY FAILURE BRINGS WITH IT THE SEED OF AN EQUIVALENT SUCCESS.

Henry Ford, poor and uneducated, dreamed of a horseless carriage, went to work with what tools he possessed, without waiting for opportunity to favor him, and now evidence of his dream belts the entire earth. He has put more wheels into operation than any man who ever lived, because he was not afraid to back his dreams.

Thomas Edison dreamed of a lamp that could be operated by electricity, began where he stood to put his dream into action, and despite more than *ten thousand failures*, he stood by that dream until he made it a physical reality. Practical dreamers DO NOT QUIT!

Whelan dreamed of a chain of cigar stores, transformed his dream into action, and now the United Cigar Stores occupy the best corners in America.

Lincoln dreamed of freedom for the black slaves, put his dream into action, and barely missed living to see a united North and South translate his dream into reality.

The Wright brothers dreamed of a machine that would fly through the air. Now one may see evidence all over the world, that they dreamed soundly.

Marconi dreamed of a system for harnessing the intangible forces of the ether. Evidence that he did not dream in vain, may be found in every wireless and radio in the world. Moreover, Marconi's dream brought the humblest cabin, and the most stately manor house side by side. It made the people of every nation on earth back-door neighbors. It gave the President of the United States a medium by which he may talk to all the people of America at one time, and on short notice. It may interest you to know that Marconi's "friends" had him taken into custody, and examined in a psychopathic hospital, when he announced he had discovered a principle through which he could send messages through the air, without the aid of wires, or other direct physical means of communication. The dreamers of today fare better.

The world has become accustomed to new discoveries. Nay, it has shown a willingness to reward the dreamer who gives the world a new idea.

"The greatest achievement was, at first, and for a time, but a dream."

"The oak sleeps in the acorn. The bird waits in the egg, and in the highest vision of the soul, a waking angel stirs. DREAMS ARE THE SEEDLINGS OF REALITY."

Awake, arise, and assert yourself, you dreamers of the world. Your star is now in the ascendency. The world depression brought the opportunity you have been waiting for. It taught people humility, tolerance, and open-mindedness.

The world is filled with an abundance of OPPORTUNITY which the dreamers of the past never knew.

A BURNING DESIRE TO BE, AND TO DO is the starting point from which the dreamer must take off. Dreams are not born of indifference, laziness, or lack of ambition.

The world no longer scoffs at the dreamer, nor

calls him impractical. If you think it does, take a trip to Tennessee, and witness what a dreamer President has done in the way of harnessing, and using the great water power of America. A score of years ago, such a dream would have seemed like madness.

You have been disappointed, you have undergone defeat during the depression, you have felt the great heart within you crushed until it bled. Take courage, for these experiences have tempered the spiritual metal of which you are made—they are assets of incomparable value.

Remember, too, that all who succeed in life get off to a bad start, and pass through many heart-breaking struggles before they "arrive." The turning point in the lives of those who succeed, usually comes at the moment of some crisis, through which they are introduced to their "other selves."

John Bunyan wrote the Pilgrim's Progress, which is among the finest of all English literature, after he had been confined in prison and sorely punished, because of his views on the subject of religion.

O. Henry discovered the genius which slept within his brain, after he had met with great misfortune, and was confined in a prison cell, in Columbus, Ohio. Being FORCED, through misfortune, to become acquainted with his "other self," and to use his IMAGINATION, he discovered himself to be a great author instead of a miserable criminal and outcast. Strange and varied are the ways of life, and stranger still are the ways of Infinite Intelligence, through which men are sometimes forced to undergo all sorts of punishment before discovering their own brains, and their own capacity to create useful ideas through imagination.

Edison, the world's greatest inventor and scientist, was a "tramp" telegraph operator, he failed innumerable times before he was driven, finally, to the discovery of the genius which slept within his brain.

Charles Dickens began by pasting labels on blacking pots. The tragedy of his first love penetrated the depths of his soul, and converted him into one of the world's truly great authors. That tragedy produced, first, David Copperfield, then a succession of other works that made this a richer and better world for all who read his books. Disappointment over love affairs, generally has the effect of driving men to drink, and women to ruin; and this, because most people never learn the art of transmuting their strongest emotions into dreams of a constructive nature.

Helen Keller became deaf, dumb, and blind shortly after birth. Despite her greatest misfortune, she has written her name indelibly in the pages of the history of the great. Her entire life has served as evidence that *no one ever is defeated until defeat has been accepted as a reality.*

Robert Burns was an illiterate country lad, he was cursed by poverty, and grew up to be a drunkard in the bargain. The world was made better for his having lived, because he clothed beautiful thoughts in poetry, and thereby plucked a thorn and planted a rose in its place.

Booker T. Washington was born in slavery, handicapped by race and color. Because he was tolerant, had an open mind at all times, on all subjects, and was a DREAMER, he left his impress for good on an entire race.

Beethoven was deaf, Milton was blind, but their names will last as long as time endures, because they dreamed and translated their dreams into organized thought.

Before passing to the next chapter, kindle anew in your mind the fire of hope, faith, courage, and tolerance. If you have these states of mind, and a working knowledge of the principles described, all else that you need will come to you, when you are READY for it. Let Emerson state the thought in these words, "Every proverb, every book, every byword that belongs to thee for aid and comfort shall surely come home through open or winding passages. Every friend whom not thy fantastic will, but the great and tender soul in thee craveth, shall lock thee in his embrace."

There is a difference between WISHING for a thing and being READY to receive it. No one is *ready* for a thing, until he *believes* he can acquire it. The state of mind must be BELIEF, not mere hope or wish. Open-mindedness is essential for belief. Closed minds do not inspire faith, courage, and belief.

Remember, no more effort is required to aim high in life, to demand abundance and prosperity, than is required to accept misery and poverty. A great poet has correctly stated this universal truth through these lines:

> "I bargained with Life for a penny,
> And Life would pay no more,

However I begged at evening
When I counted my scanty store.

"For Life is a just employer,
He gives you what you ask,
But once you have set the wages,
Why, you must bear the task.

"I worked for a menial's hire,
Only to learn, dismayed,
That any wage I had asked of Life,
Life would have willingly paid."

DESIRE OUTWITS MOTHER NATURE

As a fitting climax to this chapter, I wish to introduce one of the most unusual persons I have ever known. I first saw him twenty-four years ago, a few minutes after he was born. He came into the world without any physical sign of ears, and the doctor admitted, when pressed for an opinion, that the child might be deaf, and mute for life.

I challenged the doctor's opinion. I had the right to do so, I was the child's father. I, too, reached a decision, and rendered an opinion, but I expressed the opinion silently, in the secrecy of my own heart. I decided that my son would hear and speak. Nature could send me a child without ears, but Nature *could not induce me to accept* the reality of the affliction.

In my own mind I knew that my son would hear and speak. How? I was sure there must be a way, and I knew I would find it. I thought of the words of the immortal Emerson, "The whole course of things goes to teach us faith. We need only obey.

There is guidance for each of us, and by lowly listening, we shall hear *the right word.*"

The right word? DESIRE! More than anything else, I DESIRED that my son should not be a deaf mute. From that desire I never receded, not for a second.

Many years previously, I had written, "Our only limitations are those we set up in our own minds." For the first time, I wondered if that statement were true. Lying on the bed in front of me was a newly born child, without the natural equipment of hearing. Even though he might hear and speak, he was obviously disfigured for life. Surely, this was a limitation which that child had not set up in his own mind.

What could I do about it? Somehow I would find a way to transplant into that child's mind my own BURNING DESIRE for ways and means of conveying sound to his brain without the aid of ears.

As soon as the child was old enough to cooperate, I would fill his mind so completely with a BURNING DESIRE to hear, that Nature would, by methods of her own, translate it into physical reality.

All this thinking took place in my own mind, but I spoke of it to no one. Every day I renewed the pledge I had made to myself, not to accept a deaf mute for a son.

As he grew older, and began to take notice of things around him, we observed that he had a slight degree of hearing. When he reached the age when children usually begin talking, he made no attempt to speak, but we could tell by his actions that he could hear certain sounds slightly. That was all I wanted to know! I was convinced that if he could hear, even slightly, he might develop still greater hearing capacity. Then something happened which gave me hope. It came from an entirely unexpected source.

We bought a victrola. When the child heard the music for the first time, he went into ecstasies, and promptly appropriated the machine. He soon showed a preference for certain records, among them, "It's a Long Way to Tipperary." On one occasion, he played that piece over and over, for almost two hours, standing in front of the victrola, *with his teeth clamped on the edge of the case.* The significance of this self-formed habit of his did not become clear to us until years afterward, for we had never heard of the principle of "bone conduction" of sound at that time.

Shortly after he appropriated the victrola, I discovered that he could hear me quite clearly when I spoke with my lips touching his mastoid bone, or at the base of the brain. These discoveries placed in my possession the necessary media by which I began to translate into reality my *Burning Desire* to help my son develop hearing and speech. By that time he was making stabs at speaking certain words. The outlook was far from encouraging, but DESIRE BACKED BY FAITH knows no such word as impossible.

Having determined that he could hear the sound of my voice plainly, I began, immediately, to transfer to his mind the desire to hear and speak. I soon discovered that the child enjoyed bedtime stories, so I went to work, creating stories designed to develop in him self-reliance, imagination, and a *keen desire to hear and to be normal.*

There was one story in particular, which I emphasized by giving it some new and dramatic coloring each time it was told. It was designed to plant in his mind the thought that his affliction was not a liability, but an asset of great value. Despite the fact that all the philosophy I had examined clearly indicated that EVERY ADVERSITY BRINGS WITH IT THE SEED OF AN EQUIVALENT ADVANTAGE, I must confess that I had not the slightest idea *how* this affliction could ever become an asset. However, I continued my practice of wrapping that philosophy in bedtime stories, hoping the time would come when he would find some plan by which his handicap could be made to serve some useful purpose.

Reason told me plainly, that there was no adequate compensation for the lack of ears and natural hearing equipment. DESIRE backed by FAITH, pushed reason aside, and inspired me to carry on.

As I analyze the experience in retrospect, I can see now, that my son's *faith in me* had much to do with the astounding results. He did not question anything I told him. I sold him the idea that he had a distinct *advantage* over his older brother, and that this advantage would reflect itself in many ways. For example, the teachers in school would observe that he had no ears, and, because of this, they would show him special attention and treat him with extraordinary kindness. They always did. His mother saw to that, by visiting the teachers and arranging with them to give the child the extra attention necessary. I sold him the idea, too, that when he became old enough to sell newspapers, (his older brother had already become a newspaper merchant), he would have a big advantage over his brother, for the reason that people would pay him extra money for his wares, because they could see that he was a bright, industrious boy, despite the fact he had no ears.

We could notice that, gradually, the child's hearing was improving. Moreover, he had not the slightest tendency to be self-conscious, because of his affliction. When he was about seven, he showed the first evidence that our method of servicing his mind was bearing fruit. For several months he begged for the privilege of selling newspapers, but his mother would not give her consent. She was afraid that his deafness made it unsafe for him to go on the street alone.

Finally, he took matters in his own hands. One afternoon, when he was left at home with the servants, he climbed through the kitchen window, shinnied to the ground, and set out on his own. He borrowed six cents in capital from the neighborhood shoemaker, invested it in papers, sold out, reinvested, and kept repeating until late in the evening. After balancing his accounts, and paying back the six cents he had borrowed from his banker, he had a net profit of forty-two cents. When we got home that night, we found him in bed asleep, with the money tightly clenched in his hand.

His mother opened his hand, removed the coins, and cried. Of all things! Crying over her son's first victory seemed so inappropriate. My reaction was the reverse. I laughed heartily, for I knew that my endeavor to plant in the child's mind an attitude of faith in himself had been successful.

His mother saw, in his first business venture, a little deaf boy who had gone out in the streets and risked his life to earn money. I saw a brave, ambitious, self-reliant little business man whose stock in himself had been increased a hundred percent, because he had gone into business on his own initiative, and had won. The transaction pleased me, because I knew that he had given evidence of a trait of resourcefulness that would go with him all through life. Later events proved this to be true. When his older brother wanted something, he would lie down on the floor, kick his feet in the air, cry for it—and get it. When the "little deaf boy" wanted something, he would plan a way to earn the money, then buy it for himself. He still follows that plan!

Truly, my own son has taught me that handicaps can be converted into stepping stones on which one may climb toward some worthy goal, unless they are accepted as obstacles, and used as alibis.

The little deaf boy went through the grades, high school, and college without being able to hear his teachers, excepting when they shouted loudly, at close range. He did not go to a school for the deaf. WE WOULD NOT PERMIT HIM TO LEARN THE SIGN LANGUAGE. We were determined that he should live a normal life, and associate with normal children, and we stood by that decision, although it cost us many heated debates with school officials.

[57]

While he was in high school, he tried an electrical hearing aid, but it was of no value to him; due, we believed, to a condition that was disclosed when the child was six, by Dr. J. Gordon Wilson, of Chicago, when he operated on one side of the boy's head, and discovered that there was no sign of natural hearing equipment.

During his last week in college, (eighteen years after the operation), something happened which marked the most important turning-point of his life. Through what seemed to be mere chance, he came into possession of another electrical hearing device, which was sent to him on trial. He was slow about testing it, due to his disappointment with a similar device. Finally he picked the instrument up, and more or less carelessly, placed it on his head, hooked up the battery, and lo! as if by a stroke of magic, his lifelong DESIRE FOR NORMAL HEARING BECAME A REALITY! For the first time in his life he heard practically as well as any person with normal hearing. "God moves in mysterious ways, His wonders to perform."

Overjoyed because of the Changed World which had been brought to him through his hearing device, he rushed to the telephone, called his mother, and heard her voice perfectly. The next day he plainly heard the voices of his professors in class, for the first time in his life! Previously he could hear them only when they shouted, at short range. He heard the radio. He *heard* the talking pictures. For the first time in his life, he could converse freely with other people, without the necessity of their having to speak loudly. Truly, he had come into possession of a Changed World. We had refused to accept Nature's error, and, by PERSISTENT DESIRE, we had induced Nature to correct that error, through the only practical means available.

DESIRE had commenced to pay dividends, but the victory was not yet complete. The boy still had to find a definite and practical way to convert his handicap into an *equivalent asset*.

Hardly realizing the significance of what had already been accomplished, but intoxicated with the joy of his newly discovered world of sound, he wrote a letter to the manufacturer of the hearing-aid, enthusiastically describing his experience. Something in his letter; something, perhaps which was not written on the lines, but back of them; caused the company to invite him to New York. When he arrived, he was escorted through the factory, and while talking with the Chief Engineer, telling him about his changed world, a hunch, an idea, or an inspiration—call it what you wish—flashed into his mind. It was *this impulse of thought* which converted his affliction into an asset, destined to pay dividends in both money and happiness to thousands for all time to come.

The sum and substance of that impulse of thought was this: It occurred to him that he might be of help to the millions of deafened people who go through life without the benefit of hearing devices, if he could find a way to tell them the story of his Changed World. Then and there, he reached a decision to devote the remainder of his life to rendering useful service to the hard of hearing.

For an entire month, he carried on an intensive

research, during which he analyzed the entire marketing system of the manufacturer of the hearing device, and created ways and means of communicating with the hard of hearing all over the world for the purpose of sharing with them his newly discovered "Changed World." When this was done, he put in writing a two-year plan, based upon his findings. When he presented the plan to the company, he was instantly given a position, for the purpose of carrying out his ambition.

Little did he dream, when he went to work, that he was destined to bring hope and practical relief to thousands of deafened people who, without his help, would have been doomed forever to deaf mutism.

Shortly after he became associated with the manufacturer of his hearing aid, he invited me to attend a class conducted by his company, for the purpose of teaching deaf mutes to hear, and to speak. I had never heard of such a form of education, therefore I visited the class, skeptical but hopeful that my time would not be entirely wasted. Here I saw a demonstration which gave me a greatly enlarged vision of what I had done to arouse and keep alive in my son's mind the DESIRE for normal hearing. I saw deaf mutes actually being taught to hear and to speak, through application of the self-same principle I had used, more than twenty years previously, in saving my son from deaf mutism.

Thus, through some strange turn of the Wheel of Fate, my son, Blair, and I have been destined to aid in correcting deaf mutism for those as yet unborn, because we are the only living human beings, as far as I know, who have established definitely the fact that deaf mutism can be corrected to the extent of restoring to normal life those who suffer with this affliction. It has been done for one; it will be done for others.

There is no doubt in my mind that Blair would have been a deaf mute all his life, if his mother and I had not managed to shape his mind as we did. The doctor who attended at his birth told us, confidentially, the child might never hear or speak. A few weeks ago, Dr. Irving Voorhees, a noted specialist on such cases, examined Blair very thoroughly. He was astounded when he learned how well my son now hears, and speaks, and said his examination indicated that "theoretically, the boy should not be able to hear at all." But the lad does hear, despite the fact that X-ray pictures show there is no opening in the skull, whatsoever, from where his ears should be to the brain.

When I planted in his mind the DESIRE to hear and talk, and live as a normal person, there went with that impulse some strange influence which caused Nature to become bridge-builder, and span the gulf of silence between his brain and the outer world, by some means which the keenest medical specialists have not been able to interpret. It would be sacrilege for me to even conjecture as to how Nature performed this miracle. It would be unforgiveable if I neglected to tell the world as much as I know of the humble part I assumed in the strange experience. It is my duty, and a privilege to say I believe, and not without reason, that nothing is impossible to the person who backs DESIRE with enduring FAITH.

Verily, a BURNING DESIRE has devious ways of transmuting itself into its physical equivalent. Blair DESIRED normal hearing; now he has it! He was born with a handicap which might easily have sent one with a less defined DESIRE to the street with a bundle of pencils and a tin cup. That handicap now promises to serve as the medium by which he will render useful service to many millions of hard of hearing, also, to give him useful employment at adequate financial compensation the remainder of his life.

The little "white lies" I planted in his mind when he was a child, by leading him to BELIEVE his affliction would become a great asset, which he could capitalize, has justified itself. Verily, there is nothing, right or wrong, which BELIEF, plus BURNING DESIRE, cannot make real. These qualities are free to everyone.

In all my experience in dealing with men and women who had personal problems, I never handled a single case which more definitely demonstrates the power of DESIRE. Authors sometimes make the mistake of writing of subjects of which they have but superficial, or very elementary knowledge. It has been my good fortune to have had the privilege of testing the soundness of the POWER OF DESIRE, through the affliction of my own son. Perhaps it was providential that the experience came as it did, for surely no one is better prepared than he, to serve as an example of what happens when DESIRE is put to the test. *If Mother Nature bends to the will of desire, is it logical that mere men can defeat a burning desire?*

Strange and imponderable is the power of the human mind! We do not understand the method by which it uses every circumstance, every individual, every physical thing within its reach, as a means of transmuting DESIRE into its physical counterpart. Perhaps science will uncover this secret.

I planted in my son's mind the DESIRE to hear and to speak as any normal person hears and speaks. That DESIRE has now become a reality. I planted in his mind the DESIRE to convert his greatest handicap into his greatest asset. That DESIRE has been realized. The modus operandi by which this astounding result was achieved is not hard to describe. It consisted of three very definite facts; first, I MIXED FAITH with the DESIRE for normal hearing, which I passed on to my son. Second, I communicated my desire to him in every conceivable way available, through persistent, continuous effort, over a period of years. Third, HE BELIEVED ME!

As this chapter was being completed, news came of the death of Mme. Schuman-Heink. One short paragraph in the news dispatch gives the clue to this unusual woman's stupendous success as a singer. I quote the paragraph, because the clue it contains is none other than DESIRE.

Early in her career, Mme. Schuman-Heink visited the director of the Vienna Court Opera, to have him test her voice. But, he did not test it. After taking one look at the awkward and poorly dressed girl, he exclaimed, none too gently, "With such a face, and with no personality at all, how can you ever expect to succeed in opera? My good child, give up the idea. Buy a sewing machine, and go to work. YOU CAN NEVER BE A SINGER."

Never is a long time! The director of the Vienna Court Opera knew much about the technique of singing. He knew little about the power of desire, when it assumes the proportion of an obsession. If he had known more of that power, he would not have made the mistake of condemning genius without giving it an opportunity.

Several years ago, one of my business associates became ill. He became worse as time went on, and finally was taken to the hospital for an operation. Just before he was wheeled into the operating room, I took a look at him, and wondered how anyone as thin and emaciated as he, could possibly go through a major operation successfully. The doctor warned me that there was little if any chance of my ever seeing him alive again. But that was the DOCTOR'S OPINION. It was not the opinion of the patient. Just before he was wheeled away, he whispered feebly, "Do not be disturbed, Chief, I will be out of here in a few days." The attending nurse looked at me with pity. But the patient did come through safely. After it was all over, his physician said, "Nothing but his own desire to live saved him. He never would have pulled through if he had not refused to accept the possibility of death."

I believe in the power of DESIRE backed by FAITH, because I have seen this power lift men from lowly beginnings to places of power and wealth; I have seen it rob the grave of its victims; I have seen it serve as the medium by which men staged a comeback after having been defeated in a hundred different ways; I have seen it provide my own son with a normal, happy, successful life, despite Nature's having sent him into the world without ears.

How can one harness and use the power of DESIRE? This has been answered through this, and the subsequent chapters of this book. This message is going out to the world at the end of the longest, and perhaps, the most devastating depression America has ever known. It is reasonable to presume that the message may come to the attention of many who have been wounded by the depression, those who have lost their fortunes, others who have lost their positions, and great numbers who must reorganize their plans and stage a comeback. To all these I wish to convey the thought that all achievement, no matter what may be its nature, or its purpose, must begin with an intense, BURNING DESIRE for something definite.

Through some strange and powerful principle of "mental chemistry" which she has never divulged, Nature wraps up in the impulse of STRONG DESIRE "that something" which recognizes no such word as impossible, and accepts no such reality as failure.

CHAPTER 3

FAITH

VISUALIZATION OF, AND BELIEF
IN ATTAINMENT OF DESIRE
The Second Step toward Riches

FAITH is the head chemist of the mind. When FAITH is blended with the vibration of thought, the subconscious mind instantly picks up the vibration, translates it into its spiritual equivalent, and transmits it to Infinite Intelligence, as in the case of prayer.

The emotions of FAITH, LOVE, and SEX are the most powerful of all the major positive emotions. When the three are blended, they have the effect of "coloring" the vibration of thought in such a way that it instantly reaches the subconscious mind, where it is changed into its spiritual equivalent, the only form that induces a response from Infinite Intelligence.

Love and faith are psychic; related to the spiritual side of man. Sex is purely biological, and related only to the physical. The mixing, or blending, of these three emotions has the effect of opening a direct line of communication between the finite, thinking mind of man, and Infinite Intelligence.

HOW TO DEVELOP FAITH

There comes, now, a statement which will give a better understanding of the importance the principle of auto-suggestion assumes in the transmutation of desire into its physical, or monetary equivalent;

namely: FAITH is a state of mind which may be induced, or created, by affirmation or repeated instructions to the subconscious mind, through the principle of auto-suggestion.

As an illustration, consider the purpose for which you are, presumably, reading this book. The object is, naturally, to acquire the ability to transmute the intangible thought impulse of DESIRE into its physical counterpart, money. By following the instructions laid down in the chapters on auto-suggestion, and the subconscious mind, summarized in the chapter on auto-suggestion, you may CONVINCE the subconscious mind that you *believe* you will receive that for which you ask, and it will act upon that belief, which your subconscious mind passes back to you in the form of "FAITH," followed by definite plans for procuring that which you desire.

The method by which one develops FAITH, where it does not already exist, is extremely difficult to describe, almost as difficult, in fact, as it would be to describe the color of red to a blind man who has never seen color, and has nothing with which to compare what you describe to him. Faith is a state of mind which you may develop at will, after you have mastered the thirteen principles, because it is a state of mind which develops voluntarily, through application and use of these principles.

Repetition of affirmation of orders to your subconscious mind is the only known method of voluntary development of the emotion of faith.

Perhaps the meaning may be made clearer

through the following explanation as to the way men sometimes become criminals. Stated in the words of a famous criminologist, "When men first come into contact with crime, they abhor it. If they remain in contact with crime for a time, they become accustomed to it, and endure it. If they remain in contact with it long enough, they finally embrace it, and become influenced by it."

This is the equivalent of saying that any impulse of thought which is repeatedly passed on to the subconscious mind is, finally, accepted and acted upon by the subconscious mind, which proceeds to translate that impulse into its physical equivalent, by the most practical procedure available.

In connection with this, consider again the statement, ALL THOUGHTS WHICH HAVE BEEN EMOTIONALIZED, (given feeling) AND MIXED WITH FAITH, begin immediately to translate themselves into their physical equivalent or counterpart.

The emotions, or the "feeling" portion of thoughts, are the factors which give thoughts vitality, life and action. The emotions of Faith, Love, and Sex, when mixed with any thought impulse, give it greater action than any of these emotions can do singly.

Not only thought impulses which have been mixed with FAITH, but those which have been mixed with any of the positive emotions, or any of the negative emotions, may reach, and influence the subconscious mind.

From this statement, you will understand that the subconscious mind will translate into its physical equivalent, a thought impulse of a negative or destructive nature, just as readily as it will act upon thought impulses of a positive or constructive nature. This accounts for the strange phenomenon which so many millions of people experience, referred to as "misfortune," or "bad luck."

There are millions of people who BELIEVE themselves "doomed" to poverty and failure, because of some strange force over which they BELIEVE they have no control. They are the creators of their own "misfortunes," because of this negative BELIEF, which is picked up by the subconscious mind, and translated into its physical equivalent.

This is an appropriate place at which to suggest again that you may benefit, by passing on to your subconscious mind, any DESIRE which you wish translated into its physical, or monetary equivalent, in a state of expectancy or BELIEF that the transmutation will actually take place. Your BELIEF, or FAITH, is the element which determines the action of your subconscious mind. There is nothing to hinder you from "deceiving" your subconscious mind when giving it instructions through autosuggestion, as I deceived my son's subconscious mind.

To make this "deceit" more realistic, conduct yourself just as you would, if you were ALREADY IN POSSESSION OF THE MATERIAL THING WHICH YOU ARE DEMANDING, when you call upon your subconscious mind.

The subconscious mind will transmute into its physical equivalent, by the most direct and practical media available, any order which is given to it in a state of BELIEF, or FAITH that the order will be carried out.

Surely, enough has been stated to give a starting point from which one may, through experiment and practice, acquire the ability to mix FAITH with any order given to the subconscious mind. Perfection will come through practice. It *cannot* come by merely *reading* instructions.

If it be true that one may become a criminal by association with crime, (and this is a known fact), it is equally true that one may develop faith by voluntarily suggesting to the subconscious mind that one has faith. The mind comes, finally, to take on the nature of the influences which dominate it. Understand this truth, and you will know why it is essential for you to encourage the *positive emotions* as dominating forces of your mind, and discourage— and *eliminate* negative emotions.

A mind dominated by positive emotions, becomes a favorable abode for the state of mind known as faith. A mind so dominated may, at will, give the subconscious mind instructions, which it will accept and act upon immediately.

FAITH IS A STATE OF MIND WHICH MAY BE INDUCED BY AUTO-SUGGESTION

All down the ages, the religionists have admonished struggling humanity to "have faith" in this, that, and the other dogma or creed, but they have failed to tell people HOW to have faith. They have not stated that "faith is a state of mind, and that it may be induced by self-suggestion."

In language which any normal human being can understand, we will describe all that is known about the principle through which FAITH may be developed, where it does not already exist.

Have Faith in yourself; Faith in the Infinite.

Before we begin, you should be reminded again that:

FAITH is the "eternal elixir" which gives life, power, and action to the impulse of thought!

The foregoing sentence is worth reading a second time, and a third, and a fourth. It is worth reading aloud!

FAITH is the starting point of all accumulation of riches!

FAITH is the basis of all "miracles," and all mysteries which cannot be analyzed by the rules of science!

FAITH is the only known antidote for FAILURE!

FAITH is the element, the "chemical" which, when mixed with prayer, gives one direct communication with Infinite Intelligence.

FAITH is the element which transforms the ordinary vibration of thought, created by the finite mind of man, into the spiritual equivalent.

FAITH is the only agency through which the cosmic force of Infinite Intelligence can be harnessed and used by man.

EVERY ONE OF THE FOREGOING STATEMENTS IS CAPABLE OF PROOF!

The proof is simple and easily demonstrated. It is wrapped up in the principle of auto-suggestion. Let us center our attention, therefore, upon the subject of self-suggestion, and find out what it is, and what it is capable of achieving.

It is a well known fact that one comes, finally, to BELIEVE whatever one repeats to one's self, *whether the statement be true or false.* If a man repeats a lie over and over, he will eventually accept the lie as truth. Moreover, he will BELIEVE it to be the truth. Every man is what he is, because of the DOMINATING THOUGHTS which he permits to occupy his mind. Thoughts which a man deliberately places in his own mind, and encourages with sympathy, and with which he mixes any one or more of the emotions, constitute the motivating forces, which direct and control his every movement, act, and deed!

Comes, now, a very significant statement of truth:

THOUGHTS WHICH ARE MIXED WITH ANY OF THE FEELINGS OF EMOTIONS, CONSTITUTE A "MAGNETIC" FORCE WHICH ATTRACTS, FROM THE VIBRATIONS OF THE ETHER, OTHER SIMILAR, OR RELATED THOUGHTS. A thought thus "magnetized" with emotion may be compared to a seed which, when planted in fertile soil, germinates, grows, and multiples itself over and over again, until that which was originally one small seed, becomes countless millions of seeds of the SAME BRAND!

The ether is a great cosmic mass of eternal forces of vibration. It is made up of both destructive vibrations and constructive vibrations. It carries, at all times, vibrations of fear, poverty, disease, failure, misery; and vibrations of prosperity, health, success, and happiness, just as surely as it carries the sound of hundreds of orchestrations of music, and hundreds of human voices, all of which maintain their own individuality, and means of identification, through the medium of radio.

From the great storehouse of the ether, the human mind is constantly attracting vibrations which harmonize with that which DOMINATES the human mind. Any thought, idea, plan, or purpose which one *holds* in one's mind attracts, from the vibrations of the ether, a host of its relatives, adds these "relatives" to its own force, and grows until it becomes the dominating, MOTIVATING MASTER of the individual in whose mind it has been housed.

Now, let us go back to the starting point, and become informed as to how the original seed of an idea, plan, or purpose may be planted in the mind. The information is easily conveyed: any idea, plan, or purpose may be placed in the mind *through repetition of thought.* This is why you are asked to write out a statement of your major purpose, or Definite Chief Aim, commit it to memory, and repeat it, in audible words, day after day, until these vibrations of sound have reached your subconscious mind.

We are what we are, because of the vibrations of thought which we pick up and register, through the stimuli of our daily environment.

Resolve to throw off the influences of any unfortunate environment, and to build your own life to ORDER. Taking inventory of mental assets and liabilities, you will discover that your greatest weakness is lack of self-confidence. This handicap can be surmounted, and timidity translated into courage, through the aid of the principle of auto-suggestion. The application of this principle may be made through a simple arrangement of positive thought impulses stated in writing, memorized, and repeated, until they become a part of the working equipment of the subconscious faculty of your mind.

SELF-CONFIDENCE FORMULA

First. I know that I have the ability to achieve the object of my Definite Purpose in life, therefore, I DEMAND of myself persistent, continuous action toward its attainment, and I here and now promise to render such action.

Second. I realize the dominating thoughts of my mind will eventually reproduce themselves in outward, physical action, and gradually transform themselves into physical reality, therefore, I will concentrate my thoughts for thirty minutes daily, upon the task of thinking of the person I intend to become, thereby creating in my mind a clear mental picture of that person.

Third. I know through the principle of auto-suggestion, any desire that I persistently hold in my mind will eventually seek expression through some practical means of attaining the object back of it, therefore, I will devote ten minutes daily to demanding of myself the development of SELF-CONFIDENCE.

Fourth. I have clearly written down a description of my DEFINITE CHIEF AIM in life, and I will never stop trying, until I shall have developed sufficient self-confidence for its attainment.

Fifth. I fully realize that no wealth or position can long endure, unless built upon truth and justice, therefore, I will engage in no transaction which does not benefit all whom it affects. I will succeed by attracting to myself the forces I wish to use, and the cooperation of other people. I will induce others to serve me, because of my willingness to serve others. I will eliminate hatred, envy, jealousy, selfishness, and cynicism, by developing love for all humanity, because I know that a negative attitude toward others can never bring me success. I will cause others to believe in me, because I will believe in them, and in myself.

I will sign my name to this formula, commit it to memory, and repeat it aloud once a day, with full FAITH that it will gradually influence my THOUGHTS and ACTIONS so that I will become a self-reliant, and successful person.

Back of this formula is a law of Nature which no man has yet been able to explain. It has baffled the scientists of all ages. The psychologists have named this law "auto-suggestion," and let it go at that.

The name by which one calls this law is of little importance. The important fact about it is—it

WORKS for the glory and success of mankind, IF it is used constructively. On the other hand, if used destructively, it will destroy just as readily. In this statement may be found a very significant truth, namely; that those who go down in defeat, and end their lives in poverty, misery, and distress, do so because of negative application of the principle of auto-suggestion. The cause may be found in the fact that ALL IMPULSES OF THOUGHT HAVE A TENDENCY TO CLOTHE THEMSELVES IN THEIR PHYSICAL EQUIVALENT.

The subconscious mind, (the chemical laboratory in which all thought impulses are combined, and made ready for translation into physical reality), makes no distinction between constructive and destructive thought impulses. It works with the material we feed it, through our thought impulses. The subconscious mind will translate into reality a thought driven by FEAR just as readily as it will translate into reality a thought driven by COURAGE, or FAITH.

The pages of medical history are rich with illustrations of cases of "suggestive suicide." A man may commit suicide through negative suggestion, just as effectively as by any other means. In a midwestern city, a man by the name of Joseph Grant, a bank official, "borrowed" a large sum of the bank's money, without the consent of the directors. He lost the money through gambling. One afternoon, the Bank Examiner came and began to check the accounts. Grant left the bank, took a room in a local hotel, and when they found him, three days later, he was lying in bed, wailing and moaning, repeating over and over these words, "My God, this will kill me! I cannot stand the disgrace." In a short time he was dead. The doctors pronounced the case one of "mental suicide."

Just as electricity will turn the wheels of industry, and render useful service if used constructively; or sniff out life if wrongly used, so will the law of auto-suggestion lead you to peace and prosperity, or down into the valley of misery, failure, and death, according to your degree of understanding and application of it.

If you fill your mind with FEAR, doubt and unbelief in your ability to connect with, and use the forces of Infinite Intelligence, the law of auto-suggestion will take this spirit of unbelief and use it as a pattern by which your subconscious mind will translate it into its physical equivalent.

THIS STATEMENT IS AS TRUE AS THE STATEMENT THAT TWO AND TWO ARE FOUR!

Like the wind which carries one ship East, and another West, the law of auto-suggestion will lift you up or pull you down, according to the way you set your sails of THOUGHT.

The law of auto-suggestion, through which any person may rise to altitudes of achievement which stagger the imagination, is well described in the following verse:

"If you *think* you are beaten, you are,
   If you *think* you dare not, you don't
If you like to win, but you *think* you can't
   It is almost certain you won't.

"If you *think* you'll lose, you're lost
    For out of the world we find,
Success begins with a fellow's will—
    It's all in the *state of mind.*

"If you *think* you are outclassed, you are,
    You've got to *think* high to rise,
You've got to be *sure of yourself* before
    You can ever win a prize.

"Life's battles don't always go
    To the stronger or faster man,
But soon or late the man who wins
    Is the man WHO THINKS HE CAN!"

Observe the words which have been emphasized, and you will catch the deep meaning which the poet had in mind.

Somewhere in your make-up (perhaps in the cells of your brain) there lies *sleeping,* the seed of achievement which, if aroused and put into action, would carry you to heights, such as you may never have hoped to attain.

Just as a master musician may cause the most beautiful strains of music to pour forth from the strings of a violin, so may you arouse the genius which lies asleep in your brain, and cause it to drive you upward to whatever goal you may wish to achieve.

Abraham Lincoln was a failure at everything he tried, until he was well past the age of forty. He was a Mr. Nobody from Nowhere, until a great experience came into his life, aroused the sleeping genius within his heart and brain, and gave the world one of its really great men. That "experience" was mixed with the emotions of sorrow and LOVE. It came to him through Anne Rutledge, the only woman whom he ever truly loved.

It is a known fact that the emotion of LOVE is closely akin to the state of mind known as FAITH, and this for the reason that Love comes very near to translating one's thought impulses into their spiritual equivalent. During his work of research, the author discovered, from the analysis of the life-work and achievements of hundreds of men of outstanding accomplishment, that there was the influence of a woman's love back of nearly EVERY ONE OF THEM. The emotion of love, in the human heart and brain, creates a favorable field of magnetic attraction, which causes an influx of the higher and finer vibrations which are afloat in the ether.

If you wish evidence of the power of FAITH, study the achievements of men and women who have employed it. At the head of the list comes the Nazarene. Christianity is the greatest single force which influences the minds of men. The basis of Christianity is FAITH, no matter how many people may have perverted, or misinterpreted the meaning of this great force, and no matter how many dogmas and creeds have been created in its name, which do not reflect its tenets.

The sum and substance of the teachings and the achievements of Christ, which may have been inter-preted as "miracles," were nothing more nor less than FAITH. If there are any such phenomena as "miracles" they are produced only through the state of mind known as FAITH! Some teachers of religion, and many who call themselves Christians, neither understand nor practice FAITH.

Let us consider the power of FAITH, as it is now being demonstrated, by a man who is well known to all of civilization, Mahatma Gandhi, of India. In this man the world has one of the most astounding examples known to civilization, of the possibilities of FAITH. Gandhi wields more potential power than any man living at this time, and this, despite the fact that he has none of the orthodox tools of power, such as money, battle ships, soldiers, and materials of warfare. Gandhi has no money, he has no home, he does not own a suit of clothes, but HE DOES HAVE POWER. How does he come by that power?

HE CREATED IT OUT OF HIS UNDER-STANDING OF THE PRINCIPLE OF FAITH, AND THROUGH HIS ABILITY TO TRANSPLANT THAT FAITH INTO THE MINDS OF TWO HUNDRED MILLION PEOPLE.

Gandhi has accomplished, through the influence of FAITH, that which the strongest military power on earth could not, and never will accomplish through soldiers and military equipment. He has accomplished the astounding feat of INFLUENCING two hundred million minds to COALESCE AND MOVE IN UNISON, AS A SINGLE MIND.

What other force on earth, except FAITH could do as much?

There will come a day when employees as well as employers will discover the possibilities of FAITH. That day is dawning. The whole world has had ample opportunity, during the recent business depression, to witness what the LACK OF FAITH will do to business.

Surely, civilization has produced a sufficient number of intelligent human beings to make use of this great lesson which the depression has taught the world. During this depression, the world had evidence in abundance that widespread FEAR will paralyze the wheels of industry and business. Out of this experience will arise leaders in business and industry who will profit by the example which Gandhi has set for the world, and they will apply to business the same tactics which he has used in building the greatest following known in the history of the world. These leaders will come from the rank and file of the unknown men, who now labor in the steel plants, the coal mines, the automobile factories, and in the small towns and cities of America.

Business is due for a reform, make no mistake about this! The methods of the past, based upon economic combinations of FORCE and FEAR, will be supplanted by the better principles of FAITH and cooperation. Men who labor will receive more than daily wages; they will receive dividends from the business, the same as those who supply the capital for business; but, first they must GIVE MORE TO THEIR EMPLOYERS, and stop this bickering and bargaining by force, at the expense of the public. *They must earn the right to dividends!*

Moreover, and this is the most important thing of all—THEY WILL BE LED BY LEADERS WHO WILL UNDERSTAND AND APPLY THE PRINCIPLES EMPLOYED BY MAHATMA

GANDHI. Only in this way may leaders get from their followers the spirit of FULL cooperation which constitutes power in its highest and most enduring form.

This stupendous machine age in which we live, and from which we are just emerging, has taken the soul out of men. Its leaders have driven men as though they were pieces of cold machinery; they were forced to do so by the employees who have bargained, at the expense of all concerned, to *get* and not to *give*. The watchword of the future will be HUMAN HAPPINESS AND CONTENTMENT, and when this state of mind shall have been attained, the production will take care of itself, more effectively than anything that has ever been accomplished where men did not, and could not mix FAITH and individual interest with their labor.

Because of the need for faith and cooperation in operating business and industry, it will be both interesting and profitable to analyze an event which provides an excellent understanding of the method by which industrialists and business men accumulate great fortunes, by *giving* before they try to *get*.

The event chosen for this illustration dates back to 1900, when the United States Steel Corporation was being formed. As you read the story, keep in mind these fundamental facts and you will understand how IDEAS have been converted into huge fortunes.

First, the huge United States Steel Corporation was born in the mind of Charles M. Schwab, in the form of an IDEA he created through his IMAGINATION! Second, he mixed FAITH with his

IDEA. Third, he formulated a PLAN for the transformation of his IDEA into physical and financial
reality. Fourth, he put his plan into action with his
famous speech at the University Club. Fifth, he
applied, and followed-through on his PLAN with
PERSISTENCE, and backed it with firm DECISION
until it had been fully carried out. Sixth, he prepared
the way for success by a BURNING DESIRE for
success.

If you are one of those who have often wondered
how great fortunes are accumulated, this story of the
creation of the United States Steel Corporation will
be enlightening. If you have any doubt that men can
THINK AND GROW RICH, this story should dispel
that doubt, because you can plainly see in the story
of the United States Steel, the application of a major
portion of the thirteen principles described in this
book.

This astounding description of the power of an
IDEA was dramatically told by John Lowell, in the
New York World-Telegram, with whose courtesy it is
here reprinted.

"A Pretty After-Dinner Speech for a Billion Dollars

"When, on the evening of December 12, 1900, some
eighty of the nation's financial nobility gathered in
the banquet hall of the University Club on Fifth
Avenue to do honor to a young man from out of the
West, not half a dozen of the guests realized they were
to witness the most significant episode in American
industrial history.

"J. Edward Simmons and Charles Stewart Smith,

their hearts full of gratitude for the lavish hospitality bestowed on them by Charles M. Schwab during a recent visit to Pittsburgh, had arranged the dinner to introduce the thirty-eight-year-old steel man to eastern banking society. But they didn't expect him to stampede the convention. They warned him, in fact, that the bosoms within New York's stuffed shirts would not be responsive to oratory, and that, if he didn't want to bore the Stillmans and Harrimans and Vanderbilts, he had better limit himself to fifteen or twenty minutes of polite vaporings and let it go at that.

"Even John Pierpont Morgan, sitting on the right hand of Schwab as became his imperial dignity, intended to grace the banquet table with his presence only briefly. And so far as the press and public were concerned, the whole affair was of so little moment that no mention of it found its way into print the next day.

"So the two hosts and their distinguished guests ate their way through the usual seven or eight courses. There was little conversation and what there was of it was restrained. Few of the bankers and brokers had met Schwab, whose career had flowered along the banks of the Monongahela, and none knew him well. But before the evening was over, they—and with them Money Master Morgan— were to be swept off their feet, and a billion-dollar baby, the United States Steel Corporation, was to be conceived.

"It is perhaps unfortunate, for the sake of history, that no record of Charlie Schwab's speech at the dinner ever was made. He repeated some parts of it at a later date during a similar meeting of Chicago bankers. And still later, when the Government brought suit to dissolve the Steel Trust, he gave his own version, from the witness stand, of the remarks that stimulated Morgan into a frenzy of financial activity.

"It is probable, however, that it was a 'homely' speech, somewhat ungrammatical (for the niceties of language never bothered Schwab), full of epigram and threaded with wit. But aside from that it had a galvanic force and effect upon the five billions of estimated capital that was represented by the diners. After it was over and the gathering was still under its spell, although Schwab had talked for ninety minutes, Morgan led the orator to a recessed window where, dangling their legs from the high, uncomfortable seat, they talked for an hour more.

"The magic of the Schwab personality had been turned on, full force, but what was more important and lasting was the full-fledged, clear-cut program he laid down for the aggrandizement of Steel. Many other men had tried to interest Morgan in slapping together a steel trust after the pattern of the biscuit, wire and hoop, sugar, rubber, whisky, oil or chewing gum combinations. John W. Gates, the gambler, had urged it, but Morgan distrusted him. The Moore boys, Bill and Jim, Chicago stock jobbers who had glued together a match trust and a cracker corporation, had urged it and failed. Elbert H. Gary, the sanctimonious country lawyer, wanted to foster it, but he wasn't big enough to be impressive. Until Schwab's eloquence took J. P.

Morgan to the heights from which he could visualize the solid results of the most daring financial undertaking ever conceived, the project was regarded as a delirious dream of easy-money crackpots.

"The financial magnetism that began, a generation ago, to attract thousands of small and sometimes inefficiently managed companies into large and competition-crushing combinations, had become operative in the steel world through the devices of that jovial business pirate, John W. Gates. Gates already had formed the American Steel and Wire Company out of a chain of small concerns, and together with Morgan had created the Federal Steel Company. The National Tube and American Bridge companies were two more Morgan concerns, and the Moore Brothers had forsaken the match and cookie business to form the 'American' group—Tin Plate, Steel Hoop, Sheet Steel—and the National Steel Company.

"But by the side of Andrew Carnegie's gigantic vertical trust, a trust owned and operated by fifty-three partners, those other combinations were picayune. They might combine to their heart's content but the whole lot of them couldn't make a dent in the Carnegie organization, and Morgan knew it.

"The eccentric old Scot knew it, too. From the magnificent heights of Skibo Castle he had viewed, first with amusement and then with resentment, the attempts of Morgan's smaller companies to cut into his business. When the attempts became too bold, Carnegie's temper was translated into anger and retaliation. He decided to duplicate every mill owned by his rivals. Hitherto, he hadn't been interested in wire, pipe, hoops, or sheet. Instead, he was content to sell such companies the raw steel and let them work it into whatever shape they wanted. Now, with Schwab as his chief and able lieutenant, he planned to drive his enemies to the wall.

"So it was that in the speech of Charles M. Schwab, Morgan saw the answer to his problem of combination. A trust without Carnegie—giant of them all—would be no trust at all, a plum pudding, as one writer said, without the plums.

"Schwab's speech on the night of December 12, 1900, undoubtedly carried the inference, though not the pledge, that the vast Carnegie enterprise could be brought under the Morgan tent. He talked of the world future for steel, of reorganization for efficiency, of specialization, of the scrapping of unsuccessful mills and concentration of effort on the flourishing properties, of economies in the ore traffic, of economies in overhead and administrative departments, of capturing foreign markets.

"More than that, he told the buccaneers among them wherein lay the errors of their customary piracy. Their purposes, he inferred, had been to create monopolies, raise prices, and pay themselves fat dividends out of privilege. Schwab condemned the system in his heartiest manner. The shortsightedness of such a policy, he told his hearers, lay in the fact that it restricted the market in an era when everything cried for expansion. By cheapening the cost of steel, he argued, an ever-expanding market would be created; more uses for steel would be devised, and a goodly portion of the world trade could be captured. Actually, though he did not know it, Schwab was an apostle of modern mass production.

"So the dinner at the University Club came to an end. Morgan went home, to think about Schwab's rosy predictions. Schwab went back to Pittsburgh to run the steel business for 'Wee Andra Carnegie,' while Gary and the rest went back to their stock tickers, to fiddle around in anticipation of the next move.

"It was not long coming. It took Morgan about one week to digest the feast of reason Schwab had placed before him. When he had assured himself that no financial indigestion was to result, he sent for Schwab—and found that young man rather coy. Mr. Carnegie, Schwab indicated, might not like it if he found his trusted company president had been flirting with the Emperor of Wall Street, the Street upon which Carnegie was resolved never to tread. Then it was suggested by John W. Gates the go-between, that if Schwab 'happened' to be in the Bellevue Hotel in Philadelphia, J.P. Morgan might also 'happen' to be there. When Schwab arrived, however, Morgan was inconveniently ill at his New York home, and so, on the elder man's pressing invitation, Schwab went to New York and presented himself at the door of the financier's library.

"Now certain economic historians have professed the belief that from the beginning to the end of the drama, the stage was set by Andrew Carnegie—that the dinner to Schwab, the famous speech, the Sunday night conference between Schwab and the Money King, were events arranged by the canny

Scot. The truth is exactly the opposite. When Schwab was called in to consummate the deal, he didn't even know whether 'the little boss,' as Andrew was called, would so much as listen to an order to sell, particularly to a group of men whom Andrew regarded as being endowed with something less than holiness. But Schwab did take into the conference with him, in his own handwriting, six sheets of copper-plate figures, representing to his mind the physical worth and the potential earning capacity of every steel company he regarded as an essential star in the new metal firmament.

"Four men pondered over these figures all night. The chief, of course, was Morgan, steadfast in his belief in the Divine Right of Money. With him was his aristocratic partner, Robert Bacon, a scholar and a gentleman. The third was John W. Gates whom Morgan scorned as a gambler and used as a tool. The fourth was Schwab, who knew more about the processes of making and selling steel than any whole group of men then living. Throughout that conference, the Pittsburgher's figures were never questioned. If he said a company was worth so much, then it was worth that much and no more. He was insistent, too, upon including in the combination only those concerns he nominated. He had conceived a corporation in which there would be no duplication, not even to satisfy the greed of friends who wanted to unload their companies upon the broad Morgan shoulders. Thus he left out, by design, a number of the larger concerns upon which the Walruses and Carpenters of Wall Street had cast hungry eyes.

"When dawn came, Morgan rose and straightened his back. Only one question remained.

" 'Do you think you can persuade Andrew Carnegie to sell?' he asked.

" 'I can try,' said Schwab.

" 'If you can get him to sell, I will undertake the matter,' said Morgan.

"So far so good. But would Carnegie sell? How much would he demand? (Schwab thought about $320,000,000). What would he take payment in? Common or preferred stocks? Bonds? Cash? Nobody could raise a third of a billion dollars in cash.

"There was a golf game in January on the frost-cracking heath of the St. Andrews links in Westchester, with Andrew bundled up in sweaters against the cold, and Charlie talking volubly, as usual, to keep his spirits up. But no word of business was mentioned until the pair sat down in the cozy warmth of the Carnegie cottage hard by. Then, with the same persuasiveness that had hypnotized eighty millionaires at the University Club, Schwab poured out the glittering promises of retirement in comfort, of untold millions to satisfy the old man's social caprices. Carnegie capitulated, wrote a figure on a slip of paper, handed it to Schwab and said, 'all right, that's what we'll sell for.'

"The figure was approximately $400,000,000, and was reached by taking the $320,000,000 mentioned by Schwab as a basic figure, and adding to it $80,000,000 to represent the increased capital value over the previous two years.

"Later, on the deck of a trans-Atlantic liner, the

Scotsman said ruefully to Morgan, 'I wish I had asked you for $100,000,000 more.'

" 'If you had asked for it, you'd have gotten it,' Morgan told him cheerfully.

*　　*　　*　　*　　*　　*　　*

"There was an uproar, of course. A British correspondent cabled that the foreign steel world was 'appalled' by the gigantic combination. President Hadley, of Yale, declared that unless trusts were regulated the country might expect 'an emperor in Washington within the next twenty-five years.' But that able stock manipulator, Keene, went at his work of shoving the new stock at the public so vigorously that all the excess water—estimated by some at nearly $600,000,000—was absorbed in a twinkling. So Carnegie had his millions, and the Morgan syndicate had $62,000,000 for all its 'trouble,' and all the 'boys,' from Gates to Gary, had their millions.

*　　*　　*　　*　　*　　*　　*

"The thirty-eight-year-old Schwab had his reward. He was made president of the new corporation and remained in control until 1903."

The dramatic story of "Big Business" which you have just finished, was included in this book, because it is a perfect illustration of the method by which DESIRE CAN BE TRANSMUTED INTO ITS PHYSICAL EQUIVALENT!

I imagine some readers will question the statement that a mere, intangible DESIRE can be converted into its physical equivalent. Doubtless some will say, "You cannot convert NOTHING into

SOMETHING!" The answer is in the story of United States Steel.

That giant organization was created in the mind of one man. The plan by which the organization was provided with the steel mills that gave it financial stability was created in the mind of the same man. His FAITH, his DESIRE, his IMAGINATION, his PERSISTENCE were the real ingredients that went into United States Steel. The steel mills and mechanical equipment acquired by the corporation, AFTER IT HAD BEEN BROUGHT INTO LEGAL EXISTENCE, were incidental, but careful analysis will disclose the fact that the appraised value of the properties acquired by the corporation increased in value by an estimated SIX HUNDRED MILLION DOLLARS, by the mere transaction which consolidated them under one management.

In other words, Charles M. Schwab's IDEA, plus the FAITH with which he conveyed it to the minds of J.P. Morgan and the others, was marketed for a profit of approximately $600,000,000. Not an insignificant sum for a single IDEA!

What happened to some of the men who took their share of the millions of dollars of profit made by this transaction, is a matter with which we are not now concerned. The important feature of the astounding achievement is that it serves as unquestionable evidence of the soundness of the philosophy described in this book, because this philosophy was the warp and the woof of the entire transaction. Moreover, the practicability of the philosophy has been established by the fact that the

United States Steel Corporation prospered, and became one of the richest and most powerful corporations in America, employing thousands of people, developing new uses for steel, and opening new markets; thus providing that the $600,000,000 in profit which the Schwab IDEA produced was earned.

RICHES begin in the form of THOUGHT!

The amount is limited only by the person in whose mind the THOUGHT is put into motion. FAITH removes limitations! Remember this when you are ready to bargain with Life for whatever it is that you ask as your price for having passed this way.

Remember, also, that the man who created the United States Steel Corporation was practically unknown at the time. He was merely Andrew Carnegie's "Man Friday" until he gave birth to his famous IDEA. After that he quickly rose to a position of power, fame, and riches.

THERE ARE NO LIMI-
TATIONS TO THE
MIND EXCEPT THOSE
WE *ACKNOWLEDGE*

BOTH *POVERTY* AND
RICHES ARE THE
OFFSPRING OF
THOUGHT

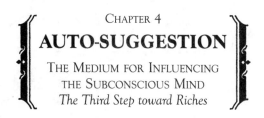

CHAPTER 4

AUTO-SUGGESTION

THE MEDIUM FOR INFLUENCING
THE SUBCONSCIOUS MIND
The Third Step toward Riches

AUTO-SUGGESTION is a term which applies to all suggestions and all self-administered stimuli which reach one's mind through the five senses. Stated in another way, auto-suggestion is self-suggestion. It is the agency of communication between that part of the mind where conscious thought takes place, and that which serves as the seat of action for the subconscious mind.

Through the dominating thoughts which one *permits* to remain in the conscious mind, (whether these thoughts be negative or positive, is immaterial), the principle of auto-suggestion voluntarily reaches the subconscious mind and influences it with these thoughts.

NO THOUGHT, whether it be negative or positive, CAN ENTER THE SUBCONSCIOUS MIND WITHOUT THE AID OF THE PRINCIPLE OF AUTO-SUGGESTION, with the exception of thoughts picked up from the ether. Stated differently, all sense impressions which are perceived through the five senses, are stopped by the CONSCIOUS thinking mind, and may be either passed on to the subconscious mind, or rejected, at will. The conscious faculty serves, therefore, as an outerguard to the approach of the subconscious.

Nature has so built man that he has ABSOLUTE CONTROL over the material which reaches his subconscious mind, through his five senses, although this is not meant to be constructed as a statement that man always EXERCISES this control. In the great majority of instances, he does NOT exercise it, which explains why so many people go through life in poverty.

Recall what has been said about the subconscious mind resembling a fertile garden spot, in which weeds will grow in abundance, if the seeds of more desirable crops are not sown therein. AUTO-SUGGES-TION is the agency of control through which an individual may voluntarily feed his subconscious mind on thoughts of a creative nature, or, by neglect, permit thoughts of a destructive nature to find their way into this rich garden of the mind.

You were instructed, in the last of the six steps described in the chapter on Desire, to read ALOUD twice daily the WRITTEN statement of your DESIRE FOR MONEY, and to SEE AND FEEL yourself ALREADY in possession of the money! By following these instructions, you communicate the object of your DESIRE directly to your SUBCON-SCIOUS mind in a spirit of absolute FAITH. Through repetition of this procedure, you voluntarily create thought habits which are favorable to your efforts to transmute desire into its monetary equivalent.

Go back to these six steps described in chapter two, and read them again, very carefully, before you proceed further. Then (when you come to it), read very carefully the four instructions for the organization of your "Master Mind" group, described in the chapter on Organized Planning. By comparing these two sets of instructions with that which has been stated on auto-suggestion, you, of course, will see that the instructions involve the application of the principle of auto-suggestion.

Remember, therefore, when reading aloud the statement of your desire (through which you are endeavoring to develop a "money consciousness"), that the mere reading of the words is of NO CONSEQUENCE—UNLESS you mix emotion, or feeling with your words. If you repeat a million times the famous Emil Coué formula, "Day by day, in every way, I am getting better and better," without mixing emotion and FAITH with your words, you will experience no desirable results. Your subconscious mind recognizes and acts upon ONLY thoughts which have been well-mixed with emotion or feeling.

This is a fact of such importance as to warrant repetition in practically every chapter, because the lack of understanding of this is the main reason the majority of people who try to apply the principle of auto-suggestion get no desirable results.

Plain, unemotional words do not influence the subconscious mind. You will get no appreciable results until you learn to reach your subconscious mind with thoughts, or spoken words which have been well emotionalized with BELIEF.

Do not become discouraged, if you cannot control and direct your emotions the first time you try to do so. Remember, there is no such possibility as SOMETHING FOR NOTHING. Ability to reach, and influence your subconscious mind has its price, and you MUST PAY THAT PRICE. You cannot cheat, even if you desire to do. The price of ability to influence your subconscious mind is everlasting PERSISTENCE in applying the principles described here. You cannot develop the desired ability for a lower price. You, and YOU ALONE, must decide whether or not the reward for which you are striving (the "money conscious"), is worth the price you must pay for it in effort.

Wisdom and "cleverness" alone, will not attract and retain money except in a few very rare instances, where the law of averages favors the attraction of money through these sources. The method of attracting money described here, does not depend upon the law of averages. Moreover, the method plays no favorites. It will work for one person as effectively as it will for another. Where failure is experienced, it is the individual, *not the method*, which has failed. If you try and fail, make another effort, and still another, until you succeed.

Your ability to use the principle of auto-suggestion will depend, very largely, upon your capacity to CONCENTRATE upon a given DESIRE until that desire becomes a BURNING OBSESSION.

When you begin to carry out the instructions in connection with the six steps described in the second chapter, it will be necessary for you to make use of the principle of CONCENTRATION.

Let us here offer suggestions for the effective use of concentration. When you begin to carry out the first of the six steps, which instructs you to "fix in your own mind the EXACT amount of money you desire," hold your thoughts on that amount of money by CONCENTRATION, or fixation of attention, with your eyes closed, until you can ACTUALLY SEE the physical appearance of the money. Do this at least once each day. As you go through these exercises, follow the instructions given in the chapter on FAITH, and see yourself actually IN POSSESSION OF THE MONEY!

Here is a most significant fact—the subconscious mind takes any orders given it in a spirit of absolute FAITH, and acts upon those orders, although the orders often have to be presented *over and over again,* through repetition, before they are interpreted by the subconscious mind. Following the preceding statement, consider the possibility of playing a perfectly legitimate "trick" on your subconscious mind, by making it believe, *because you believe it,* that you must have the amount of money you are visualizing, that this money is already awaiting your claim, that the subconscious mind MUST hand over to you practical plans for acquiring the money which is yours.

Hand over the thought suggested in the preceding paragraph to your IMAGINATION, and see what your imagination can, or will do, to create practical plans for the accumulation of money through transmutation of your desire.

DO NOT WAIT for a definite plan, through which you intend to exchange services or merchandise in return for the money you are visualizing, but begin at once to see yourself in possession of the money, DEMANDING and EXPECTING meanwhile, that your subconscious mind will hand over the plan, or plans you need. Be on the alert for these plans, and when they appear, put them into ACTION IMMEDIATELY. When the plans appear, they will probably "flash" into your mind through the sixth sense, in the form of an "inspiration." This inspiration may be considered a direct "telegram," or message from Infinite Intelligence. Treat it with respect, and act upon it as soon as you receive it. Failure to do this will be FATAL to your success.

In the fourth of the six steps, you were instructed to "Create a definite plan for carrying out your desire, and begin at once to put this plan into action." You should follow this instruction in the manner described in the preceding paragraph. Do not trust to your "reason" when creating your plan for accumulating money through the transmutation of desire. Your reason is faulty. Moreover, your reasoning faculty may be lazy, and, if you depend entirely upon it to serve you, it may disappoint you.

When visualizing the money you intend to accumulate, (with closed eyes), *see yourself rendering the service, or delivering the merchandise you intend to give in return for this money. This is important!*

SUMMARY OF INSTRUCTIONS

The fact that you are reading this book is an indication that you earnestly seek knowledge. It is also an indication that you are a student of this subject. If you are only a student, there is a chance that you may learn much that you did not know, but you will learn only by assuming an attitude of humility. If you choose to follow some of the instructions but neglect, or refuse to follow others—*you will fail!* To get satisfactory results, you must follow ALL instructions in a spirit of FAITH.

The instructions given in connection with the six steps in the second chapter will now be summarized, and blended with the principles covered by this chapter, as follows:

First. Go into some quiet spot (preferably in bed at night) where you will not be disturbed or interrupted, close your eyes, and repeat aloud, (so you may hear your own words) the written statement of the amount of money you intend to accumulate, the time limit for its accumulation, and a description of the service or merchandise you intend to give in return for the money. As you carry out these instructions, SEE YOURSELF ALREADY IN POSSESSION OF THE MONEY.

For example:—Suppose that you intend to accumulate $50,000 by the first of January, five years hence, that you intend to give personal services in return for the money, in the capacity of a salesman. Your written statement of your purpose should be similar to the following:

"By the first day of January, 19..., I will have in my possession $50,000, which will come to me in various amounts from time to time during the interim.

"In return for this money I will give the most efficient service of which I am capable, rendering the fullest possible quantity, and the best possible quality of service in the capacity of salesman of . . . . (describe the service or merchandise you intend to sell).

"I believe that I will have this money in my possession. My faith is so strong that I can now see this money before my eyes. I can touch it with my hands. It is now awaiting transfer to me at the time, and in the proportion that I deliver the service I intend to render in return for it. I am awaiting a plan by which to accumulate this money, and I will follow that plan, when it is received."

Second. Repeat this program night and morning until you can see, (in your imagination) the money you intend to accumulate.

Third. Place a written copy for your statement where you can see it night and morning, and read it just before retiring, and upon arising until it has been memorized.

Remember, as you carry out these instructions, that you are applying the principle of auto-suggestion, for the purpose of giving orders to your subconscious mind. Remember, also, that your subconscious mind will act ONLY upon instructions which are emotionalized, and handed over to it with "feeling." FAITH is the strongest, and most productive of the emotions. Follow the instructions given in the chapter on FAITH.

These instructions may, at first, seem abstract. Do not let this disturb you. Follow the instructions, no matter how abstract or impractical they may, at first, appear to be. The time will soon come, if you do as you have been instructed, *in spirit as well as in act*, when a whole new universe of power will unfold to you.

Scepticism, in connection will ALL new ideas, is characteristic of all human beings. But if you follow the instructions outlined, your skepticism will soon be replaced by belief, and this, in turn, will soon become crystallized into ABSOLUTE FAITH. Then you will have arrived at the point where you may truly say, "I am the master of my fate, I am the captain of my soul!"

Many philosophers have made the statement, that man is the master of his own *earthly* destiny, but most of them have failed to say *why* he is the master. The reason that man may be the master of his own earthly status, and especially his financial status, is thoroughly explained in this chapter. Man may become the master of himself, and of his environment, because he has the POWER TO INFLUENCE HIS OWN SUBCONSCIOUS MIND, and through it, gain the cooperation of Infinite Intelligence.

You are now reading the chapter which represents the keystone to the arch of this philosophy. The instructions contained in this chapter must be understood and APPLIED WITH PERSISTENCE, if you succeed in transmuting desire into money.

The actual performance of transmuting DESIRE into money, involves the use of auto-suggestion as an agency by which one may reach, and influence, the subconscious mind. The other principles are simply tools with which to apply auto-suggestion. Keep this thought in mind, and you will, at all times, be conscious of the important part the principle of auto-suggestion is to play in your efforts to accumulate money through the methods described in this book.

Carry out these instructions as though you were a small child. Inject into your efforts something of the FAITH of a child. The author has been most careful, to see that no impractical instructions were included, because of his sincere desire to be helpful.

After you have read the entire book, come back to this chapter, and follow in spirit, and in action, this instruction:

READ THE ENTIRE CHAPTER ALOUD ONCE EVERY NIGHT, UNTIL YOU BECOME THOR-OUGHLY CONVINCED THAT THE PRINCIPLE OF AUTO-SUGGESTION IS SOUND, THAT IT WILL ACCOMPLISH FOR YOU ALL THAT HAS BEEN CLAIMED FOR IT. AS YOU READ, *UNDERSCORE WITH A PENCIL* EVERY SENTENCE WHICH IMPRESSES YOU FAVORABLY.

Follow the foregoing instruction to the letter, and it will open the way for a complete understanding, and mastery of the principles of success.

CHAPTER 5

SPECIALIZED KNOWLEDGE

PERSONAL EXPERIENCES OR
OBSERVATIONS
The Fourth Step toward Riches

THERE are two kinds of knowledge. One is general, the other is specialized. General knowledge, no matter how great in quantity or variety it may be, is of but little use in the accumulation of money. The faculties of the great universities possess, in the aggregate, practically every form of general knowledge known to civilization. *Most of the professors have but little or no money.* They specialize on *teaching* knowledge, but they do not specialize on the organization, or the *use* of knowledge.

KNOWLEDGE will not attract money, unless it is organized, and intelligently directed, through practical PLANS OF ACTION, to the DEFINITE END of accumulation of money. Lack of understanding of this fact has been the source of confusion to millions of people who falsely believe that "knowledge is power." It is nothing of the sort! Knowledge is only *potential* power. It becomes power only when, and if, it is organized into definite plans of action, and directed to a definite end.

This "missing link" in all systems of education known to civilization today, may be found in the failure of educational institutions to teach their students HOW TO ORGANIZE AND USE KNOWLEDGE AFTER THEY ACQUIRE IT.

Many people make the mistake of assuming that,

because Henry Ford had but little "schooling," he is not a man of "education." Those who make this mistake do not know Henry Ford, nor do they understand the real meaning of the word "educate." That word is derived from the Latin word "educo," meaning to educe, to draw out, to DEVELOP FROM WITHIN.

An educated man is not, necessarily, one who has an abundance of general or specialized knowledge. An educated man is one who has so developed the faculties of his mind that he may acquire anything he wants, or its equivalent, without violating the rights of others. Henry Ford comes well within the meaning of this definition.

During the world war, a Chicago newspaper published certain editorials in which, among other statements, Henry Ford was called "an ignorant pacifist." Mr. Ford objected to the statements, and brought suit against the paper for libeling him. When the suit was tried in the Courts, the attorneys for the paper pleaded justification, and placed Mr. Ford, himself, on the witness stand, for the purpose of proving to the jury that he was ignorant. The attorneys asked Mr. Ford a great variety of questions, all of them intended to prove, by his own evidence, that, while he might possess considerable specialized knowledge pertaining to the manufacture of automobiles, he was, in the main, ignorant.

Mr. Ford was plied with such questions as the following:

"Who was Benedict Arnold?" and "How many soldiers did the British send over to America to put down the Rebellion of 1776?" In answer to the last question, Mr. Ford replied, "I do not know the exact number of soldiers the British sent over, but I have heard that it was a considerably larger number than ever went back."

Finally, Mr. Ford became tired of this line of questioning, and in reply to a particularly offensive question he leaned over, pointed his finger at the lawyer who has asked the question, and said, "If I should really WANT to answer the foolish question you have just asked, or any of the other questions you have been asking me, let me remind you that I have a row of electric push-buttons on my desk, and by pushing the right button, I can summon to my aid men who can answer ANY question I desire to ask concerning the business to which I am devoting most of my efforts. Now, will you kindly tell me, WHY I should clutter up my mind with general knowledge, for the purpose of being able to answer questions, when I have men around me who can supply any knowledge I require?"

There certainly was good logic to that reply.

That answer floored the lawyer. Every person in the courtroom realized it was the answer, not of an ignorant man, but of a man of EDUCATION. Any man is educated who knows where to get knowledge when he needs it, and how to organize that knowledge into definite plans of action. Through the assistance of his "Master Mind" group, Henry Ford had at his command all the specialized knowledge he needed to enable him to become one of the wealthiest men in America. *It was not essential that he have this knowledge in his own mind.* Surely no person who has sufficient inclination and intelligence to read a book of this nature can possibly miss the significance of this illustration.

Before you can be sure of your ability to transmute DESIRE into its monetary equivalent, you will require SPECIALIZED KNOWLEDGE of the service, merchandise, or profession which you intend to offer in return for fortune. Perhaps you may need much more specialized knowledge than you have the ability or the inclination to acquire, and if this should be true, you may bridge your weakness through the aid of your "Master Mind" group.

Andrew Carnegie stated that he, personally, knew nothing about the technical end of the steel business; moreover, he did not particularly care to know anything about it. The specialized knowledge which he required for the manufacture and marketing of steel, he found available through the individual units of his MASTER MIND GROUP.

The accumulation of great fortunes calls for POWER, and power is acquired through highly organized and intelligently directed specialized knowledge, but that knowledge does not, necessarily, have to be in the possession of the man who accumulates the fortune.

The preceding paragraph should give hope and encouragement to the man with ambition to accumulate a fortune, who has not possessed himself of the necessary "education" to supply such specialized knowledge as he may require. Men sometimes go through life suffering from "inferiority complexes, because they are not men of "education." The man who can organize and direct a "Master Mind" group of men who possess knowledge useful in the accumulation of money, is just as much a man of education as any man in the group. REMEMBER THIS, if you suffer from a feeling of inferiority, because your schooling has been limited.

Thomas A. Edison had only three months of "schooling" during his entire life. He did not lack education, neither did he die poor.

Henry Ford had less than a sixth grade "schooling" but he has managed to do pretty well by himself, financially.

SPECIALIZED KNOWLEDGE is among the most plentiful, and the cheapest forms of service which may be had! If you doubt this, consult the payroll of any university.

It Pays to Know How to Purchase Knowledge

First of all, decide the sort of specialized knowledge you require, and the purpose for which it is needed. To a large extent your major purpose in life, the goal toward which you are working, will help determine what knowledge you need. With this question settled, your next move requires that you have accurate information concerning dependable sources of knowledge. The more important of these are:

(a) One's own experience and education
(b) Experience and education available through cooperation of others (Master Mind Alliance)
(c) Colleges and Universities
(d) Public Libraries (Through books and periodicals in which may be found all the knowledge organized by civilization)

(e) Special Training Courses (Through night schools and home study schools in particular.)

As knowledge is acquired, it must be organized and put into use, for a definite purpose, through practical plans. Knowledge has no value except that which can be gained from its application toward some worthy end. This is one reason why college degrees are not valued more highly. They represent nothing but miscellaneous knowledge.

If you contemplate taking additional schooling, first determine the purpose for which you want the knowledge you are seeking, then learn where this particular sort of knowledge can be obtained, from reliable sources.

Successful men, in all callings, never stop acquiring specialized knowledge related to their major purpose, business, or profession. Those who are not successful usually make the mistake of believing that the knowledge acquiring period ends when one finishes school. The truth is that schooling does but little more than to put one in the way of learning how to acquire practical knowledge.

With this Changed World which began at the end of the economic collapse, came also astounding changes in educational requirements. The order of the day is SPECIALIZATION! This truth was emphasized by Robert P. Moore, secretary of appointments of Columbia University.

"Specialists Most Sought

"Particularly sought after by employing companies are candidates who have specialized in some field—business-school graduates with training in accounting and statistics, engineers of all varieties, journalists, architects, chemists, and also outstanding leaders and activity men of the senior class.

"The man who has been active on the campus, whose personality is such that he gets along with all kinds of people and who has done an adequate job with his studies has a most decided edge over the strictly academic student. Some of these, because of their all-around qualifications, have received several offers of positions, a few of them as many as six.

"In departing from the conception that the 'straight A' student was invariably the one to get the choice of the better jobs, Mr. Moore said that most companies look not only to academic records but to activity records and personalities of the students.

"One of the largest industrial companies, the leader in its field, in writing to Mr. Moore concerning prospective seniors at the college, said:

" 'We are interested primarily in finding men who can make exceptional progress in management work. For this reason we emphasize qualities of character, intelligence and personality far more than specific educational background.'

" 'APPRENTICESHIP' PROPOSED

"Proposing a system of 'apprenticing' students in offices, stores and industrial occupations during the summer vacation, Mr. Moore asserts that after the first two or three years of college, every student should be asked 'to choose a definite future course and to call a halt if he has been merely pleasantly drifting without purpose through an unspecialized academic curriculum.'

"Colleges and universities must face the practical consideration that all professions and occupations now demand specialists," he said, urging that educational institutions accept more direct responsibility for vocational guidance.

One of the most reliable and practical sources of knowledge available to those who need specialized schooling, is the night schools operated in most large cities. The correspondence schools give specialized training anywhere the U.S. mails go, on all subjects that can be taught by the extension method. One advantage of home study training is the flexibility of the study programme which permits one to study during spare time. Another stupendous advantage of home study training (if the school is carefully chosen), is the fact that most courses offered by home study schools carry with them generous privileges of consultation which can be priceless value to those needing specialized knowledge. No matter where you live, you can share the benefits.

Anything acquired without effort, and without cost is generally unappreciated, often discredited; perhaps this is why we get so little from our marvelous opportunity in public schools. The SELF-DISCIPLINE one receives from a definite programme of specialized study makes up to some extent, for the wasted opportunity when knowledge was available without cost. Correspondence schools are highly organized business institutions. Their tuition fees are so low that they are forced to insist upon prompt payments. Being asked to pay, whether the student makes good grades or poor, has the effect of causing one to follow through with the course when he would otherwise drop it. The correspondence schools have not stressed this point sufficiently, for the truth is that their collection departments constitute the very finest sort of training on DECISION, PROMPTNESS, ACTION and THE HABIT OF FINISHING THAT WHICH ONE BEGINS.

I learned this from experience, more than twenty-five years ago. I enrolled for a home study course in Advertising. After completing eight or ten lessons I stopped studying, but the school did not stop sending me bills. Moreover, it insisted upon payment, whether I kept up my studies or not. I decided that if I had to pay for the course (which I had legally obligated myself to do), I should complete the lessons and get my money's worth. I felt, at the time, that the collection system of the school was somewhat too well organized, but I learned later in life that it was a valuable part of my training for which no charge had been made. Being forced to pay, I went ahead and completed the course. Later in life I discovered that the efficient collection system of that school had been worth much in the form of money earned, because of the training in advertising I had so reluctantly taken.

We have in this country what is said to be the greatest public school system in the world. We have invested fabulous sums for fine buildings, we have provided convenient transportation for children living in the rural districts, so they may attend the best schools, but there is one astounding weakness to this marvelous system—IT IS FREE! One of the strange things about human beings is that they value only that which has a price. The free schools of America, and the free public libraries, do not impress people *because they are free*. This is the major reason why so many people find it necessary to acquire additional training after they quit school and go to work. It is also one of the major reasons why EMPLOYERS GIVE GREATER CONSIDERATION TO EMPLOYEES WHO TAKE HOME STUDY COURSES. They have learned, from experience, that any person who has the ambition to give up a part of his spare time to studying at home has in him those qualities which make for leadership. This recognition is not a charitable gesture, it is sound business judgment upon the part of the employers.

There is one weakness in people in which there is no remedy. It is the universal weakness of LACK OF AMBITION! Persons, especially salaried people, who schedule their spare time, to provide for home study, seldom remain at the bottom very long. Their action opens the way for the upward climb, removes many obstacles from their path, and gains the friendly interest of those who have the power to put them in the way of OPPORTUNITY.

The home study method of training is especially suited to the needs of employed people who find, after leaving school, that they must acquire additional specialized knowledge, but cannot spare the time to go back to school.

The changed economic conditions prevailing since

the depression have made it necessary for thousands of people to find additional, or new sources of income. For the majority of these, the solution to their problem may be found only by acquiring specialized knowledge. Many will be forced to change their occupations entirely. When a merchant finds that a certain line of merchandise is not selling, he usually supplants it with another that is in demand. The person whose business is that of marketing personal services must also be an efficient merchant. If his services do not bring adequate returns in one occupation, he must change to another, where broader opportunities are available.

Stuart Austin Wier prepared himself as a Construction Engineer and followed this line of work until the depression limited his market to where it did not give him the income he required. He took inventory of himself, decided to change his profession to law, went back to school and took special courses by which he prepared himself as a corporation lawyer. Despite the fact the depression had not ended, he completed his training, passed the Bar Examination, and quickly built a lucrative law practice, in Dallas, Texas; in fact he is turning away clients.

Just to keep the record straight, and to anticipate the alibis of those who will say, "I couldn't go to school because I have a family to support," or "I'm too old," I will add the information that Mr. Wier was past forty, and married when he went back to school. Moreover, by carefully selecting highly specialized courses, in colleges best prepared to teach the subjects chosen, Mr. Wier completed in two years the work for which the majority of law students require four years. IT PAYS TO KNOW HOW TO PURCHASE KNOWLEDGE!

The person who stops studying merely because he has finished school is forever hopelessly doomed to mediocrity, no matter what may be his calling. The way of success is the way of continuous pursuit of knowledge.

Let us consider a specific instance.

During the depression a salesman in a grocery store found himself without a position. Having had some bookkeeping experience, he took a special course in accounting, familiarized himself with all the latest bookkeeping and office equipment, and went into business for himself. Starting with the grocer for whom he had formerly worked, he made contracts with more than 100 small merchants to keep their books, at a very nominal monthly fee. His idea was so practical that he soon found it necessary to set up a portable office in a light delivery truck, which he equipped with modern bookkeeping machinery. He now has a fleet of these bookkeeping offices "on wheels" and employs a large staff of assistants, thus providing small merchants with accounting service equal to the best that money can buy, at very nominal cost.

Specialized knowledge, plus imagination, were the ingredients that went into this unique and successful business. Last year the owner of that business paid an income tax of almost ten times as much as was paid by the merchant for whom he worked when the depression forced upon him a temporary adversity which proved to be a blessing in disguise.

The beginning of this successful business was an IDEA!

Inasmuch as I had the privilege of supplying the unemployed salesman with that idea, I now assume the further privilege of suggesting another idea which has within it the possibility of even greater income. Also the possibility of rendering useful service to thousands of people who badly need that service.

The idea was suggested by the salesman who gave up selling and went into the business of keeping books on a wholesale basis. When the plan was suggested as a solution of his unemployment problem, he quickly exclaimed, "I like the idea, but I would not know how to turn it into cash." In other words, he complained he would not know how to market his bookkeeping knowledge *after he acquired it.*

So, that brought up another problem which had to be solved. With the aid of a young woman typist, clever at hand lettering, and who could put the story together, a very attractive book was prepared, describing the advantages of the new system of book-keeping. The pages were neatly typed and pasted in an ordinary scrapbook, which was used as a silent salesman with which the story of this new business was so effectively told that its owner soon had more accounts than he could handle.

There are thousands of people, all over the country, who need the services of a merchandising specialist capable of preparing an attractive brief for use in marketing personal services. The aggregate annual income from such a service might easily exceed that received by the largest employment agency, and the benefits of the service might be made far greater to the purchaser than any to be obtained from an employment agency.

The IDEA here described was born of necessity, to bridge an emergency which had to be covered, but it did not stop by merely serving one person. The woman who created the idea has a keen IMAGINA-TION. She saw in her newly born brain-child the making of a new profession, one that is destined to render valuable service to thousands of people who need practical guidance in marketing personal services.

Spurred to action by the instantaneous success of her first, "PREPARED PLAN TO MARKET PERSONAL SERVICES," this energetic woman turned next to the solution of a similar problem for her son who had just finished college, but had been totally unable to find a market for his services. The plan she originated for his use was the finest specimen of merchandising of personal services I have ever seen.

When the plan book had been completed, it contained nearly fifty pages of beautifully typed, properly organized information, telling the story of her son's native ability, schooling, personal experiences, and a great variety of other information too extensive for description. The plan book also contained a complete description of the position her son desired, together with a marvelous word picture of the exact plan he would use in filling the position.

The preparation of the plan book required several week's labor, during which time its creator sent her son to the public library almost daily, to procure data needed in selling his services to best advantage. She sent him, also to all the competitors of his prospective employer, and gathered from them vital information concerning their business methods which was of great value in the formation of the plan he intended to use in filling the position he sought. When the plan had been finished, it contained more than half a dozen very fine suggestions for the use and benefit of the prospective employer. (The suggestions were put into use by the company).

One may be inclined to ask, "Why go to all this trouble to secure a job?" The answer is straight to the point, also it is dramatic, because it deals with a subject which assumes the proportion of a tragedy with millions of men and women whose sole source of income is personal services.

The answer is, "DOING A THING WELL NEVER IS TROUBLE! THE PLAN PREPARED BY THIS WOMAN FOR THE BENEFIT OF HER SON, HELPED HIM GET THE JOB FOR WHICH HE APPLIED, AT THE FIRST INTERVIEW, AT A SALARY FIXED BY HIMSELF."

Moreover—and this, too, is important—THE POSITION DID NOT REQUIRE THE YOUNG MAN TO START AT THE BOTTOM. HE BEGAN AS A JUNIOR EXECUTIVE, AT AN EXECUTIVE'S SALARY.

"Why go to all this trouble?" do you ask?

Well, for one thing, the PLANNED PRESENTATION of this young man's application for a position clipped off no less than ten years of time he would have required to get to where he began, had he "started at the bottom and worked his way up."

This idea of starting at the bottom and working one's way up may appear to be sound, but the major objection to it is this—too many of those who begin at the bottom never manage to lift their heads high enough to be seen by OPPORTUNITY, so they remain at the bottom. It should be remembered, also, that the outlook from the bottom is not so very bright or encouraging. It has a tendency to kill off ambition. We call it "getting into a rut," which means that we accept our fate because we form the HABIT of daily routine, a habit that finally becomes so strong we cease to try to throw it off. And that is another reason why it pays to start one or two steps above the bottom. By so doing one forms the HABIT of looking around, of observing how others get ahead, of seeing OPPORTUNITY, and of embracing it without hesitation.

Dan Halpin is a splendid example of what I mean. During his college days, he was manager of the famous 1930 National championship Notre Dame football team, when it was under the direction of the late Knute Rockne.

Perhaps he was inspired by the great football coach to aim high, and NOT MISTAKE TEMPORARY DEFEAT FOR FAILURE, just as Andrew Carnegie, the great industrial leader, inspired his young business lieutenants to set high goals for themselves. At any rate, young Halpin finished college at a mighty unfavorable time, when the depression had made jobs scarce, so, after a fling at investment banking and motion pictures, he took the first opening with a potential future he could find—selling electrical hearing aids on a commission

basis. ANYONE COULD START IN THAT SORT OF
JOB, AND HALPIN KNEW IT, but it was enough to
open the door of opportunity to him.

For almost two years, he continued in a job not to
his liking, and he would never have risen above that
job if he had not done something about his dissatis-
faction. He aimed, first, at the job of Assistant Sales
Manager of his company, and got the job. That one
step upward placed him high enough above the
crowd to enable him to see still greater opportunity,
also, it placed him where OPPORTUNITY COULD
SEE HIM.

He made such a fine record selling hearing aids,
that A. M. Andrews, Chairman of the Board of
Dictograph Products Company, a business
competitor of the company for which Halpin
worked, wanted to know something about that
man Dan Halpin who was taking big sales away
from the long established Dictograph company.
He sent for Halpin. When the interview was over,
Halpin was the new Sales Manager, in charge of the
Acousticon division. Then, to test young Halpin's
metal, Mr. Andrews went away to Florida for three
months, leaving him to sink or swim in his new
job. He did not sink! Knute Rockne's spirit of "All
the world loves a winner, and has no time for a
loser," inspired him to put so much into his job
that he was recently elected Vice-President of the
company, and General Manager of the Acousticon
and Silent Radio Division, a job which most men
would be proud to earn through ten years of loyal
effort. Halpin turned the trick in little more than
six months.

It is difficult to say whether Mr. Andrews or Mr. Halpin is more deserving of eulogy, for the reason that both showed evidence of having an abundance of that very rare quality known as IMAGINATION. Mr. Andrews deserves credit for seeing, in young Halpin, a "go-getter" of the highest order. Halpin deserves credit for REFUSING TO COMPROMISE WITH LIFE BY ACCEPTING AND KEEPING A JOB HE DID NOT WANT, and that is one of the major points I am trying to emphasize through this entire philosophy—that we rise to high positions or remain at the bottom BECAUSE OF CONDITIONS WE CAN CONTROL IF WE DESIRE TO CONTROL THEM.

I am also trying to emphasize another point, namely, that both success and failure are largely the results of HABIT! I have not the slightest doubt that Dan Halpin's close association with the greatest football coach America ever knew, planted in his mind the same brand of DESIRE to excel which made the Notre Dame football team world famous. Truly, there is something to the idea that hero-worship is helpful, provided one worships a WINNER. Halpin tells me that Rockne was one of the world's greatest leaders of men in all history.

My belief in the theory that business associations are vital factors, both in failure and in success, was recently demonstrated, when my son Blair was negotiating with Dan Halpin for a position. Mr. Halpin offered him a beginning salary of about one half what he could have gotten from a rival company. I brought parental pressure to bear, and induced him to accept the place with Mr. Halpin, because

I BELIEVE THAT CLOSE ASSOCIATION WITH ONE WHO REFUSES TO COMPROMISE WITH CIRCUM-STANCES HE DOES NOT LIKE, IS AN ASSET THAT CAN NEVER BE MEASURED IN TERMS OF MONEY.

The bottom is a monotonous, dreary, unprofitable place for any person. That is why I have taken the time to describe how lowly beginnings may be circumvented by proper planning. Also, that is why so much space has been devoted to a description of this new profession, created by a woman who was inspired to do a fine job of PLANNING because she wanted her son to have a favorable "break."

With the changed conditions ushered in by the world economic collapse, came also the need for newer and better ways of marketing PERSONAL SERVICES. It is hard to determine why someone had not previously discovered this stupendous need, in view of the fact that more money changes hands in return for personal services than for any other purpose. The sum paid out monthly, to people who work for wages and salaries, is so huge that it runs into hundreds of millions, and the annual distribution amounts to billions.

Perhaps some will find, in the IDEA here briefly described, the nucleus of the riches they DESIRE! Ideas with much less merit have been the seedlings from which great fortunes have grown. Woolworth's Five and Ten Cent Store idea, for example, had far less merit, but it piled up a fortune for its creator.

Those seeing OPPORTUNITY lurking in this sugges-tion will find valuable aid in the chapter on Organized Planning. Incidentally, an efficient merchandiser of personal services would find a growing demand for his services wherever there are men and women who seek better markets for their services. By applying the Master Mind principle, a few people with suitable talent, could form an alliance, and have a paying business very quickly. One would need to be a fair writer, with a flair for advertising and selling, one handy at typing and hand lettering, and one should be a first class business getter who would let the world know about the service. If one person possessed all these abilities, he might carry on the business alone, until it outgrew him.

The woman who prepared the "Personal Service Sales Plan" for her son now receives requests from all parts of the country for her cooperation in preparing similar plans for others who desire to market their personal services for more money. She has a staff of expert typists, artists, and writers who have the ability to dramatize the case history so effectively that one's personal services can be marketed for much more money than the prevailing wages for similar services. She is so confident of her ability that she accepts, as the major portion of her fee, a percentage of the *increased* pay she helps her clients to earn.

It must not be supposed that her plan merely consists of clever salesmanship by which she helps men and women to demand and receive more money for the same services they formerly sold for less pay. She looks after the interests of the purchaser as well as the seller of personal services, and so prepares her plans that the employer receives full value for the additional money he pays. The method by which she accomplishes this astonishing result is a professional secret which she discloses to no one excepting her own clients.

If you have the IMAGINATION, and seek a more profitable outlet for your personal services, this suggestion may be the stimulus for which you have been searching. The IDEA is capable of yielding an income far greater than that of the "average" doctor, lawyer, or engineer whose education required several years in college. The idea is saleable to those seeking new positions, in practically all positions calling for managerial or executive ability, and those desiring re-arrangement of incomes in their present positions.

There is no fixed price for sound IDEAS!

Back of all IDEAS is specialized knowledge. Unfortunately, for those who do not find riches in abundance, specialized knowledge is more abundant and more easily acquired than IDEAS. Because of this very truth, there is a universal demand and an ever-increasing opportunity for the person capable of helping men and women to sell their personal services advantageously. Capability means IMAGINATION, the one quality needed to combine specialized knowledge with IDEAS, in the form of ORGANIZED PLANS designed to yield riches.

If you have IMAGINATION this chapter may present you with an idea sufficient to serve as the beginning of the riches you desire. Remember, the IDEA is the main thing. Specialized knowledge may be found just around the corner—any corner!

CHAPTER 6

IMAGINATION

THE WORKSHOP OF THE MIND

The Fifth Step toward Riches

THE imagination is literally the workshop wherein are fashioned all plans created by man. The impulse, the DESIRE, is given shape, form, and ACTION through the aid of the imaginative faculty of the mind.

It has been said that men can create anything which he can imagine.

Of all the ages of civilization, this is the most favorable for the development of the imagination, because it is an age of rapid change. On every hand one may contact stimuli which develops the imagination.

Through the aid of his imaginative faculty, man has discovered, and harnessed, more of Nature's forces during the past fifty years than during the entire history of the human race, previous to that time. He has conquered the air so completely, that the birds are a poor match for him in flying. He has harnessed the ether, and made it serve as a means of instantaneous communication with any part of the world. He has analyzed, and weighed the sun at a distance of millions of miles, and has determined, through the aid of IMAGINATION, the elements of which it consists. He has discovered that his own brain is both a broadcasting, and a receiving station for the vibration of thought, and he is beginning now to learn how to make practical use of this discovery. He has increased the speed of locomotion, until he may now travel at a speed of more than three hundred miles an hour. The time will soon come when a man may breakfast in New York, and lunch in San Francisco.

MAN'S ONLY LIMITATION, within reason, LIES IN HIS DEVELOPMENT AND USE OF HIS IMAGINA-TION. He has not yet reached the apex of development in the use of his imaginative faculty. He has merely discovered that he has an imagination, and has commenced to use it in a very elementary way.

Two Forms of Imagination ·

The imaginative faculty functions in two forms. One is known as "synthetic imagination," and the other as "creative imagination."

SYNTHETIC IMAGINATION:—Through this faculty, one may arrange old concepts, ideas, or plans into new combinations. This faculty *creates* nothing. It merely works with the material of experience, education, and observation with which it is fed. It is the faculty used most by the inventor, with the exception of the "genius" who draws upon the creative imagination, when he cannot solve his problem through synthetic imagination.

CREATIVE IMAGINATION:—Through the faculty of creative imagination, the finite mind of man has direct communication with Infinite Intelligence. It is the faculty through which "hunches" and "inspirations" are received. It is by this faculty that all basic, or new ideas are handed over to man.

It is through this faculty that thought vibrations from the minds of others are received. It is through this faculty that one individual may "tune in," or communicate with the subconscious minds of other men.

The creative imagination works automatically in the manner described in subsequent pages. This faculty functions ONLY when the conscious mind is vibrating at an exceedingly rapid rate, as for example, when the conscious mind is stimulated through the emotion of a *strong desire*.

The creative faculty becomes more alert, more receptive to vibrations from the sources mentioned, in proportion to its development through USE. This statement is significant! Ponder over it before passing on.

Keep in mind as you follow these principles, that the entire story of how one may convert DESIRE into money cannot be told in one statement. The story will be complete, only when one has MASTERED, ASSIMILATED, and BEGUN TO MAKE USE of all the principles.

The great leaders of business, industry, finance, and the great artists, musicians, poets, and writers became great, because they developed the faculty of creative imagination.

Both the synthetic and creative faculties of imagination become more alert with use, just as any muscle or organ of the body develops through use.

Desire is only a thought, an impulse. It is nebulous and ephemeral. It is abstract, and of no value, until it has been transformed into its physical counterpart. While the synthetic imagination is the one which will be used most frequently, in the process of transforming the impulse of DESIRE into money, you must keep in mind the fact, that you may face circumstances and situations which demand use of the creative imagination as well.

Your imaginative faculty may have become weak through inaction. It can be revived and made alert through USE. This faculty does not die, though it may become quiescent through lack of use.

Center your attention, for the time being, on the development of the synthetic imagination, because this is the faculty which you will use more often in the process of converting desire into money.

Transformation of the intangible impulse, of DESIRE, into the tangible reality, of MONEY, calls for the use of a plan, or plans. These plans must be formed with the aid of the imagination, and mainly, with the synthetic faculty.

Read the entire book through, then come back to this chapter, and begin at once to put your imagination to work on the building of a plan, or plans, for the transformation of your DESIRE into money. Detailed instructions for the building of plans have been given in almost every chapter. Carry out the instructions best suited to your needs, reduce your plan to writing, if you have not already done so. The moment you complete this, you will have DEFI-NITELY given concrete form to the intangible DESIRE. Read the preceding sentence once more. Read it aloud, very slowly, and as you do so, remember that the moment you reduce the statement of your desire, and a plan for its realization, to writing, you have actually TAKEN THE FIRST of a series of steps, which will enable you to convert the thought into its physical counterpart.

The earth on which you live, you, yourself, and every other material thing are the result of evolutionary change, through which microscopic bits of matter have been organized and arranged in an orderly fashion.

Moreover—and this statement is of stupendous importance—this earth, every one of the billions of individual cells of your body, and every atom of matter, *began as an intangible form of energy.*

DESIRE is thought impulse! Thought impulses are forms of energy. When you begin with the thought impulse, DESIRE, to accumulate money, you are drafting into your service the same "stuff" that Nature used in creating this earth, and every material form in the universe, including the body and brain in which the thought impulses function.

As far as science has been able to determine, the entire universe consists of but two elements—matter and energy.

Through the combination of energy and matter, has been created everything perceptible to man, from the largest star which floats in the heavens, down to, and including man, himself.

You are now engaged in the task of trying to profit by Nature's method. You are (sincerely and earnestly, we hope), trying to adapt yourself to Nature's laws, by endeavoring to convert DESIRE into its physical or monetary equivalent. YOU CAN DO IT! IT HAS BEEN DONE BEFORE!

You can build a fortune through the aid of laws which are immutable. But, first, you must become familiar with these laws, and learn to USE them. Through repetition, and by approaching the description of these principles from every conceivable angle, the author hopes to reveal to you the secret through which every great fortune has been accumulated. Strange and paradoxical as it may seem, the "secret" is NOT A SECRET. Nature, herself, advertises it in the earth on which we live, the stars, the planets suspended within our view, in the elements above and around us, in every blade of grass, and every form of life within our vision.

Nature advertises this "secret" in the terms of biology, in the conversion of a tiny cell, so small that it may be lost on the point of a pin, into the HUMAN BEING now reading this line. The conversion of desire into its physical equivalent is, certainly, no more miraculous!

Do not become discouraged if you do not fully comprehend all that has been stated. Unless you have long been a student of the mind, it is not to be expected that you will assimilate all that is in this chapter upon a first reading.

But you will, in time, make good progress.

The principles which follow will open the way for understanding of imagination. Assimilate that which you understand, as you read this philosophy for the first time, then, when you reread and study it, you will discover that something has happened to clarify it, and give you a broader understanding of the whole. Above all, DO NOT STOP, nor hesitate in your study of these principles until you have read the book at least THREE times, for then, you will not want to stop.

How to Make Practical Use of Imagination

Ideas are the beginning points of all fortunes. Ideas are products of the imagination. Let us examine a few well known ideas which have yielded huge fortunes, with the hope that these illustrations will convey definite information concerning the method by which imagination may be used in accumulating riches.

The Enchanted Kettle

Fifty years ago, an old country doctor drove to town, hitched his horse, quietly slipped into a drug store by the back door, and began "dickering" with the young drug clerk.

His mission was destined to yield great wealth to many people. It was destined to bring to the South the most far-flung benefit since the Civil War.

For more than an hour, behind the prescription counter, the old doctor and the clerk talked in low tones. Then the doctor left. He went out to the buggy and brought back a large, old fashioned kettle, a big wooden paddle (used for stirring the contents of the kettle), and deposited them in the back of the store.

The clerk inspected the kettle, reached into his inside pocket, took out a roll of bills, and handed it over to the doctor. The roll contained exactly $500.00—the clerk's entire savings!

The doctor handed over a small slip of paper on which was written a secret formula. The words on that small slip of paper were worth a King's ransom! *But not to the doctor!* Those magic words were needed to start the kettle to boiling, but neither the doctor nor the young clerk knew what fabulous fortunes were destined to flow from that kettle.

The old doctor was glad to sell the outfit for five hundred dollars. The money would pay off his debts, and give him freedom of mind. The clerk was taking a big chance by staking his entire life's savings on a mere scrap of paper and an old kettle! He never dreamed his investment would start a kettle to overflowing with gold that would surpass the miraculous performance of Aladdin's lamp.

What the clerk *really purchased* was an IDEA!

The old kettle and the wooden paddle, and the secret message on a slip of paper were incidental. The strange performance of that kettle began to take place after the new owner mixed with the secret instructions an ingredient of which the doctor knew nothing.

Read this story carefully, give your imagination a test! See if you can discover what it was that the young man added to the secret message, which caused the kettle to overflow with gold. Remember, as you read, that this is not a story from Arabian Nights. Here you have a story of facts, stranger than fiction, facts which began in the form of an IDEA.

Let us take a look at the vast fortunes of gold this idea has produced. It has paid, and still pays huge fortunes to men and women all over the world, who distribute the contents of the kettle to millions of people.

The Old Kettle is now one of the world's largest consumers of sugar, thus providing jobs of a permanent nature to thousands of men and women engaged in growing sugar cane, and in refining and marketing sugar.

The Old Kettle consumes, annually, millions of glass bottles, providing jobs to huge numbers of glass workers.

The Old Kettle gives employment to an army of clerks, stenographers, copy writers, and advertising experts throughout the nation. It has brought fame and fortune to scores of artists who have created magnificent pictures describing the product.

The Old Kettle has converted a small Southern city into the business capital of the South, where it now benefits, directly, or indirectly, every business and practically every resident of the city.

The influence of this idea now benefits every civilized country in the world, pouring out a continuous stream of gold to all who touch it.

Gold from the kettle built and maintains one of the most prominent colleges of the South, where thousands of young people receive the training essential for success.

The Old Kettle has done other marvelous things.

All through the world depression, when factories, banks and business houses were folding up and quitting by the thousands, the owner of this Enchanted Kettle went marching on, *giving continuous employment* to an army of men and women all over the world, and paying out extra portions of gold to those who, long ago, *had faith in the idea.*

If the product of that old brass kettle could talk, it would tell thrilling tales of romance in every language. Romances of love, romances of business, romances of professional men and women who are daily being stimulated by it.

The author is sure of at least one such romance, for he was a part of it, and it all began not far from the very spot on which the drug clerk purchased the old kettle. It was here that the author met his wife, and it was she who first told him of the Enchanted Kettle. It was the product of that Kettle they were drinking when he asked her to accept him "for better or worse."

Now that you know the contents of the Enchanted Kettle is a world famous drink, it is fitting that the author confess that the home city of the drink supplied him with a wife, also that the drink itself provides him with *stimulation of thought without intoxication,* and thereby it serves to give the refreshment of mind which an author must have to do his best work.

Whoever you are, wherever you may live, whatever occupation you may be engaged in, just remember in the future, every time you see the words "Coca-Cola," that its vast empire of wealth and influence grew out of a single IDEA, and that the mysterious ingredient the drug clerk—Asa Candler—mixed with the secret formula was... IMAGINATION!

Stop and think of that, for a moment.

Remember, also, that the thirteen steps to riches, described in this book, were the media through which the influence of Coca-Cola has been extended to every city, town, village, and cross-roads of the world, and that ANY IDEA you may create, as *sound and meritorious* as Coca-Cola, has the possibility of duplicating the stupendous record of this world-wide thirst-killer.

Truly, thoughts are things, and their scope of operation is the world, itself.

What I Would Do If I Had a Million Dollars

This story proves the truth of that old saying, "where there's a will, there's a way." It was told to me by that beloved educator and clergyman, the late Frank W. Gunsaulus, who began his preaching career in the stockyards region of South Chicago.

While Dr. Gunsaulus was going through college, he observed many defects in our educational system, defects which he believed he could correct, if he were the head of a college. His *deepest desire* was to become the directing head of an educational institution in which young men and women would be taught to "learn by doing."

He made up his mind to organize a new college in which he could carry out his ideas, without being handicapped by orthodox methods of education.

He needed a million dollars to put the project across! Where was he to lay his hands on so large a sum of money? That was the question that absorbed most of this ambitious young preacher's thought.

But he couldn't seem to make any progress.

Every night he took that thought to bed with him. He got up with it in the morning. He took it with him everywhere he went. He turned it over and over in his mind until it became a consuming *obsession* with him. A million dollars is a lot of money. He recognized that fact, but he also recognized the truth that *the only limitation is that which one sets up in one's own mind.*

Being a philosopher as well as a preacher, Dr. Gunsaulus recognized, as do all who succeed in life, that DEFINITENESS OF PURPOSE is the starting point from which one must begin. He recognized, too, that definiteness of purpose takes on animation, life, and power when backed by a BURNING DESIRE to translate that purpose into its material equivalent.

He knew all these great truths, yet he did not know where, or how to lay his hands on a million dollars. The natural procedure would have been to give up and quit, by saying, "Ah well, my idea is a good one, but I cannot do anything with it, because I never can procure the necessary million dollars." That is exactly what the majority of people would have said, but it is not what Dr. Gunsaulus said. What he said, and what he did are so important that I now introduce him, and let him speak for himself.

"One Saturday afternoon I sat in my room thinking of ways and means of raising the money to carry out my plans. For nearly two years, I had been thinking, but I *had done nothing but think!*

"The time had come for ACTION!

"I made up my mind, then and there, that I would get the necessary million dollars within a week. How? I was not concerned about that. The main thing of importance was the *decision* to get the money within a specified time, and I want to tell you that the moment I reached a definite decision to get the money within a specified time, a strange feeling of assurance came over me, such as I had never before experienced. Something inside me seemed to say, 'Why didn't you reach that decision a long time ago? The money was waiting for you all the time!'

"Things began to happen in a hurry. I called the newspapers and announced I would preach a sermon the following morning, entitled, 'What I would do if I had a Million Dollars.'

"I went to work on the sermon immediately, but I must tell you, frankly, the task was not difficult, because I had been preparing that sermon for almost two years. The spirit back of it was a part of me!

"Long before midnight I had finished writing the sermon. I went to bed and slept with a feeling of confidence, for *I could see myself already in possession of the million dollars.*

"Next morning I arose early, went into the bathroom, read the sermon, then kelt on my knees and asked that my sermon might come to the attention of someone who would supply the needed money.

"While I was praying I again had that feeling of assurance that the money would be forthcoming. In my excitement, I walked out without my sermon, and did not discover the oversight until I was in my pulpit and about ready to begin delivering it.

"It was too late to go back for my notes, and what a blessing that I couldn't go back! Instead, my own subconscious mind yielded the material I needed. When I arose to begin my sermon, I closed my eyes, and spoke with all my heart and soul of my dreams. I not only talked to my audience, but I fancy I talked also to God. I told what I would do with a million dollars if that amount were placed in my hands. I described the plan I had in mind for organizing a great educational institution, where young people would learn to do practical things, and at the same time develop their minds.

"When I had finished and sat down, a man slowly arose from his seat, about three rows from the rear, and made his way toward the pulpit. I wondered what he was going to do. He came into the pulpit, extended his hand, and said, 'Reverend, I liked your sermon. I believe you can do everything you said you would, if you had a million dollars. To prove that I believe in you and your sermon, if you will come to my office tomorrow morning, I will give you the million dollars. My name is Phillip D. Armour.' "

Young Gunsaulus went to Mr. Armour's office and the million dollars was presented to him. With the money, he founded the Armour Institute of Technology.

That is more money than the majority of preachers ever see in an entire lifetime, yet the thought impulse back of the money was created in the young preacher's mind in a fraction of a minute. The necessary million dollars came as a result of an idea. Back of the idea was a DESIRE which young Gunsaulus had been nursing in his mind for almost two years.

Observe this important fact...HE GOT THE MONEY WITHIN THIRTY-SIX HOURS AFTER HE REACHED A DEFINITE DE-CISION IN HIS OWN MIND TO GET IT, AND

DECIDED UPON A DEFINITE PLAN FOR GETTING IT!

There was nothing new or unique about young Gunsaulus' vague thinking about a million dollars, and weakly hoping for it. Others before him, and many since his time, have had similar thoughts. But there was something very unique and different about the decision he reached on that memorable Saturday, when he put vagueness into the background, and definitely said, "I WILL get that money within a week!"

God seems to throw Himself on the side of the man who knows *exactly* what he wants, *if he is determined* to get JUST THAT!

Moreover, the principle through which Dr. Gunsaulus got his million dollars is still alive! It is available to you! This universal law is as workable today as it was when the young preacher made use of it so successfully. This book describes, step by step, the thirteen elements of this great law, and suggests how they may be put to use.

Observe that Asa Candler and Dr. Frank Gunsaulus had one characteristic in common. Both knew the astounding truth that IDEAS CAN BE TRANSMUTED INTO CASH THROUGH THE POWER OF DEFINITE PURPOSE, PLUS DEFINITE PLANS.

If you are one of those who believe that hard work and honesty, alone, will bring riches, perish the thought! It is not true! Riches, when they come in huge quantities, are never the result of HARD work! Riches, come, if they come at all, in response to definite demands, based upon the application of definite principles, and not by chance or luck.

Generally speaking, an idea is an impulse of thought that impels action, by an appeal to the imagination. All master salesmen know that ideas can be sold where merchandise cannot. Ordinary salesmen do not know this—that is why they are "ordinary."

A publisher of books, which sell for a nickel, made a discovery that should be worth much to publishers generally. He learned that many people buy titles, and not contents of books. By merely changing the name of one book that was not moving, his sales on that book jumped upward more than a million copies. The inside of the book was not changed in any way. He merely ripped off the cover bearing the title that did not sell, and put on a new cover with a title that had "box-office" value.

That, as simple as it may seem, was an IDEA! It was IMAGINATION.

There is no standard price on ideas. The creator of ideas makes his own price, and, if he is smart, gets it.

The moving picture industry created a whole flock of millionaires. Most of them were men who couldn't create ideas—BUT—they had the imagination to recognize ideas when they saw them.

The next flock of millionaires will grow out of the radio business, which is new and not overburdened with men of keen imagination. The money will be made by those who discover or create new and more meritorious radio programmes and have the imagination to recognize merit, and to give the radio listeners a chance to profit by it.

The sponsor! That unfortunate victim who now

pays the cost of all radio "entertainment," soon will become idea conscious, and demand something for his money. The man who beats the sponsor to the draw, and supplies programmes that render useful service, is the man who will become rich in this new industry.

Crooners and light chatter artists who now pollute the air with wisecracks and silly giggles, will go the way of all light timbers, and their places will be taken by real artists who interpret carefully planned programmes which have been designed to service the minds of men, as well as provide entertainment.

Here is a wide open field of opportunity screaming its protest at the way it is being butchered, because of lack of imagination, and begging for rescue at any price. Above all, the thing that radio needs is new IDEAS!

If this new field of opportunity intrigues you, perhaps you might profit by the suggestion that the successful radio programmes of the future will give more attention to creating "buyer" audiences, and less attention to "listener" audiences. Stated more plainly, the builder of radio programmes who succeeds in the future, must find practical ways to convert "listeners" into "buyers." Moreover, the successful producer of radio programmes in the future must key his features so that he can definitely show its effect upon the audience.

Sponsors are becoming a bit weary of buying glib selling talks, based upon statements grabbed out of thin air. They want, and in the future will demand, indisputable proof that the Whoosit programme not only gives millions of people the silliest giggle ever, but that the silly giggler can sell merchandise!

Another thing that might as well be understood by those who contemplate entering this new field of opportunity, radio advertising is going to be handled by an entirely new group of advertising experts, separate and distinct from the old time newspaper and magazine advertising agency men. The old timers in the advertising game *cannot read* the modern radio scripts, because they have been schooled to SEE ideas. The new radio technique demands men who can interpret ideas from a *written* manuscript in terms of SOUND! It cost the author a year of hard labor, and many thousands of dollars to learn this.

Radio, right now, is about where the moving pictures were, when Mary Pickford and her curls first appeared on the screen. There is plenty of room in radio for those who can *produce or recognize* IDEAS.

If the foregoing comment on the opportunities of radio has not started your idea factory at work, you had better forget it. Your opportunity is in some other field. If the comment intrigued you in the slightest degree, then go further into it, and you may find the one IDEA you need to round out your career.

Never let it discourage you if you have no experience in radio. Andrew Carnegie knew very little about making steel—I have Carnegie's own word for this—but he made practical use of two of the principles described in this book, and made the steel business yield him a fortune.

The story of practically every great fortune starts with the day when a creator of ideas and a seller of ideas got together and worked in harmony. Carnegie surrounded himself with men who could do all that he could not do. Men who created ideas, and men who put ideas into operation, and made himself and the others fabulously rich.

Millions of people go through life hoping for favorable "breaks." Perhaps a favorable break can get one an opportunity, but the safest plan is not to depend upon luck. It was a favorable "break" that gave me the biggest opportunity of my life—*but*—twenty-five years of *determined effort* had to be devoted to that opportunity before it became an asset.

The "break" consisted of my good fortune in meeting and gaining the cooperation of Andrew Carnegie. On that occasion Carnegie planted in my mind the *idea* of organizing the principles of achievement into a philosophy of success. Thousands of people have profited by the discoveries made in the twenty-five years of research, and several fortunes have been accumulated through the application of the philosophy. The beginning was simple. It was an IDEA which anyone might have developed.

The favorable break came through Carnegie, but what about the DETERMINATION, DEFINITE-NESS OF PURPOSE, and the DESIRE TO ATTAIN THE GOAL, and the PERSISTENT EFFORT OF TWENTY-FIVE YEARS? It was no ordinary DESIRE that survived disappointment, discouragement, temporary defeat, criticism, and the constant reminding of "waste of time." It was a BURNING DESIRE! an OBSESSION!

When the idea was first planted in my mind by Mr. Carnegie, it was coaxed, nursed, and enticed to *remain alive*. Gradually, the idea became a giant under its own power, and it coaxed, nursed, and drove me. Ideas are like that. First you give life and action and guidance to ideas, then they take on power of their own and sweep aside all opposition.

Ideas are intangible forces, but they have more power than the physical brains that give birth to them. They have the power to live on, after the brain that creates them has returned to dust. For example, take the power of Christianity. That began with a simple idea, born in the brain of Christ. Its chief tenet was, "do unto others as you would have others do unto you." Christ has gone back to the source from whence He came, but His IDEA goes marching on. Some day, it may grow up, and come into its own, then it will have fulfilled Christ's deepest DESIRE. The IDEA has been developing only two thousand years. Give it time!

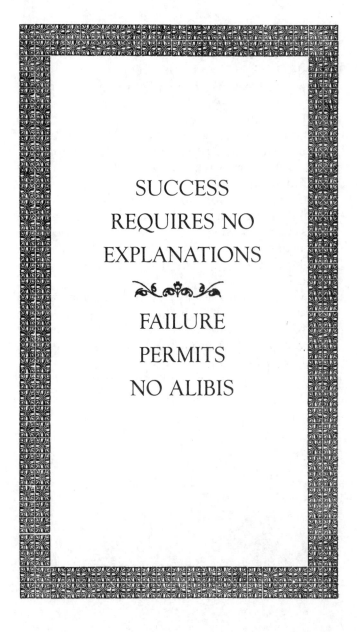

SUCCESS
REQUIRES NO
EXPLANATIONS

FAILURE
PERMITS
NO ALIBIS

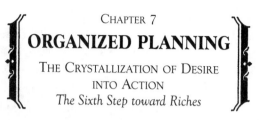

CHAPTER 7

ORGANIZED PLANNING

THE CRYSTALLIZATION OF DESIRE
INTO ACTION
The Sixth Step toward Riches

YOU have learned that everything man creates or acquires, begins in the form of DESIRE, that desire is taken on the first lap of its journey, from the abstract to the concrete, into the workshop of the IMAGINATION, where PLANS for its transition are created and organized.

In Chapter two, you were instructed to take six definite, practical steps, as your first move in translating the desire for money into its monetary equivalent. One of these steps is the formation of a DEFINITE, practical plan, or plans, through which this transformation may be made.

You will now be instructed how to build plans which will be practical, viz:—

(a)   Ally yourself with a group of as many people as you may need for the creation, and carrying out of your plan, or plans for the accumulation of money—making use of the "Master Mind" principle described in a later chapter. (Compliance with this instruction is *absolutely essential.* Do not neglect it.)

(b)   Before forming your "Master Mind" alliance, decide what advantages, and benefits, *you* may offer the individual members of your group, in return for their cooperation. No one will work indefinitely without some form of compensation. No intelligent person will either request or expect another to work without adequate compensation, although this may not always be in the form of money.

(c) Arrange to meet with the members of your "Master Mind" group at least twice a week, and more often if possible, until you have jointly perfected the necessary plan, or plans for the accumulation of money.

(d) Maintain PERFECT HARMONY between yourself and every member of your "Master Mind" group. If you fail to carry out this instruction to the letter, you may expect to meet with failure. The "Master Mind" principle *cannot* obtain where PERFECT HARMONY does not prevail.

Keep in mind these facts:—

First. You are engaged in an undertaking of major importance to you. To be sure of success you must have plans which are faultless.

Second. You must have the advantage of the experience, education, native ability and imagination of other minds. This is in harmony with the methods followed by every person who has accumulated a great fortune.

No individual has sufficient experience, education, native ability, and knowledge to insure the accumulation of a great fortune, without the cooperation of other people. Every plan you adopt, in your endeavor to accumulate wealth, should be the joint creation of yourself and every other member of your "Master Mind" group. You may originate your own plans, either in whole or in part, but SEE THAT THOSE PLANS ARE CHECKED, AND APPROVED BY THE MEMBERS OF YOUR "MASTER MIND" ALLIANCE.

If the first plan which you adopt does not work successfully, replace it with a new plan, if this new plan fails to work, replace it, in turn with still another, and so on, until you find a plan which DOES WORK. Right here is the point at which the majority of men meet with failure, because of their lack of PERSISTENCE in creating new plans to take the place of those which fail.

The most intelligent man living cannot succeed in accumulating money—nor in any other under-taking—without plans which are practical and workable. Just keep this fact in mind, and remember when your plans fail, that temporary defeat is not permanent failure. It may only mean that your plans have not been sound. Build other plans. Start all over again.

Thomas A. Edison "failed" ten thousand times before he perfected the incandescent electric light bulb. That is—he met with *temporary defeat* ten thousand times, before his efforts were crowned with success.

Temporary defeat should mean only one thing, the certain knowledge that there is something wrong with your plan. Millions of men go through life in misery and poverty, because they lack a sound plan through which to accumulate a fortune.

Henry Ford accumulated a fortune, not because

of his superior mind, but because he adopted and followed a PLAN which proved to be sound. A thousand men could be pointed out, each with a better education than Ford's, yet each of whom lives in poverty, because he does not possess the RIGHT plan for the accumulation of money.

Your achievement can be no greater than your PLANS are sound. That may seem to be an axiomatic statement, but it is true. Samuel Insull lost his fortune of over one hundred million dollars. The Insull fortune was built on plans which were sound. The business depression forced Mr. Insull to CHANGE HIS PLANS; and the CHANGE brought "temporary defeat," because his new plans were NOT SOUND. Mr. Insull is now an old man, he may, consequently, accept "failure" instead of "temporary defeat," but if his experience turns out to be FAILURE, it will be for the reason that he lacks the fire of PERSISTENCE to rebuild his plans.

No man is ever whipped, until he QUITS—*in his own mind.*

This fact will be repeated many times, because it is so easy to "take the count" at the first sign of defeat.

James J. Hill met with temporary defeat when he first endeavored to raise the necessary capital to build a railroad from the East to the West, but he, too turned defeat into victory *through new plans.*

Henry Ford met with temporary defeat, not only at the beginning of his automobile career, but after he had gone far toward the top. He created new plans, and went marching on to financial victory.

We see men who have accumulated great fortunes, but we often recognize only their triumph, overlooking the temporary defeats which they had to surmount before "arriving."

NO FOLLOWER OF THIS PHILOSOPHY CAN REASONABLY EXPECT TO ACCUMULATE A FORTUNE WITHOUT EXPERIENCING "TEMPORARY DEFEAT." When defeat comes, accept it as a signal that your plans are not sound, rebuild those plans, and set sail once more toward your coveted goal. If you give up before your goal has been reached, you are a "quitter." A QUITTER NEVER WINS—AND—A WINNER NEVER QUITS. Lift this sentence out, write it on a piece of paper in letters an inch high, and place it where you will see it every night before you go to sleep, and every morning before you go to work.

When you begin to select members for your "Master Mind" group, endeavor to select those who do not take defeat seriously.

Some people foolishly believe that only MONEY can make money. This is not true! DESIRE, transmuted into its monetary equivalent, through the principles laid down here, is the agency through which money is "made." Money, of itself, is nothing but inert matter. It cannot move, think, or talk, but it can "hear" when a man who DESIRES it, calls it to come!

Planning the Sale of Services

The remainder of this chapter has been given over to a description of ways and means of marketing personal services. The information here conveyed will be of practical help to any person having any form of personal services to market, but it will be of priceless benefit to those who aspire to leadership in their chosen occupations.

Intelligent planning is essential for success in any undertaking designed to accumulate riches. Here will be found detailed instructions to those who must begin the accumulation of riches by selling personal services.

It should be encouraging to know that practically all the great fortunes began in the form of compensation for personal services or from the sale of IDEAS. What else, except ideas and personal services, would one not possessed of property have to give in return for riches?

Broadly speaking, there are two types of people in the world. One type is known as LEADERS, and the other as FOLLOWERS. Decide at the outset whether you intend to become a leader in your chosen calling, or remain a follower. The difference in compensation is vast. The follower cannot reasonably expect the compensation to which a leader is entitled, although many followers make the mistake of expecting such pay.

It is no disgrace to be a follower. On the other hand, it is no credit to remain a follower. Most great leaders began in the capacity of followers. They became great leaders because they were INTELLIGENT FOLLOWERS. With few exceptions, the man who cannot follow a leader intelligently, cannot become an efficient leader. The man who can follow a leader most efficiently, is usually the man who develops into leadership most rapidly. An intelligent follower has many advantages, among them the OPPORTUNITY TO ACQUIRE KNOWLEDGE FROM HIS LEADER.

The Major Attributes of Leadership

The following are important factors of leadership:—

1. UNWAVERING COURAGE based upon knowledge of self, and of one's occupation. No follower wishes to be dominated by a leader who lacks self-confidence and courage. No intelligent follower will be dominated by such a leader very long.

2. SELF-CONTROL. The man who cannot control himself, can never control others. Self-control sets a mighty example for one's followers, which the more intelligent will emulate.

3. A KEEN SENSE OF JUSTICE. Without a sense of fairness and justice, no leader can command and retain the respect of his followers.

4. DEFINITENESS OF DECISION. The man who wavers in his decisions, shows that he is not sure of himself. He cannot lead others successfully.

5. DEFINITENESS OF PLANS. The successful leader must plan his work, and *work his plan.* A leader who moves by guesswork, without practical, definite plans, is comparable to a ship without a rudder. Sooner or later he will land on the rocks.

6. THE HABIT OF DOING MORE THAN PAID FOR. One of the penalties of leadership is the necessity of willingness, upon the part of the leader, to do more than he requires of his followers.

7. A PLEASING PERSONALITY. No slovenly, careless person can become a successful leader. Leadership calls for respect. Followers will not respect a leader who does not grade high on all of the factors of a Pleasing Personality.

8. SYMPATHY AND UNDERSTANDING. The successful leader must be in sympathy with his followers. Moreover, he must understand them and their problems.

9. MASTERY OF DETAIL. Successful leadership calls for mastery of details of the leader's position.

10. WILLINGNESS TO ASSUME FULL RESPONSIBILITY. The successful leader must be willing to assume responsibility for the mistakes and the shortcomings of his followers. If he tries to shift this responsibility, he will not remain the leader. If one of his followers makes a mistake, and shows himself incompetent, the leader must consider that it is *he* who failed.

11. COOPERATION. The successful leader must understand, and *apply* the principle of cooperative effort and be able to induce his followers to do the same. Leadership calls for POWER, and power calls for COOPERATION.

There are two forms of Leadership. The first, and by far the most effective, is LEADERSHIP BY CONSENT of, and with the sympathy of the followers. The second is LEADERSHIP BY FORCE, without the consent and sympathy of the followers.

History is filled with evidences that Leadership by Force cannot endure. The downfall and disappearance of "Dictators" and kings is significant. It means that people will not follow forced leadership indefinitely.

The world has just entered a new era of relationship between leaders and followers, which very clearly calls for new leaders, and a new brand of leadership in business and industry. Those who belong to the old school of leadership-by-force, must acquire an understanding of the new brand of leadership (cooperation) or be relegated to the rank and file of the followers. There is no other way out for them.

The relationship of employer and employee, or of leader and follower, in the future, will be one of mutual cooperation, based upon an equitable division of the profits of business. In the future, the relationship of employer and employee will be more like a partnership than it has been in the past.

Napoleon, Kaiser Wilhelm of Germany, the Czar of Russia, and the King of Spain were examples of leadership by force. Their leadership passed. Without much difficulty, one might point to the prototypes of these ex-leaders, among the business, financial, and labor leaders of America who have been dethroned or slated to go. *Leadership-by-*

consent of the followers is the only brand which can endure!

Men may follow the forced leadership temporarily, but they will not do so willingly.

The new brand of LEADERSHIP will embrace the eleven factors of leadership, described in this chapter, as well as some other factors. The man who makes these the basis of his leadership, will find abundant opportunity to lead in any walk of life. The depression was prolonged, largely, because the world lacked LEADERSHIP of the new brand. At the end of the depression, the demand for leaders who are competent to apply the new methods of leadership has greatly exceeded the supply. Some of the old type of leaders will reform and adapt themselves to the new brand of leadership, but generally speaking, the world will have to look for new timber for its leadership.

This necessity may be your OPPORTUNITY!

The 10 Major Causes of Failure in Leadership

We come now to the major faults of leaders who fail, because it is just as essential to know WHAT NOT TO DO as it is to know what to do.

1. INABILITY TO ORGANIZE DETAILS. Efficient leadership calls for ability to organize and to master details. No genuine leader is ever "too busy" to do anything which may be required of him in his capacity as leader. When a man, whether he is a leader or follower, admits that he is "too busy" to change his plans, or to give attention to any emergency, he admits his

inefficiency. The successful leader must be the master of all details connected with his position. That means, of course, that he must acquire the habit of relegating details to capable lieutenants.

2. UNWILLINGNESS TO RENDER HUMBLE SERVICE. Truly great leaders are willing, when occasion demands, to perform any sort of labor which they would ask another to perform. "The greatest among ye shall be the servant of all" is a truth which all able leaders observe and respect.

3. EXPECTATION OF PAY FOR WHAT THEY "KNOW" INSTEAD OF WHAT THEY DO WITH THAT WHICH THEY KNOW. The world does not pay men for that which they "know." It pays them for what they DO, or induce others to do.

4. FEAR OF COMPETITION FROM FOLLOWERS. The leader who fears that one of his followers may take his position is practically sure to realize that fear sooner or later. The able leader trains understudies to whom he may delegate, at will, any of the details of his position. Only in this way may a leader multiply himself and prepare himself to be at many places, and give attention to many things at one time. It is an eternal truth that men receive more pay for their ABILITY TO GET OTHERS TO PERFORM, than they could possibly earn by their own efforts. An efficient leader may, through his knowledge of his job

and the magnetism of his personality, greatly increase the efficiency of others, and induce them to render more service and better service than they could render without his aid.

5. LACK OF IMAGINATION. Without imagination, the leader is incapable of meeting emergencies, and of creating plans by which to guide his followers efficiently.

6. SELFISHNESS. The leader who claims all the honor for the work of his followers, is sure to be met by resentment. The really great leader CLAIMS NONE OF THE HONORS. He is contented to see the honors, when there are any, go to his followers, because he knows that most men will work harder for commendation and recognition than they will for money alone.

7. INTEMPERANCE. Followers do not respect an intemperate leader. Moreover, intemperance in any of its various forms, destroys the endurance and the vitality of all who indulge in it.

8. DISLOYALTY. Perhaps this should have come at the head of the list. The leader who is not loyal to his trust, and to his associates, those above him, and those below him, cannot long maintain his leadership. Disloyalty marks one as being less then the dust of the earth, and brings down on one's head the contempt he deserves. Lack of loyalty is one of the major causes of failure in every walk of life.

9. EMPHASIS OF THE "AUTHORITY" OF LEADERSHIP. The efficient leader leads by

encouraging, and not by trying to instill fear in the hearts of his followers. The leader who tries to impress his followers with his "authority" comes within the category of leadership through FORCE. If a leader is a REAL LEADER, he will have no need to advertise that fact except by his conduct—his sympathy, understanding, fairness, and a demonstration that he knows his job.

10. EMPHASIS OF TITLE. The competent leader requires no "title" to give him the respect of his followers. The man who makes too much over his title generally has little else to emphasize. The doors to the office of the real leader are open to all who wish to enter, and his working quarters are free from formality or ostentation.

These are among the more common of the causes of failure in leadership. Any one of these faults is sufficient to induce failure. Study the list carefully if you aspire to leadership, and make sure that you are free of these faults.

SOME FERTILE FIELDS IN WHICH "NEW LEADERSHIP" WILL BE REQUIRED

Before leaving this chapter, your attention is called to a few of the fertile fields in which there has been a decline of leadership, and in which the new type of leader may find an abundance of OPPORTUNITY.

First. In the field of politics there is a most insistent demand for new leaders; a demand which indicates nothing less than an emergency. The majority of politicians have, seemingly, become high-grade, legalized racketeers. They have increased taxes and debauched the machinery of industry and business until the people can no longer stand the burden.

Second. The banking business is undergoing a reform. The leaders in this field have almost entirely lost the confidence of the public. Already the bankers have sensed the need of reform, and they have begun it.

Third. Industry calls for new leaders. The old type of leaders thought and moved in terms of dividends instead of thinking and moving in terms of human equations! The future leader in industry, to endure, must regard himself as a quasi-public official whose duty it is to manage his trust in such a way that it will work hardship on no individual, or group of individuals. Exploitation of working men is a thing of the past. Let the man who aspires to leadership in the field of business, industry, and labor remember this.

Fourth. The religious leader of the future will be forced to give more attention to the temporal needs of his followers, in the solution of their economic and personal problems of the present, and less attention to the dead past, and the yet unborn future.

Fifth. In the professions of law, medicine, and education, a new brand of leadership, and to some extent, new leaders will become a necessity. This is especially true in the field of education. The leader in that field must, in the future, find ways and means of teaching people HOW TO APPLY the knowledge they receive in school. He must deal more with PRACTICE and less with THEORY.

Sixth. New leaders will be required in the field of Journalism. Newspapers of the future, to be conducted successfully, must be divorced from "special privilege" and relieved from the subsidy of advertising. They must cease to be organs of propaganda for the interests which patronize their advertising columns. The type of newspaper which publishes scandal and lewd pictures will eventually go the way of all forces which debauch the human mind.

These are but a few of the fields in which opportunities for new leaders and a new brand of leadership are now available. The world is undergoing a rapid change. This means that the media through which the changes in human habits are promoted, must be adapted to the changes. The media here described, are the ones which, more than any others, determine the trend of civilization.

WHEN AND HOW TO APPLY FOR A POSITION

The information described here is the net result of many years of experience during which thousands of men and women were helped to market their services effectively. It can, therefore, be relied upon as sound and practical.

Media through Which Services May Be Marketed

Experience has proved that the following media offer the most direct and effective methods of bringing the buyer and seller of personal services together.

1. EMPLOYMENT BUREAUS. Care must be taken to select only reputable bureaus, the management of which can show adequate records of achievement of satisfactory results. There are comparatively few such bureaus.

2. ADVERTISING in newspapers, trade journals, magazines, and radio. Classified advertising may usually be relied upon to produce satisfactory results in the case of those who apply for clerical or ordinary salaried positions. Display advertising is more desirable in the case of those who seek executive connections, the copy to appear in the section of the paper which is most apt to come to the attention of the class of employer being sought. The copy should be prepared by an expert, who understands how to inject sufficient selling qualities to produce replies.

3. PERSONAL LETTERS OF APPLICATION, directed to particular firms or individuals most apt to need such services as are being offered. Letters should be *neatly typed*, ALWAYS, and signed by hand. With the letter, should be sent a complete "brief" or outline of the applicant's qualifications. Both the letter of application and the brief of experience or qualifications should

be prepared by an expert. (See instructions as to information to be supplied).

4. APPLICATION THROUGH PERSONAL AC-QUAINTANCES. When possible, the applicant should endeavor to approach prospective employers through some mutual acquaintance. This method of approach is particularly advantageous in the case of those who seek executive connections and do not wish to appear to be "peddling" themselves.

5. APPLICATION IN PERSON. In some instances, it may be more effective if the applicant offers personally, his services to prospective employers, in which event a complete written statement of qualifications for the position should be presented, for the reason that prospective employers often wish to discuss with associates, one's record.

INFORMATION TO BE SUPPLIED IN A WRITTEN "BRIEF"

This brief should be prepared as carefully as a lawyer would prepare the brief of a case to be tried in court. Unless the applicant is experienced in the preparation of such briefs, an expert should be consulted, and his services enlisted for this purpose. Successful merchants employ men and women who understand the art and the psychology of advertising to present the merits of their merchandise. One who has personal services for sale should do the same. The following information should appear in the brief:

1. *Education.* State briefly, but definitely, what schooling you have had, and in what subjects you specialized in school, giving the reasons for that specialization.

2. *Experience.* If you have had experience in connection with positions similar to the one you seek, describe it fully, state names and addresses of former employers. Be sure to bring out clearly any *special* experience you may have had which would equip you to fill the position you seek.

3. *References.* Practically every business firm desires to know all about the previous records, antecedents, etc., of prospective employees who seek positions of responsibility. Attach to your brief photostatic copies of letters from:

    a. Former employers
    b. Teachers under whom you studied
    c. Prominent people whose judgment may be relied upon.

4. *Photograph of self.* Attach to your brief a recent, unmounted photograph of yourself.

5. *Apply for a specific position.* Avoid application for a position without describing EXACTLY what particular position you seek. Never apply for "just a position." That indicates you lack specialized qualifications.

6. *State your qualifications* for the particular position for which you apply. Give full details as to the reason you believe you are qualified for the particular position you seek. This is THE MOST IMPORTANT DETAIL OF YOUR

APPLICATION. It will determine, more than anything else, what consideration you receive.

7. *Offer to go to work on probation.* In the majority of instances if you are determined to have the position for which you apply, it will be most effective if you offer to work for a week, or a month, or for a sufficient length of time to enable your prospective employer to judge your value WITHOUT PAY. This may appear to be a radical suggestion, but experience has proved that it seldom fails to win at least a trial. If you are SURE OF YOUR QUALIFICATIONS, a trial is all you need. Incidentally, such an offer indicates that you have confidence in your ability to fill the position you seek. It is most convincing. If your offer is accepted, and you make good, more than likely you will be paid for your "probation" period. Make clear the fact that your offer is based upon:

  a. Your confidence in your ability to fill the position.
  b. Your confidence in your prospective employer's decision to employ you after trail.
  c. Your DETERMINATION to have the position you seek.

8. *Knowledge of your prospective employer's business.* Before applying for a position, do sufficient research in connection with the business to familiarize yourself thoroughly with that business, and indicate in your brief the knowledge you have acquired in this field. This will be impressive, as it will indicate that you have im-

agination, and a real interest in the position you seek.

Remember that it is not the lawyer who knows the most law, but the one who best prepares his case, who wins. If your "case" is properly prepared and presented, your victory will have been more than half won at the outset.

Do not be afraid of making your brief too long. Employers are just as much interested in purchasing the services of well-qualified applicants as you are in securing employment. In fact, the success of most successful employers is due, in the main, to their ability to select well-qualified lieutenants. They want all the information available.

Remember another thing; neatness in the preparation of your brief will indicate that you are a painstaking person. I have helped to prepare briefs for clients which were so striking and out of the ordinary that they resulted in the employment of the applicant without a personal interview.

When your brief has been completed, have it neatly bound by an experienced binder, and lettered by an artist, or printer similar to the following:

BRIEF OF THE QUALIFICATIONS OF
Robert K. Smith
APPLYING FOR THE POSITION OF
$$\left\{ \begin{array}{c} \text{Private Secretary to} \\ \text{The President of} \\ \text{THE BLANK COMPANY, Inc.} \end{array} \right\}$$
Change names each time brief is shown.

This personal touch is sure to command attention. Have your brief neatly typed or mimeographed on the finest paper you can obtain, and bound with a heavy paper of the book-cover variety, the binder to be changed, and the proper firm name to be inserted if it is to be shown to more than one company. Your photograph should be pasted on one of the pages of your brief. Follow these instructions to the letter, improving upon them wherever your imagination suggests.

Successful salesmen groom themselves with care. They understand that first impressions are lasting. Your brief is your salesman. Give it a good suit of clothes, so it will stand out in bold contrast to anything your prospective employer ever saw, in the way of an application for a position. If the position you seek is worth having, it is worth going after with care. Moreover, if you sell yourself to an employer in a manner that impresses him with your individuality, you probably will receive more money for your services from the very start, than you would if you applied for employment in the usual conventional way.

If you seek employment through an advertising agency, or an employment agency, have the agent use copies of your brief in marketing your services. This will help to gain preference for you, both with the agent, and the prospective employers.

How to Get the Exact Position You Desire

Everyone enjoys doing the kind of work for which he is best suited. An artist loves to work with paints, a craftsman with his hands, a writer loves to write. Those with less definite talents have their preferences for certain fields of business and industry. If America does anything well, it offers a full range of occupations, tilling the soil, manufacturing, marketing, and the professions.

First. Decide EXACTLY what kind of a job you want. If the job doesn't already exist, perhaps you can create it.

Second. Choose the company, or individual for whom you wish to work.

Third. Study your prospective employer, as to policies, personnel, and chances of advancement.

Fourth. By analysis of yourself, your talents and capabilities, figure WHAT YOU CAN OFFER, and plan ways and means of giving advantages, services, developments, ideas that *you believe* you can successfully deliver.

Fifth. Forget about "a job." Forget whether or not there is an opening. Forget the usual routine of "have you got a job for me?" Concentrate on what *you can give.*

Sixth. Once you have your plan in mind, arrange with an experienced writer to put it on paper in neat form, and in full detail.

Seventh. Present it to the *proper person with authority* and he will do the rest. Every company is looking for men who can give something of value, whether it be ideas, services, or "connections." Every company has room for the man who has a definite plan of action which is to the advantage of that company.

This line of procedure may take a few days or weeks of extra time, but the difference in income, in advancement, and in gaining recognition will save years of hard work at small pay. It has many advantages, the main one being that it will often save from one to five years of time in reaching a chosen goal.

Every person who starts, or "gets in" half way up the ladder, does so by deliberate and careful planning, (excepting, of course, the Boss' son).

THE NEW WAY OF MARKETING SERVICES
"JOBS" ARE NOW "PARTNERSHIPS"

Men and women who market their services to best advantage in the future, must recognize the stupendous change which has taken place in connection with the relationship between employer and employee.

In the future, the "Golden Rule," and not the "Rule of Gold" will be the dominating factor in the marketing of merchandise as well as personal services. The future relationship between employers and their employees will be more in the nature of a partnership consisting of:

    a. The employer
    b. The employee
    c. The public they serve

This new way of marketing personal services is called new for many reasons, first, both the employer and the employee of the future will be considered as fellow-employees whose business it will be to SERVE THE PUBLIC EFFICIENTLY. In times past, employers, and employees have bartered among themselves, driving the best bargains they could with one another, not considering that in the final analysis they were, in reality, BARGAINING AT THE EXPENSE OF THE THIRD PARTY, THE PUBLIC THEY SERVED.

The depression served as a mighty protest from an injured public, whose rights had been trampled upon in every direction by those who were clamoring for individual advantages and profits. When the debris of the depression shall have been cleared away, and business shall have been once again restored to balance, both employers and employees will recognize that they are NO LONGER PRIVILEGED TO DRIVE BARGAINS AT THE EXPENSE OF THOSE WHOM THEY SERVE. The real employer of the future will be the public. This should be kept uppermost in mind by every person seeking to market personal services effectively.

Nearly every railroad in America is in financial difficulty. Who does not remember the day when, if a citizen enquired at the ticket office, the time of departure of a train, he was abruptly referred to the bulletin board instead of being politely given the information?

The street car companies have experienced a "change of times" also. There was a time not so very long ago when street car conductors took pride in giving argument to passengers. Many of the street car tracks have been removed and passengers ride on a bus, whose driver is "the last word in politeness."

All over the country street car tracks are rusting

from abandonment, or have been taken up. Wherever street cars are still in operation, passengers may now ride without argument, and one may even hail the car in the middle of the block, and the motorman will OBLIGINGLY pick him up.

HOW TIMES HAVE CHANGED! That is just the point I am trying to emphasize. TIMES HAVE CHANGED! Moreover, the change is reflected not merely in railroad offices and on street cars, but in other walks of life as well. The "public-be-damned" policy is now passé. It has been supplanted by the "we-are-obligingly-at-your-service, sir," policy.

The bankers have learned a thing or two during this rapid change which has taken place during the past few years. Impoliteness on the part of a bank official, or bank employee today is as rare as it was conspicuous a dozen years ago. In the years past, some bankers (not all of them, of course), carried an atmosphere of austerity which gave every would-be borrower a chill when he even thought of approaching his banker for a loan.

The thousands of bank failures during the depression had the effect of removing the mahogany doors behind which bankers formerly barricaded themselves. They now sit at desks in the open, where they may be seen and approached at will by any depositor, or by anyone who wishes to see them, and the whole atmosphere of the bank is one of courtesy and understanding.

It used to be customary for customers to have to stand and wait at the corner grocery until the clerks were through passing the time of day with friends, and the proprietor had finished making up his bank deposit, before being waited upon. Chain stores, managed by COURTEOUS MEN who do everything in the way of service, short of shining the customer's shoes, have PUSHED THE OLD-TIME MERCHANTS INTO THE BACKGROUND. TIME MARCHES ON!

"Courtesy" and "Service" are the watch-words of merchandising today, and apply to the person who is marketing personal services even more directly than to the employer whom he serves, because, in the final analysis, both the employer and his employees are EMPLOYED BY THE PUBLIC THEY SERVE. If they fail to serve well, they pay by the loss of their privilege of serving.

We can all remember the time when the gas-meter reader pounded on the door hard enough to break the panels. When the door was opened, he pushed his way in, uninvited, with a scowl on his face which plainly said, "what-the-hell-did-you-keep-me-waiting-for?" All that has undergone a change. The meter-man now conducts himself as a gentleman who is "delighted-to-be-at-your-service-sir." Before the gas companies learned that their scowling meter-men were accumulating liabilities never to be cleared away, the polite salesmen of oil burners came along and did a land office business.

During the depression, I spent several months in the anthracite coal region of Pennsylvania, studying conditions which all but destroyed the coal industry. Among several very significant discoveries, was the fact that greed on the part of operators and their employees was the chief cause of the loss of business for the operators, and loss of jobs for the miners.

Through the pressure of a group of overzealous labor leaders, representing the employees, and the greed for profits on the part of the operators, the anthracite business suddenly dwindled. The coal operators and their employees drove sharp bargains with one another, adding the cost of the "bargaining" to the price of the coal, until, finally, they discovered they had BUILT UP A WONDERFUL BUSINESS FOR THE MANUFAC-TURERS OF OIL BURNING OUTFITS AND THE PRODUCERS OF CRUDE OIL.

"The wages of sin is death!" Many have read this in the Bible, but few have discovered its meaning. Now, and for several years, the entire world had been listening BY FORCE, to a sermon which might well be called "WHATSOEVER A MAN SOWETH, THAT SHALL HE ALSO REAP."

Nothing as widespread and effective as the depression could possibly be "just a coincidence." Behind the depression was a CAUSE. Nothing ever happens without a CAUSE. In the main, the cause of the depression is traceable directly to the world-wide habit of trying to REAP without SOWING.

This should not be mistaken to mean that the depression represents a crop which the world is being FORCED to reap without having SOWN. The trouble is that the world *sowed the wrong sort of seed.* Any farmer knows he cannot sow the seed of thistles, and reap a harvest of grain. Beginning at the outbreak of the world war, the people of the world began to sow the seed of service inadequate in both quality and quantity. Nearly everyone was engaged in the pastime of trying to GET WITHOUT GIVING.

These illustrations are brought to the attention of those who have personal services to market, to show that we are where we are, and what we are, because of *our own conduct!* If there is a principle of cause and effect, which controls business, finance, and transportation, this same principle controls individuals and determines their economic status.

What Is Your "QQS" Rating?

The causes of success in marketing services EFFECTIVELY and permanently, have been clearly described. Unless those causes are studied, analyzed, understood and APPLIED, no man can market his services effectively and permanently. Every person must be his own salesman of personal services. The QUALITY and the QUANTITY of service rendered, and the SPIRIT in which it is rendered, determine to a large extent, the price, and the duration of employment. To market Personal services effectively, (which means a permanent market, at a satisfactory price, under pleasant conditions), one must adopt and follow the "QQS" formula which means the QUALITY, plus QUANTITY, plus the proper SPIRIT of cooperation, equals perfect salesmanship of service. Remember the "QQS" formula, but do more—APPLY IT AS A HABIT!

Let us analyze the formula to make sure we understand exactly what it means.

1. *QUALITY* of service shall be constructed to mean the performance of every detail, in connection with your position, in the most efficient manner possible, with the object of greater efficiency always in mind.

2. *QUANTITY* of service shall be understood to mean the HABIT of rendering all the service of which you are capable, at all times, with the purpose of increasing the amount of service rendered as greater skill is developed through practice and experience. Emphasis is again placed on the word HABIT.

3. *SPIRIT* of service shall be constructed to mean the HABIT of agreeable, harmonious conduct which will induce cooperation from associates and fellow employees.

Adequacy of QUALITY and QUANTITY of service is not sufficient to maintain a permanent market of your services. The conduct, or the SPIRIT in which you deliver service, is a strong determining factor in connection with both the price you receive, and the duration of employment.

Andrew Carnegie stressed this point more than others in connection with his description of the factors which lead to success in the marketing of personal services. He emphasized again, and again, the necessity for HARMONIOUS CONDUCT. He stressed the fact that he would not retain any man, no matter how great a QUANTITY, or how efficient the QUALITY of his work, *unless* he worked in a spirit of HARMONY. Mr. Carnegie insisted upon men being AGREEABLE.

To prove that he placed a high value upon this quality, he permitted many men *who conformed to his standards* to become very wealthy. Those who did not conform, had to make room for others.

The importance of a pleasing personality has been stressed, because it is a factor which enables one to render service in the proper SPIRIT. If one has a personality which PLEASES, and renders service in a spirit of HARMONY, these assets often make up for deficiencies in both the QUALITY, and the QUANTITY of service one renders. Nothing, however, can be SUCCESSFULLY SUBSTITUTED FOR PLEASING CONDUCT.

The Capital Value of Your Services

The person whose income is derived entirely from the sale of personal services is no less a merchant than the man who sells commodities, and it might well be added, such a person is subjected to EXACTLY THE SAME RULES of conduct as the merchant who sells merchandise.

This has been emphasized, because the majority of people who live by the sale of personal services make the mistake of considering themselves free from the rules of conduct, and the responsibilities attached to those who are engaged in marketing commodities.

The new way of marketing services has practically forced both employer and employee into partnership alliances, through which both take into consideration the rights of the third party, THE PUBLIC THEY SERVE.

The day of the "go-getter" has passed. He has

been supplanted by the "go-giver." High-pressure methods in business finally blew the lid off. There will never be the need to put the lid back on, because, in the future, business will be conducted by methods that will require no pressure.

The actual capital value of your brains may be determined by the amount of income you can produce (by marketing your services). A fair estimate of the capital value of your services may be made by multiplying your annual income by sixteen and two-thirds, as it is reasonable to estimate that your annual income represents six percent of your capital value. Money rents for 6% per annum. Money is worth no more than brains. It is often worth much less.

Competent "brains," if effectively marketed, represent a much more desirable form of capital than that which is required to conduct a business dealing in commodities, because "brains" are a form of capital which cannot be permanently depreciated through depressions, nor can this form of capital be stolen or spent. Moreover, the money which is essential for the conduct of business is as worthless as a sand dune, until it has been mixed with efficient "brains."

THE THIRTY MAJOR CAUSES OF FAILURE
How Many of These Are Holding You Back?

Life's greatest tragedy consists of men and women who earnestly try, and fail! The tragedy lies in the overwhelmingly large majority of people who fail, as compared to the few who succeed.

I have had the privilege of analyzing several

thousand men and women, 98% of whom were classed as "failures." There is something radically wrong with a civilization, and a system of education, which permit 98% of the people to go through life as failures. But I did not write this book for the purpose of moralizing on the rights and wrongs of the world; that would require a book a hundred times the size of this one.

My analysis work proved that there are thirty major reasons for failure, and thirteen major principles through which people accumulate fortunes. In this chapter, a description of the thirty major causes of failure will be given. As you go over the list, check yourself by it, point by point, for the purpose of discovering how many of these causes-of-failure stand between you and success.

1. UNFAVORABLE HEREDITARY BACKGROUND. There is but little, if anything, which can be done for people who are born with a deficiency in brain power. This philosophy offers but one method of bridging this weakness—through the aid of the Master Mind. Observe with profit, however, that this is the ONLY one of the thirty causes of failure which may not be *easily corrected* by any individual.

2. LACK OF A WELL-DEFINED PURPOSE IN LIFE. There is no hope of success for the person who does not have a central purpose, or *definite goal* at which to aim. Ninety-eight out of every hundred of those whom I have analyzed, had no such aim. Perhaps this was the MAJOR CAUSE OF THEIR FAILURE.

3. LACK OF AMBITION TO AIM ABOVE MEDIOC-RITY. We offer no hope for the person who is so indifferent as not to want to get ahead in life, and who is not willing to pay the price.

4. INSUFFICIENT EDUCATION. This is a hand-icap which may be overcome with comparative ease. Experience has proven that the best-educated people are often those who are known as "self-made," or self-educated. It takes more than a college degree to make one a person of education. Any person who is educated is one who has learned to get what-ever he wants in life without violating the rights of others. Education consists, not so much of knowledge, but of knowledge effec-tively and persistently APPLIED. Men are paid, not merely for what they know, but more particularly for WHAT THEY DO WITH THAT WHICH THEY KNOW.

5. LACK OF SELF-DISCIPLINE. Discipline comes through self-control. This means that one must control all negative qualities. Before you can control conditions, you must first control yourself. Self-mastery is the hardest job you will ever tackle. If you do not conquer self, you will be conquered by self. You may see at one and the same time both your best friend and your greatest enemy, by stepping in front of a mirror.

6. ILL HEALTH. No person may enjoy out-standing success without good health. Many

of the causes of ill health are subject to mastery and control. These, in the main are:

    a. Overeating of foods not conducive to health.

    b. Wrong habits of thought; giving expression to negatives.

    c. Wrong use of, and over indulgence in sex.

    d. Lack of proper physical exercise.

    e. An inadequate supply of fresh air, due to improper breathing.

7. UNFAVORABLE ENVIRONMENTAL INFLUENCES DURING CHILDHOOD. "As the twig is bent, so shall the tree grow." Most people who have criminal tendencies acquire them as the result of bad environment, and improper associates during childhood.

8. PROCRASTINATION. This is one of the most common causes of failure. "Old Man Procrastination" stands within the shadow of every human being, waiting his opportunity to spoil one's chances of success. Most of us go through life as failures, because we are waiting for the "time to be right" to start doing something worthwhile. Do not wait. The time will never be "just right." Start where you stand, and work with whatever tools you may have at your command, and better tools will be found as you go along.

9. LACK OF PERSISTENCE. Most of us are good "starters" but poor "finishers" of everything we begin. Moreover, people are prone to give up at the first signs of defeat. There is

no substitute for PERSISTENCE. The person who makes PERSISTENCE his watch-word, discovers that "Old Man Failure" finally becomes tired, and makes his departure. Failure cannot cope with PERSISTENCE.

10. NEGATIVE PERSONALITY. There is no hope of success for the person who repels people through a negative personality. Success comes through the application of POWER, and power is attained through the cooperative efforts of other people. A negative personality will not induce cooperation.

11. LACK OF CONTROLLED SEXUAL URGE. Sex energy is the most powerful of all the stimuli which move people into ACTION. Because it is the most powerful of the emotions, it must be controlled, through transmutation, and converted into other channels.

12. UNCONTROLLED DESIRE FOR "SOMETHING FOR NOTHING." The gambling instinct drives millions of people to failure. Evidence of this may be found in a study of the Wall Street crash of '29, during which millions of people tried to make money by gambling on stock margins.

13. LACK OF A WELL DEFINED POWER OF DECISION. Men who succeed reach decisions promptly, and change them, if at all, very slowly. Men who fail, reach decisions, if at all, very slowly, and change them frequently, and quickly. Indecision and procrastination are twin brothers. Where one is found, the other

may usually be found also. Kill off this pair before they completely "hog-tie" you to the treadmill of FAILURE.

14. ONE OR MORE OF THE SIX BASIC FEARS. These fears have been analyzed for you in a later chapter. They must be mastered before you can market your services effectively.

15. WRONG SELECTION OF A MATE IN MARRIAGE. This a most common cause of failure. The relationship of marriage brings people intimately into contact. Unless this relationship is harmonious, failure is likely to follow. Moreover, it will be a form of failure that is marked by misery and unhappiness, destroying all signs of AMBITION.

16. OVER-CAUTION. The person who takes no chances, generally has to take whatever is left when others are through choosing. Over-caution is as bad as under-caution. Both are extremes to be guarded against. Life itself is filled with the element of chance.

17. WRONG SELECTION OF ASSOCIATES IN BUSINESS. This is one of the most common causes of failure in business. In marketing personal services, one should use great care to select an employer who will be an inspiration, and who is, himself, intelligent and successful. We emulate those with whom we associate most closely. Pick an employer who is worth emulating.

18. SUPERSTITION AND PREJUDICE. Superstition is a form of fear. It is also a sign of

ignorance. Men who succeed keep open minds and are afraid of nothing.

19. WRONG SELECTION OF A VOCATION. No man can succeed in a line of endeavor which he does not like. The most essential step in the marketing of personal services is that of selecting an occupation into which you can throw yourself wholeheartedly.

20. LACK OF CONCENTRATION OF EFFORT. The "jack-of-all-trades" seldom is good at any. Concentrate all of your efforts on one DEFINITE CHIEF AIM.

21. THE HABIT OF INDISCRIMINATE SPENDING. The spend-thrift cannot succeed, mainly because he stands eternally in FEAR OF POVERTY. Form the habit of systematic saving by putting aside a definite percentage of your income. Money in the bank gives one a very safe foundation of COURAGE when bargaining for the sale of personal services. Without money, one must take what one is offered, and be glad to get it.

22. LACK OF ENTHUSIASM. Without enthusiasm one cannot be convincing. Moreover, enthusiasm is contagious, and the person who has it, under control, is generally welcome in any group of people.

23. INTOLERANCE. The person with a "closed" mind on any subject seldom gets ahead. Intolerance means that one has stopped acquiring knowledge. The most damaging forms of in-

tolerance are those connected with religious, racial, and political differences of opinion.

24. INTEMPERANCE. The most damaging forms of intemperance are connected with eating, strong drink, and sexual activities. Over-indulgence in any of these is fatal to success.

25. INABILITY TO COOPERATE WITH OTHERS. More people lose their positions and their big opportunities in life, because of this fault, than for all other reasons combined. It is a fault which no well-informed business man, or leader will tolerate.

26. POSSESSION OF POWER THAT WAS NOT ACQUIRED THROUGH SELF EFFORT. (Sons and daughters of wealthy men, and others who inherit money which they did not earn). Power in the hands of one who did not acquire it gradually, is often fatal to success. QUICK RICHES are more dangerous than poverty.

27. INTENTIONAL DISHONESTY. There is no substitute for honesty. One may be temporarily dishonest by force of circumstances over which one has no control, without permanent damage. But, there is NO HOPE for the person who is dishonest by choice. Sooner or later, his deeds will catch up with him, and he will pay by loss of reputation, and perhaps even loss of liberty.

28. EGOTISM AND VANITY. These qualities serve as red lights which warn others to keep away. THEY ARE FATAL TO SUCCESS.

29. GUESSING INSTEAD OF THINKING. Most people are too indifferent or lazy to acquire FACTS with which to THINK ACCURATELY. They prefer to act on "opinions" created by guesswork or snap-judgments.

30. LACK OF CAPITAL. This is a common cause of failure among those who start out in business for the first time, without sufficient reserve of capital to absorb the shock of their mistakes, and to carry them over until they have established a REPUTATION.

31. Under this, name any particular cause of failure from which you have suffered that has not been included in the foregoing list.

In these thirty major causes of failure is found a description of the tragedy of life, which obtains for practically every person who tries and fails. It will be helpful if you can induce someone who knows you well to go over this list with you, and help to analyze you by the thirty causes of failure. It may be beneficial if you try this alone. Most people cannot see themselves as others see them. You may be one who cannot.

The oldest of admonitions is "Man, know thyself!" If you market merchandise successfully, you must know the merchandise. The same is true in marketing personal services. You should know all of your weaknesses in order that you may either bridge them or eliminate them entirely. You should know your strength in order that you may call attention to it when selling your services. You can know yourself only through *accurate* analysis.

The folly of ignorance in connection with self was displayed by a young man who applied to the manager of a well known business for a position. He made a very good impression until the manager asked him what salary he expected. He replied that he had no fixed sum in mind (*lack of a definite aim*). The manager then said, "We will pay you all you are worth, after we try you out for a week."

"I will not accept it," the applicant replied, "because I AM GETTING MORE THAN THAT WHERE I AM NOW EMPLOYED."

Before you even start to negotiate for a readjustment of your salary in your present position, or to seek employment elsewhere, BE SURE THAT YOU ARE WORTH MORE THAN YOU NOW RECEIVE.

It is one thing to WANT money—everyone wants more—but it is something entirely different to be WORTH MORE! Many people mistake their WANTS for their JUST DUES. Your financial requirements or wants have nothing whatever to do with your WORTH. Your value is established entirely by your ability to render useful service or your capacity to induce others to render such service.

TAKE INVENTORY OF YOURSELF
28 QUESTIONS YOU SHOULD ANSWER

Annual self-analysis is an essential in the effective marketing of personal services, as is annual inventory in merchandising. Moreover, the yearly analysis should disclose a DECREASE IN FAULTS, and an increase in VIRTUES. One goes ahead, stands still, or goes backward in life. One's object should be, of course, to go ahead. Annual self-analysis will disclose whether advancement has been made, and if so, how much. It will also disclose any backward steps one may have made. The effective marketing of personal services requires one to move forward even if the progress is slow.

Your annual self-analysis should be made at the end of each year, so you can include in your New Year's Resolutions any improvements which the analysis indicates should be made. Take this inventory by asking yourself the following questions, and by checking your answers with the aid of someone who will not permit you to deceive yourself as to their accuracy.

Self-Analysis Questionnaire for Personal Inventory

1. Have I attained the goal which I established as my objective for this year? (You should work with a definite yearly objective to be attained as a part of your major life objective).

2. Have I delivered service of the best possible QUALITY of which I was capable, or could I have improved any part of this service?

3. Have I delivered service in the greatest possible QUANTITY of which I was capable?

4. Has the spirit of my conduct been harmonious, and cooperative at all times?

5. Have I permitted the habit of PROCRASTINA-TION to decrease my efficiency, and if so, to what extent?

6. Have I improved my PERSONALITY, and if so, in what ways?

7. Have I been PERSISTENT in following my plans through to completion?

8. Have I reached DECISIONS PROMPTLY AND DEFINITELY on all occasions?

9. Have I permitted any one or more of the six basic fears to decrease my efficiency?

10. Have I been either "over-cautious," or "under-cautious?"

11. Has my relationship with my associates in work been pleasant, or unpleasant? If it has been unpleasant, has the fault been partly, or wholly mine?

12. Have I dissipated any of my energy through lack of CONCENTRATION of effort?

13. Have I been open minded and tolerant in connection with all subjects?

14. In what way have I improved my ability to render service?

15. Have I been intemperate in any of my habits?

16. Have I expressed, either openly or secretly, any form of EGOTISM?

17. Has my conduct toward my associates been such that it has induced them to RESPECT me?

18. Have my opinions and DECISIONS been based upon guesswork, or accuracy of analysis and THOUGHT?

19. Have I followed the habit of budgeting my

time, my expenses, and my income, and have I
been conservative in these budgets?

20. How much time have I devoted to UNPROF-
ITABLE effort which I might have used to better
advantage?

21. How may I RE-BUDGET my time, and change
my habits so I will be more efficient during the
coming year?

22. Have I been guilty of any conduct which was
not approved by my conscience?

23. In what ways have I rendered MORE SERVICE
AND BETTER SERVICE than I was paid to render?

24. Have I been unfair to anyone, and if so, in what
way?

25. If I had been the purchaser of my own services
for the year, would I be satisfied with my
purchase?

26. Am I in the right vocation, and if not, why not?

27. Has the purchaser of my services been satisfied
with the service I have rendered, and if not, why
not?

28. What is my present rating on the fundamental
principles of success? (Make this rating fairly,
and frankly, and have it checked by someone
who is courageous enough to do it accurately).

Having read and assimilated the information
conveyed through this chapter, you are now ready
to create a practical plan for marketing your
personal services. In this chapter will be found an

adequate description of every principle essential in planning the sale of personal services, including the major attributes of leadership; the most common causes of failure in leadership; a description of the fields of opportunity for leadership; the main causes of failure in all walks of life, and the important questions which should be used in self-analysis.

This extensive and detailed presentation of accurate information has been included, because it will be needed by all who must begin the accumulation of riches by marketing personal services. Those who have lost their fortunes, and those who are just beginning to earn money, have nothing but personal services to offer in return for riches, therefore it is essential that they have available the practical information needed to market services to best advantage.

The information contained in this chapter will be of great value to all who aspire to attain leadership in any calling. It will be particularly helpful to those aiming to market their services as business or industrial executives.

Complete assimilation and understanding of the information here conveyed will be helpful in marketing one's own services, and it will also help one to become more analytical and capable of judging people. The information will be priceless to personnel directors, employment managers, and other executives charged with the selection of employees, and the maintenance of efficient organizations. If you doubt this statement, test its soundness by answering in writing the twenty-eight self-analysis questions. That might be both interesting and profitable, even though you do not doubt the soundness of the statement.

WHERE AND HOW ONE MAY FIND OPPORTUNITIES TO ACCUMULATE RICHES

Now that we have analyzed the principles by which riches may be accumulated, we naturally ask, "where may one find favorable opportunities to apply these principles?" Very well, let us take inventory and see what the United States of America offer the person seeking riches, great or small.

To begin with, let us remember, *all of us,* that we live in a country where *every law-abiding citizen enjoys freedom of thought and freedom of deed unequaled anywhere in the world.* Most of us have never taken inventory of the advantages of this freedom. We have never compared our unlimited freedom with the curtailed freedom in other countries.

Here we have freedom of thought, freedom in the choice and enjoyment of education, freedom in religion, freedom in politics, freedom in the choice of a business, profession or occupation, freedom to accumulate and own without molestation, *ALL THE PROPERTY WE CAN ACCUMULATE,* freedom to choose our place of residence, freedom in marriage, freedom through equal opportunity to all races, freedom of travel from one state to another, freedom in our choice of foods, and freedom to *AIM FOR ANY STATION IN LIFE FOR WHICH WE HAVE PREPARED OURSELVES* even for the presidency of the United States.

We have other forms of freedom, but this list will give a bird's eye view of the most important, which constitute OPPORTUNITY of the highest order. This advantage of freedom is all the more conspicuous because the United States is the only country guaranteeing to every citizen, whether native born or naturalized, so broad and varied a list of freedom.

Next, let us recount some of the blessings which our widespread freedom has placed within our hands. Take the average American family for example (meaning, the family of average income) and sum up the benefits available to every member of the family, in this land of OPPORTUNITY and plenty!

a. FOOD. Next to freedom of thought and deed comes FOOD, CLOTHING, and SHELTER, the three basic necessities of life.

Because of our universal freedom the average American family has available, at its very door, the choicest selection of food to be found anywhere in the world, and at prices within its financial range.

A family of two, living in the heart of Times Square district of New York City, far removed from the source of production of foods, took careful inventory of the cost of a simple breakfast, with this astonishing result:

Articles of food;   Cost at the
                                breakfast table:
Grape Fruit Juice, (From Florida)...... .02

Rippled Wheat Breakfast food (Kansas
Farm). 02
Tea (From China) 02
Bananas (From South America). . . . . .02 ½
Toasted Bread (From Kansas Farm). 01
Fresh Country Eggs (From Utah) 07
Sugar (From Cuba, or Utah) . . . . .00 ½
Butter and Cream (From New
England) 03
                                                    ___
                    Grand total 20

It is not very difficult to obtain FOOD in a country where two people can have breakfast consisting of all they want or need for a dime apiece! Observe that this simple breakfast was gathered, by some strange form of magic (?) from China, South America, Utah, Kansas and the New England States, and delivered on the breakfast table, ready for consumption, in the very heart of the most crowded city in America, at a cost well within the means of the most humble laborer.

The cost included all federal, state and city taxes! (Here is a fact the politicians did not mention when they were crying out to the voters to throw their opponents out of office because the people were being taxed to death).

b. SHELTER. This family lives in a comfortable apart-
    ment, heated by steam, lighted with electricity,
    with gas for cooking, all for $65.00 a month. In
    a smaller city, or a more sparsely settled part of
    New York City, the same apartment could be
    had for as low as $20.00 a month.

The toast they had for breakfast in the food estimate was toasted on an electric toaster, which cost but a few dollars, the apartment is cleaned with a vacuum sweeper that is run by electricity. Hot and cold water is available, at all times, in the kitchen and the bathroom. The food is kept cool in a refrigerator that is run by electricity. The wife curls her hair, washes her clothes and irons them with easily operated electrical equipment, on power obtained by sticking a plug in the wall. The husband shaves with an electric shaver, and they receive entertainment from all over the world, twenty four hours a day, if they want it, without cost, by merely turning the dial of their radio.

There are other conveniences in this apartment, but the foregoing list will give a fair idea of some of the concrete evidences of the freedom we, of America, enjoy. (*And this is neither political nor economic propaganda*).

c. CLOTHING. Anywhere in the United States, the woman of average clothing requirements can dress very comfortably and neatly for less than $200.00 a year, and the average man can dress for the same, or less.

Only the three basic necessities of food, clothing, and shelter have been mentioned. The average American citizen has other privileges and advantages available in return for modest effort, not exceeding eight hours per day of labor. Among these is the privilege of automobile transportation, with which one can go and come at will, at very small cost.

The average American has security of property rights not found in any other country in the world. He can place his surplus money in a bank with the assurance that his government will protect it, and make good to him if the bank fails. If an American citizen wants to travel from one state to another he needs no passport, no one's permission. He may go when he pleases, and return at will. Moreover, he may travel by train, private automobile, bus, airplane, or ship, as his pocketbook permits. In Germany, Russia, Italy, and most of the other European and Oriental countries, the people cannot travel with so much freedom, and at so little cost.

The "Miracle" That Has Provided These Blessings

We often hear politicians proclaiming the freedom of America, when they solicit votes, but seldom do they take the time or devote sufficient effort to the analysis of the source or nature of this "freedom." Having no axe to grind, no grudge to express, no ulterior motives to be carried out, I have the privilege of going into a frank analysis of that mysterious, abstract, greatly misunderstood "SOMETHING" which gives to every citizen of America more blessings, more opportunities to accumulate wealth, more freedom of every nature, than may be found in any other country.

I have the right to analyze the source and nature of this UNSEEN POWER, because I know, and have known for more than a quarter of a century, many of the men who organized that power, and many who are now responsible for its maintenance.

The name of this mysterious benefactor of mankind is CAPITAL!

CAPITAL consists not alone of money, but more particularly of highly organized, intelligent groups of men who plan ways and means of using money efficiently for the good of the public, and profitably to themselves.

These groups consist of scientists, educators, chemists, inventors, business analysts, publicity men, transportation experts, accountants, lawyers, doctors, and both men and women who have highly specialized knowledge in all fields of industry and business. They pioneer, experiment, and blaze trails in new fields of endeavor. They support colleges, hospitals, public schools, build good roads, publish newspapers, pay most of the cost of government, and take care of the multitudinous detail essential to human progress. Stated briefly, the capitalists are the brains of civilization, because they supply the entire fabric of which all education, enlightenment and human progress consists.

Money, without brains, always is dangerous. Properly used, it is the most important essential of civilization. The simple breakfast here described could not have been delivered to the New York family at a dime each, *or at any other price,* if organized capital had not provided the machinery, the ships, the railroads, and the huge armies of trained men to operate them.

Some slight idea of the importance of ORGAN-

IZED CAPITAL may be had by trying to imagine yourself burdened with the responsibility of collecting, without the aid of capital, and delivering to the New York City family, the simple breakfast described.

To supply the tea, you would have to make a trip to China or India, both a very long way from America. Unless you are an excellent swimmer, you would become rather tired before making the round trip. Then, too, another problem would confront you. What would you use for money, even if you had the physical endurance to swim the ocean?

To supply the sugar, you would have to take another long swim to Cuba, or a long walk to the sugar beet section of Utah. But even then, you might come back without the sugar, because organized effort and money are necessary to produce sugar, to say nothing of what is required to refine, transport, and deliver it to the breakfast table anywhere in the United States.

The eggs, you could deliver easily enough from the barn yards near New York City, but you would have a very long walk to Florida and return, before you could serve the two glasses of grapefruit juice.

You would have another long walk, to Kansas, or one of the other wheat growing states, when you went after the four slices of wheat bread.

The Rippled Wheat Biscuits would have to be omitted from the menu, because they would not be available except through the labor of a trained organization of men and suitable machinery, ALL OF WHICH CALL FOR CAPITAL.

While resting, you could take off for another little

swim down to South America, where you would pick up a couple of bananas, and on your return, you could take a short walk to the nearest farm having a dairy and pick up some butter and cream. Then your New York City family would be ready to sit down and enjoy breakfast, and *you could collect your two dimes for your labor!*

Seems absurd, doesn't it? Well, the procedure described would be the only possible way these simple items of food could be delivered to the heart of New York City, if we had no capitalistic system.

The sum of money required for the building and maintenance of the railroads and steam ships used in the delivery of that simple breakfast is so huge that it staggers one's imagination. It runs into hundreds of millions of dollars, not to mention the armies of trained employees required to man the ships and trains. But, transportation is only a part of the requirements of modern civilization in capitalistic America. Before there can be anything to haul, something must be grown from the ground, or manufactured and prepared for market. This calls for more millions of dollars for equipment, machinery, boxing, marketing, and for the wages of millions of men and women.

Steam ships and railroads do not spring up from the earth and function automatically. They come in response to the call of civilization, through the labor and ingenuity and organizing ability of men who have IMAGINATION, FAITH, ENTHUSI-ASM, DECISION, PERSISTENCE! These men are known as capitalists. They are motivated by the desire to build, construct, achieve, render useful service, earn profits and accumulate riches. And, because they RENDER SERVICE WITHOUT WHICH THERE WOULD BE NO CIVILIZA- TION, they put themselves in the way of great riches.

Just to keep the record simple and understand- able, I will add that these capitalists are the self-same men of whom most of us have heard soap-box orators speak. They are the same men to whom radicals, racketeers, dishonest politicians and grafting labor leaders refer as "the predatory interests," or "Wall Street."

I am not attempting to present a brief for or against any group of men or any system of economics. I am not attempting to condemn collective bargaining when I refer to "grafting labor leaders," nor do I aim to give a clean bill of health to all individuals known as capitalists.

The purpose of this book—*A purpose to which I have faithfully devoted over a quarter of a century*—is to present to all who want the knowledge, the most dependable philosophy through which individ- uals may accumulate riches in whatever amounts they desire.

I have here analyzed the economic advantages of the capitalistic system for the two-fold purpose of showing:

1. that all who seek riches must recognize and adapt themselves to the system that controls all approaches to fortunes, large or small, and

2. to present the side of the picture opposite to that being shown by politicians and demagogues

who deliberately becloud the issues they bring up, by referring to organized capital as if it were something poisonous.

This is a capitalistic country, it was developed through the use of capital, and we who claim the right to partake of the blessings of freedom and opportunity, we who seek to accumulate riches here, may as well know that neither riches nor opportunity would be available to us if ORGANIZED CAPITAL had not provided these benefits.

For more than twenty years it has been a somewhat popular and growing pastime for radicals, self-seeking politicians, racketeers, crooked labor leaders, and on occasion religious leaders, to take pot-shots at "WALL STREET, THE MONEY CHANGERS, and BIG BUSINESS."

The practice became so general that we witnessed during the business depression, the unbelievable sight of high government officials lining up with the cheap politicians, and labor leaders, with the openly avowed purpose of throttling the system which has made Industrial America the richest country on earth. The line-up was so general and so well organized that it prolonged the worst depression America has ever known. It cost millions of men their jobs, because those jobs were inseparably a part of the industrial and capitalistic system which form the very backbone of the nation.

During this unusual alliance of government officials and self-seeking individuals who were endeavoring to profit by declaring "open season" on the American system of industry, a certain type of labor leader joined forces with the politicians and offered to deliver voters in return for legislation designed to permit men to TAKE RICHES AWAY FROM INDUSTRY BY ORGANIZED FORCE OF NUMBERS, INSTEAD OF THE BETTER METHOD OF GIVING A FAIR DAY'S WORK FOR A FAIR DAY'S PAY.

Millions of men and women throughout the nation are still engaged in this popular pastime of trying to GET without GIVING. Some of them are lined up with labor unions, where they demand SHORTER HOURS AND MORE PAY! Others do not take the trouble to work at all. THEY DEMAND GOVERNMENT RELIEF AND ARE GETTING IT. Their idea of their rights of freedom was demonstrated in New York City, where violent complaint was registered with the Postmaster, by a group of "relief beneficiaries," because the Postmen awakened them at 7:30 A.M. to deliver Government relief checks. They DEMANDED that the time of delivery be set up to 10:00 o'clock.

If you are one of those who believe that riches can be accumulated by the mere act of men who organize themselves into groups and demand MORE PAY for LESS SERVICE, if you are one of those who DEMAND Government relief without early morning disturbance when the money is delivered to you, if you are one of those who believe in trading their votes to politicians in return for the passing of laws which permit the raiding of the public treasury, you may rest securely on your belief, with certain knowledge that no one will disturb you, because THIS IS A FREE COUNTRY WHERE EVERY MAN MAY THINK AS HE PLEASES, where nearly everybody can live with but little effort, where many may live well without doing any work whatsoever.

However, you should know the full truth concerning this FREEDOM of which so many people boast, and so few understand. As great as it is, as far as it reaches, as many privileges as it provides, IT DOES NOT, AND CANNOT BRING RICHES WITHOUT EFFORT.

There is but one dependable method of accumulating, and legally holding riches, and that is by rendering useful service. No system has ever been created by which men can legally acquire riches through mere force of numbers, or without giving in return an equivalent value of one form or another.

There is a principle known as the law of ECONOMICS! This is more than a theory. It is a law no man can beat.

Mark well the name of the principle, and remember it, because it is far more powerful than all the politicians and political machines. It is above and beyond the control of all the labor unions. It cannot be swayed, nor influenced nor bribed by racketeers or self-appointed leaders in any calling. Moreover, IT HAS AN ALL-SEEING EYE, AND A PERFECT SYSTEM OF BOOKKEEPING, in which it keeps an accurate account of the transactions of every human being engaged in the business of trying to get without giving. Sooner or later its auditors come around, look over the records of individuals both great and small, and demand an accounting.

"Wall Street, Big Business, Capital Predatory Interests," or whatever name you choose to give the system which has given us AMERICAN FREEDOM, represents a group of men who understand, respect, and adapt themselves to this powerful LAW OF ECONOMICS! Their financial continuation depends upon their respecting the law.

Most people living in America like this country, its capitalistic system and all. I must confess I know of no better country, where one may find greater opportunities to accumulate riches. Judging by their acts and deeds, there are some in this country who do not like it. That, of course is their privilege; if they do not like this country, its capitalistic system, its boundless opportunities, THEY HAVE THE PRIVILEGE OF CLEARING OUT! Always there are other countries, such as Germany, Russia, and Italy, where one may try one's hand at enjoying freedom, and accumulating riches providing one is not too particular.

America provides all the freedom and all the opportunity to accumulate riches that any honest person may require. When one goes hunting for game, one selects hunting grounds where game is plentiful. When seeking riches, the same rule would naturally obtain.

If it is riches you are seeking, do not overlook the possibilities of a country whose citizens are so rich that women, alone, spend over two hundred million dollars annually for lip-sticks, rouge and cosmetics. Think twice, you who are seeking riches, before trying to destroy the Capitalistic System of a country whose citizens spend over fifty million dollars a year for GREETING CARDS, with which to express their appreciation of their FREEDOM!

If it is money you are seeking, consider carefully a country that spends hundreds of millions of dollars annually for cigarettes, the bulk of the income from which goes to only four major companies engaged in supplying this national builder of "nonchalance" and "quiet nerves."

By all means give plenty of consideration to a country whose people spend annually more than fifteen million dollars for the privilege of seeing moving pictures, and toss in a few additional millions for liquor, narcotics, and other less potent soft drinks and giggle-waters.

Do not be in too big a hurry to get away from a country whose people willingly, even eagerly, hand over millions of dollars annually for football, base-ball, and prize fights.

And, by all means, STICK by a country whose inhabitants give up more than a million dollars a year for chewing gum, and another million for safety razor blades.

Remember, also, that this is but the beginning of the available sources for the accumulation of wealth. Only a few of the luxuries and non-essentials have been mentioned. But, remember that the business of producing, transporting, and marketing these few items of merchandise gives regular employment to MANY MILLIONS OF MEN AND WOMEN, who receive for their services MANY MILLIONS OF DOLLARS MONTHLY, and spend it freely for both the luxuries and the necessities.

Especially remember, that back of all this exchange of merchandise and personal services may be found an abundance of OPPORTUNITY to accumulate riches. Here our AMERICAN FREEDOM comes to one's aid. There is nothing to stop you, or anyone from engaging in any portion of the effort necessary to carry on these businesses. If one has superior talent, training, experience, one may accumulate riches in large amounts. Those not so fortunate may accumulate smaller amounts. Anyone may earn a living in return for a very nominal amount of labor.

So—there you are!

OPPORTUNITY has spread its wares before you. Step up to the front, select what you want, create your plan, put the plan into action, and follow through with PERSISTENCE. "Capitalistic" America will do the rest. You can depend upon this much—CAPITALISTIC AMERICA INSURES EVERY PERSON THE OPPORTUNITY TO RENDER USEFUL SERVICE, AND TO COLLECT RICHES IN PROPORTION TO THE VALUE OF THE SERVICE.

The "System" denies no one this right, but it does not, and cannot promise SOMETHING FOR NOTHING, because the system, itself is irrevocably controlled by the LAW OF ECONOMICS which neither recognizes nor tolerates for long, GETTING WITHOUT GIVING.

The LAW OF ECONOMICS was passed by Nature! There is no Supreme Court to which violators of this law may appeal. The law hands out both penalties for its violation, and appropriate rewards for its observance, *without interference or the possibility of interference by any human being.* The law cannot be repealed. It is as fixed as the stars in the heavens, and subject to, and a part of the same system that controls the stars.

May one refuse to adapt one's self to the LAW OF ECONOMICS?

Certainly! This is a free country, where all men are born with equal rights, including the privilege of ignoring the LAW OF ECONOMICS.

What happens then?

Well, nothing happens until large numbers of men join forces for the avowed purpose of ignoring the law, and taking what they want by force. THEN COMES THE DICTATOR, WITH WELL ORGANIZED FIRING SQUADS AND MACHINE GUNS!

We have not yet reached that stage in America! But we have heard all we want to know about how the system works. Perhaps we shall be fortunate enough not to demand personal knowledge of so gruesome a reality. Doubtless we shall prefer to continue with our FREEDOM OF SPEECH, FREEDOM OF DEED, and FREEDOM TO RENDER USEFUL SERVICE IN RETURN FOR RICHES.

The practice, by Government officials of extending to men and women the privilege of raiding the public treasury in return for votes, sometimes results in election, but as night follows day, the final payoff comes; when every penny wrongfully used, must be repaid with compound interest on compound interest. If those who make the grab are not forced to repay, the burden falls on their children, and their children's children, "even unto the third and fourth generations." There is no way to avoid the debt.

Men can, and sometimes do, form themselves into groups for the purpose of crowding wages up, and working hours down. There is a point beyond which they cannot go. It is the point at which the LAW OF ECONOMICS steps in, and the sheriff gets both the employer and the employees.

For six years, from 1929, to 1935, the people of America, both rich and poor, barely missed seeing the Old Man Economics hand over to the sheriff all the businesses, and industries and banks. It was not a pretty sight! It did not increase our respect for mob psychology through which men cast reason to the winds and start trying to GET without GIVING.

We who went through those six discouraging years, when FEAR WAS IN THE SADDLE, AND FAITH WAS ON THE GROUND, cannot forget how ruthlessly the LAW OF ECONOMICS exacted its toll from both rich and poor, weak and strong, old and young. We shall not wish to go through another such experience.

These observations are not founded upon short-time experience. They are the result of twenty-five years of careful analysis of the methods of both the most successful and the most unsuccessful men America has known.

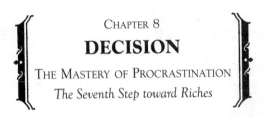

CHAPTER 8

DECISION

THE MASTERY OF PROCRASTINATION
The Seventh Step toward Riches

ACCURATE analysis of over 25,000 men and women who had experienced failure, disclosed the fact that LACK OF DECISION was near the head of the list of the 30 major causes of FAILURE. This is no mere statement of a theory—*it is a fact.*

PROCRASTINATION, the opposite of DECISION, is a common enemy which practically every man must conquer.

You will have an opportunity to test your capacity to reach *quick* and *definite* DECISIONS when you finish reading this book, and are ready to begin putting into ACTION the principles which it describes.

Analysis of several hundred people who had accumulated fortunes well beyond the million dollar mark, disclosed the fact that *every one of them* had the habit of REACHING DECISIONS PROMPTLY, and of changing these decisions SLOWLY, if, and when they were changed. People who fail to accumulate money, *without exception* have the habit of reaching decisions, IF AT ALL, very *slowly*, and of *changing these decisions quickly and often.*

One of Henry Ford's most outstanding qualities is his *habit* of reaching decisions quickly and definitely, and changing them slowly. This quality is so pronounced in Mr. Ford, that it has given him the reputation of being obstinate. It was this quality which prompted Mr. Ford to continue to manufacture his famous Model "T" (the world's ugliest car), when all of his advisors, and many of the purchasers of the car, were urging him to change it.

Perhaps, Mr. Ford delayed too long in making the change, but the other side of the story is, that Mr. Ford's firmness of decision yielded a huge fortune, before the change in model became *necessary*. There is but little doubt that Mr. Ford's habit of definiteness of decision assumes the proportion of obstinacy, but this quality is preferable to slowness in reaching decisions and quickness in changing them.

The majority of people who fail to accumulate money sufficient for their needs, are, generally easily influenced by the "opinions" of others. They permit the newspapers and the "gossiping" neighbors to do their "thinking" for them. "Opinions" are the cheapest commodities on earth. Everyone has a flock of opinions ready to be wished upon anyone who will accept them. If you are influenced by "opinions" when you reach DECISIONS, you will not succeed in any undertaking, much less in that of transmuting YOUR OWN DESIRE into money.

If you are influenced by the opinions of others, you will have no DESIRE of your own.

Keep your own counsel, when you begin to put into practice the principles described here, by *reaching your own decisions and following them*. Take no one into your confidence, EXCEPT the members of your "Master Mind" group, and be very sure in your selection of this group, that you choose ONLY those who will be in COMPLETE SYMPATHY AND HARMONY WITH YOUR PURPOSE.

Close friends and relatives, while not meaning to do so, often handicap one through "opinions" and sometimes through ridicule, which is meant to be humorous. Thousands of men and women carry inferiority complexes with them all through life, because some well-meaning, but ignorant person destroyed their confidence through "opinions" or ridicule.

You have a brain and mind of your own. USE IT, and reach your own decisions. If you need facts or information from other people, to enable you to reach decisions, as you probably will in many instances; acquire these facts or secure the information you need quietly, without disclosing your purpose.

It is characteristic of people who have but a smattering or a veneer of knowledge to try to give the impression that they have much knowledge. Such people generally do TOO MUCH talking, and TOO LITTLE listening. Keep your eyes and ears wide open—and your mouth CLOSED, if you wish to acquire the habit of prompt DECISION. Those who talk too much do little else. If you talk more than you listen, you not only deprive yourself of many opportunities to accumulate useful knowledge, but you also disclose your PLANS and PURPOSES to people who will take great delight in defeating you, because they envy you.

Remember, also, that every time you open your mouth in the presence of a person who has an abundance of knowledge, you display to that person, your exact stock of knowledge, or your LACK of it! Genuine wisdom is usually conspicuous through *modesty and silence.*

Keep in mind the fact that every person with whom you associate is, like yourself, seeking the opportunity to accumulate money. If you talk about your plans too freely, you may be surprised when you learn that some other person has beaten you to your goal by PUTTING INTO ACTION AHEAD OF YOU, the plans of which you talked unwisely.

Let one of your first decisions be to KEEP A CLOSED MOUTH AND OPEN EARS AND EYES.

As a reminder to yourself to follow this advice, it will be helpful if you copy the following epigram in large letters and place it where you will see it daily.

"TELL THE WORLD WHAT YOU INTEND TO DO, BUT FIRST SHOW IT."

This is the equivalent of saying that "deeds, and not words, are what count most."

Freedom or Death on a Decision

The value of decisions depends upon the courage required to render them. The great decisions, which served as the foundation of civilization, were reached by assuming great risks, which often meant the possibility of death.

Lincoln's decision to issue his famous Proclamation of Emancipation, which gave freedom to the colored people of America, was rendered with full understanding that his act would turn thousands of friends and political supporters against him. He knew, too, that the carrying out of that proclamation would mean death to thousands of men on the battlefield. In the end, it cost Lincoln his life. That required courage.

Socrates' decision to drink the cup of poison, rather than compromise in his personal belief was a decision of courage. It turned Time ahead a thousand years, and gave to people then unborn, the right to freedom of thought and of speech.

The decision of Gen. Robert E. Lee, when he came to the parting of the way with the Union, and took up the cause of the South, was a decision of courage, for he well knew that it might cost him his own life, that it would surely cost the lives of others.

But, the greatest decision of all time, as far as any American citizen is concerned, was reached in Philadelphia, July 4, 1776, when fifty-six men signed their names to a document, which they well knew would bring freedom to all Americans, or *leave every one of the fifty-six hanging from a gallows!*

You have heard of this famous document, but may not have drawn from it the great lesson in personal achievement it so plainly taught.

We all remember the date of this momentous decision, but few of us realize what courage that decision required. We remember our history, as it was taught; we remember dates, and the names

(503)

of the men who fought; we remember Valley Forge, and Yorktown; we remember George Washington, and Lord Cornwallis. But we know little of the real forces back of these names, dates, and places. We know still less of that intangible POWER, which insured us freedom *long before Washington's armies reached Yorktown.*

We read the history of the revolution and falsely imagine that George Washington was the Father of our Country, that it was he who won our freedom, while the truth is—Washington was only an accessory after the fact, because victory for his armies had been insured long before Lord Cornwallis surrendered. This is not intended to rob Washington of any of the glory he so richly merited. Its purpose, rather, is to give greater attention to the astounding POWER that was the real cause of his victory.

It is nothing short of tragedy that the writers of history have missed, entirely, even the slightest reference to the irresistible POWER, which gave birth and freedom to the nation destined to set up new standards of independence for all the peoples of the earth. I say it is a tragedy, because it is the self-same POWER which must be used by every individual who surmounts the difficulties of Life, and forces Life to pay the price asked.

Let us briefly review the events which gave birth to this POWER. The story begins with an incident in Boston, March 5, 1770. British soldiers were patrolling the streets, by their presence, openly threatening the citizens. The colonists resented armed men marching in their midst. They began to express their resentment openly, hurling stones as well as epithets, at the marching soldiers, until the commanding officer gave orders, "Fix bayonets.... Charge!"

The battle was on. It resulted in the death and injury of many. The incident aroused such resentment that the Provincial Assembly (made up of prominent colonists), called a meeting for the purpose of taking definite action. Two of the members of that Assembly were, John Hancock, and Samuel Adams—LONG LIVE THEIR NAMES! They spoke up courageously, and declared that a move must be made to eject all British soldiers from Boston.

Remember this—a DECISION, in the minds of two men, might properly be called the beginning of the freedom which we, of the United States now enjoy. Remember, too, that the DECISION of these two men called for FAITH, and COURAGE, because it was dangerous.

Before the Assembly adjourned, Samuel Adams was appointed to call on the Governor of the Province, Hutchinson, and demand the withdrawal of the British troops.

The request was granted, the troops were removed from Boston, but the incident was not closed. It had caused a situation destined to change the entire trend of civilization. Strange, is it not, how the great changes, such as the American Revolution, and the World War, often have their beginnings in circumstances which seem unimportant? It is interesting, also, to observe that these important changes usually begin in the form of a

DEFINITE DECISION in the minds of a relatively small number of people. Few of us know the history of our country well enough to realize that John Hancock, Samuel Adams, and Richard Henry Lee (of the Province of Virginia) were the real Fathers of our country.

Richard Henry Lee became an important factor in this story by reason of the fact that he and Samuel Adams communicated frequently (by correspondence) sharing freely their fears and their hopes concerning the welfare of the people of their Provinces. From this practice, Adams conceived the idea that a mutual exchange of letters between the thirteen Colonies might help to bring about the coordination of effort so badly needed in connection with the solution of their problems. Two years after the clash with the soldiers in Boston (March '72), Adams presented this idea to the Assembly, in the form of a motion that a Correspondence Committee be established among the Colonies, with definitely appointed correspondents in each Colony, "for the purpose of friendly cooperation for the betterment of the Colonies of British America."

Mark well this incident! It was the beginning of the organization of the far-flung POWER destined to give freedom to you, and to me. The Master Mind had already been organized. It consisted of Adams, Lee, and Hancock. "I tell you further, that if two of you agree upon the earth concerning anything for which you ask, it will come to you from My Father, who is in Heaven."

The Committee of Correspondence was organized. Observe that this move provided the way for increasing the power of the Master Mind by adding to it men from all the Colonies. Take notice that this procedure constituted the first ORGANIZED PLAN-NING of the disgruntled Colonists.

In union there is strength! The citizens of the Colonies had been waging disorganized warfare against the British soldiers, through incidents similar to the Boston riot, but nothing of benefit had been accomplished. Their individual griev-ances had not been consolidated under one Master Mind. No group of individuals had put their hearts, minds, souls, and bodies together in one definite DECISION to settle their difficulty with the British once and for all, until Adams, Hancock, and Lee got together.

Meanwhile, the British were not idle. They, too, were doing some PLANNING and "Master-Minding" on their own account, with the advantage of having back of them money, and organized soldiery.

The Crown appointed Gage to supplant Hutchin-son as the Governor of Massachusetts. One of the new Governor's first acts was to send a messenger to call on Samuel Adams, for the purpose of endeav-oring to stop his opposition—by FEAR.

We can best understand the spirit of what happened by quoting the conversation between Col. Fenton, (the messenger sent by Gage), and Adams.

Col Fenton: "I have been authorized by Governor Gage, to assure you, Mr. Adams, that the Governor has been empowered to confer upon you such benefits as would be satisfactory, [endeavor to win Adams by promise of bribes], upon the condition that you engage to cease in your opposition to the measures of the government. It is the Governor's advice to you, Sir, not to incur the further displeasure of his majesty. Your conduct has been such as makes you liable to penalties of an Act of Henry VIII, by which persons can be sent to England for trial for treason, or misprision of treason, at the discretion of a governor of a province. But, BY CHANGING YOUR POLITICAL COURSE, you will not only receive great personal advantages, but you will make your peace with the King."

Samuel Adams had the choice of two DECISIONS. He could cease his opposition, and receive personal bribes, or he could CONTINUE, AND RUN THE RISK OF BEING HANGED!

Clearly, the time had come when Adams was *forced* to reach *instantly*, a DECISION which could have cost his life. The majority of men would have found it difficult to reach such a decision. The majority would have sent back an evasive reply, but not Adams! He insisted upon Col. Fenton's word of honor, that the colonel would deliver to the Governor the answer exactly as Adams would give it to him.

Adams' answer, "Then you may tell Governor Gage that I trust I have long since made my peace with the King of Kings. No personal consideration shall induce me to abandon the righteous cause of my Country. And, TELL GOVERNOR GAGE IT IS THE ADVICE OF SAMUEL ADAMS TO HIM, no longer to insult the feelings of an exasperated people."

Comment as to the character of this man seems

unnecessary. It must be obvious to all who read this astounding message that its sender possessed loyalty of the highest order. *This is important.* (Racketeers and dishonest politicians have prostituted the honor for which such men as Adams died).

When Governor Gage received Adams' caustic reply, he flew into a rage, and issued a proclamation which read, "I do, hereby, in his majesty's name, offer and promise his most gracious pardon to all persons who shall forthwith lay down their arms, and return to the duties of peaceable subjects, excepting only from the benefit of such pardon, SAMUEL ADAMS AND JOHN HANCOCK, whose offences are of too flagitious a nature to admit of any other consideration but that of condign punishment."

As one might say, in modern slang, Adams and Hancock were "on the spot!" The threat of the irate Governor forced the two men to reach another DECISION, equally as dangerous. They hurriedly called a secret meeting of their staunchest followers, (here the Master Mind began to take on momentum). After the meeting had been called to order, Adams locked the door, placed the key in his pocket, and informed all present that it was imperative that a Congress of the Colonists be organized, and that NO MAN SHOULD LEAVE THE ROOM UNTIL THE DECISION FOR SUCH A CONGRESS HAD BEEN REACHED.

Great excitement followed. Some weighed the possible consequences of such radicalism. (Old Man Fear). Some expressed grave doubt as to the wisdom of so *definite a decision* in defiance of the Crown. Locked in that room were TWO MEN immune to Fear, blind to the possibility of Failure. Hancock and Adams. Through the influence of their minds, the others were induced to agree that, through the Correspondence Committee, arrangements should be made for a meeting of the First Continental Congress, to be held in Philadelphia, September 5, 1774.

Remember this date. It is more important than July 4, 1776. If there had been no DECISION to hold a Continental Congress, there could have been no signing of the Declaration of Independence.

Before the first meeting of the new Congress, another leader, in a different section of the country was deep in the throes of publishing a "Summary View of the Rights of British America." He was Thomas Jefferson, of the Province of Virginia, whose relationship to Lord Dunmore, (representative of the Crown in Virginia), was as strained as that of Hancock and Adams with their Governor.

Shortly after his famous Summary of Rights was published, Jefferson was informed that he was subject to prosecution for high treason against his majesty's government. Inspired by the threat, one of Jefferson's colleagues, Patrick Henry, boldly spoke his mind, concluding his remarks with a sentence which shall remain forever a classic, "*If this be treason, then make the most of it.*"

It was such men as these who, without power, without authority, without military strength, without money, sat in solemn consideration of the destiny of the colonies, beginning at the opening of the First Continental Congress, and continuing at intervals for two years—until on June 7, 1776, Richard Henry Lee arose, addressed the Chair, and to the startled Assembly made this motion:

"Gentlemen, I make the motion that these United Colonies are, and of right ought to be free and independent states, that they be absolved from allegiance to the British Crown, and that all political connection between them and the state of Great Britain is, and ought to be totally dissolved."

Lee's astounding motion was discussed fervently, and at such length that he began to lose patience. Finally, after days of argument, he again, took the floor, and declared, in a clear, firm voice, "Mr. President, we have discussed this issue for days. It is the only course for us to follow. Why, then Sir, do we longer delay? Why still deliberate? Let this happy day give birth to an American Republic. Let her arise, not to devastate and to conquer, but to re-establish the reign of peace, and of law. The eyes of Europe are fixed upon us. She demands of us a living example of freedom, that may exhibit a contrast, in the felicity of the citizen, to the ever increasing tyranny."

Before his motion was finally voted upon, Lee was called back to Virginia, because of serious family illness, but before leaving, he placed his cause in the hands of his friend, Thomas Jefferson, who promised to fight until favorable action was taken. Shortly thereafter the President of the Congress (Hancock), appointed Jefferson as Chairman of a Committee to draw up a Declaration of Independence.

Long and hard the Committee labored, on a document which would mean, when accepted by the Congress, that EVERY MAN WHO SIGNED IT, WOULD BE SIGNING HIS OWN DEATH WARRANT, should the Colonies lose in the fight with Great Britain, which was sure to follow.

The document was drawn, and on June 28, the original draft was read before the Congress. For several days it was discussed, altered, and made ready. On July 4, 1776, Thomas Jefferson stood before the Assembly, and fearlessly read the most momentus DECISION ever placed upon paper.

"When in the course of human events it is necessary for one people to dissolve the political bands which have connected them with another, and to assume, among the powers of the earth, the separate and equal station to which the laws of Nature, and of Nature's God entitle them, a decent respect to the opinions of mankind requires that they should declare the causes which impel them to the separation..."

When Jefferson finished, the document was voted upon, accepted, and signed by the fifty-six men, every one staking his own life upon his DECISION to write his name. By that DECISION came into existence a nation destined to bring to mankind forever, the privilege of making DECISIONS.

By decisions made in a similar spirit of Faith, and only by such decisions, can men solve their personal problems, and win for themselves high estates of material and spiritual wealth. Let us not forget this!

Analyze the events which led to the Declaration

of Independence, and be convinced that this nation, which now holds a position of commanding respect and power among all nations of the world, was born of a DECISION created by a Master Mind, consisting of fifty-six men. Note well, the fact that it was their DECISION which insured the success of Washington's armies, because the *spirit* of that decision was in the heart of every soldier who fought with him, and served as a spiritual power which recognizes no such thing as FAILURE.

Note, also, (with great personal benefit), that the POWER which gave this nation its freedom, is the self-same power that must be used by every individual who becomes self-determining. This POWER is made up of the principles described in this book. It will not be difficult to detect, in the story of the Declaration of Independence, at least six of these principles; DESIRE, DECISION, FAITH, PERSIST-ENCE, THE MASTER MIND, and ORGANIZED PLANNING.

Throughout this philosophy will be found the suggestion that thought, backed by strong DESIRE, has a tendency to transmute itself into its physical equivalent. Before passing on, I wish to leave with you the suggestion that one may find in this story, and in the story of the organization of the United States Steel Corporation, a perfect description of the method by which thought makes this astounding transformation.

In your search for the secret of the method, do not look for a miracle, because you will not find it. You will find only the eternal laws of Nature. These laws are available to every person who has the FAITH and the COURAGE to use them. They may be used to bring freedom to a nation, or to accumulate riches. There is no charge save the time necessary to understand and appropriate them.

Those who reach DECISIONS promptly and definitely, know what they want, and generally get it. The leaders in every walk of life DECIDE quickly, and firmly. That is the major reason why they are leaders. The world has the habit of making room for the man whose words and actions show that he knows where he is going.

INDECISION is a habit which usually begins in youth. The habit takes on permanency as the youth goes through graded school, high school, and even through college, without DEFINITENESS OF PURPOSE. The major weakness of all educational systems is that they neither teach nor encourage the habit of DEFINITE DECISION.

It would be beneficial if no college would permit the enrollment of any student, unless and until the student declared his major purpose in matriculating. It would be of still greater benefit, if every student who enters the graded schools were compelled to accept training in the HABIT OF DECISION, and forced to pass a satisfactory examination on this subject before being permitted to advance in the grades.

The habit of INDECISION acquired because of the deficiencies of our school systems, goes with the student into the occupation he chooses...IF...in fact, he chooses his occupation. Generally, the youth just out of school seeks any job that he can find. He takes the first place he finds, because he has fallen into the habit of INDECISION. Ninety-eight out of every hundred people working for wages today, are in the positions they hold, because they lacked the DEFINITENESS OF DECISION to PLAN A DEFINITE POSITION, and the knowledge of how to choose an employer.

DEFINITENESS OF DECISION always requires courage, sometimes very great courage. The fifty-six men who signed the Declaration of Independence staked their lives on the DECISION to affix their signatures to that document. The person who reaches a DEFINITE DECISION to procure the particular job, and make life pay the price he asks, does not stake his life on that decision; he stakes his ECONOMIC FREEDOM. Financial independence, riches, desirable business and professional positions are not within reach of the person who neglects or refuses to EXPECT, PLAN, and DEMAND these things. The person who desires riches in the same spirit that Samuel Adams desired freedom for the Colonies, is sure to accumulate wealth.

In the chapter on Organized Planning, you will find complete instructions for marketing every type of personal services. You will find also detailed information on how to choose the employer you prefer, and the particular job you desire. These instructions will be of no value to you UNLESS YOU DEFINITELY DECIDE to organize them into a plan of action.

CHAPTER 9
PERSISTENCE
THE SUSTAINED EFFORT NECESSARY
TO INDUCE FAITH
The Eighth Step toward Riches

PERSISTENCE is an essential factor in the procedure of transmuting DESIRE into its monetary equivalent. The basis of persistence is the POWER OF WILL.

Will-power and desire, when properly combined, makes an irresistible pair. Men who accumulate great fortunes are generally known as cold-blooded, and sometimes ruthless. Often they are misunderstood. What they have is will-power, which they mix with persistence, and place back of their desires to *insure* the attainment of their objectives.

Henry Ford has been generally misunderstood to be ruthless and cold-blooded. This misconception grew out of Ford's habit of following through in all of his plans with PERSISTENCE.

The majority of people are ready to throw their aims and purposes overboard, and give up at the first sign of opposition or misfortune. A few carry on DESPITE all opposition, until they attain their goal. These few are the Fords, Carnegies, Rockefellers, and Edisons.

There may be no heroic connotation to the word "persistence," but the quality is to the character of man what carbon is to steel.

The building of a fortune, generally, involves the application of the entire thirteen factors of this philosophy. These principles must be understood, they must be applied with PERSISTENCE by all who accumulate money.

If you are following this book with the intention of applying the knowledge it conveys, your first test as to your PERSISTENCE will come when you begin to follow the six steps described in the second chapter. Unless you are one of the two out of every hundred who already have a DEFINITE GOAL at which you are aiming, and a DEFINITE PLAN for its attainment, you may read the instructions, and then pass on with your daily routine, and never comply with those instructions.

The author is checking you up at this point, because lack of persistence is one of the major causes of failure. Moreover, experience with thousands of people has proved that lack of persistence is a weakness common to the majority of men. It is a weakness which may be overcome by effort. The ease with which lack of persistence may be conquered will depend *entirely* upon the INTENSITY OF ONE'S DESIRE.

The starting point of all achievement is DESIRE. Keep this constantly in mind. Weak desires bring weak results, just as a small amount of fire makes a small amount of heat. If you find yourself lacking in persistence, this weakness may be remedied by building a stronger fire under your desires.

Continue to read through to the end, then go back to Chapter two, and start *immediately* to carry out the instructions given in connection with the six steps. The eagerness with which you follow these instructions will indicate clearly, how much, or how little you really DESIRE to accumulate money. If you find that you are indifferent, you may be sure that you have not yet acquired the "money consciousness" which you must possess, before you can be sure of accumulating a fortune.

Fortunes gravitate to men whose minds have been prepared to "attract" them, just as surely as water gravitates to the ocean. In this book may be found all the stimuli necessary to "attune" any normal mind to the vibrations which will attract the object of one's desires.

If you find you are weak in PERSISTENCE, center your attention upon the instructions contained in the chapter on "Power"; surround yourself with a "MASTER MIND" group, and through the cooperative efforts of the members of this group, you can develop persistence. You will find additional instructions for the development of persistence in the chapters on auto-suggestion, and the subconscious mind. Follow the instructions outlined in these chapters until your habit nature hands over to your subconscious mind, a clear picture of the object of your DESIRE. From that point on, you will not be handicapped by lack of persistence.

Your subconscious mind works continuously, while you are awake, and while you are asleep.

Spasmodic, or occasional effort to apply the rules will be of no value to you. To get RESULTS, you must apply all of the rules until their application becomes a fixed habit with you. In no other way can you develop the necessary "money consciousness."

POVERTY is attracted to the one whose mind is

favorable to it, as money is attracted to him whose mind has been deliberately prepared to attract it, and through the same laws. POVERTY CONSCIOUSNESS WILL VOLUNTARILY SEIZE THE MIND WHICH IS NOT OCCUPIED WITH THE MONEY CONSCIOUSNESS. A poverty consciousness develops without *conscious* application of habits favorable to it. The money consciousness must be created to order, unless one is born with such a consciousness.

Catch the full significance of the statements in the preceding paragraph, and you will understand the importance of PERSISTENCE in the accumulation of a fortune. Without PERSISTENCE, you will be defeated, even before you start. With PERSISTENCE you will win.

If you have ever experienced a nightmare, you will realize the value of persistence. You are lying in bed, half awake, with a feeling that you are about to smother. You are unable to turn over, or to move a muscle. You realize that you MUST BEGIN to regain control over your muscles. Through persistent effort of will-power, you finally manage to move the fingers of one hand. By continuing to move your fingers, you extend your control to the muscles of one arm, until you can lift it. Then you gain control of the other arm in the same manner. You finally gain control over the muscles of one leg, and then extend it to the other leg. THEN—WITH ONE SUPREME EFFORT OF WILL—you regain complete control over your muscular system, and "snap" out of your nightmare. The trick has been turned step by step.

You may find it necessary to "snap" out of your mental inertia, through a similar procedure, moving slowly at first, then increasing your speed, until you gain complete control over your will. Be PERSISTENT no matter how slowly you may, at first, have to move. WITH PERSISTENCE WILL COME SUCCESS.

If you select your "Master Mind" group with care, you will have in it, at least one person who will aid you in the development of PERSISTENCE. Some men who have accumulated great fortunes, did so because of NECESSITY. They developed the habit of PERSISTENCE, because they were so closely driven by circumstances, that they *had to become persistent.*

THERE IS NO SUBSTITUTE FOR PERSISTENCE! It cannot be supplanted by any other quality! Remember this, and it will hearten you, in the beginning, when the going may seem difficult and slow.

Those who have cultivated the HABIT of persistence seem to enjoy insurance against failure. No matter how many times they are defeated, they finally arrive up toward the top of the ladder. Sometimes it appears that there is a hidden Guide whose duty is to test men through all sorts of discouraging experiences. Those who pick themselves up after defeat and keep on trying, arrive; and the world cries, "Bravo! I knew you could do it!" The hidden Guide lets no one enjoy great achievement without passing the PERSISTENCE TEST. Those who can't take it, simply do not make the grade.

Those who can "take it" are bountifully rewarded for their PERSISTENCE. They receive, as their compensation, whatever goal they are pursuing. That is not all! They receive something infinitely more important than material compensation—the knowledge that "EVERY FAILURE BRINGS WITH IT THE SEED OF AN EQUIVALENT ADVANTAGE."

There are exceptions to this rule; a few people know from experience the soundness of persistence. They are the ones who have not accepted defeat as being anything more than temporary. They are the ones whose DESIRES are so PERSISTENTLY APPLIED that defeat is finally changed into victory. We who stand on the side-lines of Life see the overwhelmingly large number who go down in defeat, never to rise again. We see the few who take the punishment of defeat *as an urge to greater effort*. These, fortunately, never learn to accept Life's reverse gear. But what we DO NOT SEE, what most of us never suspect of existing, is the silent but irresistible POWER which comes to the rescue of those who fight on in the face of discouragement. If we speak of this power at all we call it PERSISTENCE, and let it go at that. One thing we all know, if one does not possess PERSISTENCE, one does not achieve noteworthy success in any calling.

As these lines are being written, I look up from my work, and see before me, less than a block away, the great mysterious "Broadway," the "Graveyard of Dead Hopes," and the "Front Porch of Opportunity." From all over the world people have come to Broadway, seeking fame, fortune, power, love, or whatever it is that human beings call success. Once in a great while someone steps out from the long procession of seekers, and the world hears that another person has mastered Broadway. But Broadway is not easily nor quickly conquered. She acknowledges talent, recognizes genius, pays off in money, only *after* one has refused to QUIT.

Then we know he has discovered the secret of how to conquer Broadway. The secret is always inseparably attached to one word, PERSISTENCE!

The secret is told in the struggle of Fannie Hurst, whose PERSISTENCE conquered the Great White Way. She came to New York in 1915, to convert writing into riches. The conversion did not come quickly, BUT IT CAME. For four years Miss Hurst learned about "The Sidewalks of New York" from firsthand experience. She spent her days laboring, and her nights HOPING. When hope grew dim, she did not say, "Alright Broadway, you win!" She said, "Very well, Broadway, you may whip some, but not me. I'm going to force you to give up."

One publisher (The Saturday Evening Post) sent her *thirty six* rejection slips, before she "broke the ice" and got a story across. The average writer, like the "average" in other walks of life, would have given up the job when the first rejection slip came. She pounded the pavements for four years to the tune of the publishers "NO," because she was determined to win.

Then came the "payoff." The spell had been broken, the unseen Guide had tested Fannie Hurst, and she could take it. From that time on publishers made a beaten path to her door. Money came so fast she hardly had time to count it. Then the moving picture men discovered her, and money came not in small change, but in floods. The moving picture rights to her latest novel, "Great Laughter," brought $100,000.00 said to be the highest price ever paid for a story before publication. Her royalties from the sale of the book probably will run much more.

Briefly, you have a description of what PERSIST-ENCE is capable of achieving. Fannie Hurst is no exception. Wherever men and women accumulate great riches, you may be sure they first acquired PERSISTENCE. Broadway will give any beggar a cup of coffee and a sandwich, but it demands PERSISTENCE of those who go after the big stakes.

Kate Smith will say "amen" when she reads this. For years she sang, without money, and without price, before any microphone she could reach. Broadway said to her, "Come and get it, if you can take it." She did take it until one happy day Broadway got tired and said, "Aw, what's the use? You don't know when you're whipped, so name your price, and go to work in earnest." Miss Smith named her price! It was plenty. Away up in figures so high that one week's salary is far more than most people make in a whole year.

Verily it pays to be PERSISTENT!

And here is an encouraging statement which carries with it a suggestion of great significance— THOUSANDS OF SINGERS WHO EXCEL

KATE SMITH ARE WALKING UP AND DOWN BROADWAY LOOKING FOR A "BREAK"—WITHOUT SUCCESS. Countless others have come and gone, many of them sang well enough, but they failed to make the grade because they lacked the courage to keep on keeping on, until Broadway became tired of turning them away.

Persistence is a state of mind, therefore it can be cultivated. Like all states of mind, persistence is based upon definite causes, among them these:—

a. DEFINITENESS OF PURPOSE. Knowing what one wants is the first and, perhaps, the most important step toward the development of persistence. A strong motive forces one to surmount many difficulties.

b. DESIRE. It is comparatively easy to acquire and to maintain persistence in pursuing the object of intense desire.

c. SELF-RELIANCE. Belief in one's ability to carry out a plan encourages one to follow the plan through with persistence. (Self-reliance can be developed through the principle described in the chapter on auto-suggestion).

d. DEFINITENESS OF PLANS. Organized plans, even though they may be weak and entirely impractical, encourage persistence.

e. ACCURATE KNOWLEDGE. Knowing that one's plans are sound, based upon experience or observation, encourages persistence; "guessing" instead of "knowing" destroys persistence.

f. CO-OPERATION. Sympathy, understanding, and harmonious cooperation with others tend to develop persistence.

g. WILL-POWER. The habit of concentrating one's thoughts upon the building of plans for the attainment of a definite purpose, leads to persistence.

h. HABIT. Persistence is the direct result of habit. The mind absorbs and becomes a part of the daily experiences upon which it feeds. Fear, the worst of all enemies, can be effectively cured by *forced repetition of acts of courage*. Everyone who has seen active service in war knows this.

Before leaving the subject of PERSISTENCE, take inventory of yourself, and determine in what particular, if any, you are lacking in this essential quality. Measure yourself courageously, point by point, and see how many of the eight factors of persistence you lack. The analysis may lead to discoveries that will give you a new grip on yourself.

SYMPTOMS OF LACK OF PERSISTENCE

Here you will find the real enemies which stand between you and noteworthy achievement. Here you will find not only the "symptoms" indicating weakness of PERSISTENCE, but also the deeply seated subconscious causes of this weakness. Study the list carefully, and face yourself squarely IF YOU REALLY WISH TO KNOW WHO YOU ARE, AND WHAT YOU ARE CAPABLE OF DOING. These are the weaknesses which must be mastered by all who accumulate riches.

1. Failure to recognize and to clearly define exactly what one wants.

2. Procrastination, with or without cause. (Usually backed up with a formidable array of alibis and excuses).

3. Lack of interest in acquiring specialized knowledge.

4. Indecision, the habit of "passing the buck" on all occasions, instead of facing issues squarely. (Also backed by alibis).

5. The habit of relying upon alibis instead of creating definite plans for the solution of problems.

6. Self-satisfaction. There is but little remedy for this affliction, and no hope for those who suffer from it.

7. Indifference, usually reflected in one's readiness to compromise on all occasions, rather than meet opposition and fight it.

8. The habit of blaming others for one's mistakes, and accepting unfavorable circumstances as being unavoidable.

9. WEAKNESS OF DESIRE, due to neglect in the choice of MOTIVES that impel action.

10. Willingness, even eagerness, to quit at the first sign of defeat. (Based upon one or more of the 6 basic fears).

11. Lack of ORGANIZED PLANS, placed in writing where they may be analyzed.

12. The habit of neglecting to move on ideas, or to grasp opportunity when it presents itself.

13. WISHING instead of WILLING.

14. The habit of compromising with POVERTY instead of aiming at riches. General absence of ambition to *be*, to *do*, and to *own*.

15. Searching for all the short-cuts to riches, trying to GET without GIVING a fair equivalent, usually reflected in the habit of gambling, endeavoring to drive "sharp" bargains.

16. FEAR OF CRITICISM, failure to create plans and to put them into action, because of what other people will think, do, or say. This enemy belongs at the head of the list, because it generally exits in one's subconscious mind, where its presence is not recognized. (See the Six Basic Fears in a later chapter).

Let us examine some of the symptoms of the Fear of Criticism. The majority of people permit relatives, friends, and the public at large to so influence them that they cannot live their own lives, because they fear criticism.

Huge numbers of people make mistakes in marriage, stand by the bargain, and go through life miserable and unhappy, because they fear criticism which may follow if they correct the mistake. (Anyone who has submitted to this form of fear knows the irreparable damage it does, by destroying ambition, self-reliance, and the desire to achieve).

Millions of people neglect to acquire belated educations, after having left school, because they fear criticism.

Countless numbers of men and women, both young and old, permit relatives to wreck their lives in the name of DUTY, because they fear criticism. (Duty does not require any person to submit to the destruction of his personal ambitions and the right to live his own life in his own way).

People refuse to take chances in business, because they fear the criticism which may follow if they fail. *The fear of criticism, in such cases is stronger than the DESIRE for success.*

Too many people refuse to set high goals for themselves, or even neglect selecting a career, because they fear the criticism of relatives and "friends" who may say "Don't aim so high, people will think you are crazy."

When Andrew Carnegie suggested that I devote twenty years to the organization of a philosophy of individual achievement my first impulse of thought was fear of what people might say. The suggestion set up a goal for me, far out of proportion to any I have ever conceived. As quick as a flash, my mind began to create alibis and excuses, all of them traceable to the inherent FEAR OF CRITICISM. Something inside of me said, "You can't do it—the job is too big, and requires too much time—what will your relatives think of you?—how will you earn a living?—no one has ever organized a philosophy of success, what right have you to believe you can do it?—who are you, anyway, to aim so high?— remember your humble birth—what do you know about philosophy—people will think you are crazy—(and they did)—why hasn't some other person done this before now?"

These, and many other questions flashed into my mind, and demanded attention. It seemed as if the whole world had suddenly turned its attention to me with the purpose of ridiculing me into giving up all desire to carry out Mr. Carnegie's suggestion.

I had a fine opportunity, then and there, to kill off ambition before it gained control of me. Later in life, after having analyzed thousands of people, I discovered that MOST IDEAS ARE STILL-BORN, AND NEED THE BREATH OF LIFE INJECTED INTO THEM THROUGH DEFINITE PLANS OF IMMEDIATE ACTION. The time to nurse an idea is at the time of its birth. Every minute it lives gives it a better chance of surviving. The FEAR OF CRITICISM is at the bottom of the destruction of most ideas which never reach the PLANNING and ACTION stage.

Many people believe that material success is the result of favorable "breaks." There is an element of ground for the belief, but those depending entirely upon luck, are nearly always disappointed, because they overlook another important factor which must be present before one can be sure of success. It is the knowledge with which favorable "breaks" can be made to order.

During the depression, W.C. Fields, the comedian, lost all his money, and found himself without income, without a job, and his means of earning a living (vaudeville) no longer existed. Moreover, he was past sixty, when many men consider themselves "old." He was so eager to stage a comeback that he offered to work without pay, in a new field (movies). In addition to his other troubles, he fell and injured his neck. To many that would have been the place to give up and QUIT. But Fields was PERSISTENT. He knew that if he carried on he would get the "breaks" sooner or later, and he did get them, but not by chance.

Marie Dressler found herself down and out, with her money gone, with no job, when she was about sixty. She, too, went after the "breaks," and got them. Her PERSISTENCE brought an astounding triumph late in life, long beyond the age when most men and women are done with ambition to achieve.

Eddie Cantor lost his money in the 1929 stock crash, but he still had his PERSISTENCE and his courage. With these, plus two prominent eyes, he exploited himself back into an income of $10,000 a week! Verily, if one has PERSISTENCE, one can get along very well without many other qualities.

The only "break" anyone can afford to rely upon is a self-made "break." These come through the application of PERSISTENCE. The starting point is DEFINITENESS OF PURPOSE.

Examine the first hundred people you meet, ask them what they want most in life, and ninety eight of them will not be able to tell you. If you press them for an answer, some will say—SECURITY, many will say—MONEY, a few will say—HAPPINESS, others will say—FAME AND POWER, and still others will say— SOCIAL RECOGNITION, EASE IN LIVING, ABILITY TO SING, DANCE, or WRITE, but none of them will be able to define these terms, or give the slightest indication of a PLAN by which they hope to attain these vaguely expressed wishes. Riches do not respond to wishes. They respond only to definite plans, backed by definite desires, through constant PERSISTENCE.

How to Develop Persistence

There are four simple steps which lead to the habit of PERSISTENCE. They call for no great amount of intelligence, no particular amount of education, and but little time or effort. The necessary steps are:—

1. A DEFINITE PURPOSE BACKED BY BURNING DESIRE FOR ITS FULFILLMENT.

2. A DEFINITE PLAN, EXPRESSED IN CONTINUOUS ACTION.

3. A MIND CLOSED TIGHTLY AGAINST ALL NEGATIVE AND DISCOURAGING INFLUENCES, including negative suggestions of relatives, friends and acquaintances.

4. A FRIENDLY ALLIANCE WITH ONE OR MORE PERSONS WHO WILL ENCOURAGE ONE TO FOLLOW THROUGH WITH BOTH PLAN AND PURPOSE.

These four steps are essential for success in all walks of life. The entire purpose of the thirteen principles of this philosophy is to enable one to take these four steps as a matter of *habit*.

These are the steps by which one may control one's economic destiny.

They are the steps that lead to freedom and independence of thought.

They are the steps that lead to riches, in small or great quantities.

They lead the way to power, fame, and worldly recognition.

They are the four steps which guarantee favorable "breaks."

They are the steps that convert dreams into physical realities.

They lead, also, to the mastery of FEAR, DISCOUR-AGEMENT, INDIFFERENCE.

There is a magnificent reward of all who learn to take these four steps. It is the privilege of writing one's own ticket, and of making Life yield whatever price is asked.

I have no way of knowing the facts, but I venture to conjecture that Mrs. Wallis Simpson's great love for a man was not accidental, nor the result of favorable "breaks" alone. There was a burning desire, and careful searching at every step of the way. Her first duty was to love. What is the greatest thing on earth? The Master called it love—not manmade rules, criticism, bitterness, slander, or political "marriages," but love.

She knew what she wanted, not after she met the Prince of Wales, but long before that. Twice when she had failed to find it, she had the courage to continue her search. "To thine own self be true, and it must follow, as the night the day, thou canst not then be false to any man."

Her rise from obscurity was of the slow, progressive, PERSISTENT order, but it was SURE! She triumphed over unbelievably long odds; and, no matter who you are, or what you may think of Wallis Simpson, or the king who gave up his Crown for her love, she is an astounding example of applied PERSISTENCE, an instructor on the rules of self-determination, from whom the entire world might profitably take lessons.

When you think of Wallis Simpson, think of one who knew what she wanted, and shook the greatest empire on earth to get it. Women who complain that this is a man's world, that women do not have an equal chance to win, owe it to themselves to study carefully the life of this unusual women, who, at an age which most women consider "old," captured the affections of the most desirable bachelor in the entire world.

And what of King Edward? What lesson may we learn from his part in the world's greatest drama of recent times? Did he pay too high a price for the affections of the woman of his choice?

Surely no one but he can give the correct answer.

The rest of us can only conjecture. This much we know, the king came into the world without his own consent. He was born to great riches, without requesting them. He was persistently sought in marriage; politicians and statesmen throughout Europe tossed dowagers and princesses at his feet. Because he was the first born of his parents, he inherited a crown, which he did not seek, and perhaps did not desire. For more than forty years he was not a free agent, could not live his life in his own way, had but little privacy, and finally assumed duties inflicted upon him when he ascended the throne.

Some will say, "With all these blessings, King Edward should have found peace of mind, contentment, and joy of living."

The truth is that back of all the privileges of a crown, all the money, the fame, and the power inherited by King Edward, there was an emptiness which could be filled only by love.

His greatest DESIRE was for love. Long before he met Wallis Simpson, he doubtless felt this great universal emotion tugging at the strings of his heart, beating upon the door of his soul, and crying out for expression.

And when he met a kindred spirit, crying out for this same Holy privilege of expression, he recognized it, and without fear or apology, opened his heart and bade it enter. All the scandal-mongers in the world cannot destroy the beauty of this international drama, through which two people found love, and had the courage to face open criticism, renounce ALL ELSE to give it *holy* expression.

King Edward's DECISION to give up the crown of the world's most powerful empire, for the privilege of going the remainder of the way through life with the women of his choice, was a decision that required courage. The decision also had a price, but who has the right to say the price was too great? Surely not He who said, "He among you who is without sin, let him cast the first stone."

As a suggestion to any evil-minded person who chooses to find fault with the Duke of Windsor, because his DESIRE was for LOVE, and for openly declaring his love for Wallis Simpson, and giving up his throne for her, let it be remembered that the OPEN DECLARATION was not essential. He could have followed the custom of clandestine liaison which has prevailed in Europe for centuries, without giving up either his throne, or the woman of his choice, and there would have been NO COM-

PLAINT FROM EITHER CHURCH OR LAITY. But this unusual man was built of sterner stuff. His love was clean. It was deep and sincere. It represented the one thing which, above ALL ELSE he truly DESIRED, therefore, he took what he wanted, and paid the price demanded.

If Europe had been blessed with more rulers with the human heart and the traits of honesty of ex-king Edward, for the past century, that unfortunate hemisphere now seething with greed, hate, lust, political connivance, and threats of war, would have a DIFFERENT AND A BETTER STORY TO TELL. A story in which Love and not Hate would rule.

In the words of Stuart Austin Wier we raise our cup and drink this toast to ex-king Edward and Wallis Simpson:

"Blessed is the man who has come to know that our muted thoughts are our sweetest thoughts.

"Blessed is the man who, from the blackest depths, can see the luminous figure of LOVE, and seeing, sing; and singing, say: "Sweeter far than uttered lays are the thoughts I have of you.'"

In these words would we pay tribute to the two people who, more than all others of modern times, have been the victims of criticism and the recipients of abuse, because they found Life's greatest treasure, and claimed it.*

Most of the world will applaud the Duke of Windsor and Wallis Simpson, because of their PERSISTENCE in searching until they found life's greatest reward. ALL OF US CAN PROFIT by

*Mrs. Simpson read and approved this analysis.

following their example in our own search for that which we demand of life.

What mystical power gives to men of PERSISTENCE the capacity to master difficulties? Does the quality of PERSISTENCE set up in one's mind some form of spiritual, mental or chemical activity which gives one access to supernatural forces? Does Infinite Intelligence throw itself on the side of the person who still fights on, after the battle has been lost, with the whole world on the opposing side?

These and many other similar questions have arisen in my mind as I have observed men like Henry Ford, who started at scratch, and built an Industrial Empire of huge proportions, with little else in the way of a beginning but PERSISTENCE. Or, Thomas A. Edison, who, with less than three months of schooling, became the world's leading inventor and converted PERSISTENCE into the talking machine, the moving picture machine, and the incandescent light, to say nothing of half a hundred other useful inventions.

I had the happy privilege of analyzing both Mr. Edison and Mr. Ford, year by year, over a long period of years, and therefore, the opportunity to study them at close range, so I speak from actual knowledge when I say that I found no quality save PERSISTENCE, in either of them, that even remotely suggested the major source of their stupendous achievements.

As one makes an impartial study of the prophets, philosophers, "miracle" men, and religious leaders of the past, one is drawn to the inevitable conclusion that PERSISTENCE, concentration of effort, and DEFINITENESS OF PURPOSE, were the major sources of their achievements.

Consider, for example, the strange and fascinating story of Mohammed; analyze his life, compare him with men of achievement in this modern age of industry and finance, and observe how they have one outstanding trait in common, PERSISTENCE!

If you are keenly interested in studying the strange power which gives potency to PERSISTENCE, read a biography of Mohammed, especially the one by Essad Bey. This brief review of that book, by Thomas Sugrue, in the Herald-Tribune, will provide a preview of the rare treat in store for those who take the time to read the entire story of one of the most astounding examples of the power of PERSISTENCE known to civilization.

The Last Great Prophet
Reviewed by Thomas Sugrue

.   .   .   .   .

"Mohammed was a prophet, but he never performed a miracle. He was not a mystic; he had no formal schooling; he did not begin his mission until he was forty. When he announced that he was the Messenger of God, bringing word of the true religion, he was ridiculed and labeled a lunatic. Children tripped him and women threw filth upon him. He was banished from his native city, Mecca, and his followers were stripped of their worldly goods and sent into the desert after him. When he had been preaching ten years he had nothing to show for it but banishment, poverty and ridicule. Yet before another ten years had passed, he was dictator of all Arabia, ruler of Mecca, and the head of a New World religion which was to sweep to the Danube and the Pyrenees before exhausting the impetus he gave it. That impetus was three-fold: the power of words, the efficacy of prayer and man's kinship with God.

"His career never made sense. Mohammed was born to impoverished members of a leading family of Mecca. Because Mecca, the crossroads of the world, home of the magic stone called the Caaba, great city of trade and the center of trade routes, was unsanitary, its children were sent to be raised in the desert by Bedouins. Mohammed was thus nurtured, drawing strength and health from the milk of nomad, vicarious mothers. He tended sheep and soon hired out to a rich widow as leader of her caravans. He traveled to all parts of the Eastern World, talked with many men of diverse beliefs and observed the decline of Christianity into warring sects. When he was twenty-eight, Khadija, the widow, looked upon him with favor, and married him. Her father would have objected to such a marriage, so she got him drunk and held him up while he gave the paternal blessing. For the next twelve years Mohammed lived as a rich and respected and very shrewd trader. Then he took to wandering in the desert, and one day he returned with the first verse of the Koran and told Khadija that the archangel Gabriel had appeared to him and said that he was to be the Messenger of God.

"The Koran, the revealed word of God, was the closest thing to a miracle in Mohammed's life. He had not been a poet; he had no gift of words. Yet the verses of the Koran, as he received them and recited them to the faithful, were better than any verses which the professional poets of the tribes could produce. This, to the Arabs, was a miracle. To them the gift of words was the greatest gift, the poet was all-powerful. In addition the Koran said that all men were equal before God, that the world should be a democratic state–Islam. It was this political heresy, plus Mohammed's desire to destroy all the 360 idols in the courtyard of the Caaba, which brought about his banishment. The idols brought the desert tribes to Mecca, and that meant trade. So the business men of Mecca, the capitalists, of which he had been one, set upon Mohammed. Then he retreated to the desert and demanded sovereignty over the world.

"The rise of Islam began. Out of the desert came a flame which would not be extinguished—a democratic army fighting as a unit and prepared to die without wincing. Mohammed had invited the Jews and Christians to join him; for he was not building a new religion. He was calling all who believed in one God to join in a single faith. If the Jews and Christians had accepted his invitation Islam would have conquered the world. They didn't. They would not even accept Mohammed's innovation of humane warfare. When the armies of the prophet entered Jerusalem not a single person was killed because of his faith. When the crusaders entered the city, centuries later, not a Moslem man, woman, or child was spared. But the Christians did accept one Moslem idea—the place of learning, the university."

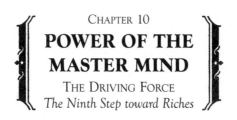

CHAPTER 10

POWER OF THE MASTER MIND

THE DRIVING FORCE
The Ninth Step toward Riches

POWER is essential for success in the accumulation of money.

PLANS are inert and useless, without sufficient POWER to translate them into ACTION. This chapter will describe the method by which an individual may attain and apply POWER.

POWER may be defined as "organized and intelligently directed KNOWLEDGE." Power, as the term is here used, refers to ORGANIZED effort, sufficient to enable an individual to transmute DESIRE into its monetary equivalent. ORGANIZED effort is produced through the coordination of effort of two or more people, who work toward a DEFINITE end, in a spirit of harmony.

POWER IS REQUIRED FOR THE ACCUMULATION OF MONEY! POWER IS NECESSARY FOR THE RETENTION OF MONEY AFTER IT HAS BEEN ACCUMULATED!

Let us ascertain how power may be acquired. If power is "organized knowledge," let us examine the sources of knowledge:

a. INFINITE INTELLIGENCE. This source of knowledge may be contacted through the procedure described in another chapter, with the aid of Creative Imagination.

b. ACCUMULATED EXPERIENCE. The accumulated experience of man, (or that portion of it which has been organized and recorded), may be found in any well-equipped public library. An important part of this accumulated experience is taught in public schools and colleges, where it has been classified and organized.

c. EXPERIMENT AND RESEARCH. In the field of science, and in practically every other walk of life, men are gathering, classifying, and organizing new facts daily. This is the source to which one must turn when knowledge is not available through "accumulated experience." Here, too, the Creative Imagination must often be used.

Knowledge may be acquired from any of the foregoing sources. It may be converted into POWER by organizing it into definite PLANS and by expressing those plans in terms of ACTION.

Examination of the three major sources of knowledge will readily disclose the difficulty an individual would have, if he depended upon his efforts alone, in assembling knowledge and expressing it through definite plans in terms of ACTION. If his plans are comprehensive, and if they contemplate large proportions, he must, generally, induce others to cooperate with him, before he can inject into them the necessary element of POWER.

GAINING POWER THROUGH THE "MASTER MIND"

The "Master Mind" may be defined as: "Coordination of knowledge and effort, in a spirit of harmony, between two or more people, for the attainment of a definite purpose."

No individual may have great power without availing himself of the "Master Mind." In a preceding chapter, instructions were given for the creation of PLANS for the purpose of translating DESIRE into its monetary equivalent. If you carry out these instructions with PERSISTENCE and intelligence, and use discrimination in the selection of your "Master Mind" group, your objective will have been half-way reached, even before you begin to recognize it.

So you may better understand the "intangible" potentialities of power available to you, through a properly chosen "Master Mind" group, we will here explain the two characteristics of the Master Mind principle, one of which is economic in nature, and the other psychic. The economic feature is obvious. Economic advantages may be created by any person who surrounds himself with the advice, counsel, and personal cooperation of a group of men who are willing to lend him wholehearted aid, in a spirit of PERFECT HARMONY. This form of cooperative alliance has been the basis of nearly every great fortune. Your understanding of this great truth may definitely determine your financial status.

The psychic phase of the Master Mind principle is much more abstract, much more difficult to comprehend, because it has reference to the spiritual forces with which the human race, as a whole, is not well acquainted. You may catch a significant suggestion from this statement: "No two minds ever come together without, thereby, creating a third, invisible, intangible force which may be likened to a third mind."

Keep in mind the fact that there are only two known elements in the whole universe, energy and matter. It is a well known fact that matter may be broken down into units of molecules, atoms, and electrons. There are units of matter which may be isolated, separated, and analyzed.

Likewise, there are units of energy.

The human mind is a form of energy, a part of it being spiritual in nature. When the minds of two people are coordinated in a SPIRIT OF HARMONY, the spiritual units of energy of each mind form an affinity, which constitutes the "psychic" phase of the Master Mind.

The Master Mind principle, or rather the economic feature of it, was first called to my attention by Andrew Carnegie, over twenty-five year ago. Discovery of this principle was responsible for the choice of my life's work.

Mr. Carnegie's Master Mind group consisted of a staff of approximately fifty men, with whom he surrounded himself, for the DEFINITE PURPOSE of manufacturing and marketing steel. He attributed his entire fortune to the POWER he accumulated through this "Master Mind."

Analyze the record of any man who has accumulated a great fortune, and many of those who have accumulated modest fortunes, and you will find that they have either consciously, or unconsciously employed the "Master Mind" principle.

GREAT POWER CAN BE ACCUMULATED THROUGH NO OTHER PRINCIPLE!

ENERGY is Nature's universal set of building blocks, out of which she constructs every material thing in the universe, including man, and every form of animal and vegetable life. Through a process which only Nature completely understands, she translates energy into matter.

Nature's building blocks are available to man, in the energy involved in THINKING! Man's brain may be compared to an electric battery. It absorbs energy from the ether, which permeates every atom of matter, and fills the entire universe.

It is a well known fact that a group of electric batteries will provide more energy than a single battery. It is also a well known fact that an individual battery will provide energy in proportion to the number and capacity of the cells it contains.

The brain functions in a similar fashion. This accounts for the fact that some brains are more efficient than others, and leads to this significant statement—a group of brains coordinated (or connected) in a spirit of harmony, will provide more thought-energy than a single brain, just as a group of electric batteries will provide more energy than a single battery.

Through this metaphor it becomes immediately obvious that the Master Mind principle holds the secret of the POWER wielded by men who surround themselves with other men of brains.

There follows, now, another statement which will lead still nearer to an understanding of the psychic phase of the Master Mind principle: When a group of individual brains are coordinated and function in Harmony, the increased energy created through that alliance, becomes available to every individual brain in the group.

It is a well known fact that Henry Ford began his business career under the handicap of poverty, illiteracy, and ignorance. It is an equally well known fact that, within the inconceivably short period of ten years, Mr. Ford mastered these three handicaps, and that within twenty-five years he made himself one of the richest men in America. Connect with this fact, the additional knowledge that Mr. Ford's most rapid strides became notice-able, from the time he became a personal friend of Thomas A. Edison, and you will begin to under-stand what the influence of one mind upon another can accomplish. Go a step further, and consider the fact that Mr. Ford's most outstanding achievements began from the time that he formed the acquaintances of Harvey Firestone, John Burroughs, and Luther Burbank, (each a man of great brain capacity), and you will have further evidence that POWER may be produced through friendly alliance of minds.

There is little if any doubt that Henry Ford is one of the best informed men in the business and indus-trial world. The question of his wealth needs no discussion. Analyze Mr. Ford's intimate personal friends, some of whom have already been mentioned, and you will be prepared to understand the following statement:—

"Men take on the nature and the habits and the POWER OF THOUGHT of those with whom they associate in a spirit of sympathy and harmony."

Henry Ford whipped poverty, illiteracy, and

ignorance by allying himself with great minds, whose vibrations of thought he absorbed into his own mind. Through his association with Edison, Burbank, Burroughs, and Firestone, Mr. Ford added to his own brain power, the sum and substance of the intelligence, experience, knowledge, and spiritual forces of these four men. Moreover, he appropriated, and made use of the Master Mind principle through the methods of procedure described in this book.

This principle is available to you!

We have already mentioned Mahatma Gandhi. Perhaps the majority of those who have heard of Gandhi, look upon him as merely an eccentric little man, who goes around without formal wearing apparel, and makes trouble for the British Government.

In reality, Gandhi is not eccentric, but HE IS THE MOST POWERFUL MAN NOW LIVING. (Estimated by the number of his followers and their faith in their leader.) Moreover, he is probably the most powerful man who has ever lived. His power is passive, but it is real.

Let us study the method by which he attained his stupendous POWER. It may be explained in a few words. He came by POWER through inducing over two hundred million people to coordinate, with mind and body, in a spirit of HARMONY, for a DEFI-NITE PURPOSE.

In brief, Gandhi has accomplished a MIRACLE, for it is a miracle when two hundred million people can be induced—not forced—to cooperate in a spirit of HARMONY, for a limitless time. If you doubt that this is a miracle, try to induce ANY TWO PEOPLE to cooperate in a spirit of harmony for *any length of time.*

Every man who manages a business knows what a difficult matter it is to get employees to work together in a spirit even remotely resembling HARMONY.

The list of the chief sources from which POWER may be attained is, as you have seen, headed by INFINITE INTELLIGENCE. When two or more people coordinate in a spirit of HARMONY, and work toward a definite objective, they place themselves in position, through that alliance, to absorb power directly from the great universal storehouse of Infinite Intelligence. This is the greatest of all sources of POWER. It is the source to which the genius turns. It is the source to which every great leader turns, (whether he may be conscious of the fact or not).

The other two major sources from which the knowledge, necessary for the accumulation of POWER, may be obtained are no more reliable than the five senses of man. The senses are not always reliable. Infinite Intelligence DOES NOT ERR.

In subsequent chapters, the methods by which Infinite Intelligence may be most readily contacted will be adequately described.

This is not a course on religion. No fundamental principle described in this book should be interpreted as being intended to interfere either directly, or indirectly, with any man's religious habits. This book has been confined, exclusively, to instructing the reader how to transmute the DEFINITE PUR-

POSE OF DESIRE FOR MONEY, into its monetary equivalent.

Read, *THINK*, and meditate as you read. Soon, the entire subject will unfold, and you will see it in perspective. You are now seeing the detail of the individual chapters.

Money is as shy and elusive as the "old time" maiden. It must be wooed and won by methods not unlike those used by a determined lover, in pursuit of the girl of his choice. And, coincidental as it is, the POWER used in the "wooing" of money is not greatly different than that used in wooing a maiden. That power, when successfully used in the pursuit of money must be mixed with FAITH. It must be mixed with DESIRE. It must be mixed with PERSISTENCE. It must be applied through a plan, and that plan must be set into ACTION.

When money comes in quantities known as "the big money," it flows to the one who accumulates it, as easily as water flows down hill. There exists a great unseen stream of POWER, which may be compared to a river; except that one side flows in one direction, carrying all who get into that side of the stream, onward and upward to WEALTH–and the other side flows in the opposite direction, carrying all who are unfortunate enough to get into it (and not able to extricate themselves from it), downward to misery and POVERTY.

Every man who has accumulated a great fortune, has recognized the existence of this stream of life. It consists of one's THINKING PROCESS. The positive emotions of thought form the side of the stream which carries one to fortune. The negative emotions form the side which carries one down to poverty.

This carries a thought of stupendous importance to the person who is following this book with the object of accumulating a fortune.

If you are in the side of the stream of POWER which leads to poverty, this may serve as an oar, by which you may propel yourself over into the other side of the stream. It can serve you ONLY through application and use. Merely reading, and passing judgment on it, either one way or another, will in no way benefit you.

Some people undergo the experience of alternating between the positive and negative sides of the stream, being at times on the positive side, and at times on the negative side. The Wall Street crash of '29 swept millions of people from the positive to the negative side of the steam. These millions are struggling, some of them in desperation and fear, to get back to the positive side of the stream. This book was written especially for those millions.

Poverty and riches often change places. The Crash taught the world this truth, although the world will not long remember the lesson. Poverty may, and generally does, voluntarily take the place of riches. When riches take the place of poverty, the change is usually brought about through well-conceived and carefully executed PLANS. Poverty needs no plan. It needs no one to aid it, because it is bold and ruthless. Riches are shy and timid. They have to be "attracted."

A NYBODY can WISH for riches, and most people do, but only a few know that a definite plan, plus a BURNING DESIRE for wealth, are the only dependable means of accumulating wealth.

CHAPTER 11
THE MYSTERY OF SEX TRANSMUTATION

The Tenth Step toward Riches

THE meaning of the word "transmute" is, in simple language, "the changing, or transferring of one element, or form of energy, into another."

The emotion of sex brings into being a state of mind.

Because of ignorance on the subject, this state of mind is generally associated with the physical, and because of improper influences, to which most people have been subjected, in acquiring knowledge of sex, things essentially physical have highly biased the mind.

The emotion of sex has back of it the possibility of three constructive potentialities, they are:—

1. The perpetuation of mankind.

2. The maintenance of health, (as a therapeutic agency, it has no equal).

3. The transformation of mediocrity into genius through transmutation.

Sex transmutation is simple and easily explained. It means the switching of the mind from thoughts of physical expression, to thoughts of some other nature.

Sex desire is the most powerful of human desires.

When driven by this desire, men develop keenness of imagination, courage, will-power, persistence, and creative ability unknown to them at other times. So strong and impelling is the desire for sexual contact that men freely run the risk of life and reputation to indulge it. When harnessed, and redirected along other lines, this motivating force maintains all of its attributes of keenness of imagination, courage, etc., which may be used as powerful creative forces in literature, art, or in any other profession or calling, including, of course, the accumulation of riches.

The transmutation of sex energy calls for the exercise of will-power, to be sure, but the reward is worth the effort. The desire for sexual expression is inborn and natural. The desire cannot, and should not be submerged or eliminated. But it should be given an outlet through forms of expression which enrich the body, mind, and spirit of man. If not given this form of outlet, through transmutation, it will seek outlets through purely physical channels.

A river may be dammed, and its water controlled for a time, but eventually, it will force an outlet. The same is true of the emotion of sex. It may be submerged and controlled for a time, but its very nature causes it to be ever seeking means of expression. If it is not transmuted into some creative effort it will find a less worthy outlet.

Fortunate, indeed, is the person who has discovered how to give sex emotion an outlet through some form of creative effort, for he has, by that discovery, lifted himself to the status of a genius.

Scientific research has disclosed these significant facts:

1. The men of greatest achievement are men with highly developed sex natures; men who have learned the art of sex transmutation.

2. The men who have accumulated great fortunes and achieved outstanding recognition in literature, art, industry, architecture, and the professions, were motivated by the influence of a woman.

The research from which these astounding discoveries were made, went back through the pages of biography and history for more than two thousand years. Wherever there was evidence available in connection with the lives of men and women of great achievement, it indicated most convincingly that they possessed highly developed sex natures.

The emotion of sex is an "irresistible force," against which there can be no such opposition as an "immovable body." When driven by this emotion, men become gifted with a super power for action. Understand this truth, and you will catch the significance of the statement that sex transmutation will lift one to the status of a genius.

The emotion of sex contains the secret of creative ability.

Destroy the sex glands, whether in man or beast, and you have removed the major source of action. For proof of this, observe what happens to any animal after it has been castrated. A bull becomes as docile as a cow after it has been altered sexually. Sex alteration takes out of the male, whether man or beast, all the FIGHT that was in him. Sex alteration of the female has the same effect.

THE TEN MIND STIMULI

The human mind responds to stimuli, through which it may be "keyed up" to high rates of vibration, known as enthusiasm, creative imagination, intense desire, etc. The stimuli to which the mind responds most freely are:—

1. The desire for sex expression
2. Love
3. A burning desire for fame, power, or financial gain, MONEY
4. Music
5. Friendship between either those of the same sex, or those of the opposite sex.
6. A Master Mind alliance based upon the harmony of two or more people who ally themselves for spiritual or temporal advancement.
7. Mutual suffering, such as that experienced by people who are persecuted.
8. Auto-suggestion
9. Fear
10. Narcotics and alcohol.

The desire for sex expression comes at the head of the list of stimuli, which most effectively "step-up" the vibrations of the mind and start the "wheels" of physical action. Eight of these stimuli are natural and constructive. Two are destructive. The list is here presented for the purpose of enabling you to make a comparative study of the major sources of mind stimulation. From this study, it will be readily seen that the emotion of sex is, by great odds, the most intense and powerful of all mind stimuli.

This comparison is necessary as a foundation for proof of the statement that transmutation of sex energy may lift one to the status of a genius. Let us find out what constitutes a genius.

Some wiseacre has said that a genius is a man who "wears long hair, eats queer food, lives alone, and serves as a target for the joke makers." A better definition of a genius is, "a man who has discovered how to increase the vibrations of thought to the point where he can freely communicate with sources of knowledge not available through the ordinary rate of vibration of thought."

The person who thinks will want to ask some questions concerning this definition of genius. The first question will be, "How may one communicate with sources of knowledge which are not available through the ORDINARY rate of vibration of thought?"

The next question will be, "Are there known sources of knowledge which are available only to genii, and if so, WHAT ARE THESE SOURCES, and exactly how may they be reached?"

We shall offer proof of the soundness of some of the more important statements made in this book—or at least we shall offer evidence through which you may secure your own proof through experimentation, and in doing so, we shall answer both of these questions.

"Genius" Is Developed through the Sixth Sense

The reality of a "sixth sense" has been fairly well established. This sixth sense is "Creative Imagination." The faculty of creative imagination is one which the majority of people never use during an entire lifetime, and if used at all, it usually happens by mere accident. A relatively small number of people use, WITH DELIBERATION AND PURPOSE AFORETHOUGHT, the faculty of creative imagination. Those who use this faculty voluntarily, and with understanding of its functions, are GENII.

The faculty of creative imagination is the direct link between the finite mind of man and Infinite Intelligence. All so-called revelations, referred to in the realm of religion, and all discoveries of basic or new principles in the field of invention, take place through the faculty of creative imagination.

When ideas or concepts flash into one's mind, through what is popularly called a "hunch," they come from one or more of the following sources:—

1. Infinite Intelligence

2. One's subconscious mind, wherein is stored every sense impression and thought impulse which ever reached the brain through any of the five senses

3. From the mind of some other person who has just released the thought, or picture of the idea or concept, through conscious thought, or

4. From his subconscious storehouse.

There are no other KNOWN sources from which "inspired" ideas or "hunches" may be received.

The creative imagination functions best when the mind is vibrating (due to some form of mind stimulation) at an exceedingly high rate. That is, when the mind is functioning at a rate of vibration higher than that of ordinary, normal thought.

When brain action has been stimulated, through one or more of the ten mind stimulants, it has the effect of lifting the individual far above the horizon of ordinary thought, and permits him to envision distance, scope, and quality of THOUGHTS not available on the lower plane, such as that occupied while one is engaged in the solution of the problems of business and professional routine.

When lifted to this higher level of thought, through any form of mind stimulation, an individual occupies, relatively, the same position as one who has ascended in an airplane to a height from which he may see over and beyond the horizon line which limits his vision, while on the ground. Moreover, while on this higher level of thought, the individual is not hampered or bound by any of the stimuli which circumscribe and limit his vision while wrestling with the problems of gaining the three basic necessities of food, clothing, and shelter. He is in a world of thought in which the ORDINARY, work-a-day thoughts have been as effectively removed as are the hills and valleys and other limitations of physical vision, when he rises in an airplane.

While on this exalted plane of THOUGHT, the creative faculty of the mind is given freedom for action. The way has been cleared for the sixth sense to function, it becomes receptive to ideas which could not reach the individual under any other circumstances. The "sixth sense" is the faculty which marks the difference between a genius and an ordinary individual.

The creative faculty becomes more alert and receptive to vibrations, originating outside the individual's subconscious mind, the more this faculty is used, and the more the individual relies upon it, and makes demands upon it for thought impulses. This faculty can be cultivated and developed only through use.

That which is known as one's "conscience" operates entirely through the faculty of the sixth sense.

The great artists, writers, musicians, and poets become great, because they acquire the habit of relying upon the "still small voice" which speaks from within, through the faculty of creative imagination. It is a fact well known to people who have "keen" imaginations that their best ideas come through so-called "hunches."

There is a great orator who does not attain to greatness, until he closes his eyes and begins to rely entirely upon the faculty of Creative Imagination. When asked why he closed his eyes just before the climaxes of his oratory, he replied, "I do it, because, then I speak through ideas which come to me from within."

One of America's most successful and best known financiers followed the habit of closing his eyes for two or three minutes before making a decision.

When asked why he did this, he replied, "With my eyes closed, I am able to draw upon a source of superior intelligence."

The late Dr. Elmer R. Gates, of Chevy Chase, Maryland, created more than 200 useful patents, many of them basic, through the process of cultivating and using the creative faculty. His method is both significant and interesting to one interested in attaining to the status of genius, in which category Dr. Gates, unquestionably belonged. Dr. Gates was one of the really great, though less publicized scientists of the world.

In his laboratory, he had what he called his "personal communication room." It was practically sound proof, and so arranged that all light could be shut out. It was equipped with a small table, on which he kept a pad of writing paper. In front of the table, on the wall, was an electric pushbutton, which controlled the lights. When Dr. Gates desired to draw upon the forces available to him through his Creative Imagination, he would go into this room, seat himself at the table, shut off the lights, and CONCENTRATE upon the KNOWN factors of the invention on which he was working, remaining in that position until ideas began to "flash" into his mind in connection with the UNKNOWN factors of the invention.

On one occasion, ideas came through so fast that he was forced to write for almost three hours. When the thoughts stopped flowing, and he examined his notes, he found they contained a minute description of principles which had not a parallel among the known data of the scientific world.

Moreover, the answer to his problem was intelligently presented in those notes. In this manner Dr. Gates completed over 200 patents, which had been begun, but not completed, by "half-baked" brains. Evidence of the truth of this statement is in the United States Patent Office.

Dr. Gates earned his living by "sitting for ideas" for individuals and corporations. Some of the largest corporations in America paid him substantial fees, by the hour, for "sitting for ideas."

The reasoning faculty is often faulty, because it is largely guided by one's accumulated experience. Not all knowledge, which one accumulates through "experience," is accurate. Ideas received through the creative faculty are much more reliable, for the reason that they come from sources more reliable than any which are available to the reasoning faculty of the mind.

The major difference between the genius and the ordinary "crank" inventor, may be found in the fact that the genius works through his faculty of creative imagination, while the "crank" knows nothing of this faculty. The scientific inventor (such as Mr. Edison, and Dr. Gates), makes use of both the synthetic and the creative faculties of imagination.

For example, the scientific inventor, or "genius," begins an invention by organizing and combining the known ideas, or principles accumulated through experience, through the synthetic faculty (the reasoning faculty). If he finds this accumulated knowledge to be insufficient for the completion of his invention, he then draws upon the sources of knowledge available to him through his *creative* faculty. The method by which he does this varies with the individual, but this is the sum and substance of his procedure:

1. HE STIMULATES HIS MIND SO THAT IT VIBRATES ON A HIGHER-THAN-AVERAGE PLANE, using one or more of the ten mind stimulants or some other stimulant of his choice.

2. HE CONCENTRATES upon the known factors (the finished part) of his invention, and creates in his mind a perfect picture of unknown factors (the unfinished part), of his invention. He holds the picture in mind until it has been taken over by the subconscious mind, then relaxes by clearing his mind of ALL thought, and waits for his answer to "flash" into his mind.

Sometimes the results are both definite and immediate. At other times, the results are negative, depending upon the state of development of the "sixth sense," or creative faculty.

Mr. Edison tried out more than 10,000 different combinations of ideas through the synthetic faculty of his imagination before he "tuned in" through the creative faculty, and got the answer which perfected the incandescent light. His experience was similar when he produced the talking machine.

There is plenty of reliable evidence that the faculty of creative imagination exists. This evidence is available through accurate analysis of men who have become leaders in their respective callings, without having had extensive educations. Lincoln was a notable example of a great leader who achieved greatness, through the discovery, and use of his faculty of creative imagination. He discovered, and began to use this faculty as the result of the stimulation of love which he experienced after he met Anne Rutledge, a statement of the highest significance, in connection with the study of the source of genius.

The pages of history are filled with the records of great leaders whose achievements may be traced directly to the influence of women who aroused the creative faculties of their minds, through the stimulation of sex desire. Napoleon Bonaparte was one of these. When inspired by his first wife, Josephine, he was irresistible and invincible. When his "better judgment" or reasoning faculty prompted him to put Josephine aside, he began to decline. His defeat and St. Helena were not far distant.

If good taste would permit, we might easily mention scores of men, well known to the American people, who climbed to great heights of achievement under the stimulating influences of their wives, only to drop back to destruction AFTER money and power went to their heads, and they put aside the old wife for a new one. Napoleon was not the only man to discover that sex influence, *from the right source*, is more powerful than any substitute of expediency, which may be created by mere reason.

The human mind responds to stimulation!

Among the greatest, and most powerful of these stimuli is the urge of sex. When harnessed and transmuted, this driving force is capable of lifting men into that higher sphere of thought which enables them to master the sources of worry and petty annoyance which beset their pathway on the lower plane.

Unfortunately, only the genii have made the discovery. Others have accepted the experience of sex urge, without discovering one of its major potentialities—a fact which accounts for the great number of "others" as compared to the limited number of genii.

For the purpose of refreshing the memory, in connection with the facts available from the biographies of certain men, we here present the names of a few men of outstanding achievement, each of whom was known to have been of a highly sexed nature. The genius which was their's, undoubtedly found its source of power in transmuted sex energy:

GEORGE WASHINGTON	THOMAS JEFFERSON
NAPOLEON BONAPARTE	ELBERT HUBBARD
WILLIAM SHAKESPEARE	ELBERT H. GARY
ABRAHAM LINCOLN	OSCAR WILDE
RALPH WALDO EMERSON	WOODROW WILSON
ROBERT BURNS	JOHN H. PATTERSON
ANDREW JACKSON	ENRICO CARUSO

Your own knowledge of biography will enable you to add to the list. Find, if you can, a single man, in all history of civilization, who achieved outstanding success in any calling, who was not driven by a well developed sex nature.

If you do not wish to rely upon biographies of men not now living, take inventory of those whom you know to be men of great achievement, and see if you can find one among them who is not highly sexed.

Sex energy is the creative energy of all genii. *There never has been, and never will be a great leader, builder, or artist lacking in this driving force of sex.*

Surely no one will misunderstand these statements to mean that ALL who are highly sexed are genii! Man attains to the status of a genius ONLY when, and IF, he stimulates his mind so that it draws upon the forces available, through the creative faculty of the imagination. Chief among the stimuli with which this "stepping up" of the vibrations may be produced is sex energy. The mere *possession* of this energy is not sufficient to produce a genius. The energy must be *transmuted* from desire for physical contact, into some *other* form of desire and action, before it will lift one to the status of a genius.

Far from becoming genii, because of great sex desires, the majority of men *lower* themselves, through misunderstanding and misuse of this great force, to the status of the lower animals.

WHY MEN SELDOM SUCCEED BEFORE FORTY

I discovered, from the analysis of over 25,000 people that men who succeed in an outstanding way, seldom do so before the age of forty, and more often they do not strike their real pace until they are well beyond the age of fifty. This fact was so astounding that it prompted me to go into the study of its cause most carefully, carrying the investigation over a period of more than twelve years.

This study disclosed the fact that the major reason why the majority of men who succeed do not begin to do so before the age of forty to fifty, is their tendency to DISSIPATE their energies through over indulgence in physical expression of the emotion of sex. The majority of men *never* learn that the urge of sex has other possibilities, which far transcend in importance, that of mere physical expression. The majority of those who make this discovery, do so *after having wasted many years* at a period when the sex energy is at its height, prior to the age of forty-five to fifty. This usually is followed by noteworthy achievement.

The lives of many men up to, and sometimes well past the age of forty, reflect a continued dissipation of energies, which could have been more profitably turned into better channels. Their finer and more powerful emotions are sown wildly to the four winds. Out of this habit of the male, grew the term, "sowing his wild oats."

The desire for sexual expression is by far the strongest and most impelling of all the human emotions, and for this very reason this desire, when *harnessed and transmuted* into action, other than that of physical expression, may raise one to the status of a genius.

One of America's most able business men frankly admitted that his attractive secretary was responsible for most of the plans he created. He admitted that her presence lifted him to heights of creative imagination, such as he could experience under no other stimulus.

One of the most successful men in America owes most of his success to the influence of a very charming young woman, who has served as his source of inspiration for more than twelve years. Everyone knows the man to whom this reference is made, but not everyone knows the REAL SOURCE of his achievements.

History is not lacking in examples of men who attained to the status of genii, as the result of the use of artificial mind stimulants in the form of alcohol and narcotics. Edgar Allen Poe wrote the "Raven" while under the influence of liquor, "dreaming dreams that mortal never dared to dream before." James Whitcomb Riley did his best writing while under the influence of alcohol. Perhaps it was thus he saw "the ordered intermingling of the real and the dream, the mill above the river, and the mist above the stream." Robert Burns wrote best when intoxicated, "For Auld Lang Syne, my dear, we'll take a cup of kindness yet, for Auld Lang Syne."

But let it be remembered that many such men have destroyed themselves in the end. Nature has prepared her own potions with which men may safely stimulate their minds so they vibrate on a plane that enables them to tune in to fine and rare thoughts which come from—no man knows where! No satisfactory substitute for Nature's stimulants has ever been found.

It is a fact well known to psychologists that there is a very close relationship between sex desires and spiritual urges—a fact which accounts for the peculiar behavior of people who participate in the orgies known as religious "revivals," common among the primitive types.

The world is ruled, and the destiny of civilization is established, by the human emotions. People are influenced in their actions, not by reason so much as by "feelings." The creative faculty of the mind is set into action entirely by emotions, and *not by cold reason.* The most powerful of all human emotions is that of sex. There are other mind stimulants, some of which have been listed, but no one of them, nor all of them combined, can equal the driving power of sex.

A mind stimulant is any influence which will either temporarily, or permanently, increase the vibrations of thought. The ten major stimulants, described, are those most commonly resorted to. Through these sources one may commune with Infinite Intelligence, or enter, at will, the storehouse of the subconscious mind, either one's own, or that of another person, a procedure *which is all there is of genius.*

A teacher, who has trained and directed the efforts of more than 30,000 sales people, made the astounding discovery that highly sexed men are the most efficient salesmen. The explanation is, that the factor of personality known as "personal magnetism" is nothing more nor less than sex energy. Highly sexed people always have a plentiful supply of magnetism. Through cultivation and understanding, this vital force may be drawn upon and used to great advantage in the relationships between people. This energy may be communicated to others through the following media:

1. The hand-shake. The touch of the hand indicates, instantly, the presence of magnetism, or the lack of it.

2. The tone of voice. Magnetism, or sex energy, is the factor with which the voice may be colored, or made musical and charming.

3. Posture and carriage of the body. Highly sexed people move briskly, and with grace and ease.

4. The vibrations of thought. Highly sexed people mix the emotion of sex with their thoughts, or may do so at will, and in that way, may influence those around them.

5. Body adornment. People who are highly sexed are usually very careful about their personal appearance. They usually select clothing of a style becoming to their personality, physique, complexion, etc.

When employing salesmen, the more capable sales manager looks for the quality of personal magnetism as the *first requirement* of a salesman. People who lack sex energy will never become enthusiastic nor inspire others with enthusiasm, and enthusiasm is one of the most important requisites in salesmanship, no matter what one is selling.

The public speaker, orator, preacher, lawyer, or salesman who is lacking in sex energy is a "flop," as far as being able to influence others is concerned. Couple with this the fact, that most people can be influenced only through an appeal to their emotions, and you will understand the importance of sex energy as a part of the salesman's native ability. Master salesmen attain the status of mastery in selling, because they, either consciously, or unconsciously, *transmute* the energy of sex into SALES ENTHUSIASM! In this statement may be found a very practical suggestion as to the actual meaning of sex transmutation.

The salesman who knows how to take his mind off the subject of sex, and direct it in sales effort with as much enthusiasm and determination as he would apply to its original purpose, has acquired the art of sex transmutation, whether he knows it or not. The majority of salesmen who transmute their sex energy do so without being in the least aware of what they are doing, or how they are doing it.

Transmutation of sex energy calls for more will power than the average person cares to use for this purpose. Those who find it difficult to summon will-power sufficient for transmutation, may gradually acquire this ability. Though this requires will-power, the reward for the practice is more than worth the effort.

The entire subject of sex is one with which the majority of people appear to be unpardonably ignorant. The urge of sex has been grossly misunderstood, slandered, and burlesqued by the ignorant and the evil minded, for so long that the very word sex is seldom used in polite society. Men and women who are known to be blessed—yes, BLESSED—with highly sexed natures, are usually looked upon as being people who will bear watching. Instead of being called blessed, they are usually called cursed.

Millions of people, even in this age of enlightenment, have inferiority complexes which they developed because of this false belief that a highly sexed nature is a curse. These statements, of the virtue of sex energy, should not be construed as justification for the libertine. The emotion of sex is a virtue ONLY when used intelligently, and with discrimination. It may be misused, and often is, to such an extent that it debases, instead of enriches, both body and mind. The better use of this power is the burden of this chapter.

It seemed quite significant to the author, when he made the discovery that practically every great leader, whom he had the privilege of analyzing, was a man whose achievements were largely inspired by a woman. In many instances, the "woman in the case" was a modest, self-denying wife, of whom the public had heard but little or nothing. In a few instances, the source of inspiration has been traced to the "other woman." Perhaps such cases may not be entirely unknown to you.

Intemperance in sex habits is just as detrimental as intemperance in habits of drinking and eating. In this age in which we live, an age which began with the world war, intemperance in habits of sex is common. This orgy of indulgence may account for the shortage of great leaders. No man can avail himself of the forces of his creative imagination, while dissipating them. Man is the only creature on earth which violates Nature's purpose in this connection. Every other animal indulges its sex nature in moderation, and with purpose which harmonizes with the laws of nature. Every other animal responds to the call of sex only in "season." Man's inclination is to declare "open season."

Every intelligent person knows that stimulation in excess, through alcoholic drink and narcotics, is a form of intemperance which destroys the vital organs of the body, including the brain. Not every person knows, however, that over indulgence in sex expression may become a habit as destructive and as detrimental to creative effort as narcotics or liquor.

A sex-mad man is not essentially different than a dope-mad man! Both have lost control over their faculties of reason and will-power. Sexual over-indulgence may not only destroy reason and will-power, but it may also lead to either temporary, or permanent insanity. Many cases of hypochondria (imaginary illness) grow out of habits developed in ignorance of the true function of sex.

From these brief references to the subject, it may be readily seen that ignorance on the subject of sex transmutation, forces stupendous penalties upon the ignorant on the one hand, and withholds from them equally stupendous benefits, on the other.

Widespread ignorance on the subject of sex is due to the fact that the subject has been surrounded with mystery and beclouded by dark silence. The conspiracy of mystery and silence has had the same effect upon the minds of young people that the psychology of prohibition had. The result has been increased curiosity, and desire to acquire more knowledge on this "verboten" subject; and to the shame of all lawmakers, and most physicians—by training best qualified to educate youth on the subject—information has not been easily available. Seldom does an individual enter upon highly creative effort in any field of endeavor before the age of forty. The average man reaches the period of his greatest capacity to create between forty and sixty. These statements are based upon analysis of thousands of men and women who have been carefully observed. They should be encouraging to those who fail to arrive before the age of forty, and to those who become frightened at the approach of "old age," around the forty-year mark. The years between forty and fifty are, as a rule, the most fruitful. Man should approach this age, not with fear and trembling, but with hope and eager anticipation.

If you want evidence that most men do not begin to do their best work before the age of forty, study the records of the most successful men known to the American people, and you will find it. Henry Ford had not "hit his pace" of achievement until he had passed the age of forty. Andrew Carnegie was well past forty before he began to reap the reward of his efforts. James J. Hill was still running a telegraph key at the age of forty. His stupendous achievements took place after that age. Biographies of America industrialists and financiers are filled with evidence that the period from forty to sixty is the most productive age of man.

Between the ages of thirty and forty, man begins to learn (if he ever learns), the art of sex transmutation. This discovery is generally accidental, and more often than otherwise, the man who makes it is totally unconscious of his discovery. He may observe that his powers of achievement have increased around the age of thirty-five to forty, but in most cases, he is not familiar with the cause of this change; that Nature begins to harmonize the emotions of love and sex in the individual, between the ages of thirty and forty, so that he may draw upon these great forces, and apply them jointly as stimuli to action.

Sex, alone, is a mighty urge to action, but its forces are like a cyclone—they are often uncontrollable. When the emotion of love begins to mix itself with the emotion of sex, the result is calmness of purpose, poise, accuracy of judgment, and balance. What person, who has attained to the age of forty, is so unfortunate as to be unable to analyze these statements, and to corroborate them by his own experience?

When driven by his desire to please a woman, based solely upon the emotion of sex, a man may be, and usually is, capable of great achievement, but his actions may be disorganized distorted, and totally destructive. When driven by his desire to please a woman, based upon the motive of sex alone, a man may steal, cheat, and even commit murder. But when the emotion of LOVE is mixed with the emotion of sex, that same man will guide his actions with more sanity, balance, and reason.

Criminologists have discovered that the most hardened criminals can be reformed through the influence of a woman's *love*. There is no record of a criminal having been reformed solely through the sex influence. These facts are well known, but their cause is not. Reformation comes, if at all, through the *heart*, or the emotional side of man, *not* through his head, or reasoning side. Reformation means, "a change of heart." It does not mean a "change of head." A man may, because of reason, make certain changes in his personal conduct to avoid the consequences of undesirable effects, but GENUINE REFORMATION comes only through a change of heart—through a DESIRE to change.

Love, Romance, and Sex are all emotions capable of driving men to heights of super achievement. Love is the emotion which serves as a safety valve, and insures balance, poise, and constructive effort. When combined, these three emotions may lift one to an altitude of a genius. There are genii, however, who know but little of the emotion of love. Most of them may be found engaged in some form of action which is destructive, or at least, not based upon justice and fairness toward others. If good taste would permit, a dozen genii could be named in the field of industry and finance, who ride ruthlessly over the rights of their fellow men. They seem totally lacking in conscience. The reader can easily supply his own list of such men.

The emotions are states of mind. Nature has provided man with a "chemistry of the mind" which operates in a manner similar to the principles of chemistry of matter. It is a well known fact that, through the aid of chemistry of matter, a chemist may create a deadly poison by mixing certain elements, none of which are—in themselves—

harmful in the right proportions. The emotions may, likewise, be combined so as to create a deadly poison. The emotions of sex and jealousy, when mixed, may turn a person into an insane beast.

The presence of any one or more of the destructive emotions in the human mind, through the chemistry of the mind, sets up a poison which may destroy one's sense of justice and fairness. In extreme cases, the presence of any combination of these emotions in the mind may destroy one's reason.

The road to genius consists of the development, control, and use of sex, love, and romance. Briefly, the process may be stated as follows:

Encourage the presence of these emotions as the dominating thoughts in one's mind, and discourage the presence of all the destructive emotions. The mind is a creature of habit. It thrives upon the *dominating* thoughts fed it. Through the faculty of will-power, one may discourage the presence of any emotion, and encourage the presence of any other. Control of the mind, through the power of will, is not difficult. Control comes from persistence, and habit. The secret of control lies in understanding the process of transmutation. When any negative emotion presents itself in one's mind, it can be transmuted into a positive, or constructive emotion, by the simple procedure of changing one's thoughts.

THERE IS NO OTHER ROAD TO GENIUS THAN THROUGH VOLUNTARY SELF EFFORT! A man may attain to great heights of financial or business achievement, solely by the driving force of sex energy, but history is filled with evidence that he may, and usually does, carry with him certain traits of character which rob him of the ability to either hold, or enjoy his fortune. This is worthy of analysis, thought, and meditation, for it states a truth, the knowledge of which may be helpful to women as well as men. Ignorance of this has cost thousands of people their privilege of HAPPINESS, even though they possessed riches.

The emotions of love and sex leave their unmistakable marks upon the features. Moreover, these signs are so visible, that all who wish may read them. The man who is driven by the storm of passion, based upon sex desires alone, plainly advertises that fact to the entire world, by the expression of his eyes, and the lines of his face. The emotion of love, when mixed with the emotion of sex, softens, modifies, and beautifies the facial expression. No character analyst is needed to tell you this—you may observe it for yourself.

The emotion of love brings out, and develops, the artistic and the aesthetic nature of man. It leaves its impress upon one's very soul, even after the fire has been subdued by time and circumstance.

Memories of love never pass. They linger, guide, and influence long after the source of stimulation has faded. There is nothing new in this. Every person, who has been moved by GENUINE LOVE, knows that it leaves enduring traces upon the human heart. The effect of love endures, because love is spiritual in nature. The man who cannot be stimulated to great heights of achievement by love, is hopeless—he is dead, though he may seem to live.

Even the memories of love are sufficient to lift one to a higher plane of creative effort. The major force of love may spend itself and pass away, like a fire which has burned itself out, but it leaves behind indelible marks as evidence that it passed that way. Its departure often prepares the human heart for a still greater love.

Go back into your yesterdays, at times, and bathe your mind in the beautiful memories of past love. It will soften the influence of the present worries and annoyances. It will give you a source of escape from the unpleasant realities of life, and maybe—who knows?—your mind will yield to you, during this temporary retreat into the world of fantasy, ideas, or plans which may change the entire financial or spiritual status of your life.

If you believe yourself unfortunate, because you have "loved and lost," perish the thought. One who has loved truly, can never lose entirely. Love is whimsical and temperamental. Its nature is ephemeral, and transitory. It comes when it pleases, and goes away without warning. Accept and enjoy it while it remains, but spend no time worrying about its departure. Worry will never bring it back.

Dismiss, also, the thought that love never comes but once. Love may come and go, times without number, but there are no two love experiences which affect one in just the same way. There may be, and there usually is, one love experience which leaves a deeper imprint on the heart than all the others, but all love experiences are beneficial, except to the person who becomes resentful and cynical when love makes its departure.

There should be no disappointment over love, and there would be none if people understood the difference between the emotions of love and sex. The major difference is that love is spiritual, while sex is biological. No experience, which touches the human heart with a spiritual force, can possibly be harmful, except through ignorance, or jealousy.

Love is, without question, life's greatest experience. It brings one into communion with Infinite Intelligence. When mixed with the emotions of romance and sex, it may lead one far up the ladder of creative effort. The emotions of love, sex, and romance, are sides of the eternal triangle of achievement-building genius. Nature creates genii through no other force.

Love is an emotion with many sides, shades, and colors. The love which one feels for parents, or children is quite different than that which one feels for one's sweetheart. The one is mixed with the emotion of sex, while the other is not.

The love which one feels in true friendship is not the same as that felt for one's sweetheart, parents, or children, but it, too, is a form of love.

Then, there is the emotion of love for things inanimate, such as the love of Nature's handiwork. But the most intense and burning of all these various kinds of love, is that experienced in the blending of the emotions of love and sex. Marriages, not blessed with the eternal affinity of love, properly balanced and proportioned, with sex, cannot be happy ones—and seldom endure. Love, alone, will not bring happiness in marriage, nor will sex alone. When these two beautiful emotions are blended, marriage may bring about a state of mind, closest to the spiritual that one may ever know on this earthly plane.

When the emotion of romance is added to those of love and sex, the obstructions between the finite mind of man and Infinite Intelligence are removed. Then a genius has been born!

What a different story is this, than those usually associated with the emotion of sex. Here is an interpretation of the emotion which lifts it out of the commonplace, and makes of it potter's clay in the hands of God, from which He fashions all that is beautiful and inspiring. It is an interpretation which would, when properly understood, bring harmony out of the chaos which exists in too many marriages. The disharmonies often expressed in the form of nagging, may usually be traced to *lack of knowledge* on the subject of sex. Where love, romance and the proper understanding of the emotion and function of sex abide, there is no disharmony between married people.

Fortunate is the husband whose wife understands the true relationship between the emotions of love, sex, and romance. When motivated by this holy triumvirate, no form of labor is burdensome, because even the most lowly form of effort takes on the nature of a labor of love.

It is a very old saying that "a man's wife may either make him or break him," but the reason is not always understood. The "making" and "breaking" is the result of the wife's understanding, or lack of understanding of the emotions of love, sex, and romance.

Despite the fact that men are polygamous, by the very nature of their biological inheritance, it is true that no woman has as great an influence on a man as his wife, unless he is married to a woman totally unsuited to his nature. If a woman permits her husband to lose interest in her, and become more interested in other women, it is usually because of her ignorance, or indifference toward the subjects of sex, love, and romance. This statement presupposes, of course, that genuine love once existed between a man and his wife. The facts are equally applicable to a man who permits his wife's interest in him to die.

Married people often bicker over a multitude of trivialities. If these are analyzed accurately, the real cause of the trouble will often be found to be indifference, or ignorance on these subjects.

Man's greatest motivating force is his desire to please woman! The hunter who excelled during prehistoric days, before the dawn of civilization, did so, because of his desire to appear great in the eyes of woman. Man's nature has not changed in this respect. The "hunter" of today brings home no skins of wild animals, but he indicates his desire for her favor by supplying fine clothes, motor cars, and wealth. Man has the same desire to please woman that he had before the dawn of civilization. The only thing that has changed, is his method of pleasing. Men who accumulate large fortunes, and attain to great heights of power and fame, do so, mainly, to satisfy their *desire to please women.*

Take women out of their lives, and great wealth would be useless to most men. *It is this inherent desire of man to please woman, which gives woman the power to make or break a man.*

The woman who understands man's nature and tactfully caters to it, need have no fear of competition from other women. Men may be "giants" with indomitable will-power when dealing with other men, but they are easily managed by the women of their choice.

Most men will not admit that they are easily influenced by the women they prefer, because it is in the nature of the male to want to be recognized as the stronger of the species. Moreover, the intelligent woman recognizes this "manly trait" and very wisely makes no issue of it.

Some men know that they are being influenced by the women of their choice—their wives, sweethearts, mothers or sisters—but they tactfully refrain from rebelling against the influence because they are intelligent enough to know that NO MAN IS HAPPY OR COMPLETE WITHOUT THE MODIFYING INFLUENCE OF THE RIGHT WOMAN. The man who does not recognize this important truth deprives himself of the power which has done more to help men achieve success than all other forces combined.

CHAPTER 12
THE SUBCONSCIOUS MIND
THE CONNECTING LINK
The Eleventh Step toward Riches

THE SUBCONSCIOUS MIND consists of a field of consciousness, in which every impulse of thought that reaches the objective mind through any of the five senses, is classified and recorded, and from which thoughts may be recalled or withdrawn as letters may be taken from a filing cabinet.

It receives, and files, sense impressions or thoughts, regardless of their nature. You may VOLUNTARILY plant in your subconscious mind any plan, thought, or purpose which you desire to translate into its physical or monetary equivalent. The subconscious acts first on the dominating desires which have been mixed with emotional feeling, such as faith.

Consider this in connection with the instructions given in the chapter on DESIRE, for taking the six steps there outlined, and the instructions given in the chapter on the building and executive of plans, and you will understand the importance of the thought conveyed.

THE SUBCONSCIOUS MIND WORKS DAY AND NIGHT. Through a method of procedure, unknown to man, the subconscious mind draws upon the forces of Infinite Intelligence for the power with which it voluntarily transmutes one's desires into their physical equivalent, making use, always of the most practical media by which this end may be accomplished.

You cannot *entirely* control your subconscious mind, but you can voluntarily hand over to it any plan, desire, or purpose which you wish transformed into concrete form. Read, again, instructions for using the subconscious mind, in the chapter on auto-suggestion.

There is plenty of evidence to support the belief that the subconscious mind is the connecting link between the finite mind of man and Infinite Intelligence. It is the intermediary through which one may draw upon the forces of Infinite Intelligence at will. It, alone, contains the secret process by which mental impulses are modified and changed into their spiritual equivalent. It, alone, is the medium through which prayer may be transmitted to the source capable of answering prayer.

The possibilities of creative effort connected with the subconscious mind are stupendous and imponderable. They inspire one with awe.

I never approach the discussion of the subconscious mind without a feeling of littleness and inferiority due, perhaps, to the fact that man's entire stock of knowledge on this subject is so pitifully limited. The very fact that the subconscious mind is the medium of communication between the thinking mind of man and Infinite Intelligence is, of itself, a thought which almost paralyzes one's reason.

After you have accepted, as a reality, the existence of the subconscious mind, and understand its possibilities, as a medium for transmuting your

DESIRES into their physical or monetary equivalent, you will comprehend the full significance of the instructions given in the chapter on DESIRE. You will also understand why you have been repeatedly admonished to MAKE YOUR DESIRES CLEAR, AND TO REDUCE THEM TO WRITING. You will also understand the necessity of PERSISTENCE in carrying out instructions.

The thirteen principles are the stimuli with which you acquire the ability to reach, and to influence your subconscious mind. Do not become discouraged, if you cannot do this upon the first attempt. Remember that the subconscious mind may be voluntarily directed *only through habit*, under the directions given in the chapter on FAITH. You have not yet had time to master faith. Be patient. Be persistent.

A good many statements in the chapters on faith and auto-suggestion will be repeated here, for the benefit of YOUR subconscious mind. Remember, your subconscious mind functions voluntarily, *whether you make any effort to influence it or not*. This, naturally, suggests to you that thoughts of fear and poverty, and all negative thoughts serve as stimuli to your subconscious mind, *unless*, you master these impulses and give it more desirable food upon which it may feed.

The subconscious mind will not remain idle! If you fail to plant DESIRES in your subconscious mind, it will feed upon the thoughts which reach it as the *result of your neglect*. We have already explained that thought impulses, both negative and positive are reaching the subconscious mind continuously, from the four sources which were mentioned in the chapter on Sex Transmutation.

For the present, it is sufficient if you remember that you are living *daily*, in the midst of all manner of thought impulses which are reaching your subconscious mind, without your knowledge. Some of these impulses are negative, some are positive. You are now engaged in trying to help shut off the flow of negative impulses, and to aid in voluntarily influencing your subconscious mind, through positive impulses of DESIRE.

When you achieve this, you will possess the key which unlocks the door to your subconscious mind. Moreover, you will control that door so completely, that no undesirable thought may influence your subconscious mind.

Everything which man creates, BEGINS in the form of a thought impulse. Man can create nothing which he does not first conceive in THOUGHT. Through the aid of the imagination, thought impulses may be assembled into plans. The imagination, when under control, may be used for the creation of plans of purposes that lead to success in one's chosen occupation.

All thought impulses, intended for transmutation into their physical equivalent, voluntarily planted in the subconscious mind, must pass through the imagination, and be mixed with faith. The "mixing" of faith with a plan, or purpose, intended for submission to the subconscious mind, may be done ONLY through the imagination.

From these statements, you will readily observe that voluntary use of the subconscious mind calls for coordination and application of all the principles.

Ella Wheeler Wilcox gave evidence of her under-standing of the power of the subconscious mind when she wrote:

"You never can tell what a thought will do
    In bringing you hate or love—
For thoughts are things, and their airy wings
    Are swifter than carrier doves.
They follow the law of the universe—
    Each thing creates its kind,
And they speed O'er the track to bring you back
    Whatever went out from your mind."

Mrs. Wilcox understood the truth, that thoughts which go out from one's mind, also imbed them-selves deeply in one's subconscious mind, where they serve as a magnet, pattern, or blueprint by which the subconscious mind is influenced while translating them into their physical equivalent. Thoughts are truly things, for the reason that every material thing begins in the form of thought-energy.

The subconscious mind is more susceptible to influence by impulses of thought mixed with "feeling" or emotion, than by those originating solely in the reasoning portion of the mind. In fact, there is much evidence to support the theory, that ONLY emotionalized thoughts have any ACTION influ-ence upon the subconscious mind. It is a well known fact that emotion or feeling, rules the majority of people. If it is true that the subconscious mind responds more quickly to, and is influenced more readily by thought impulses which are well mixed with emotion, it is essential to become familiar with the more important of the emotions. There are seven major positive emotions, and seven major negative emotions. The negatives *voluntarily* inject themselves into the thought impulses, which insure passage into the subconscious mind. The positives must be injected, through the principle of auto-suggestion, into the thought impulses which an individual wishes to pass on to his subconscious mind. (Instructions have been given in the chapter on auto-suggestion.)

These emotions, or feeling impulses, may be likened to yeast in a loaf of bread, because they constitute the ACTION element, which transforms thought impulses from the passive to the active state. Thus may one understand why thought impulses, which have been well mixed with emotion, are acted upon more readily than thought impulses originating in "cold reason."

You are preparing yourself to influence and control the "inner audience" of your subconscious mind, in order to hand over to it the DESIRE for money, which you wish transmuted into its monetary equivalent. It is essential, therefore, that you understand the method of approach to this "inner audience." You must speak its language, or it will not heed your call. It understands best the language of emotion or feeling. Let us, therefore describe here the seven major positive emotions, and the seven major negative emotions, so that you may draw upon the positives, and avoid the negatives, when giving instructions to your subconscious mind.

THE SUBCONSCIOUS MIND

THE SEVEN MAJOR POSITIVE EMOTIONS

The emotion of DESIRE
The emotion of FAITH
The emotion of LOVE
The emotion of SEX
The emotion of ENTHUSIASM
The emotion of ROMANCE
The emotion of HOPE

There are other positive emotions, but these are the seven most powerful, and the ones most commonly used in creative effort. Master these seven emotions (they can be mastered only by USE), and the other positive emotions will be at your command when you need them. Remember, in this connection, that you are studying a book which is intended to help you develop a "money consciousness" by *filling your mind with positive emotions.* One does not become money conscious by filling one's mind with negative emotions.

THE SEVEN MAJOR NEGATIVE EMOTIONS
(To be avoided)

The emotion of FEAR
The emotion of JEALOUSY
The emotion of HATRED
The emotion of REVENGE
The emotion of GREED
The emotion of SUPERSTITION
The emotion of ANGER

Positive and negative emotions cannot occupy the mind at the same time. One or the other must dominate. It is your responsibility to make sure that positive emotions constitute the dominating influence of your mind. Here the law of HABIT will come to your aid. *Form the habit* of applying and using the positive emotions! Eventually, they will dominate your mind so completely, that the negatives *cannot enter it.*

Only by following these instructions literally, and continuously, can you gain control over your subconscious mind. The presence of a single negative in your conscious mind is sufficient to *destroy* all chances of constructive aid from your subconscious mind.

If you are an observing person, you must have noticed that most people resort to prayer ONLY after everything else has FAILED! Or else they pray by a ritual of meaningless words. And, because it is a fact that most people who pray, do so ONLY AFTER EVERYTHING ELSE HAS FAILED, they go to prayer with their minds filled with FEAR and DOUBT, *which are the emotions the subconscious mind acts upon,* and passes on to Infinite Intelligence. Likewise, that is the emotion which Infinite Intelligence receives, and ACTS UPON.

If you pray for a thing, but have fear as you pray, that you may not receive it, or that your prayer will not be acted upon by Infinite Intelligence, your prayer *will have been in vain.*

Prayer does, sometimes, result in the realization of that for which one prays. If you have ever had the experience of receiving that for which you prayed, go back in your memory, and recall your actual STATE OF MIND, while you were praying, and you will know, for sure, that the theory here described is more than a theory.

The time will come when the schools and educational institutions of the country will teach the "science of prayer." Moreover, then prayer may be, and will be reduced to a science. When that time comes, (it will come as soon as mankind is ready for it, and demands it), no one will approach the Universal Mind in a state of fear, for the very good reason that there will be no such emotion as fear. Ignorance, superstition, and false teaching will have disappeared, and man will have attained his true status as a child of Infinite Intelligence. A few have already attained this blessing.

If you believe this prophesy is far-fetched, take a look at the human race in retrospect. Less than a hundred years ago, men believed the lightning to be evidence of the wrath of God, and feared it. Now, thanks to the power of FAITH, men have harnessed the lightning and made it turn the wheels of industry. Much less than a hundred years ago, men believed the space between the planets to be nothing but a great void, a stretch of dead nothingness. Now, thanks to this same power of FAITH, men know that far from being either dead or a void, the space between the planets is very much alive, that it is the highest form of vibration known, excepting, perhaps, the vibration of THOUGHT. Moreover, men know that this living, pulsating, vibratory energy which permeates every atom of matter, and fills every niche of space, connects every human brain with every other human brain.

What reason have men to believe that this same

energy does not connect every human brain with Infinite Intelligence?

There are no toll-gates between the finite mind of man and Infinite Intelligence. The communication costs nothing except Patience, Faith, Persistence, Understanding, and a SINCERE DESIRE to communicate. Moreover, the approach can be made only by the individual himself. Paid prayers are worthless. Infinite Intelligence does no business by proxy. You either go direct, or you do not communicate.

You may buy prayer books and repeat them until the day of your doom, without avail. Thoughts which you wish to communicate to Infinite Intelligence, must undergo transformation, such as can be given only through your own subconscious mind.

The method by which you may communicate with Infinite Intelligence is very similar to that through which the vibration of sound is communicated by radio. If you understand the working principle of radio, you of course, know that sound cannot be communicated through the ether until it has been "stepped up," or changed into a rate of vibration which the human ear cannot detect. The radio sending station picks up the sound of the human voice, and "scrambles," or modifies it by stepping up the vibration millions of times. Only in this way, can the vibration of sound be communicated through the ether. After this transformation has taken place, the ether "picks up" the energy (which originally was in the form of vibrations of sound), carries that energy to radio receiving stations, and these receiving sets "step" that energy back down to its original rate of vibration so it is recognized as sound.

The subconscious mind is the intermediary, which translates one's prayers into terms which Infinite Intelligence can recognize, presents the message, and brings back the answer in the form of a definite plan or idea for procuring the object of the prayer. Understand this principle, and you will know why mere words read from a prayer book cannot, and will never serve as an agency of communication between the mind of man and Infinite Intelligence.

Before your prayer will reach Infinite Intelligence (a statement of the author's theory only), it probably is transformed from its original thought vibration into terms of spiritual vibration. Faith is the only known agency which will give your thoughts a spiritual nature. FAITH and FEAR make poor bedfellows. *Where one is found, the other cannot exist.*

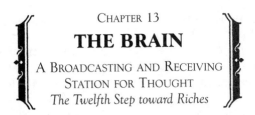

CHAPTER 13

THE BRAIN

A BROADCASTING AND RECEIVING
STATION FOR THOUGHT
The Twelfth Step toward Riches

MORE than twenty years ago, the author, working in conjunction with the late Dr. Alexander Graham Bell, and Dr. Elmer R. Gates, observed that every human brain is both a broadcasting and receiving station for the vibration of thought.

Through the medium of the ether, in a fashion similar to that employed by the radio broadcasting principle, every human brain is capable of picking up vibrations of thought which are being released by other brains.

In connection with the statement in the preceding paragraph, compare, and consider the description of the Creative Imagination, as outlined in the chapter on Imagination. The Creative Imagination is the "receiving set" of the brain, which receives thoughts, released by the brains of others. It is the agency of communication between one's conscious, or reasoning mind, and the four sources from which one may receive thought stimuli.

When stimulated, or "stepped up" to a high rate of vibration, the mind becomes more receptive to the vibration of thought which reaches it through the ether from outside sources. This "stepping up" process takes place through the positive emotions, or the negative emotions. Through the emotions, the vibrations of thought may be increased.

Vibrations of an exceedingly high rate are the only vibrations picked up and carried, by the ether, from one brain to another. Thought is energy travelling at an exceedingly high rate of vibration. Thought, which has been modified or "stepped up" by any of the major emotions, vibrates at a much higher rate than ordinary thought, and it is this type of thought which passes from one brain to another, through the broadcasting machinery of the human brain.

The emotion of sex stands at the head of the list of human emotions, as far as intensity and driving force are concerned. The brain which has been stimulated by the emotion of sex, vibrates at a much more rapid rate than it does when that emotion is quiescent or absent.

The result of sex transmutation, is the increase of the rate of vibration of thoughts to such a pitch that the Creative Imagination becomes highly receptive to ideas, which it picks up from the ether. On the other hand, when the brain is vibrating at a rapid rate, it not only attracts thoughts and ideas released by other brains through the medium of the ether, but it gives to one's own thoughts that "feeling" which is essential before those thoughts will be picked up and acted upon by one's subconscious mind.

Thus, you will see that the broadcasting principle is the factor through which you mix feeling, or emotion with your thoughts and pass them on to your subconscious mind.

The subconscious mind is the "sending station" of the brain, through which vibrations of thought are broadcast. The Creative Imagination is the "receiving set," through which the vibrations of thought are picked up from the ether.

Along with the important factors of the subconscious mind, and the faculty of the Creative Imagination, which constitute the sending and receiving sets of your mental broadcasting machinery, consider now the principle of auto-suggestion, which is the medium by which you may put into operation your "broadcasting" station.

Through the instructions described in the chapter on auto-suggestion, you were definitely informed of the method by which DESIRE may be transmuted into its monetary equivalent.

Operation of your mental "broadcasting" station is a comparatively simple procedure. You have but three principles to bear in mind, and to apply, when you wish to use your broadcasting station—the SUBCON-SCIOUS MIND, CREATIVE IMAGINATION, and AUTO-SUGGESTION. The stimuli through which you put these three principles into action have been described—the procedure begins with DESIRE.

THE GREATEST FORCES ARE "INTANGIBLE"

The depression brought the world to the very border-line of understanding of the forces which are intangible and unseen. Through the ages which have passed, man has depended too much upon his physical senses, and has limited his knowledge to physical things, which he could see, touch, weigh, and measure.

We are now entering the most marvelous of all

ages—an age which will teach us something of the intangible forces of the world about us. Perhaps we shall learn, as we pass through this age, that the "other self" is more powerful than the physical self we see when we look into a mirror.

Sometimes men speak lightly of the intangibles— the things which they cannot perceive through any of their five senses, and when we hear them, it should remind us that *all of us are controlled by forces which are unseen and intangible.*

The whole of mankind has not the power to cope with, nor to control the intangible force wrapped up in the rolling waves of the oceans. Man has not the capacity to understand the intangible force of gravity, which keeps this little earth suspended in mid-air, and keeps man from falling from it, much less the power to control that force. Man is entirely subservient to the intangible force which comes with a thunder storm, and he is just as helpless in the presence of the intangible force of electricity—nay, he does not even know what electricity is, where it comes from, or what is its purpose!

Nor is this by any means the end of man's ignorance in connection with things unseen and intangible. He does not understand the intangible force (and intelligence) wrapped up in the soil of the earth—*the force which provides him with every morsel of food he eats, every article of clothing he wears, every dollar he carries in his pockets.*

THE DRAMATIC STORY OF THE BRAIN

Last, but not least, man, with all of his boasted culture and education, understands little or nothing of the intangible force (the greatest of all the intangibles) of *thought*. He knows but little concerning the physical brain, and its vast network of intricate machinery through which the power of thought is translated into its material equivalent, but he is now entering an age which shall yield enlightenment on the subject. Already men of science have begun to turn their attention to the study of this stupendous thing called a brain, and, while they are still in the kindergarten stage of their studies, they have uncovered enough knowledge to know that the central switchboard of the human brain, the number of lines which connect the brain cells one with another, equal the figure one, followed by fifteen million ciphers.

"The figure is so stupendous," said Dr. C. Judson Herrick, of the University of Chicago, "that astronomical figures dealing with hundreds of millions of light years, become insignificant by comparison. ....It has been determined that there are from 10,000,000,000 to 14,000,000,000 nerve cells in the human cerebral cortex, and we know that these are arranged in definite patterns. These arrangements are not haphazard. They are orderly. Recently developed methods of electro-physiology draw off action currents from very precisely located cells, or fibers with micro-electrodes, amplify them with radio tubes, and record potential differences to a millionth of a volt."

It is inconceivable that such a network of intricate machinery should be in existence for the sole purpose of carrying on the physical functions incidental to growth and maintenance of the physical body. Is it not likely that the same system, which gives billions of brain cells the media for communication one with another, provides, also the means of communication with other intangible forces?

After this book had been written, just before the manuscript went to the publisher, there appeared in the New York Times, an editorial showing that at least one great University, and one intelligent investigator in the field of mental phenomena, are carrying on an organized research through which conclusions have been reached that parallel many of those described in this and the following chapter. The editorial briefly analyzed the work carried on by Dr. Rhine, and his associates at Duke University, viz:—

"WHAT IS 'TELEPATHY'?

"A month ago we cited on this page some of the remarkable results achieved by Professor Rhine and his associates in Duke University from more than a hundred thousand tests to determine the existence of 'telepathy' and 'clairvoyance.' These results were summarized in the first two articles in Harpers Magazine. In the second which has now appeared, the author, E.H. Wright, attempts to summarize what has been learned, or what it seems reasonable to infer, regarding the exact nature of these 'extra-sensory' modes of perception.

"The actual existence of telepathy and clairvoyance now seems to some scientists enormously probable as the result of Rhine's experiments. Various percipients were asked to name as many cards in a special pack as they could without looking at them and without other sensory access to them. About a score of men and women were discovered who could regularly name so many of the cards correctly that 'there was not one chance in many a million million of their having done their feats by luck or accident.'

"But how did they do them? These powers, assuming that they exist, do not seem to be sensory. There is no known organ for them. The experiments worked just as well at distances of several hundred miles as they did in the same room. These facts also dispose, in Mr. Wright's opinion, of the attempt to explain telepathy or clairvoyance through any physical theory of radiation. All known forms of radiant energy decline inversely as the square of the distance traversed. Telepathy and clairvoyance do not. But they do vary through physical causes as our mental powers do. Contrary to widespread opinion, they do not improve when the percipient is asleep or half-asleep, but, on the contrary, when he is most wide-awake and alert. Rhine discovered that a narcotic will invariably lower a percipient's score, while a stimulant will always send it higher. The most reliable performer apparently cannot make a good score unless he tries to do his best.

"One conclusion that Wright draws with some confidence is that telepathy and clairvoyance are really one and the same gift. That is, the faculty that 'sees' a card face down on a table seems to be exactly the same one that 'reads' a thought residing only in another mind. There are several grounds for believing this. So far, for example, the two gifts have been found in every person who enjoys either of them. In every one so far the two have been of equal vigor, almost exactly. Screens, walls, distances, have no effect at all on either. Wright advances from this conclusion to express what he puts forward as no more than the mere 'hunch' that other extra-sensory experiences, prophetic dreams, premonitions of disaster, and the like, may also prove to be part of the same faculty. The reader is not asked to accept any of these conclusions unless he finds it necessary, but the evidence that Rhine has piled up must remain impressive."

In view of Dr. Rhine's announcement in connection with the conditions under which the mind responds to what he terms "extra-sensory" modes of perception, I now feel privileged to add to his testimony by stating that my associates and I have discovered what we believe to be the ideal conditions under which the mind can be stimulated so that the sixth sense described in the next chapter, can be made to function in a practical way.

The conditions to which I refer consist of a close working alliance between myself and two members of my staff. Through experimentation and practice, we have discovered how to stimulate our minds (by applying the principle used in connection with the "Invisible Counselors" described in the next chapter) so that we can, by a process of blending our three minds into one, find the solution to a great variety of personal problems which are submitted by my clients.

The procedure is very simple. We sit down at a conference table, clearly state the nature of the problem we have under consideration, then begin discussing it. Each contributes whatever thoughts that may occur. The strange thing about this method of mind stimulation is that it places each participant in communication with unknown sources of knowledge definitely outside his own experience.

If you understand the principle described in the chapter on the Master Mind, you of course recognize the round-table procedure here described as being a practical application of the Master Mind.

This method of mind stimulation, through harmonious discussion of definite subjects, between three people, illustrates the simplest and most practical use of the Master Mind.

By adopting and following a similar plan any student of this philosophy may come into possession of the famous Carnegie formula briefly described in the introduction. If it means nothing to you at this time, mark this page and read it again after you have finished the last chapter.

THE "depression" was
a blessing in disguise.
It reduced the whole world
to a new starting point
that gives every one a
new opportunity.

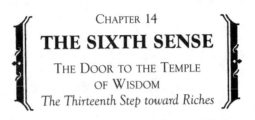

CHAPTER 14
THE SIXTH SENSE
THE DOOR TO THE TEMPLE
OF WISDOM
The Thirteenth Step toward Riches

THE "thirteenth" principle is known as the SIXTH SENSE, through which Infinite Intelligence may, and will communicate voluntarily, without any effort from, or demands by, the individual.

This principle is the apex of the philosophy. It can be assimilated, understood, and applied ONLY by first mastering the other twelve principles.

The SIXTH SENSE is that portion of the subconscious mind which has been referred to as the Creative Imagination. It has also been referred to as the "receiving set" through which ideas, plans, and thoughts flash into the mind. The "flashes" are sometimes called "hunches" or "inspirations."

The sixth sense defies description! It cannot be described to a person who has not mastered the other principles of this philosophy, because such a person has no knowledge, and no experience with which the sixth sense may be compared. Understanding of the sixth sense comes only by meditation through mind development *from within.* The sixth sense probably is the medium of contact between the finite mind of man and Infinite Intelligence, and for this reason, *it is a mixture of both the mental and the spiritual.* It is believed to be the point at which the mind of man contacts the Universal Mind.

After you have mastered the principles described in this book, you will be prepared to accept as truth a statement which may, otherwise, be incredible to you, namely:

Through the aid of the sixth sense, you will be warned of impending dangers in time to avoid them, and notified of opportunities in time to embrace them.

There comes to your aid, and to do your bidding, with the development of the sixth sense, a "guardian angel" who will open to you at all times the door to the Temple of Wisdom.

Whether or not this is a statement of truth, you will never know, except by following the instructions described in the pages of this book, or some similar method of procedure.

The author is not a believer in, nor an advocate of "miracles," for the reason that he has enough knowledge of Nature to understand that Nature *never deviates from her established laws.* Some of her laws are so incomprehensible that they produce what appears to be "miracles." The sixth sense comes as near to being a miracle as anything I have ever experienced, and it appears so, only because I do not understand the method by which this principle is operated.

This much the author does know—that there is a power, or a First Cause, or an Intelligence, which permeates every atom of matter, and embraces every unit of energy perceptible to man—that this Infinite Intelligence converts acorns into oak trees, causes water to flow down hill in response to the law of gravity, follows night with day, and winter with summer, each maintaining its proper place and relationship to the other. This Intelligence may, through the principles of this philosophy, be induced to aid in transmuting DESIRES into concrete, or material form. The author has this knowledge, because he has experimented with it—and has EXPERIENCED IT.

Step by step, through the preceding chapters, you have been led to this, the last principle. If you have mastered each of the preceding principles, you are now prepared to accept, *without being skeptical*, the stupendous claims made here. If you have not mastered the other principles, you must do so before you may determine, definitely, whether or not the claims made in this chapter are fact or fiction.

While I was passing through the age of "hero-worship" I found myself trying to imitate those whom I most admired. Moreover, I discovered that the element of FAITH, with which I endeavored to imitate my idols, gave me great capacity to do so quite successfully.

I have never entirely divested myself of this habit of hero-worship, although I have passed the age commonly given over to such. My experience has taught me that the next best thing to being truly great, is to emulate the great, by feeling and action, as nearly as possible.

Long before I had ever written a line for publication, or endeavored to deliver a speech in public, I followed the habit of reshaping my own character, by trying to imitate the nine men whose lives and life-works had been most impressive to me. These nine men were, Emerson, Paine, Edison, Darwin,

Lincoln, Burbank, Napoleon, Ford, and Carnegie. Every night, over a long period of years, I held an imaginary Council meeting with this group whom I called my "Invisible Counselors."

The procedure was this. Just before going to sleep at night, I would shut my eyes, and see, in my imagination, this group of men seated with me around my Council Table. Here I had not only an opportunity to sit among those whom I considered to be great, but I actually dominated the group, by serving as the Chairman.

I had a very DEFINITE PURPOSE in indulging my imagination through these nightly meetings. My purpose was to rebuild my own character so it would represent a composite of the characters of my imaginary counselors. Realizing, as I did, early in life, that I had to overcome the handicap of birth in an environment of ignorance and superstition, I deliberately assigned myself the task of voluntary rebirth through the method here described.

BUILDING CHARACTER THROUGH AUTO-SUGGESTION

Being an earnest student of psychology, I knew, of course, that all men have become what they are, because of their DOMINATING THOUGHTS AND DESIRES. I knew that every deeply seated desire has the effect of causing one to seek outward expression through which that desire may be transmuted into reality. I knew that self-suggestion is a powerful factor in building character, that it is, in fact, the sole principle through which character is builded.

With this knowledge of the principles of mind

operation, I was fairly well armed with the equipment needed in rebuilding my character. In these imaginary Council meetings I called on my Cabinet members for the knowledge I wished each to contribute, addressing myself to each member in audible words, as follows:—

"Mr. Emerson, I desire to acquire from you the marvelous understanding of Nature which distinguished your life. I ask that you make an impress upon my subconscious mind, of whatever qualities you possessed, which enabled you to understand and adapt yourself to the laws of Nature. I ask that you assist me in reaching and drawing upon whatever sources of knowledge are available to this end.

"Mr. Burbank, I request that you pass on to me the knowledge which enabled you to so harmonize the laws of Nature that you caused the cactus to shed its thorns, and become an edible food. Give me access to the knowledge which enabled you to make two blades of grass grow where but one grew before, and helped you to blend the coloring of the flowers with more splendor and harmony, for you, alone, have successfully guilded the lily.

"Napoleon, I desire to acquire from you, by emulation, the marvelous ability you possessed to inspire men, and to arouse them to greater and more determined spirit of action. Also to acquire the spirit of enduring FAITH, which enabled you to turn defeat into victory, and to surmount staggering obstacles. Emperor of Fate, King of Chance, Man of Destiny, I salute you!

"Mr. Paine, I desire to acquire from you the freedom of thought and the courage and clarity with which to express convictions, which so distinguished you!

"Mr. Darwin, I wish to acquire from you the marvelous patience, and ability to study cause and effect, without bias or prejudice, so exemplified by you in the field of natural science.

"Mr. Lincoln, I desire to build into my own character the keen sense of justice, the untiring spirit of patience, the sense of humor, the human understanding, and the tolerance, which were your distinguishing characteristics.

"Mr. Carnegie, I am already indebted to you for my choice of a life-work, which has brought me great happiness and peace of mind. I wish to acquire a thorough understanding of the principles of *organized effort*, which you used so effectively in the building of a great industrial enterprise.

"Mr. Ford, you have been among the most helpful of the men who have supplied much of the material essential to my work. I wish to acquire your spirit of persistence, the determination, poise, and self-confidence which have enabled you to master poverty, organize, unify, and simplify human effort, so I may help others to follow in your footsteps.

"Mr. Edison, I have seated you nearest to me, at my right, because of the personal cooperation you have given me, during my research into the causes of success and failure. I wish to acquire from you the marvelous spirit of FAITH, with which you have uncovered so many of Nature's secrets, the spirit of unremitting toil with which you have so often wrested victory from defeat."

My method of addressing the members of the

imaginary Cabinet would vary, according to the traits of character in which I was, for the moment, most interested in acquiring. I studied the records of their lives with painstaking care. After some months of this nightly procedure, I was astounded by the discovery that these imaginary figures became, apparently *real*.

Each of these nine men developed individual characteristics, which surprised me. For example, Lincoln developed the habit of always being late, then walking around in solemn parade. When he came, he walked very slowly, with his hands clasped behind him, and once in a while, he would stop as he passed, and rest his hand, momentarily, upon my shoulder. He always wore an expression of seriousness upon his face. Rarely did I see him smile. The cares of a sundered nation made him grave.

That was not true of the others. Burbank and Paine often indulged in witty repartee which seemed, at times, to shock the other members of the cabinet. One night Paine suggested that I prepare a lecture on "The Age of Reason," and deliver it from the pulpit of a church which I formerly attended. Many around the table laughed heartily at the suggestion. Not Napoleon! He drew his mouth down at the corners and groaned so loudly that all turned and looked at him with amazement. To him the church was but a pawn of the State, not to be reformed, but to be used, as a convenient inciter to mass activity by the people.

On one occasion Burbank was late. When he came, he was excited with enthusiasm, and explained that he had been late, because of an experiment he was making, through which he hoped to be able to grow apples on any sort of tree. Paine chided him by reminding him that it was an apple which started all the trouble between man and woman. Darwin chuckled heartily as he suggested that Paine should watch out for little serpents, when he went into the forest to gather apples, as they had the habit of growing into big snakes. Emerson observed—"No serpents, no apples," and Napoleon remarked, "No apples, no state!"

Lincoln developed the habit of always being the last one to leave the table after each meeting. On one occasion, he leaned across the end of the table, his arms folded, and remained in that position for many minutes. I made no attempt to disturb him. Finally, he lifted his head slowly, got up and walked to the door, then turned around, came back, and laid his hand on my shoulder and said, "My boy, you will need much courage if you remain steadfast in carrying out your purpose in life. But remember, when difficulties overtake you, the common people have common sense. Adversity will develop it."

One evening Edison arrived ahead of all the others. He walked over and seated himself at my left, where Emerson was accustomed to sit, and said, "You are destined to witness the discovery of the secret of life. When the time comes, you will observe that life consists of great swarms of energy, or entities, each as intelligent as human beings *think* themselves to be. These units of life group together like hives of bees, and remain together until they disintegrate, *through lack of harmony.*

These units have differences of opinion, the same as human beings, and often fight among themselves. These meetings which you are conducting will be very helpful to you. They will bring to your rescue some of the same units of life which served the members of your Cabinet, during their lives. These units are eternal. THEY NEVER DIE! Your own thoughts and DESIRES serve as the magnet which attracts units of life, from the great ocean of life out there. Only the friendly units are attracted—the ones which harmonize with the nature of your DESIRES."

The other members of the Cabinet began to enter the room. Edison got up, and slowly walked around to his own seat. Edison was still living when this happened. It impressed me so greatly that I went to see him, and told him about the experience. He smiled broadly, and said, "Your dream was more a reality than you may imagine it to have been." He added no further explanation to his statement.

These meetings became so realistic that I became fearful of their consequences, and discontinued them for several months. The experiences were so uncanny, I was afraid if I continued them I would lose sight of the fact that the meetings were purely *experiences of my imagination.*

Some six months after I had discontinued the practice I was awakened one night, or thought I was, when I saw Lincoln standing at my bedside. He said, "The world will soon need your services. It is about to undergo a period of chaos which will cause men and women to lose faith, and become panic stricken. Go ahead with your work and complete your philosophy. That is your mission in life. If you neglect it, for any cause whatsoever, you will be reduced to a primal state, and be compelled to retrace the cycles through which you have passed during thousands of years."

I was unable to tell, the following morning, whether I had dreamed this, or had actually been awake, and I have never since found out which it was, but I do know that the dream, if it were a dream, was so vivid in my mind the next day that I resumed my meetings the following night.

At our next meeting, the members of my Cabinet all filed into the room together, and stool at their accustomed places at the Council Table, while Lincoln raised a glass and said, "Gentlemen, let us drink a toast to a friend who has returned to the fold."

After that, I began to add new members to my Cabinet, until now it consists of more than fifty, among them Christ, St. Paul, Galileo, Copernicus, Aristotle, Plato, Socrates, Homer, Voltaire, Bruno, Spinoza, Drummond, Kant, Schopenhauer, Newton, Confucius, Elbert Hubbard, Brann, Ingersol, Wilson, and William James.

This is the first time that I have had the courage to mention this. Heretofore, I have remained quiet on the subject, because I knew, from my own attitude in connection with such matters, that I would be misunderstood if I described my unusual experience. I have been emboldened now to reduce my experience to the printed page, because I am now less concerned about what "they say" than I was in the years that have passed. One of the blessings of maturity is that it sometimes brings one greater courage to be truthful, regardless of what those who do not understand, may think or say.

Lest I be misunderstood, I wish here to state most emphatically, that I still regard my Cabinet meetings as being purely imaginary, but I feel entitled to suggest that, while the members of my Cabinet may be purely fictional, and the meetings existent only in my own imagination, they have led me into glorious paths of adventure, rekindled an appreciation of true greatness, encouraged creative endeavor, and emboldened the expression of honest thought.

Somewhere in the cell-structure of the brain, is located an organ which receives vibrations of thought ordinarily called "hunches." So far, science has not discovered where this organ of the sixth sense is located, but this is not important. The fact remains that human beings do receive accurate knowledge, through sources other than the physical senses. Such knowledge, generally, is received when the mind is under the influence of extraordinary stimulation. Any emergency which arouses the emotions, and causes the heart to beat more rapidly than normal may, and generally does, bring the sixth sense into action. Anyone who has experienced a near accident while driving, knows that on such occasions, the sixth sense often comes to one's rescue, and aids, by split seconds, in avoiding the accident.

These facts are mentioned preliminary to a statement of fact which I shall now make, namely, that during my meetings with the "Invisible Counselors" I find my mind most receptive to ideas, thoughts, and knowledge which reach me through the sixth sense. I can truthfully say that I owe entirely to my "Invisible Counselors" full credit for such ideas, facts, or knowledge as I received through "inspiration."

On scores of occasions, when I have faced emergencies, some of them so grave that my life was in jeopardy, I have been miraculously guided past these difficulties through the influence of my "Invisible Counselors."

My original purpose in conducting Council meeting with imaginary beings, was solely that of impressing my own subconscious mind, through the principle of auto-suggestion, with certain characteristics which I desired to acquire. In more recent years, my experimentation has taken on an entirely different trend. I now go to my imaginary counselors with every difficult problem which confronts me and my clients. The results are often astonishing, although I do not depend entirely on this form of Counsel.

You, of course, have recognized that this chapter covers a subject with which a majority of people are not familiar. The Sixth Sense is a subject that will be of great interest and benefit to the person whose aim is to accumulate vast wealth, but it need not claim the attention of those whose desires are more modest.

Henry Ford, undoubtedly understands and makes practical use of the sixth sense. His vast business and financial operations make it necessary for him to understand and use this principle. The late Thomas A. Edison understood and used the sixth sense in connection with the development of inventions, especially those involving basic patents, in connection with which he had no human experience and no accumulated knowledge to guide him, as was the case while he was working on the talking machine, and the moving picture machine.

Nearly all great leaders, such as Napoleon, Bismark, Joan of Arc, Christ, Buddha, Confucius, and Mohammed, understood, and probably made use of the sixth sense almost continuously. The major portion of their greatness consisted of their knowledge of this principle.

The sixth sense is not something that one can take off and put on at will. Ability to use this great power comes slowly, through application of the other principles outlined in this book. Seldom does any individual come into workable knowledge of the sixth sense before the age of forty. More often the knowledge is not available until one is well past fifty, and this, for the reason that the spiritual forces, with which the sixth sense is so closely related, do not mature and become usable except through years of meditation, self-examination, and serious thought.

No matter who you are, or what may have been your purpose in reading this book, you can profit by it without understanding the principle described in this chapter. This is especially true if your major purpose is that of accumulation of money or other material things.

The chapter on the sixth sense was included, because the book is designed for the purpose of presenting a complete philosophy by which individuals may unerringly guide themselves in attaining whatever they ask of life. The starting point of all achievement is DESIRE. The finishing point is that brand of KNOWLEDGE which leads to under-standing—understanding of self, understanding of others, understanding of the laws of Nature, recognition and understanding of HAPPINESS.

This sort of understanding comes in its fullness only through familiarity with, and use of the principle of the sixth sense, hence that principle had to be included as a part of this philosophy, for the benefit of those who demand more than money.

Having read the chapter, you must have observed that while reading it, you were lifted to a high level of mental stimulation. Splendid! Come back to this again a month from now, read it once more, and observe that your mind will soar to a still higher level of stimulation. Repeat this experience from time to time, giving no concern as to how much or how little you learn at the time, and eventually you will find yourself in possession of a power that will enable you to throw off discouragement, master fear, overcome procrastination, and draw freely upon your imagination. Then you will have felt the touch of that unknown "something" which has been the moving spirit of every truly great thinker, leader, artist, musician, writer, statesman. Then you will be in position to transmute your DESIRES into their physical or financial counterpart as easily as you may lie down and quit at the first sign of opposition.

FAITH VS. FEAR!

Previous chapters have described how to develop FAITH, through Auto-suggestion, Desire and the Subconscious. The next chapter presents detailed instructions for the mastery of FEAR.

Here will be found a full description of the six fears which are the cause of all discouragement, timidity, procrastination, indifference, indecision, and the lack of ambition, self-reliance, initiative, self-control, and enthusiasm.

Search yourself carefully as you study these six enemies, as they may exist only in your subconscious mind, where their presence will be hard to detect.

Remember, too, as you analyze the "Six Ghosts of Fear," that they are nothing but ghosts because they exist only in one's mind.

Remember, also, that ghosts—creations of uncontrolled imagination—have caused most of the damage people have done to their own minds, therefore, ghosts can be as dangerous as if they lived and walked on the earth in physical bodies.

The Ghost of the Fear of Poverty, which seized the minds of millions of people in 1929, was so real that it caused the worst business depression this country has ever known. Moreover, this particular ghost still frightens some of us out of our wits.

CHAPTER 15

HOW TO OUTWIT THE SIX GHOSTS OF FEAR

Take Inventory of Yourself, As You Read This Closing Chapter, and Find out How Many of the "Ghosts" Are Standing in Your Way

BEFORE you can put any portion of this philosophy into successful use, your mind must be prepared to receive it. The preparation is not difficult. It begins with study, analysis, and understanding of three enemies which you shall have to clear out. These are INDECISION, DOUBT, and FEAR!

The Sixth Sense will never function while these three negatives, or any of them remain in your mind. The members of this unholy trio are closely related; where one is found, the other two are close at hand.

INDECISION is the seedling of FEAR! Remember this, as you read. Indecision crystallizes into DOUBT, the two blend and become FEAR! The "blending" process often is slow. This is one reason why these three enemies are so dangerous. They germinate and grow *without their presence being observed.*

The remainder of this chapter describes an end which must be attained before the philosophy, as a whole, can be put into practical use. It also analyzes a condition which has, but lately, reduced huge numbers of people to poverty, and it states a

truth which must be understood by all who accumulate riches, whether measured in terms of money or
a state of mind of far greater value than money.

The purpose of this chapter is to turn the spotlight
of attention upon the cause and the cure of the six
basic fears. Before we can master an enemy, we must
know its name, its habits, and its place of abode. As
you read, analyze yourself carefully, and determine
which, if any, of the six common fears have attached
themselves to you.

Do not be deceived by the habits of these subtle
enemies. Sometimes they remain hidden in the
subconscious mind, where they are difficult to locate,
and still more difficult to eliminate.

THE SIX BASIC FEARS

There are six basic fears, with some combination of
which every human suffers at one time or another.
Most people are fortunate if they do not suffer from
the entire six. Named in the order of their most
common appearance, they are:—

The fear of POVERTY }
The fear of CRITICISM } at the bottom of
The fear of ILL HEALTH } most of one's worries

The fear of LOSS OF LOVE OF SOMEONE
The fear of OLD AGE
The fear of DEATH

All other fears are of minor importance, they can
be grouped under these six headings.

The prevalence of these fears, as a curse to the
world, runs in cycles. For almost six years, while
the depression was on, we floundered in the cycle

of FEAR OF POVERTY. During the world-war, we were in the cycle of FEAR OF DEATH. Just following the war, we were in the cycle of FEAR OF ILL HEALTH, as evidenced by the epidemic of disease which spread itself all over the world.

Fears are nothing more than states of mind. One's state of mind is subject to control and direction. Physicians, as everyone knows, are less subject to attack by disease than ordinary laymen, for the reason that physicians DO NOT FEAR DISEASE. Physicians, without fear or hesitation, have been known to physically contact hundreds of people, daily, who were suffering from such contagious diseases as small-pox, without becoming infected. Their immunity against the disease consisted, largely, if not solely, in their absolute lack of FEAR.

Man can create nothing which he does not first conceive in the form of an impulse of thought. Following the statement, comes another of still greater importance, namely, MAN'S THOUGHT IMPULSES BEGIN IMMEDIATELY TO TRANSLATE THEMSELVES INTO THEIR PHYSICAL EQUIVA-LENT, WHETHER THOSE THOUGHTS ARE VOLUNTARY OR INVOLUNTARY. Thought impulses which are picked up through the ether, by mere chance (thoughts which have been released by other minds) may determine one's financial, business, professional, or social destiny just as surely as do the thought impulses which one creates by intent and design.

We are here laying the foundation for the presentation of a fact of great importance to the person who does not understand why some people appear to be "lucky" while others of equal or greater ability, training, experience, and brain capacity, seem destined to ride with misfortune. This fact may be explained by the statement that *every human being has the ability to completely control his own mind,* and with this control, obviously, every person may open his mind to the tramp thought impulses which are being released by other brains, or close the doors tightly and admit only thought impulses of his own choice.

Nature has endowed man with absolute control over but one thing, and that is THOUGHT. This fact, coupled with the additional fact that everything which man creates, begins in the form of a thought, leads one very near to the principle by which FEAR may be mastered.

If it is true that ALL THOUGHT HAS A TENDENCY TO CLOTHE ITSELF IN ITS PHYSICAL EQUIVALENT (and this is true, beyond any reasonable room for doubt), it is equally true that thought impulses of fear and poverty cannot be translated into terms of courage and financial gain.

The people of America began to think of poverty, following the Wall Street crash of 1929. Slowly, but surely that mass thought was crystallized into its physical equivalent, which was known as a "depression." This had to happen, it is in conformity with the laws of Nature.

The Fear of Poverty

There can be no compromise between POVERTY

and RICHES! The two roads that lead to poverty and riches travel in opposite directions. If you want riches, you must refuse to accept any circumstance that leads toward poverty. (The word "riches" is here used in its broadest sense, meaning financial, spiritual, mental and material estates). The starting point of the path that leads to riches is DESIRE. In chapter one, you received full instructions for the proper use of DESIRE. In this chapter, on FEAR, you have complete instructions for preparing your mind to make practical use of DESIRE.

Here, then, is the place to give yourself a challenge which will definitely determine how much of this philosophy you have absorbed. Here is the point at which you can turn prophet and foretell, accurately, what the future holds in store for you. If, after reading this chapter, you are willing to accept poverty, you may as well make up your mind to receive poverty. This is one decision you cannot avoid.

If you demand riches, determine what form, and how much will be required to satisfy you. You know the road that leads to riches. You have been given a road map which, if followed, will keep you on that road. If you neglect to make the start, or stop before you arrive, no one will be to blame, but YOU. This responsibility is yours. No alibi will save you from accepting the responsibility if you now fail or refuse to demand riches of Life, because the acceptance calls for but one thing—incidentally, the only thing you can control—and that is a STATE OF MIND. A state of mind is something that one assumes. It cannot be purchased, it must be created.

Fear of poverty is a state of mind, nothing else! But it is sufficient to destroy one's chances of achievement in any undertaking, a truth which became painfully evident during the depression.

This fear paralyzes the faculty of reason, destroys the faculty of imagination, kills off self-reliance, undermines enthusiasm, discourages initiative, leads to uncertainty of purpose, encourages procrastination, wipes out enthusiasm and makes self-control an impossibility. It take the charm from one's personality, destroys the possibility of accurate thinking, diverts concentration of effort, it masters persistence, turns the will-power into nothingness, destroys ambition, beclouds the memory and invites failure in every conceivable form; it kills love and assassinates the finer emotions of the heart, discourages friendship and invites disaster in a hundred forms, leads to sleeplessness, misery and unhappiness—and all this despite the obvious truth that we live in a world of over-abundance of everything the heart could desire, with nothing standing between us and our desires, excepting lack of a definite purpose.

The Fear of Poverty is, without doubt, the most destructive of the six basic fears. It has been placed at the head of the list, because it is the most difficult to master. Considerable courage is required to state the truth about the origin of this fear, and still greater courage to accept the truth after it has been stated. The fear of poverty grew out of man's inherited tendency to PREY UPON HIS FELLOW-

MAN ECONOMICALLY. Nearly all animals lower than man are motivated by instinct, but their capacity to "think" is limited, therefore, they prey upon one another physically. Man, with his superior sense of intuition, with the capacity to think and to reason, does not eat his fellowman bodily, he gets more satisfaction out of "eating" him FINANCIALLY. Man is so avaricious that every conceivable law has been passed to safeguard him from his fellowman.

Of all the ages of the world, of which we know anything, the age in which we live seems to be one that is outstanding because of man's money-madness. A man is considered less than the dust of the earth, unless he can display a fat bank account; but if he has money—NEVER MIND HOW HE ACQUIRED IT—he is a "king" or a "big shot"; he is above the law, he rules in politics, he dominates in business, and the whole world about him bows in respect when he passes.

Nothing brings man so much suffering and humility as POVERTY! Only those who have experienced poverty understand the full meaning of this.

It is no wonder that man *fears* poverty. Through a long line of inherited experiences man has learned, for sure, that some men cannot be trusted, where matters of money and earthly possessions are concerned. This is a rather stinging indictment, the worst part of it being that it is TRUE.

The majority of marriages are motivated by the wealth possessed by one, or both of the contracting parties. It is no wonder, therefore, that the divorce courts are busy.

So eager is man to possess wealth that he will acquire it in whatever manner he can—through legal methods if possible—through other methods if necessary or expedient.

Self-analysis may disclose weaknesses which one does not like to acknowledge. This form of examination is essential to all who demand of Life more than mediocrity and poverty. Remember, as you check yourself point by point, that you are both the court and the jury, the prosecuting attorney and the attorney for the defense, and that you are the plaintiff and the defendant, also, that you are on trial. Face the facts squarely. Ask yourself definite questions and demand direct replies. When the examination is over, you will know more about yourself. If you do not feel that you can be an impartial judge in this self-examination, call upon someone who knows you well to serve as judge while you cross-examine yourself. You are after the truth. *Get it, no matter at what cost even though it may temporarily embarrass you!*

The majority of people, if asked what they fear most, would reply, "I fear nothing." The reply would be inaccurate, because few people realize that they are bound, handicapped, whipped spiritually and physically through some form of fear. So subtle and deeply seated is the emotion of fear that one may go through life burdened with it, never recognizing its presence. Only a courageous analysis will disclose the presence of this universal enemy. When you begin such an analysis, search deeply into your character. Here is a list of the symptoms for which you should look:

Symptoms of the Fear of Poverty

INDIFFERENCE. Commonly expressed through lack of ambition; willingness to tolerate poverty; acceptance of whatever compensation life may offer without protest; mental and physical laziness; lack of initiative, imagination, enthusiasm and self-control.

INDECISION. The habit of permitting others to do one's thinking. Staying "on the fence."

DOUBT. Generally expressed through alibis and excuses designed to cover up, explain away, or apologize for one's failures, sometimes expressed in the form of envy of those who are successful, or by criticizing them.

WORRY. Usually expressed by finding fault with others, a tendency to spend beyond one's income, neglect of personal appearance, scowling and frowning; intemperance in the use of alcoholic drink, sometimes through the use of narcotics; nervousness, lack of poise, self-consciousness and lack of self-reliance.

OVER-CAUTION. The habit of looking for the negative side of every circumstance, thinking and talking of possible failure instead of concentrating upon the means of succeeding. Knowing all the roads to disaster, but never searching for the plans to avoid failure. Waiting for "the right time" to begin putting ideas and plans into action, until the waiting becomes a permanent habit. Remembering those who have failed, and forgetting those who have succeeded. Seeing the hole in the doughnut, but overlooking the doughnut. Pessimism, leading to indigestion, poor elimination, auto-intoxication, bad breath and bad disposition.

PROCRASTINATION. The habit of putting off until tomorrow that which should have been done last year. Spending enough time in creating alibis and excuses to have done the job. This symptom is closely related to over-caution, doubt and worry. Refusal to accept responsibility when it can be avoided. Willingness to compromise rather than put up a stiff fight. Compromising with difficulties instead of harnessing and using them as stepping stones to advancement. Bargaining with Life for a penny, instead of demanding prosperity, opulence, riches, contentment and happiness. Planning what to do IF AND WHEN OVER-TAKEN BY FAILURE, INSTEAD OF BURNING ALL BRIDGES AND MAKING RETREAT IMPOSSIBLE. Weakness of, and often total lack of self-confidence, definiteness of purpose, self-control, initiative, enthusiasm, ambition, thrift, and sound reasoning ability. EXPECTING POVERTY INSTEAD OF DEMANDING RICHES. Association with those who accept poverty instead of seeking the company of those who demand and receive riches.

Money Talks!

Some will ask, "why did you write a book about money? Why measure riches in dollars, alone?" Some will believe, and rightly so, that there are other forms of riches more desirable than money. Yes, there are riches which cannot be measured in terms of dollars, but there are millions of people who will say, "Give me all the money I need, and I will find everything else I want."

The major reason why I wrote this book on how to get money is the fact that the world has but lately passed through an experience that left millions of men and women paralyzed with the FEAR OF POVERTY. What this sort of fear does to one was well described by Westbrook Pegler, in the New York World-Telegram, viz:

"Money is only clam shells or metal discs or scraps of paper, and there are treasures of the heart and soul which money cannot buy, but most people, being broke, are unable to keep this in mind and sustain their spirits. When a man is down and out and on the street, unable to get any job at all, something happens to his spirit which can be observed in the droop of his shoulders, the set of his hat, his walk and his gaze. He cannot escape a feeling of inferiority among people with regular employment, even though he knows they are definitely not his equals in character, intelligence or ability.

"These people—even his friends—feel, on the other hand, a sense of superiority and regard him, perhaps unconsciously, as a casualty. He may borrow for a time, but not enough to carry on his accustomed way, and he cannot continue to borrow very long. But borrowing in itself, when a man is borrowing merely to live, is a depressing experience, and the money lacks the power of earned money to revive his spirits. Of course, none of this applies

THINK AND GROW RICH

to bums or habitual ne'er-do-wells, but only to men of normal ambitions and self-respect.

"WOMEN CONCEAL DESPAIR.

"Women in the same predicament must be different. We somehow do not think of women at all in considering the down-and-outers. They are scarce in the breadlines, they rarely are seen begging on the streets, and they are not recognizable in crowds by the same plain signs which identify busted men. Of course, I do not mean the shuffling hags of the city streets who are the opposite number of the confirmed male bums. I mean reasonably young, decent and intelligent women. There must be many of them, but their despair is not apparent. Maybe they kill themselves.

"When a man is down and out he has time on his hands for brooding. He may travel miles to see a man about a job and discover that the job is filled or that it is one of those jobs with no base pay but only a commission on the sale of some useless knick-knack which nobody would buy, except out of pity. Turning that down, he finds himself back on the street with nowhere to go but just anywhere. So he walks and walks. He gazes into store windows at luxuries which are not for him, and feels inferior and gives way to people who stop to look with an active interest. He wanders into the railroad station or puts himself down in the library to ease his legs and soak up a little heat, but that isn't looking for a job, so he gets going again. He may not know it, but his aimlessness would give him away even if the very lines of his figure did not. He may be well dressed in the clothes left over from the days when he had a steady job, but the clothes cannot disguise the droop.

"MONEY MAKES DIFFERENCE.

"He sees thousands of other people, bookkeepers or clerks or chemists or wagon hands, busy at their work and envies them from the bottom of his soul. They have their independence, their self-respect and manhood, and he simply cannot convince himself that he is a good man, too, though he argue it out and arrive at a favorable verdict hour after hour.

"It is just money which makes this difference in him. With a little money he would be himself again.

"Some employers take the most shocking advantage of people who are down and out. The agencies hang out little colored cards offering miserable wages to busted men—$12 a week, $15 a week. An $18 a week job is a plum, and anyone with $25 a week to offer does not hang the job in front of an agency on a colored card. I have a want ad clipped from a local paper demanding a clerk, a good, clean penman, to take telephone orders for a sandwich shop from 11 A.M. to 2 P.M. for $8 a month—not $8 a week but $8 a month. The ad says also, 'State religion.' Can you imagine the brutal effrontery of anyone who demands a good, clean penman for 11 cents an hour inquiring into the victim's religion? But that is what busted people are offered."

THE FEAR OF CRITICISM

Just how man originally came by this fear, no

THINK AND GROW RICH

one can state definitely, but one thing is certain—he has it in a highly developed form. Some believe that this fear made its appearance about the time that politics became a "profession." Others believe it can be traced to the age when women first began to concern themselves with "styles" in wearing apparel.

This author, being neither a humorist nor a prophet, is inclined to attribute the basic fear of criticism to that part of man's inherited nature which prompts him not only to take away his fellowman's goods and wares, but to justify his action by CRITICISM of his fellowman's character. It is a well known fact that a thief will criticize the man from whom he steals—that politicians seek office, not by displaying their own virtues and qualifications, but by attempting to besmirch their opponents.

The fear of criticism takes on many forms, the majority of which are petty and trivial. Baldheaded men, for example, are bald for no other reason than their fear of criticism. Heads become bald because of the tight fitting bands of hats which cut off the circulation from the roots of the hair. Men wear hats, not because they actually need them, but mainly because "everyone is doing it." The individual falls into line and does likewise, lest some other individual CRITICISE him. Women seldom have bald heads, or even thin hair, because they wear hats which fit their heads loosely, the only purpose of the hats being adornment.

But, it must not be supposed that women are free from the fear of criticism. If any woman claims to be superior to man with reference to this fear, ask her to walk down the street wearing a hat of the vintage of 1890.

The astute manufacturers of clothing have not been slow to capitalize this basic fear of criticism, with which all mankind has been cursed. Every season the styles in many articles of wearing apparel change. Who establishes the style? Certainly not the purchaser of clothing, but the manufacturer. Why does he change the styles so often? The answer is obvious. He changes the styles so he can sell more clothes.

For the same reason the manufacturers of automobiles (with a few rare and very sensible exceptions) change styles of models every season. No man wants to drive an automobile which is not of the latest style, although the older model may actually be the better car.

We have been describing the manner in which people behave under the influence of fear of criticism as applied to the small and petty things of life. Let us now examine human behavior when this fear affects people in connection with the more important events of human relationship. Take for example practically any person who has reached the age of "mental maturity" (from 35 to 40 years of age, as a general average), and if you could read the secret thoughts of his mind, you would find a very decided disbelief in most of the fables taught by the majority of the dogmatists and theologians a few decades back.

Not often, however, will you find a person who has the courage to openly state his belief on this subject. Most people will, if pressed far enough, tell a lie rather than admit that they do not believe the stories associated with that form of religion which held people in bondage prior to the age of scientific discovery and education.

Why does the average person, even in this day of enlightenment, shy away from denying his belief in the fables which were the basis of most of the religions a few decades ago? The answer is, "because of the fear of criticism." Men and women have been burned at the stake for daring to express disbelief in ghosts. It is no wonder we have inherited a consciousness which makes us fear criticism. The time was, and not so far in the past, when criticism carried severe punishments—it still does in some countries.

The fear of criticism robs man of his initiative, destroys his power of imagination, limits his individuality, takes away his self-reliance, and does him damage in a hundred other ways. Parents often do their children irreparable injury by criticizing them. The mother of one of my boyhood chums used to punish him with a switch almost daily, always completing the job with the statement, "You'll land in the penitentiary before you are twenty." He was sent to a Reformatory at the age of seventeen.

Criticism is the one form of service, of which everyone has too much. Everyone has a stock of it which is handed out, gratis, whether called for or not. One's nearest relatives often are the worst offenders. It should be recognized as a crime (in reality it is a crime of the worst nature), for any parent to build inferiority complexes in the mind of a child, through unnecessary criticism. Employers who understand human nature, get the best there is in men, not by criticism, but by constructive suggestion. Parents may accomplish the same results with their children. Criticism will plant FEAR in the human heart, or resentment, but it will not build love or affection.

Symptoms of the Fear of Criticism

This fear is almost as universal as the fear of poverty, and its effects are just as fatal to personal achievement, mainly because this fear destroys initiative, and discourages the use of imagination. The major symptoms of the fear are:

SELF-CONSCIOUSNESS. Generally expressed through nervousness, timidity in conversation and in meeting strangers, awkward movement of the hands and limbs, shifting of the eyes.

LACK OF POISE. Expressed through lack of voice control, nervousness in the presence of others, poor posture of body, poor memory.

PERSONALITY. Lacking in firmness of decision, personal charm, and ability to express opinions definitely. The habit of side-stepping issues instead of meeting them squarely. Agreeing with others without careful examination of their opinions.

INFERIORITY COMPLEX. The habit of expressing self-approval by word of mouth and by actions, as a means of covering up a feeling of inferiority. Using "big words" to impress others, (often without knowing the real meaning of the words). Imitating others in dress, speech and manners. Boasting of imaginary achievements. This sometimes gives a surface appearance of a feeling of superiority.

EXTRAVAGANCE. The habit of trying to "keep up with the Joneses," spending beyond one's income.

LACK OF INITIATIVE. Failure to embrace opportunities for self-advancement, fear to express opinions, lack of confidence in one's own ideas, giving evasive answers to questions asked by superiors, hesitancy of manner and speech, deceit in both words and deeds.

LACK OF AMBITION. Mental and physical laziness, lack of self-assertion, slowness in reaching decisions, easily influenced by others, the habit of criticizing others behind their backs and flattering them to their faces, the habit of accepting defeat without protest, quitting an undertaking when opposed by others, suspicious of other people without cause, lacking in tactfulness of manner and speech, unwillingness to accept the blame for mistakes.

THE FEAR OF ILL HEALTH

This fear may be traced to both physical and social heredity. It is closely associated, as to its origin, with the causes of fear of Old Age and the fear of Death, because it leads one closely to the border of "terrible worlds" of which man knows not, but concerning which he has been taught some discomforting stories. The opinion is somewhat general, also, that certain unethical people engaged in the business of "selling health" have had not a little to do with keeping alive the fear of ill health. In the main, man fears ill health because of the terrible pictures which have been planted in his mind of what may happen if death should overtake him. He also fears it because of the economic toll which it may claim.

A reputable physician estimated that 75% of all people who visit physicians for professional service are suffering with hypochondria (imaginary illness). It has been shown most convincingly that the fear of disease, even where there is not the slightest cause for fear, often produces the physical symptoms of the disease feared.

Powerful and mighty is the human mind! It builds or it destroys.

Playing upon this common weakness of fear of ill health, dispensers of patent medicines have reaped fortunes. This form of imposition upon credulous humanity became so prevalent some twenty years ago that Colliers' Weekly Magazine conducted a bitter campaign against some of the worst offenders in the patent medicine business.

During the "flu" epidemic which broke out during the world war, the mayor of New York City took drastic steps to check the damage which people were doing themselves through their inherent fear of ill health. He called in the newspaper men and said to them, "Gentlemen, I feel it necessary to ask you not to publish any *scare headlines* concerning the 'flu' epidemic. Unless you cooperate with me, we will have a situation which we cannot control." The newspapers quit publishing stories about the "flu," and within one month the epidemic had been successfully checked.

Through a series of experiments conducted some years ago, it was proved that people may be made ill by suggestion. We conducted this experiment by causing three acquaintances to visit the "victims," each of whom asked the question, "What ails you? You look terribly ill." The first questioner usually provoked a grin, and a nonchalant "Oh, nothing, I'm alright," from the victim. The second questioner usually was answered with the statement, "I don't know exactly, but I do feel badly." The third questioner was usually met with the frank admission that the victim was actually feeling ill.

Try this on an acquaintance if you doubt that it will make him uncomfortable, but do not carry the experiment too far. There is a certain religious sect whose members take vengeance upon their enemies by the "hexing" method. They call it "placing a spell" on the victim.

There is overwhelming evidence that disease sometimes begins in the form of negative thought impulse. Such an impulse may be passed from one mind to another, by suggestion, or created by an individual in his own mind.

A man who was blessed with more wisdom than this incident might indicate, once said "When anyone asks me how I feel, I always want to answer by knocking him down."

Doctors send patients into new climates for their

health, because a change of "mental attitude" is necessary. The seed of fear of ill health lives in every
human mind. Worry, fear, discouragement, disappointment in love and business affairs, cause this
seed to germinate and grow. The recent business
depression kept the doctors on the run, because every
form of negative thinking may cause ill health.

Disappointments in business and in love stand at
the head of the list of causes of fear of ill health. A
young man suffered a disappointment in love which
sent him to a hospital. For months he hovered
between life and death. A specialist in suggestive ther-
apeutics was called in. The specialist changed nurses,
placing him in charge of a very *charming young woman*
who began (by pre-arrangement with the doctor) to
make love to him the first day of her arrival on the
job. Within three weeks the patient was discharged
from the hospital, still suffering, but with an entirely
different malady. HE WAS IN LOVE AGAIN. The
remedy was a hoax, but the patient and the nurse
were later married. Both are in good health at the
time of this writing.

Symptoms of the Fear of Ill Health

The symptoms of this almost universal fear are:

AUTO-SUGGESTION. The habit of negative use of
self-suggestion by looking for, and expecting to
find the symptoms of all kinds of disease.
"Enjoying" imaginary illness and speaking of
it as being real. The habit of trying all "fads"
and "isms" recommended by others as having
therapeutic value. Talking to others of opera-

tions, accidents and other forms of illness. Experimenting with diets, physical exercises, reducing systems, without professional guidance. Trying home remedies, patent medicines and "quack" remedies.

HYPOCHONDRIA. The habit of talking of illness, concentrating the mind upon disease, and expecting its appearance until a nervous break occurs. Nothing that comes in bottles can cure this condition. It is brought on by negative thinking and nothing but positive thought can affect a cure. Hypochondria, (a medical term for imaginary disease) is said to do as much damage on occasion, as the disease one fears might do. Most so-called cases of "nerves" come from imaginary illness.

EXERCISE. Fear of ill health often interferes with proper physical exercise, and results in over-weight, by causing one to avoid outdoor life.

SUSCEPTIBILITY. Fear of ill health breaks down Nature's body resistance, and creates a favorable condition for any form of disease one may contact.

The fear of ill health often is related to the fear of Poverty, especially in the case of the hypochondriac, who constantly worries about the possibility of having to pay doctor's bills, hospital bills, etc. This type of person spends much time preparing for sickness, talking about death, saving money for cemetery lots, and burial expenses, etc.

SELF-CODDLING. The habit of making a bid for sympathy, using imaginary illness as the lure. (People often resort to this trick to avoid work). The habit of feigning illness to cover plain laziness, or to serve as an alibi for lack of ambition.

INTEMPERANCE. The habit of using alcohol or narcotics to destroy pains such as headaches, neuralgia, etc., instead of eliminating the cause.

The habit of reading about illness and worrying over the possibility of being stricken by it. The habit of reading patent medicine advertisements.

THE FEAR OF LOSS OF LOVE

The original source of this inherent fear needs but little description, because it obviously grew out of man's polygamous habit of stealing his fellowman's mate, and his habit of taking liberties with her whenever he could.

Jealousy, and other similar forms of dementia praecox grow out of man's inherited fear of the loss of love of someone. This fear is the most painful of all the six basic fears. It probably plays more havoc with the body and mind than any of the other basic fears, as it often leads to permanent insanity.

The fear of the loss of love probably dates back to the stone age, when men stole women by brute force. They continue to steal females, but their technique has changed. Instead of force, they now use persuasion, the promise of pretty clothes, motor

THINK AND GROW RICH

cars, and other "bait" much more effective than physical force. Man's habits are the same as they were at the dawn of civilization, but he expresses them differently.

Careful analysis has shown that women are more susceptible to this fear than men. This fact is easily explained. Women have learned, from experience, that men are polygamous by nature, that they are not to be trusted in the hands of rivals.

Symptoms of the Fear of Loss of Love

The distinguishing symptoms of this fear are:—

JEALOUSY. The habit of being suspicious of friends and loved ones without any reasonable evidence of sufficient grounds. (Jealousy is a form of dementia praecox which sometimes becomes violent without the slightest cause). The habit of accusing wife or husband of infidelity without grounds. General suspicion of everyone, absolute faith in no one.

FAULT FINDING. The habit of finding fault with friends, relatives, business associates and loved ones upon the slightest provocation, or without any cause whatsoever.

GAMBLING. The habit of gambling, stealing, cheating, and otherwise taking hazardous chances to provide money for loved ones, with the belief that love can be bought. The habit of spending beyond one's means, or incurring debts, to provide gifts for loved ones, with the object of making a favorable showing. Insomnia, nervousness, lack of persistence, weakness of will, lack of self-control, lack of self-reliance, bad temper.

THE FEAR OF OLD AGE

In the main, this fear grows out of two sources. First, the thought that old age may bring with it POVERTY. Secondly, and by far the most common source of origin, from false and cruel teachings of the past which have been too well mixed with "fire and brimstone," and other bogies cunningly designed to enslave man through fear.

In the basic fear of old age, man has two very sound reasons for his apprehension—one growing out of his distrust of his fellowman, who may seize whatever worldly goods he may possess, and the other arising from the terrible pictures of the world beyond, which were planted in his mind, through social heredity before he came into full possession of his mind.

The possibility of ill health, which is more common as people grow older, is also a contributing cause of this common fear of old age. Erotocism also enters into the cause of the fear of old age, as no man cherishes the thought of diminishing sex attraction.

The most common cause of fear of old age is associated with the possibility of poverty. "Poor-house" is not a pretty word. It throws a chill into the mind of every person who faces the possibility of having to spend his declining years on a poor farm.

Another contributing cause of the fear of old age, is the possibility of loss of freedom and independence, as old age may bring with it the loss of both physical and economic freedom.

SYMPTOMS OF THE FEAR OF OLD AGE

The commonest symptoms of this fear are:

The tendency to slow down and develop an inferiority complex at the age of mental maturity, around the age of forty, falsely believing one's self to be "slipping" because of age. (The truth is that man's most useful years, mentally and spiritually, are those between forty and sixty).

The habit of speaking apologetically of one's self as "being old" merely because one has reached the age of forty, or fifty, instead of reversing the rule and expressing gratitude for having reached the age of wisdom and understanding.

The habit of killing off initiative, imagination, and self-reliance by falsely believing one's self too old to exercise these qualities. The habit of the man or woman of forty dressing with the aim of trying to appear much younger, and affecting mannerisms of youth; thereby inspiring ridicule by both friends and strangers.

THE FEAR OF DEATH

To some this is the cruelest of all the basic fears. The reason is obvious. The terrible pangs of fear associated with the thought of death, in the majority of cases, may be charged directly to religious fanaticism. So-called "heathen" are less afraid of death than the more "civilized." For hundreds of millions of years man has been asking the still unanswered questions, "whence" and "whither." Where did I come from, and where am I going?

During the darker ages of the past, the more cunning and crafty were not slow to offer the answer to these questions, FOR A PRICE. Witness, now, the major source of origin of the FEAR OF DEATH.

"Come into my tent, embrace my faith, accept my dogmas, and I will give you a ticket that will admit you straightaway into heaven when you die," cries a leader of sectarianism. "Remain out of my tent," says the same leader, "and may the devil take you and burn you throughout eternity."

ETERNITY is a long time. FIRE is a terrible thing. The thought of eternal punishment, with fire, not only causes man to fear death, it often causes him to lose his reason. It destroys interest in life and makes happiness impossible.

During my research, I reviewed a book entitled "A Catalogue of the Gods," in which were listed the 30,000 gods which man has worshiped. Think of it! Thirty thousand of them, represented by everything from a crawfish to a man. It is little wonder that men have become frightened at the approach of death.

While the religious leader may not be able to provide safe conduct into heaven, nor, by lack of such provision, allow the unfortunate to descend into hell, the possibility of the latter seems so terrible

THINK AND GROW RICH

that the very thought of it lays hold of the imagination in such a realistic way that it paralyzes reason, and sets up the fear of death.

In truth, NO MAN KNOWS, and no man has ever known, what heaven or hell is like, nor does any man know if either place actually exists. This very lack of positive knowledge opens the door of the human mind to the charlatan so he may enter and control that mind with his stock of legerdemain and various brands of pious fraud and trickery.

The fear of DEATH is not as common now as it was during the age when there were no great colleges and universities. Men of science have turned the spotlight of truth upon the world, and this truth is rapidly freeing men and women from this terrible fear of DEATH. The young men and young women who attend the colleges and universities are not easily impressed by "fire" and "brimstone." Through the aid of biology, astronomy, geology, and other related sciences, the fears of the dark ages which gripped the minds of men and destroyed their reason have been dispelled.

Insane asylums are filled with men and women who have gone mad, because of the FEAR OF DEATH.

This fear is useless. Death will come, no matter what anyone may think about it. Accept it as a necessity, and pass the thought out of your mind. It must be a necessity, or it would not come to all. Perhaps it is not as bad as it has been pictured.

The entire world is made up of only two things, ENERGY and MATTER. In elementary physics we learn that neither matter nor energy (the only two realities known to man) can be created nor destroyed. Both matter and energy can be transformed, but neither can be destroyed.

Life is energy, if it is anything. If neither energy nor matter can be destroyed, of course life cannot be destroyed. Life, like other forms of energy, may be passed through various processes of transition, or change, but it cannot be destroyed. Death is mere transition.

If death is not mere change, or transition, then nothing comes after death except a long, eternal, peaceful sleep, and sleep is nothing to be feared. Thus you may wipe out, forever, the fear of Death.

Symptoms of the Fear of Death

The general symptoms of this fear are:—

The habit of THINKING about dying instead of making the most of LIFE, due, generally, to lack of purpose, or lack of a suitable occupation. This fear is more prevalent among the aged, but sometimes the more youthful are victims of it. The greatest of all remedies for the fear of death is a BURNING DESIRE FOR ACHIEVEMENT, backed by useful service to others. A busy person seldom has time to think about dying. He finds life too thrilling to worry about death. Sometimes the fear of death is closely associated with the Fear of Poverty, where one's death would leave loved ones poverty-stricken. In other cases, the fear of death is caused by illness and the consequent breaking down of physical body resistance. The commonest causes of the fear

THINK AND GROW RICH

of death are: ill-health, poverty, lack of appropriate occupation, disappointment over love,
insanity, religious fanaticism.

OLD MAN WORRY

Worry is a state of mind based upon fear. It works
slowly, but persistently. It is insidious and subtle.
Step by step it "digs itself in" until it paralyzes one's
reasoning faculty, destroys self-confidence and initiative. Worry is a form of sustained fear caused by
indecision therefore it is a state of mind which can
be controlled.

An unsettled mind is helpless. Indecision makes an
unsettled mind. Most individuals lack the will-power
to reach decisions promptly, and to stand by them
after they have been made, even during normal business conditions. During periods of economic unrest
(such as the world recently experienced), the individual is handicapped, not alone by his inherent
nature to be slow at reaching decisions, but he is
influenced by the indecision of others around him
who have created a state of "mass indecision."

During the depression the whole atmosphere, all
over the world, was filled with "Fearenza" and
"Worryitis," the two mental disease germs which
began to spread themselves after the Wall Street
frenzy in 1929. There is only one known antidote for
these germs; it is the habit of prompt and firm DECI-
SION. Moreover, it is an antidote which every
individual must apply for himself.

We do not worry over conditions, once we have
reached a decision to follow a definite line of action.

I once interviewed a man who was to be electrocuted two hours later. The condemned man was the calmest of some eight men who were in the death-cell with him. His calmness prompted me to ask him how it felt to know that he was going into eternity in a short while. With a smile of confidence on his face, he said, "It feels fine. Just think, brother, my troubles will soon be over. I have had nothing but trouble all my life. It has been a hardship to get food and clothing. Soon I will not need these things. I have felt fine ever since I learned FOR CERTAIN that I must die. I made up my mind then, to accept my fate in good spirit."

As he spoke he devoured a dinner of proportions sufficient for three men, eating every mouthful of the food brought to him, and apparently enjoying it as much as if no disaster awaited him. DECISION gave this man resignation to his fate! Decision can also prevent one's acceptance of undesired circumstances.

The six basic fears become translated into a state of worry, through indecision. Relieve yourself, forever of the fear of death, by reaching a decision to accept death as an inescapable event. Whip the fear of poverty by reaching a decision to get along with whatever wealth you can accumulate WITHOUT WORRY. Put your foot upon the neck of the fear of criticism by reaching a decision NOT TO WORRY about what other people think, do, or say. Eliminate the fear of old age by reaching a decision to accept it, not as a handicap, but as a great blessing which carries with it wisdom, self-control, and understanding not known to youth.

Acquit yourself of the fear of ill health by the decision to forget symptoms. Master the fear of loss of love
by reaching a decision to get along without love, if
that is necessary.

Kill the habit of worry, in all its forms, by reaching
a general, blanket decision that nothing which life
has to offer is worth the price of worry. With this
decision will come poise, peace of mind, and calmness of thought which will bring happiness.

A man whose mind is filled with fear not only
destroys his own chances of intelligent action, but,
he transmits these destructive vibrations to the
minds of all who come into contact with him, and
destroys, also their chances.

Even a dog or a horse knows when its master lack
courage; moreover, a dog or a horse will pick up the
vibrations of fear thrown off by its master, and
behave accordingly. Lower down the line of intelligence in the animal kingdom, one finds this same
capacity to pick up the vibrations of fear. A honey-
bee immediately senses fear in the mind of a
person—for reasons unknown, a bee will sting the
person whose mind is releasing vibrations of fear,
much more readily than it will molest the person
whose mind registers no fear.

The vibrations of fear pass from one mind to
another just as quickly and as surely as the sound of
the human voice passes from the broadcasting station
to the receiving set of a radio—and BY THE SELF-
SAME MEDIUM.

Mental telepathy is a reality. Thoughts pass from
one mind to another, voluntarily, whether or not
this fact is recognized by either the person re-

leasing the thoughts, or the persons who pick up those thoughts.

The person who gives expression, by word of mouth, to negative or destructive thoughts is practically certain to experience the results of those words in the form of a destructive "kick-back." The release of destructive thought impulses, alone, without the aid of words, produces also a "kick-back" in more ways than one. First of all, and perhaps most important to be remembered, the person who releases thoughts of a destructive nature, must suffer damage through the breaking down of the faculty of creative imagination. Secondly, the presence in the mind of any destructive emotion develops a negative personality which repels people, and often converts them into antagonists. The third source of damage to the person who entertains or releases negative thoughts, lies in this significant fact—these thought-impulses are not only damaging to others, but they IMBED THEMSELVES IN THE SUBCONSCIOUS MIND OF THE PERSON RELEASING THEM, and there become a part of his character.

One is never through with a thought, merely by releasing it. When a thought is released, it spreads in every direction, through the medium of the ether, but it also plants itself *permanently* in the subconscious mind of *the person releasing it.*

Your business in life is, presumably to achieve success. To be successful, you must find peace of mind, acquire the material needs of life, and above all, attain HAPPINESS. All of these evidences of success begin in the form of thought impulses.

You may control your own mind, you have the power to feed it whatever thought impulses you choose. With this privilege goes also the responsibility of using it constructively. You are the master of your own earthly destiny just as surely as you have the power to control your own thoughts. You may influence, direct, and eventually control your own environment, making your life what you want it to be—or, you may neglect to exercise the privilege which is yours, to make your life to order, thus casting yourself upon the broad sea of "Circumstance" where you will be tossed hither and yon, like a chip on the waves of the ocean.

THE DEVIL'S WORKSHOP

THE SEVENTH BASIC EVIL

In addition to the Six Basic Fears, there is another evil by which people suffer. It constitutes a rich soil in which the seeds of failure grow abundantly. It is so subtle that its presence often is not detected. This affliction cannot properly be classed as a fear. IT IS MORE DEEPLY SEATED AND MORE OFTEN FATAL THAN ALL OF THE SIX FEARS. For want of a better name, let us call this evil SUSCEPTIBILITY TO NEGATIVE INFLUENCES.

Men who accumulate great riches always protect themselves against this evil! The poverty stricken never do! Those who succeed in any calling must prepare their minds to resist the evil. If you are reading this philosophy for the purpose of accumulating riches, you should examine yourself very carefully, to determine whether you are susceptible to negative influences. If you neglect this self-analysis, you will forfeit your right to attain the object of your desires.

Make the analysis searching. After you read the questions prepared for this self-analysis, hold yourself to a strict accounting in your answers. Go at the task as carefully as you would search for any other enemy you knew to be awaiting you in ambush and deal with your own faults as you would with a more tangible enemy.

You can easily protect yourself against highway robbers, because the law provides organized cooperation for your benefit, but the "seventh basic evil" is more difficult to master, because it strikes when you are not aware of its presence, when you are asleep, and while you are awake. Moreover, its weapon is intangible, because it consists of merely—a STATE OF MIND. This evil is also dangerous because it strikes in as many different forms as there are human experiences. Sometimes it enters the mind through the well-meant words of one's own relatives. At other times, it bores from within, through one's own mental attitude. Always it is as deadly as poison, even though it may not kill as quickly.

How to Protect Yourself Against Negative Influences

To protect yourself against negative influences, whether of your own making, or the result of the activities of negative people around you, recognize that you have a WILL-POWER, and put it into constant use, until it builds a wall of immunity against negative influences in your own mind.

Recognize the fact that you, and every other human being, is, by nature, lazy, indifferent, and susceptible to all suggestions which harmonize with your weaknesses.

Recognize that you are, by nature, susceptible to all the six basic fears, and set up habits for the purpose of counteracting all these fears.

Recognize that negative influences often work on you through your subconscious mind, therefore they are difficult to detect, and keep your mind closed against all people who depress or discourage you in any way.

Clean out your medicine chest, throw away all pill bottles, and stop pandering to colds, aches, pains and imaginary illness.

Deliberately seek the company of people who influence you to THINK AND ACT FOR YOUR-SELF.

Do not EXCEPT troubles as they have a tendency not to disappoint.

Without doubt, the most common weakness of all human beings is the habit of leaving their minds open to the negative influence of other people. This weakness is all the more damaging, because most people do not recognize that they are cursed by it, and many who acknowledge it, neglect or refuse to correct the evil until it becomes an uncontrollable part of their daily habits.

To aid those who wish to see themselves as they really are, the following list of questions has been prepared. Read the questions and state you're answers aloud, so you can hear your own voice. This will make it easier for you to be truthful with yourself.

SELF-ANALYSIS TEST QUESTIONS

Do you complain often of "feeling badly," and if so, what is the cause?

Do you find fault with other people at the slightest provocation?

Do you frequently make mistakes in your work, and if so, why?

Are you sarcastic and offensive in your conversation?

Do you deliberately avoid the association of anyone, and if so, why?

Do you suffer frequently with indigestion? If so, what is the cause?

Does life seem futile and the future hopeless to you? If so, why?

Do you like your occupation? If not, why?

Do you often feel self-pity, and if so why?

Are you envious of those who excel you?

To which do you devote most time, thinking of SUCCESS, or of FAILURE?

Are you gaining or losing self-confidence as you grow older?

Do you learn something of value from all mistakes?

Are you permitting some relative or acquaintance to worry you? If so, why?

Are you sometimes "in the clouds" and at other times in the depths of despondency?

Who has the most inspiring influence upon you? What is the cause?

Do you tolerate negative or discouraging influences which you can avoid?

Are you careless of your personal appearance? If so, when and why?

Have you learned how to "drown your troubles" by being too busy to be annoyed by them?

Would you call yourself a "spineless weakling" if you permitted others to do your thinking for you?

Do you neglect internal bathing until auto-intoxication makes you ill-tempered and irritable?

How many preventable disturbances annoy you, and why do you tolerate them?

Do you resort to liquor, narcotics, or cigarettes to "quiet your nerves"? If so, why do you not try will-power instead?

Does anyone "nag" you, and if so, for what reason?

Do you have a DEFINITE MAJOR PURPOSE, and if so, what is it, and what plan have you for achieving it?

Do you suffer from any of the Six Basic Fears? If so, which ones?

Have you a method by which you can shield yourself against the negative influence of others?

Do you make deliberate use of auto-suggestion to make your mind positive?

Which do you value most, your material possessions, or your privilege of controlling your own thoughts?

Are you easily influenced by others, against your own judgment?

Has today added anything of value to your stock of knowledge or state of mind?

Do you face squarely the circumstances which make you unhappy, or sidestep the responsibility?

Do you analyze all mistakes and failures and try to profit by them or, do you take the attitude that this is not your duty?

Can you name three of your most damaging weaknesses? What are you doing to correct them?

Do you encourage other people to bring their worries to you for sympathy?

Do you choose, from your daily experiences, lessons or influences which aid in your personal advancement?

Does your presence have a negative influence on other people as a rule?

What habits of other people annoy you most?

Do you form your own opinions or permit yourself to be influenced by other people?

Have you learned how to create a mental state of mind with which you can shield yourself against all discouraging influences?

Does your occupation inspire you with faith and hope?

Are you conscious of possessing spiritual forces of sufficient power to enable you to keep your mind free from all forms of FEAR?

Does your religion help you to keep your own mind positive?

Do you feel it your duty to share other people's worries? If so, why?

If you believe that "birds of a feather flock together" what have you learned about yourself by studying the friends whom you attract?

What connection, if any, do you see between the

people with whom you associate most closely, and any unhappiness you may experience?

Could it be possible that some person whom you consider to be a friend is, in reality, your worst enemy, because of his negative influence on your mind?

By what rules do you judge who is helpful and who is damaging to you?

Are your intimate associates mentally superior or inferior to you?

How much time out of every 24 hours do you devote to:

        a. your occupation
        b. sleep
        c. play and relaxation
        d. acquiring useful knowledge
        e. plain waste

Who among your acquaintances,

        a. encourages you most
        b. cautions you most
        c. discourages you most
        d. helps you most in other ways

What is your greatest worry? Why do you tolerate it?

When others offer you free, unsolicited advice, do you accept it without question, or analyze their motive?

What, above all else, do you most DESIRE? Do you intend to acquire it? Are you willing to subordinate all other desires for this one? How much time daily do you devote to acquiring it?

Do you change your mind often? If so, why?

Do you usually finish everything you begin?

Are you easily impressed by other people's business or professional titles, college degrees, or wealth?

Are you easily influenced by what other people think or say of you?

Do you cater to people because of their social or financial status?

Whom do you believe to be the greatest person living? In what respect is this person superior to yourself?

How much time have you devoted to studying and answering these questions? (At least one day is necessary for the analysis and the answering of the entire list.)

If you have answered all these questions truthfully, you know more about yourself than the majority of people. Study the questions carefully, come back to them once each week for several months, and be astounded at the amount of additional knowledge of great value to yourself, you will have gained by the simple method of answering the questions truthfully. If you are not certain concerning the answers to some of the questions, seek the counsel of those who know you well, especially those who have no motive in flattering you, and see yourself through their eyes. The experience will be astonishing.

You have ABSOLUTE CONTROL over but one

thing, and that is your thoughts. This is the most significant and inspiring of all facts known to man! It reflects man's Divine nature. This Divine prerogative is the sole means by which you may control your own destiny. If you fail to control your own mind, you may be sure you will control nothing else.

If you must be careless with your possessions, let it be in connection with material things. *Your mind is your spiritual estate!* Protect and use it with the care to which Divine Royalty is entitled. You were given a WILL-POWER for this purpose.

Unfortunately, there is no legal protection against those who, either by design or ignorance, poison the minds of others by negative suggestion. This form of destruction should be punishable by heavy legal penalties, because it may and often does destroy one's chances of acquiring material things which are protected by law.

Men with negative minds tried to convince Thomas A. Edison that he could not build a machine that would record and reproduce the human voice, "because" they said, "no one else had ever produced such a machine." Edison did not believe them. He knew that the mind could produce ANYTHING THE MIND COULD CONCEIVE AND BELIEVE, and the knowledge was the thing that lifted the great Edison above the common herd.

Men with negative minds told F. W. Woolworth, he would go "broke" trying to run a store on five and ten cent sales. He did not believe them. He knew that he could do anything, within reason, if he backed his plans with faith. Exercising his right to keep other men's negative suggestions out of his mind, he piled up a fortune of more than a hundred million dollars.

Men with negative minds told George Washington he could not hope to win against the vastly superior forces of the British, but he exercised his Divine right to BELIEVE, therefore this book was published under the protection of the Stars and Stripes, while the name of Lord Cornwallis has been all but forgotten.

Doubting Thomases scoffed scornfully when Henry Ford tried out his first crudely built automobile on the streets of Detroit. Some said the thing never would become practical. Others said no one would pay money for such a contraption. FORD SAID, "I'LL BELT THE EARTH WITH DEPENDABLE MOTOR CARS," AND HE DID! His decision to trust his own judgment has already piled up a fortune far greater than the next five generations of his descendents can squander. For the benefit of those seeking vast riches, let it be remembered that practically the sole difference between Henry Ford and a majority of the more than one hundred thousand men who work for him, is this—FORD HAS A MIND AND CONTROLS IT, THE OTHERS HAVE MINDS WHICH THEY DO NOT TRY TO CONTROL.

Henry Ford has been repeatedly mentioned, because he is an astounding example of what a man with a mind of his own, and a will to control it, can accomplish. His record knocks the foundation from under that time-worn alibi, "I never had a chance." Ford never had a chance, either, but he CREATED AN OPPORTUNITY AND BACKED IT WITH

PERSISTENCE UNTIL IT MADE HIM RICHER THAN CROESUS.

Mind control is the result of self-discipline and habit. You either control your mind or it controls you. There is no half-way compromise. The most practical of all methods for controlling the mind is the habit of keeping it busy with a definite purpose, backed by a definite plan. Study the record of any man who achieves noteworthy success, and you will observe that he has control over his own mind, moreover, that he exercises that control and directs it toward the attainment of definite objectives. Without this control, success is not possible.

"FIFTY-SEVEN" FAMOUS ALIBIS
BY OLD MAN IF

People who do not succeed have one distinguishing trait in common. They know *all the reason for failure*, and have what they believe to be air-tight alibis to explain away their own lack of achievement.

Some of these alibis are clever, and a few of them are justifiable by the facts. But alibis cannot be used for money. The world wants to know only one thing—HAVE YOU ACHIEVED SUCCESS?

A character analyst complied a list of the most commonly used alibis. As you read the list, examine yourself carefully, and determine how many of these alibis, if any, are your own property. Remember, too, the philosophy presented in this book makes every one of these alibis obsolete.

IF I didn't have a wife and family...

IF I had enough "pull"...

IF I had money...
IF I had a good education...
IF I could get a job...
IF I had good health...
IF I only had time...
IF times were better...
IF other people understood me...
IF conditions around me were only different...
IF I could live my life over again...
IF I did not fear what "THEY" would say...
IF I had been given a chance...
IF I now had a chance...
IF other people didn't "have it in for me"...
IF nothing happens to stop me...
IF I were only younger...
IF I could only do what I want...
IF I had been born rich...
IF I could meet "the right people"...
IF I had the talent that some people have...
IF I dared assert myself...
IF I only had embraced past opportunities...
IF people didn't get on my nerves...
IF I didn't have to keep house and look after the
  children...
IF I could save some money...
IF the boss only appreciated me...
IF I only had somebody to help me...
IF my family understood me...
IF I lived in a big city...
IF I could just get started...
IF I were only free...
IF I had the personality of some people...
IF I were not so fat...

IF my talents were known...
IF I could just get a "break"...
IF I could only get out of debt...
IF I hadn't failed...
IF I only knew how...
IF everybody didn't oppose me...
IF I didn't have so many worries...
IF I could marry the right person...
IF people weren't so dumb...
IF my family were not so extravagant...
IF I were sure of myself...
IF luck were not against me...
IF I had not been born under the wrong star...
IF it were not true that "what is to be will be"...
IF I did not have to work so hard...
IF I hadn't lost my money...
IF I lived in a different neighborhood...
IF I didn't have a "past"...
IF I only had a business of my own...
IF other people would only listen to me...
IF *** and this is the greatest of them all***
      I had the courage to see myself as I really am, I
   would *find out what is wrong with me, and correct it,*
   then I might have a chance to profit by my
   mistakes and learn something from the experience of others, for I know that there is
   something WRONG with me, or I would now
   be where *I WOULD HAVE BEEN IF* I had spent
   more time analyzing my weaknesses, and less
   time building alibis to cover them.

Building alibis with which to explain away failure
is a national pastime. The habit is as old as the

human race, and is *fatal to success!* Why do people cling to their pet alibis? The answer is obvious. They defend their alibis because THEY CREATE them! A man's alibi is the child of his own imagination. It is human nature to defend one's own brain-child.

Building alibis is a deeply rooted habit. Habits are difficult to break, especially when they provide justification for something we do. Plato had this truth in mind when he said, "The first and best victory is to conquer self. To be conquered by self is, of all things, the most shameful and vile."

Another philosopher had the same thought in mind when he said, "It was a great surprise to me when I discovered that most of the ugliness I saw in others, was but a reflection of my own nature."

"It has always been a mystery to me," said Elbert Hubbard, "why people spend so much time deliberately fooling themselves by creating alibis to cover their weaknesses. If used differently, this same time would be sufficient to cure the weakness, then no alibis would be needed."

In parting, I would remind you that "Life is a checkerboard, and the player opposite you is TIME. If you hesitate before moving, or neglect to move promptly, your men will be wiped off the board by TIME. You are playing against a partner who will not tolerate INDECISION!"

Previously you may have had a logical excuse for not having forced Life to come through with whatever you asked, but that alibi is now obsolete, because you are in possession of the Master Key that unlocks the door to Life's bountiful riches.

The Master Key is intangible, but it is powerful! It is the privilege of creating, *in your own mind*, a BURNING DESIRE for a definite form of riches. There is no penalty for the use of the Key, but there is a price you must pay if you do not use it. The price is FAILURE. There is a reward of stupendous proportions if you put the Key to use. It is the satisfaction that comes to all who *conquer self and force Life to pay whatever is asked.*

The reward is worthy of your effort. Will you make the start and be convinced?

"If we are related," said the immortal Emerson, "we shall meet." In closing, may I borrow his thought, and say, "If we are related, we have, through these pages, met."

THE END

THIS STANDING ARMY
IS AT YOUR SERVICE

It Will Bring You Fame, Fortune, Peace of Mind or Whatever You Demand of Life!

In this picture you see the most *powerful* army on earth. Observe the emphasis on the word POWERFUL. This army is standing at attention, ready to do the bidding of any person who will command it. It is YOUR army if you will take charge of it.

These soldiers are labeled: DEFINITE CHIEF AIM; HABIT OF SAVING; SELF CONFIDENCE; IMAGINATION; INITIATIVE; LEADERSHIP; ENTHUSIASM; SELF CONTROL; DOING MORE THAN PAID FOR; PLEASING PERSONALITY; ACCURATE THOUGHT; CONCENTRATION; CO-OPERATION; FAILURE; TOLERANCE; GOLDEN RULE; THE MASTER MIND.

A long, searching study of the lives of 500 great American men and women—as well as actual endorsement from nationally known leaders—proves that there are the *basic principles* upon which all true and lasting success is built.

POWER comes from organized effort. You see in this picture—in these "soldiers"—the forces which enter into all organized effort. Master these sixteen forces or personal qualities *and you may have whatever you want in life.*

A FEW WORDS FROM THE PUBLISHERS

And it is because we are going to help you TO master these forces that the publishers of "THINK AND GROW RICH" want to have a little chat with you. For over fifty years "Ralston" has supplied hundreds of thousands—yes, probably millions—of ambitious men and women with home study books that bring Health, Wealth, Power and Happiness.

We have many unusual, private, exciting Instruction Books Embracing all Human Powers. From time to time we will extend an invitation to you to read these courses. But for the time being, let us concentrate upon the inspiring message that Napoleon Hill, author of "THINK AND GROW RICH" has for you. So great a business man and master of success as John Wanamaker, merchant prince of New York and Philadelphia, said:—

"If I had a young son I would insist that he read every word of the "LAW OF SUCCESS" by Napoleon Hill, and the books by Dr.....These two men are, perhaps, the most inspirational writers in the world. I know your 17 fundamentals of success are sound because I have been applying them in my business for more than 30 years."

NAPOLEON HILL HAS WRITTEN A POST GRADUATE COURSE FOR YOU

It is because we sincerely feel that every reader of this book should go on into this post graduate course, known as THE LAW OF SUCCESS, that we take the liberty here of giving a few brief side lights upon this brilliant work.

The LAW OF SUCCESS presents, for the first time in the history of the world, the true Philosophy upon which all lasting success is built. Ideas, when translated into intelligent plans of action, are the beginning of all successful achievement. So the Law of Success proceeds to show you how to create practical ideas for every human need.

It does it in easy-to-understand lessons.

Napoleon Hill spent the better part of twenty-five years in perfecting this Philosophy of Success. During the long years he has worked on it, some parts or the whole of it, have been reviewed and praised by many of the greatest Americans of our times.

Among them are included four Presidents of the United States, Theodore Roosevelt, Woodrow Wilson, Warren G. Harding, Wm. H. Taft; Thomas Edison, Luther Burbank, Wm. J. Wrigley, Alexander Graham Bell, Judge E. H. Gary, Cyrus H. K. Curtis, Edward Bok, E.M. Statler—dozens of glowing names in Politics, Finance, Education, Invention.

ANDREW CARNEGIE STARTED IT

Over twenty-five years ago, Napoleon Hill, then a young special investigator for a nationally known

business magazine, was sent to interview Andrew Carnegie. During that interview Carnegie slyly dropped a hint of a certain master power he used; a magic law of the human mind—a little known psychological principle—which was amazing in its power.

Carnegie suggested to Hill that upon that principle he could build the philosophy of all personal success—whether it be measured in terms of Money, Power, Position, Prestige, Influence, Accumulation of Wealth.

That part of the interview never went into Hill's magazine. But it did launch the young author upon over twenty years of research. And today we open to YOU the discovery and methods of using the revolutionary force which Carnegie quietly hinted at. The thrilling methods of using it are now taught in eight textbooks known as THE LAW OF SUCCESS.

In the trail of the LAW OF SUCCESS lessons come accomplishments, not mere entertainment and time-killing diversion. There come larger businesses, bigger bank accounts, fatter pay envelopes; small, struggling enterprises given new life and power to grow; low-pay employees shown how to gain advancement by leaps and bounds.

It is impossible in this small space to give any real idea of the inspiring, revealing lessons in the eight textbooks of LAW OF SUCCESS. But, you will realize that a wonderful treat is in store for you when you read what some American leaders have said, who saw parts of the philosophy while in process of creation. (also see two pages at front of book.)

"Allow me to express my appreciation of the compliment you have paid me in sending the original manuscript of the Law of Success. I can see you have spent a great deal of time and thought in its preparation. Your philosophy is sound and you are to be congratulated for sticking to your work over so long a period of years. Your students will be amply rewarded for their labor."

(World's Greatest Inventor)   THOS. A. EDISON

"Your work and mine are peculiarly akin. I am helping the laws of Nature to create more perfect specimens of vegetation while you are using those same laws through The Law of Success to build more perfect specimens of thinkers."

(World Famous Scientist)   LUTHER BURBANK

"Certainly I will supply you with the information you request. This I consider to be not only a duty, but it is a pleasure as well. You are laboring in behalf of the people who have neither the time nor the inclination to ferret out the causes of failure and success."

(Former President
of the U.S.)   THEODORE ROOSEVELT

"Our entire business policy, in the management of our hotels, is based upon the 17 fundamentals of The Law of Success, of which I am a student.

(Founder of Great Hotel System)   E.M. STATLER

"I feel greatly indebted for the privilege of reading your Law of Success philosophy. If I had had this fifty years ago, I suppose I could have accomplished all that I have done in less than half the time. I sincerely hope the world will discover and reward you."

(Steamship Magnate: The
Dollar Lines) ROBERT DOLLAR

"Napoleon Hill has produced what I believe to be the first practical philosophy of achievement. Its major distinguishing feature is the simplicity in which it has been presented."

(Leland Stanford
University) DAVID STARR JORDAN

"The best evidence of the soundness of the Law of Success, with which I am personally acquainted is the noteworthy achievement of Mr. Curtis, who has built one of the greatest publishing businesses in the world by applying the principles of this philosophy."

(Former Editor: Ladies
Home Journal) EDWARD BOK

"You may say for Mr. Rockefeller that he endorses Mr. Hill's 17 fundamental principles of success, and that he recommends them to those who are seeking the highway to achievement."

Secretary to JOHN D. ROCKEFELLER

EVIDENCE THAT MONEY COULD NOT BUY

The foregoing is evidence and praise seldom accorded *any* course of education. Money could not buy such letters of endorsement from men who are, or have been, leaders of our times.

Millions of books have been written to amuse, to entertain, to help you while away your idle hours.

But here in the LAW OF SUCCESS are eight vibrating, power-radiating books that shape your destiny, enrich your future, and turn your hopes and dreams into solid success-realities.

Don't waste your own precious years blindly searching for the hidden road to the heights. Profit by the dearly brought experience of America's leaders. Over 500 great and prominent men of America were minutely analyzed—their methods, motives, strategy—to find out the secrets that put them on top.

No matter whether you are rich or poor—you have one asset as great as the richest man living—and that is TIME. But with each setting sun you become one day older, and have *one day less* in which to attain the success and wealth you desire. Thousands of progressive people throughout the North American continent have realized this mighty truth, and have sought the help so clearly and inspiringly taught in Napoleon Hill's "LAW OF SUCCESS."

You cannot afford to let day after day slip into eternity, without getting possession of this course. You will profit greatly from the lessons in THINK AND GROW RICH. You will take even more brilliant and gratifying rewards from the LAW OF SUCCESS. The cost is trifling; the benefits are tremendous.

May we tell you in detail about the LAW OF SUCCESS? If you say "yes"—then write us that you are a reader of this book, and would like detailed information about the LAW OF SUCCESS.

The RALSTON SOCIETY
Meriden, Conn.

For additional information about Napoleon Hill
products please contact the following locations:

Napoleon Hill World Learning Center
Purdue University Calumet
2300 173rd Street
Hammond, IN 46323-2094

Judith Williamson, Director
Uriel "Chino" Martinez, Assistant/Graphic Designer

Telephone: 219-989-3173 or 219-989-3166
email: nhf@purduecal.edu

Napoleon Hill Foundation
University of Virginia–Wise
College Relations Apt. C
1 College Avenue
Wise, VA 24293

Don Green, Executive Director
Annedia Sturgill, Executive Assistant

Telephone: 276-328-6700
email: napoleonhill@uvawise.edu

Website: www.naphill.org